D1596419

Exit Wounds

CALIFORNIA SERIES IN PUBLIC ANTHROPOLOGY

The California Series in Public Anthropology emphasizes the anthropologist's role as an engaged intellectual. It continues anthropology's commitment to being an ethnographic witness, to describing, in human terms, how life is lived beyond the borders of many readers' experiences. But it also adds a commitment, through ethnography, to reframing the terms of public debate—transforming received, accepted understandings of social issues with new insights, new framings.

Series Editor: Ieva Jusionyte (Brown University)

Founding Editor: Robert Borofsky (Hawaii Pacific University)

Advisory Board: Catherine Besteman (Colby College), Philippe Bourgois (UCLA), Jason De León (UCLA), Laurence Ralph (Princeton University), and Nancy Scheper-Hughes (UC Berkeley)

Exit Wounds

How America's Guns Fuel Violence
across the Border

Ieva Jusionyte

UNIVERSITY OF CALIFORNIA PRESS

University of California Press
Oakland, California

© 2024 by Ieva Jusionyte

Excerpt from ON EARTH WE'RE BRIEFLY GOR-
GEOUS: A NOVEL by Ocean Vuong, copyright © 2019
by Ocean Vuong. Used by permission of Penguin Press,
an imprint of Penguin Publishing Group, a division of
Penguin Random House LLC. All rights reserved.

Library of Congress Cataloging-in-Publication Data

Names: Jusionyte, Ieva, 1983- author.
Title: Exit wounds : how America's guns fuel violence
    across the border / Ieva Jusionyte.
Other titles: California series in public anthropology ; 57.
Description: Oakland, California : University of
    California Press, [2024] | Series: California series in
    public anthropology ; 57 | Includes bibliographical
    references and index.
Identifiers: LCCN 2023028617 (print) | LCCN 2023028618
    (ebook) | ISBN 9780520395954 (cloth) | ISBN
    9780520395961 (ebook)
Subjects: LCSH: Firearms—Mexican-American Border
    Region. | Gun control—Mexican-American Border
    Region. | Violence—Mexican-American Border
    Region—Prevention. | Illegal arms transfers—Mexi-
    can-American Border Region. | Firearms—Mexico. |
    Firearms—United States.
Classification: LCC TS533.4.M58 J875 2024 (print) |
    LCC TS533.4.M58 (ebook) | DDC 363.330973—dc23
    /eng/20230809
LC record available at https://lccn.loc.gov/2023028617
LC ebook record available at https://lccn.loc.gov
    /2023028618

Manufactured in the United States of America

33 32 31 30 29 28 27 26 25 24
10 9 8 7 6 5 4 3 2 1

Because a bullet without a body is a song without ears.

—Ocean Vuong, *On Earth We're Briefly Gorgeous*

Contents

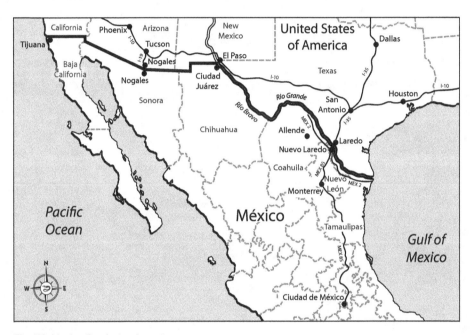

The US-Mexico Borderlands

The Workshop

I follow him downstairs in silence. We step into a room with no windows and just enough space for the two of us to stand without our hands touching. He opens the gun safe and shows me his Sakos and Berettas, lets me hold one. But we didn't come here for those and he puts the guns back in the safe and locks it. Floor-to-ceiling shelves are packed with accessories: vests he wears on hunting trips, several canisters of insect repellant, binoculars; then rows of screwdrivers, wrenches, pliers. The narrow desk in the center holds a scale and some sort of a metal instrument with a lever. He pulls out a chair and I sit, my eyes scanning the boxes of cartridges and many things he will name for me: empty casings, primers, oils, smokeless powder, and projectiles. He will teach me what each does, how they all fit together. I ask about a pair of metallic gold markers I notice on the desk in front of me and he says they are for coloring silver cartridges, to make them look like new. I now understand why I am here.

He stands behind me, points at the materials, and tells me how to do it: Roll the brass shell on a sponge-like pad smeared with a lubricant. Place the shell in the press fitted with a sizing die. Pull down the lever of the press to pop out the old primer and resize the shell. Clean the primer pocket to get rid of carbon left over from the last shot. Trim the brass casing. Pick up the cone-shaped metal instrument—he calls it the chamfer tool—and smooth the inside edge of the shell, then the outside, to remove the burr. "This step is important," he says: it prevents the bullet getting jammed in the chamber when you load the gun.

I work slowly, carefully. It feels like playing with matches. I pour the gunpowder into the container on the scale and enter "45 g." That's grains, not grams; one grain is about fifteen times lighter than a gram. The scale is so precise that adding just two or three powder kernels will change the measurement. He wants me to see this, so I drop a few extra kernels, watch the number rise, then scrupulously remove them. I pour the gunpowder into the brass shell, put the shell back into the press, seat the bullet on top and hold it with my left hand as I press the lever with the right to crimp it.

I pick it up—my first cartridge. About the size of a chile de árbol rolling in my palm. Then I put it aside and follow the procedure again, this time a little faster. He watches patiently and when I pause reminds me what to do. Those who do this regularly can reload about a hundred cartridges in one afternoon. It takes me what seemed like an hour to make four.

Later, I will learn that .308 Winchester is the ammunition of choice for military and police sniper rifles. It is the civilian version of the 7.62 × 51mm NATO round that American soldiers fed their M14s in Vietnam, that the Mexican Army still used at the turn of this century to load their G3s. Longer and more powerful than the same diameter cartridge used by AK-47s, it can hit a human-size target half a mile away, and SWAT snipers rely on its accuracy to penetrate the skulls of hostage takers. But the ones I made are not meant for people. They will most likely kill deer or antelope. Maybe an elk. Possibly a boar. Each weighs just twenty-four grams. Like five sheets of copy paper.

When I stand up to leave, I don't take them with me. They are material evidence that could implicate him, implicate me. By now I am used to this—not keeping anything. Not taking pictures. Not taking down people's names. When I write about them, I call them by names I invented for them when I scribbled their number or directions to find them in my notebook. Those are the only names I remember. Some people, though, don't even get fake names. But I can assure you that they, too, exist.

There is a principle in storytelling that suggests that noticeable details should be integrated into the plot. It is known as "Chekhov's gun." The Russian author advised young playwrights that if a gun appeared in the first act, it should be fired by the third. But that's not how it works in Mexico. The way borderland journalist Charles Bowden put it: "In

Mexico, the gun may never appear, can be fired at any moment and a body will fall to the floor with no explanation. . . . Your life will have a narrative arc and in the third act you will be killed. But no one will hear the gun go off. And no one will know why you died. And more and more often no one will know who you are."[1]

Shape of Wounds

Before I saw the guns, I saw the wounds.

The young man sat on the bench in front of me and, after looking around to make sure nobody else was listening, leaned closer. His voice, barely louder than a whisper, blended in with the hum of a large industrial fan pushing hot desert air around the building with makeshift walls and corrugated metal roof. He said his name was Raúl and that he was from Acapulco, the resort city on Guerrero's Pacific Coast.[1] He fled after men wearing balaclavas forced his father into a truck and then dumped his decapitated body onto the street. He said he had HIV and had run out of antiretrovirals. I met Raúl and many others—men, women, children; Mexican, Salvadoran, Honduran—at the aid center for migrants steps away from the US border in Nogales, Sonora, where I was providing basic medical aid as a volunteer. They came with blisters on their feet, infected wounds, fever; without their insulin or other medications. Trying to outpace fear and not lose hope along the way.

That was eight years ago. Before President Trump ordered miles of new walls to be built. Before the Covid-19 pandemic and Title 42. Before I cared to know the difference between 9mm and 7.62.

When in the summer of 2022 I returned to Nogales, the medical clinic had moved to a separate room with floor-to-ceiling cabinets full of supplies at the new spacious migrant center across the street from the old one. Alejandra was sitting on the chair by the closed door while I poured red gooey Tylenol syrup into plastic cups and handed them to each of her three small children. "Threats started coming," she said, sharing tiny pieces of her story. This family, like Raúl years earlier, had come from Guerrero, and so did many others I spoke to that day. They were farmers and taxi drivers, cooks and craftsmen, who had fled their home when they could no longer pay extortion fees, when gunmen came to take away their cattle, burned their mango orchards, when their neighbors and relatives were killed or disappeared. "There is no law," Alejandra said. There was nowhere they could turn for protection. Some had tried, went to the police, only to start receiving threats from them too. So they packed what they could carry and headed toward the US border.

Not everyone talked about the reasons they were fleeing Mexico.[2] At the clinic, we didn't ask them to say more about themselves than they wanted, focusing instead on what little we could do for them. But they didn't even have to say anything. Their bodies—exhausted, dehydrated, marked by scars—were evidence that something back home had gone seriously awry for them to risk their lives on the journey north.

Raúl and Alejandra joined more than forty-five thousand Mexicans who applied for asylum in the United States over the past two decades. Fewer than six thousand people were granted it.[3] Many crossed the border without asking for permission, knowing they would not qualify because the kind of violence they were fleeing from was not included in the mid-twentieth-century conventions still governing international humanitarian law. In 2021, US Border Patrol apprehended over 655,000 Mexicans—more than they had seen in years.[4] In 2022, that number rose to over eight hundred thousand.[5] That is more than the population of Boston. Or of San Francisco. As soon as the agents dropped them south of the border, many tried to cross again. And they would continue, until they made it or died trying.

I knew what guns could do to human bodies. As an EMT and paramedic, I had been on calls involving drive-by shootings and still have flashbacks of the scrambles inside the ambulance when our team, squeezed around the gurney, tried to save a life: starting IV lines, running fluids and pushing medications, inserting plastic tubes into tracheas to deliver air to the lungs, with lights and sirens on speeding toward the closest ER. But none of what we did mattered once the patient had lost too much blood, so we had to stop the bleeding first. And that meant feeling the body with our gloved hands to find the exit wounds.

"Always look for the exit wound," our instructors in paramedic school kept telling us. Even though they knew the frantic reality in the back of the ambulance, they made it sound elementary. The entry wound, where the bullet pierces the body, is usually round or oval and has an abrasion ring. An exit wound, in contrast, is typically larger and more irregular in shape. Due to the stretching force of the bullet overcoming the resistance of the skin, it resembles a starburst. Because the projectile never travels straight, finding the exit wound was important. It helped us understand its trajectory through the body, and suspect which organs may have been impacted, guiding our actions. Did the bullet pierce a major artery, causing critical internal bleeding that required a blood transfusion? Did it puncture a lung and we should prepare for a chest decompression? Not finding one was equally significant. No exit wound meant the bullet was still inside the body, inching its way forward through soft tissue and bone.

Locating exit wounds also has legal implications. When evaluating patients with firearm-related injuries, emergency physicians are asked to distinguish between entry and exit wounds in order to provide clues in the investigation of a crime. The appearance of the wound depends on the caliber of the weapon used, the distance from which it was fired, and the angle at which the bullet entered the body, among other factors, which makes interpreting one difficult.[6] In legal proceedings, however, the distinction becomes critical evidence. It confirms the testimonies witnesses share in court, supports narratives of crime scene investigators, establishes the truth of what occurred: Was the victim facing the perpetrator or were they shot in the back? Were they murdered or did they kill themselves? These were not the kinds of questions that mattered to paramedics while we were attending to the injured, but knowing they could arise in the courtroom we had to be mindful about what we wrote in patient care reports we completed before we left on the next call. Further investigation of the wounds was not our job—that would often be done by forensic pathologists performing autopsies and even they couldn't always tell an entry from an exit wound. As paramedics, we rarely learned the stories of the people we rushed to the ER—not why they were shot, nor if they survived.

By the time I began research on gun trafficking, several years had passed since my last shift on an ambulance, but what I was doing felt familiar—I was looking for exit wounds. Although firearms injure and kill individuals, whose bodies absorb the lethal force of the projectile, gunshot wounds reverberate through the community. The impact of a bullet exceeds the punctures and scars it leaves on the human body, penetrating social fabric, creating collective damage shared by families, neighborhoods, and passed from the present to future generations. The effects of guns are physical and social, material and political. Tracing these injuries requires peeling back legal ideologies and official state narratives that circumscribe how we think and talk about firearms. It entails finding and feeling the rough edges of the starburst that US firepower has left on the body politic bisected by the border.

We often hear that gun violence in the United States has reached alarming levels. The number of mass shootings—incidents in which four or more people are wounded—has been going up: Since 2020, there have been approximately two such events every twenty-four hours.[7] Each day, more than a hundred Americans die from firearm injuries—over half of them by suicide. Having surpassed vehicle accidents, gun violence is now the leading cause of death for children in the United States.[8] We know that Black communities have been disproportionately affected by widespread use of firearms: Black Americans are ten times more likely to be killed with guns than White Americans and they are three times more likely to be fatally shot by police.[9] Data show that, in the past five years, 20 percent of US residents have experienced gun violence, or have a family member or a friend who has.[10] Although firearm injuries kill fewer people than heart disease, cancer, or opioid overdose, social and psychological effects of the ubiquitous presence of guns in this country are incontrovertible. A survey by the American Psychological Association conducted in 2019 found that a third of Americans are so concerned about mass shootings that their fear prevents them from attending public events, and going to shopping malls, schools, and movie theaters.[11]

This gun violence epidemic doesn't stop at the border: Firearms sold in the United States also threaten and hurt people abroad—in Canada, the Caribbean, Brazil, Central America. But there is one country in particular which has been on the receiving end of American firepower with devastating effects—that's our southern neighbor, Mexico.[12]

The official counts are well known and repeated often: the quantity of firearms—sold, recovered, traced, destroyed; and the number of people—injured, disappeared, dead. Sometimes these numbers are put next to each other. Like figures in the Harper's Index, the facts, distilled into percentages and sum totals, highlight contrasts, which raise questions:

Number of people killed in Mexico in 2019: 35,588[13]

Number of people killed in the United States in 2019: 16,425[14]

Murder rate per 100,000 people in Mexico in 2019: 28.74[15]

In the United States: 5.07

Percentage of homicides in Mexico committed by firearm in the 1990s: 10[16]

In 2018: 69[17]

Number of gun stores in US states bordering Mexico: 9,940[18]

Number of gun stores in Mexico: 2[19]

Percentage of firearms recovered at crime scenes in Mexico originally purchased in the United States: 70[20]

Lowest estimated number of US firearms smuggled across the Mexican border annually: 200,000[21]

Number of outbound firearms seized by US agents on US-Mexico border in 2019: 189[22]

Seized by Mexican customs: 122[23]

In Mexico, as in the United States, gun ownership is a constitutional right. But while this right is nearly absolute in the United States, where federal gun laws are few and weak—almost anyone can buy an unlimited number of firearms of any caliber—it is much more attenuated in Mexico, where the government regulates how many and what type of guns and which citizens are allowed to have them, severely limiting domestic circulation of weapons and ammunition. This legal asymmetry between neighboring countries has created a thriving black market of firearms: In Mexico, organized crime groups that fight over drug trafficking routes, as well as citizens faced with increased levels of violence in the country, where they are unable to trust law enforcement to protect them, pay smugglers to bring them guns from one or another of the thousands of gun stores and pawn shops just north of the border, usually in Texas and Arizona, but also farther away: in Florida, Arkansas, Minnesota.[24] Although the numbers are mere estimates—nobody knows how many firearms and how much ammunition illegally crosses the US-Mexico border annually—the southbound flow of weapons is copious enough to merit being called an "iron river."[25]

Raúl, Alejandra, and many others who walked through the doors of the migrant aid center in Nogales, had traveled for thousands of miles to flee from various armed groups. The distinction between those labeled "organized crime" and those wearing uniforms with the insignia of the state, whether police or military, was irrelevant to them. It has become irrelevant to many Mexicans because often the distinction does not exist. In one particularly horrifying case, in September 2014, forty-three students from Ayotzinapa Rural Teachers' College were kidnapped and killed by members of a local gang working with the local police, while the military knew about it and did nothing. After various botched investigations, the truth commission's report released in 2022 concluded what the families of the students and human rights groups had long been saying—their murder was a "crime of the state" and its cover-up extended all the way up to the federal authorities.[26] News of the student massacre in Guerrero reached the United States, but the implications apparently did not. The United States continued selling guns to Mexican security forces and those guns continued crossing the formal line between law enforcement and organized crime.[27] Three years after I met Raúl, Acapulco's entire police force had to be disarmed, fearing that it was infiltrated by organized crime.[28] The same was happening in other parts of the country, from Baja California to Tamaulipas, from Puebla to Veracruz, where the police had become part of the mafia.

The majority of Mexicans in 2019 said they felt insecure in the cities and towns where they lived.[29] Gun violence forced people to adapt to new social norms: distrusting public officials, avoiding their neighbors, carrying cash to pay off soldiers or police or whichever armed group manned the checkpoints on the roads they had to take. As I write this, more than one hundred thousand people have been officially registered as forcibly disappeared or missing.[30] The binational community, too, has been affected, ripped apart by mistrust between US and Mexican governments and uneven dispensation of justice to people on two sides of the border. Even the language has been mangled by gun violence. The vocabulary tightened up, so that words that once meant something familiar were no longer able to describe, let alone explain, what was going on. Instead of the public square, where residents gathered to hear mariachi bands on weekend nights, *plaza* began referring to a piece of territory controlled and fought over by armed groups. *Juguetes* no longer meant toys children played with, but the guns that could kill them. Sometimes, out of caution, it was best not to say anything at all.

In August 2021, after decades of occasional criticism of how the US authorities handled guns, the Mexican government sued firearms manufacturers at the federal court in Massachusetts for "their contribution to the epidemic of gun violence" and "overall destabilizing effect on Mexican society."[31] The 135-page complaint was against companies that had been supplying most of the firearms recovered at crime scenes in Mexico, among them Smith & Wesson, Colt, Barrett, and Century Arms. These companies, the lawsuit stated, have "inflicted massive injury" to the Mexican people and the Mexican government, which has been struggling with the mounting costs of medical care and mental health services; incurred significant expenses for police, courts, and prisons; and endured extensive economic losses due to diminished property values and shuttering of businesses. It accused firearm manufacturers of acting with "conscious disregard of and indifference to the life, safety, and rights of persons in Mexico," where the guns have created "an atmosphere of fear that tears at the residents' sense of well-being and security." Firearms were, the lawsuit claimed, "the venom in the snakes that are the drug cartels."

Lawsuits against US gunmakers have been uphill battles reminiscent of civil action litigation against tobacco companies and, more recently, opioid manufacturers. Most have not been successful because gun companies, unlike the pharmaceutical industry, have federal immunity.[32] The Protection of Lawful Commerce in Arms Act (PLCAA) of 2005, approved by the US Congress with bipartisan support and two-thirds majority, shields gunmakers and dealers from civil liability for injuries their products cause to people in the United States. Mexico's lawyers argued that their country had made no such social contract exempting weapons manufacturers from responsibility. Just as US companies "may not dump toxic waste or other pollutants to poison Mexicans across the border," the complaint insisted, "they may not send their weapons of war into the hands of the cartels, causing repeated and grievous harm, and then claim immunity from accountability."

The lawsuit raised some uncomfortable questions about the US gun industry. In the public hearing on motion to dismiss the complaint, the judge wanted to know whether there was a "logical stopping point" to accountability for violence. US companies have been selling weapons to over one hundred foreign governments, including repressive regimes such as Saudi Arabia, and US-made firearms have ended up in the hands of the IRA, the Taliban, and many other groups. The judge asked whether people affected by these would also be able to sue, his question affirming that the world is awash in US weapons, most of which are exported legally.[33] Nobody brought this up at the hearing, but Mexican military and police forces, including the police in Guerrero, have also been eagerly purchasing US-made semiautomatic rifles, pistols, grenade launchers, and submachine guns, some of which were used to terrorize, injure, and kill Mexican civilians.[34] It is estimated that US exports of firearms, ammunition, and explosives to Mexico average more than 40 million US dollars annually.[35] It is only a drop in the trade between neighboring countries that in 2021 was valued at more than $276.5 billion.[36] But these are legal exports. Measuring the black market is harder and determining responsibility for it even more so. At the very least the lawsuit is not, as US defendants claim, only about "a clash of national values."[37] It hints at a longer and more complicated history of violence between the United States and Mexico—a history in which violence, rather than setting the two countries apart, is something they share.

Guns are duplicitous objects, a paradox of security: they can simultaneously be tools of aggression and of protection. At both individual and societal levels, they are relational. If the state is the only organization that can legitimately use physical violence within its borders, then firearms, in the hands of law enforcement, help maintain this monopoly.[38] When they are taken up by civilians, however, they threaten to subvert state power. Rather than being fixed, these relationships between guns and people are socially constructed: shaped by cultural and moral systems encoded in state laws (who ought to have a gun?), shifting due to political exigencies (who needs one now?), and economic asymmetries (where does it cost less?).[39]

Mexico and the United States share histories of European colonization and frontier violence fueled by gunpowder, yet firearms have come to play different roles in the development of the two states. Even before US independence from Britain, colonial governments mandated settlers in some areas to own and carry firearms, going as far as forbidding men to travel unarmed.[40] The Second Amendment, ratified in 1791, enshrined these obligations into law through the Bill of Rights. Because it mentions "well regulated militia" in the clause preceding "the right of the people to keep and bear arms," the text has led to disagreements on whether the right was meant to be collective or individual.[41] When James Madison proposed the amendment, he wrote about "state militias" that could "repel the danger" of a federal army. It wasn't until recently, until the Supreme Court's decision in *District of Columbia v. Heller* in 2008, that the interpretation of an individual right to own guns has prevailed.[42]

There was more to the history of this right than a potential check against a tyrannical government. Since independence, guns in the United States were primarily used against those with less power. In her book

Loaded: A Disarming History of the Second Amendment, historian Roxanne Dunbar-Ortiz argues that American gun culture is inextricably tied to the conquest of Indigenous territories.[43] White men, who alone enjoyed rights under the US Constitution at the time, needed firearms in order to protect themselves and their families from those who had strong motives to resist being displaced from their homelands.[44] Settlers were not allowed to sell firearms or gunpowder to the Indigenous people and faced imprisonment if they did.[45] Enslaved Black people were also forbidden to have guns. By the time these racial restrictions disappeared, practical rationale for owning firearms had also waned. It was then that Colt, Winchester, and other manufacturers turned to savvy marketing, drawing on cultural narratives of the frontier to sell guns as tokens of a uniquely American and masculine style of freedom and power.[46] Their strategy worked. Unlike in other countries, a significant portion of the US population considers private violence in the hands of civilians—whether individual citizens or militia groups—not a threat, but a potential asset to the state.[47]

In Mexico's history, too, guns have played significant material and symbolic roles. When visiting government buildings and museums in the capital city, it is hard not to notice the prominence of rifles in Diego Rivera's and José Orozco's murals of violent battle scenes. Popular images of revolutionary heroes Emiliano Zapata and Pancho Villa reproduced in books and films show them wearing ammo bandoliers. Old Winchesters and Colts are displayed in military exhibits around the country to tell the story of armed struggles that led to land reform and modern nationhood in the twentieth century. Without European and American weapons, there might have been no sovereign Mexican state. But, unlike in the United States, guns haven't been so tightly woven into the Mexican national identity. While in the United States settler colonialism was wrapped in the idea of manifest destiny and endless expansion, which entailed violent conquest of the frontier inhabited by the "Indian savage," the form it took in Mexico was somewhat different.[48] Spanish colonists, with their local allies, defeated the Mexica and their partners in the Triple Alliance, and the germs they brought from Europe caused smallpox epidemics that decimated Indigenous communities in the region. But once modern nation-building began, three centuries later, it drew on the logic of assimilation rather than extermination.[49] The ideology of *mestizaje* (mixed race) had no use for guns within the country's borders—Indigenous people, at least in theory, were to be a part of the Mexican nation. In practice, however, the Mexican government, like the United States, did not hesitate to use violence to subdue Indigenous groups who rebelled.[50] Nations inhabiting what became the US-Mexico borderlands, particularly the Apache and Comanche, were brutally persecuted by orders of both states.[51]

Compared to individualism as the core principle of gun laws in the United States, firearms in Mexico are a matter of national sovereignty. Following the country's independence from Spain in the early nineteenth century, various mandates limited possession of firearms in order to prevent armed insurrection. The right of gun ownership was first established by the Constitution of 1857 and carried over to the current Mexican Constitution passed in 1917. According to Article 10, people have the right to keep and bear arms, but it is not absolute: civilians are prohibited from having certain weapons that the law reserved for the military. Thus, with the same stroke that the Mexican Constitution created the right to own guns, it authorized laws to modulate that right. Following anti-government protests in the late 1960s and building on fears of armed resistance to the regime, the parliament passed the Federal Law of Firearms and Explosives, which further limited the type and quantity of guns and ammunition that Mexican citizens could own.[52] The 1971 law aimed to tighten the state's monopoly of violence: The Secretariat of National Defense (SEDENA) became the only institution allowed to import and sell guns, at a single store located on the military base in Mexico City.

Relationships between people and guns, inscribed in laws, reflect divergent national ideologies of power and sovereignty in Mexico and the United States. But cultural history alone, as illuminating as it is of the origins of the legal asymmetry, can't explain why so many Mexican people are wounded by US guns. We need to look at the regional political economy, a violence exchange: the relationships between things— desired, outlawed—on the two sides of the border. Prohibition of marijuana and cocaine, coupled with widespread addiction to meth and opioids in the United States created demand for these illicit substances, which since the 1980s has been largely satisfied by Mexican smugglers. Eager to swell their profits, organized crime groups in Mexico have been competing for manpower and trafficking routes, and since they could not buy the weapons they needed to fight turf battles in their own country, they got them from the United States. Mass production and scantily regulated sales of firearms through thousands of dealerships located close to the border made gun smuggling easy. Over the years, organized crime groups assembled arsenals that began rivaling those of the security forces, so the Mexican military and state police joined the arms race, importing more guns from US and European manufacturers, in addition to finally making their own. With both sides heavily armed, these confrontations between the Mexican government and organized crime groups added to the general sense of insecurity in the country. Living under siege, afraid of being killed or disappeared, those who could afford it turned to private security—yet another industry that expanded due to the availability of foreign firearms. Many more chose to abandon what little they had and flee in search of safety in the United States.

The arrival of large numbers of migrants and asylum seekers at the US-Mexico border has spurred heated political debates in the United States. More than half of the US population now thinks the country is "experiencing an invasion."[53] This paranoia has led the US government to increase investments in border security infrastructure, from additional physical walls to surveillance towers, aerostats, and drones, making the crossing—both of drugs and of people who are running away from the mayhem that the "drug war" has caused—even more difficult.[54] But rather than stopping trafficking, these border policing measures have further raised the prices and hence profits of organized crime groups that find new ways around them. And those groups continue to buy weapons from the United States. And so on and on, like an endless loop: guns and money going south and drugs and people going north.[55]

Other factors on both sides of the border perpetuate this pattern in oblique, but critical ways. One is a strong arms industry and aggressive gun lobby in the United States that oppose firearm safety laws which would curb trafficking. And then there is understaffed, underpaid, poorly trained law enforcement in Mexico, where widespread impunity for murder and police involvement in organized crime have eroded the trust of the people they purportedly serve to protect. By passing strict gun laws, the Mexican government reaffirmed its responsibility to provide security to its citizens. Yet this legal obligation is largely unmet—a failure that US guns, even though they aren't the only cause, have played a big part in. Mexican writer Cristina Rivera Garza has called her homeland a "visceraless state," one that has become disembodied, unable to recognize ties of reciprocity underlying its relationship with the people, one that no longer cares what happens to the bodies of its citizens: wounded, displaced, disappeared.[56]

The year I lived in Nogales, volunteering as a paramedic on both sides of the border while doing research about the binational work of emergency responders, I was crossing back and forth nearly every day, usually on foot. On my way back from the migrant clinic or the fire station, I would wait in line, sometimes an hour or more, to get into the United States, clutching my passport, ready to show the officers what I carried inside my bag. Going to Mexico, on the contrary, was swift, took only a minute, if that. Large signs on southbound roads warned in all caps: "WEAPONS AND AMMUNITION ILLEGAL IN MEXICO." And the same message was conveyed on a plaque with crossed-out pistol and ammo attached to an orange Jersey barrier at the DeConcini port of entry I scurried past all the time. But for many months I didn't give those signs much thought.

The realization that the people I was encountering in Nogales, Sonora, were fleeing threats enforced with guns sold in the United States came gradually. One evening after returning home from the clinic, I opened my laptop and, out of curiosity, typed the words "Mexico" and "guns" into the browser. The page filled up with alarming headlines about "cartels" and how they get their weapons from the United States, multiple references to ATF's Fast and Furious operation, and a couple of links to articles explaining Mexican gun laws. I read some of the stories and closed the computer. I began to understand why those warning signs dotted southbound lanes along the border, but gun trafficking was not something I wanted to go into any further.

I had not grown up around guns. Nobody in my Lithuanian family ever owned a firearm. Our neighbors did because they worked as bodyguards for government officials after the country freed itself from the Soviet Union and, since the occupying forces were threatening to come back, they needed those guns to defend our independence. The first firearm I held, heavy in my scrawny arms sore from climbing trees, was my neighbor's service pistol. I was maybe eight then. It only happened once, since my neighbors didn't like showing off their weapons. Moving to the United States didn't change anything. Although firearms in this country outnumber people, gun ownership rates in Massachusetts, where I have lived for years, are considerably lower than in southern or midwestern states. Nobody I knew had one. It wasn't until I became an EMT that I started encountering firearms in my life, but even then I mostly saw the wounds, not the objects that inflicted them.

Once I learned about the asymmetry between gun laws in the United States and in Mexico, however, walking past those signs when crossing the border on my way to the clinic or the firehouse wasn't the same. The cycle of violence became too obvious. As I continued seeing people who were risking their health and their life to get away from extortion, from threats of being kidnapped or killed, from the police that preyed on them instead of protecting them, the role of US guns in what I was witnessing was harder to ignore.

I had first come to Nogales to tell a different kind of border story: about binational ties between Mexican and US firefighters and paramedics, about relationships of dependence and care in the borderlands, about camaraderie and friendship between communities and people split by the monstrous wall. And yet that story barely made a dent in the narrative that still dominates the American national imagination, which paints the southern border as the site of danger, perpetual "crisis," an "invasion." Not only is this threat narrative false—border communities are safer than many urban areas around the country;[57] migrants commit fewer crimes than US citizens;[58] and it was the United States that invaded Mexico several times, never the other way around. But this false narrative also blatantly ignores the role of the United States in creating the conditions for criminal violence in Mexico and Central America that have become the pretext for seeing the border as a source of threats. To expose this role and understand why we are stuck in this loop of insecurity, it was necessary to go in the opposite direction from the people I was meeting at the border. To tell the story of US complicity—complicity of the country I've come to call home—in producing the violence that has made so many Mexicans into refugees from a wounded state, I had to follow the guns south.

Following the guns meant I had to first overcome my discomfort with them. Learning their vocabulary—like "quad rail," "hollow-point," and "bull-pup"—helped, allowing me to focus on their technical characteristics, briefly distracting from the violence those guns inflicted. I also had to unlearn the calcified lexicon of Mexican and US governments—the rhetoric of "war" and "cartels" that has put a straightjacket on people's experiences of terror and trauma. But I needed to do more than get used to new words. Although wrapped in discourse, guns are material things. I had to learn how to load them with the right ammunition, how to clear jams, how to hold them, how to breathe when I looked through the sights at the target in front, and how to shoot. I also had to learn how to disarm someone should they hold a gun to my head.

Following the guns meant getting to know people whose lives they passed through. Most Mexicans who owned illegal firearms never met the Americans who bought them and had only fleeting interactions with smugglers. Like the guns, I had to be on the move, hanging out with people in the United States and in Mexico, at gun clubs and in prisons, but also in bars, in their homes, at their workplaces, and—for long hours—in their cars driving from one place to another. Some were gun enthusiasts who smuggled firearms because they liked them better than what was legally available in Mexico. Others were members of organized crime groups who used guns to kidnap and kill. I interviewed dozens of people who worked with and around firearms, from soldiers and doctors to federal agents, attorneys, and social workers. I also poured over court transcripts and documents I obtained through public records requests, as well as investigations by US and Mexican authorities, researchers, journalists, and human rights groups. I provide a thorough description of my methods and sources at the end of the book.

Exit Wounds is my attempt to tell the story about what people do with guns and what guns do to people—people who are flawed and sometimes wrong, who have to make choices between bad options; people I didn't always agree with, but have come to care about nonetheless. Without ignoring or downplaying the gravity of the problem they have been a part of nor minimizing the human costs of gun violence, I tried to avoid both the graphic sensationalism that news media often succumb to and the stiff academic prose that is the norm for scholars. But finding a sincere voice of my own has not been easy. As an ethnographer working in proximity to violence, I have learned to use language as personal protective equipment, akin to the gloves and masks we donned as paramedics caring for the sick and injured—a shield insulating me from the brutal reality I witnessed. I hesitated to take it off.

This book delves into the lives of a handful of people I met during five years of research in Mexico and the United States. Their individual journeys, crisscrossing the border and the law, are unique, but they speak to collective experiences of violence and survival. Samara's story is about a family split apart by the border and about youth recruitment into organized crime; a story of a young woman in a violent male-dominated world. Miguel's story is about the economic elite who distrust the police and bypass laws to arm themselves with American guns. Ricky's story is about becoming a smuggler and about a binational community marked by legal asymmetries that create financial opportunities; and so is Hugo's, although he never smuggled guns. Jackson's and Alex's stories are of US federal agents investigating weapons and ammunition trafficking in the aftermath of an operation gone terribly wrong. And Juan's story is about the dangers faced by journalists who are reporting on organized crime; a story about the difficulties of producing knowledge about violence that I, as an ethnographer, am also a part of. Together, they reveal what guns have done to a society that doesn't begin or end at the international border. It is an all-American story.

Recruited

Monterrey, Nuevo León

Samara swerved left and right, maneuvering her old grey Volkswagen around potholes so large that they could swallow the car. We were in San Nicolás, on our way to colonia Carmen Romano. I didn't know the neighborhood. People more familiar with the geography of crime in Monterrey had advised me to stay away from this part of the city. Even Samara looked a bit surprised when she found me waiting for her at the street corner where the taxi driver had dropped me off that morning.

"Aren't you afraid?" she asked me.

"No," I said. Then, wary of the silence thickening between us: "Should I be?"

But she didn't answer.

I'd known Samara for almost two months, since an acquaintance introduced us via WhatsApp and we agreed to meet for lunch downtown, close to the university campus. I had never hung out with a member of an organized crime group, even a former one, before, and I didn't want to screw it up, so I arrived early and waited. "I'm on the second floor, in black shirt," I texted her then. Five minutes later, a message lit up on my phone. "I'm here," she wrote.

An unhealthy haze hung over the city that day, but instead of staying inside we picked a remote table on the terrace, as far away from the other customers as we could get, and ordered empanadas. Traffic noise on the street below—heavy engines rumbling and squealing, drivers honking at the cars that stopped or slowed, blocking their way—gave us some privacy. Samara was wearing a heart-shaped gold pendant and bright blue T-shirt with the phrase "Please cancel my subscription to your issues" printed on the front. Her thick wavy black hair was tied up, revealing fourteen stars tattooed on her neck. "For my brothers and sisters," she would tell me later, once I felt comfortable inquiring about such things.

As much as I wanted to hear her story, I hesitated. "I'm no longer ashamed," Samara said, noticing my reluctance to ask her questions. "Nor do I resent people who don't want to listen. Nor those who pass judgment. What happened, already happened." It was up to me whether I wanted to know or not. I put my phone on the table between our plates and hit "record." We stayed all afternoon and Samara only began recounting her life. After that day, we met again, and again.

In the winter of 2019, when our paths crossed, Samara had just turned twenty-three. At the time, she was commuting between home and work, about nine miles from San Nicolás in the northeast to San Pedro Garza García in the southwest, stopping midway for school. She was attending lectures at the Metropolitan University of Monterrey and that was where I usually saw her, in the city center, after her classes. But it was not the most convenient arrangement because Samara's school and work schedules could change on short notice and she would have to dash from one place to another. I didn't want to complicate matters any further, so, after a few meetings downtown, I offered to come to her neighborhood. She had told me about her grandparents' bakery and I was eager to meet her family, to see the streets she'd grown up on.

"My abuela lives there," Samara said and motioned toward the direction we were headed to on the potholed road. "That area is not very safe," she added.

Over a decade ago, when colonia Carmen Romano, like the rest of the city, was taken over by organized crime groups, armed young men would park their pickup trucks along Avenida Libaneses—the street that runs parallel to the train tracks connecting Monterrey to Matamoros—and climb onto the railcars to steal scrap metal. The stretch of the railway through San Nicolás became one of the most dangerous in the country and companies began hiring security personnel to ride on top the wagons. But their presence did not deter the bands of robbers who, in full daylight, took whatever they could find in the cargo: iron, aluminum, polyethylene. Some were brazen enough to engage in gunfights with the police. After briefly shutting down the line, the Mexican Railway Association increased the speed of the trains crossing the colonia from fifteen to thirty-five kilometers an hour. The tactics of acceleration worked: robberies went down. But it came at a cost. Residents were not used to the train speeding through the neighborhood and miscalculated how much time it would take to get through the railway crossing.

In 2019, the darkest days, when their colonia regularly appeared in crime news section, were over, but daily life in the neighborhood had changed little. There were carjackings and kidnappings and drive-by shootings. There was marijuana, cocaine, and crystal meth. Neighbors had to be careful about who they talked to and who they were seen with—the tentacles of old power structures, now under new names, still wrapped tightly around their community, ready to choke those who dared to disobey unspoken rules. Just a few days earlier someone smashed the windows of Samara's aunt's car and the family blamed it on her old acquaintances. "It was simply a dangerous area," Samara said, furious about the accusations. She wanted to believe that the incident was random, that it had nothing to do with her past.

Returning to this neighborhood hadn't been easy for her. Although she wouldn't admit it to her family, dismissing her aunt's suspicions, the people she was once associated with and their enemies had threatened her. They sent her messages, telling her they knew where she lived. They told her they would kill her. Samara changed phone numbers and social media accounts, using different spellings of her first and last names. But they knew how to find her.

One time, about two years before we met, they almost got her. She didn't have a car back then and would take the subway. If school or work ended late, her uncle would come wait for her at the metro stop and accompany her home. But that day he had another commitment and told her to call a cab. "Two trucks blocked the taxi," Samara told me. "My blood ran cold," she said. The men exited the vehicles and opened the door of the taxi. One of them started pulling her out. She dove her hand into her purse and found her pepper spray, which she pointed at the attacker, but then another guy put a gun to her head. To Samara's surprise, the taxi driver intervened. He began hitting the attacker, which gave her a chance to wrestle the pistol from his hands. "I don't think they had much experience," she said about the people who tried to kidnap her.

Still, their attempt scared her. That evening she called her father. "I was crying and shaking," she remembered. He told her to go to the bus station right away. Samara threw a change of clothes and her textbooks into a backpack and, holding her passport with a new US visa in her hands, headed to Houston to stay with her father. He lived in a trailer with her three older brothers, his new wife, and their daughter, with little room for one more. But Samara didn't despair. In the months that followed, she worked various jobs to be able to buy a phone, rent her own place, and soon save enough money for a used car. Family and friends who cared about her told her to stay in Texas, where she was safe. But Samara didn't want to.

"Why?" I asked.

"I don't want to live my life in hiding all the time," she said. "It is not my country." She admitted it was difficult for her in the United States. "I was humiliated, bullied, shouted at, called 'Mexicana,' called 'mojada.'"

She'd been back from Texas for several months now and things were better than before. She continued attending university on a tuition scholarship and had a part-time job at a clothing boutique. But she was not naive. It was possible that threats simply hadn't caught up with her yet. Or had they? Whoever vandalized her aunt's car may have done it on purpose. Samara said she always carried a pepper spray in her bag. So did I, I told her.

Past Jardines de Anáhuac, we crossed a wide intersection and Samara turned into a residential neighborhood. The house she parked in front of had her family's name on the plate. It looked like a private residence, one among multiple similar structures in the street, their concrete walls, painted in mismatched colors, butting against a crumbling sidewalk. There was no indication it was a bakery: no store sign, no hours of operation. Samara unhinged the gate and we entered the front yard.

The family had lived in the same house since the "founding" of San Nicolás, Samara said, which, she explained, was when people claimed unoccupied plots of land and built makeshift homes. Their family's lot ended up in what later became the middle of the street, so they had to move it back. Samara grew up hearing her grandparents tell stories about those old times, when there was no electricity and people had to go fetch water in buckets. That era was long gone. Now the bakery had a social media account and they were filling online orders for bread and pan dulce. There were cakes for Mother's Day and Rosca de Reyes, the sweet bread shaped as a crown, on Epiphany, and on most days there were trays full of chocolate-glazed donuts.

The bakery had been Samara's grandfather's idea. He knew how to make artisanal bread in the adobe stove and taught his wife and his daughters, starting a family business that operated for decades from under the same roof where they lived. Samara always spoke tenderly about her grandfather, whom she called "papa." He was the only person in the family she revered. When he passed away in 2018, she got a tattoo on her left arm bearing his name and the dates of his birth and death. With the anniversary of his passing approaching, her grandmother was planning a service. Samara's father would be flying in from Houston. They wanted to hire a mariachi band to sing at his grave.

I followed Samara inside, past the front store with bread and pastries lining the shelves and scents of vanilla and burnt sugar, and through the door in the back. The large adobe oven was on, a horizontal slit in the wall, heat spouting from its red mouth, as if we had walked into a room-size furnace. Samara pointed to the large trays of dough that her aunt prepared in the morning and left to ferment. I wondered how come Samara didn't get into baking, but she shrugged off my question.

We didn't have much time because Samara had to leave for work. The job at the lingerie store at the mall in San Pedro was part-time and its schedule allowed her to continue her studies. But three weeks in she was still waiting for her first paycheck and was beginning to worry how she'd afford her rent. I, too, was beginning to worry. She was not desperate, not yet. She still thought it would work out and, though she allowed me to pay for our breakfast of chilaquiles, she refused my repeated offers to help her with the groceries. Before we said our goodbyes, Samara picked a plastic bag and filled it with *dulces de cajeta* for me to take to the hotel.

I left, hoping that this would be it, the new chapter of her life, that she wouldn't have to go back to *them*.

The first time Samara saw them, on an otherwise unremarkable day in 2009, she was taking out the trash. Heavily armed, they were sitting in a car in front of the four-story apartment building she'd been living in. As soon as she noticed them, she wanted to run, but fear shackled her feet. Then she realized they were not all strangers. Some were friends of her cousins—she'd seen them hang out together. Reluctantly, she greeted them.

"What's your name?" asked one of the guys. He wore thick-rimmed glasses and a yellow Tigres jersey.

She knew he worked for the Zetas. She already knew about the Zetas. The last letter of the alphabet had been excised from the local lexicon, as if refusal to identify the group denied its existence. But the menace spread, enveloping the city like a fog, making it hard to see the shape of things. All residents could do was listen. To rumors. To threats. To the staccato of gunfire jolting them at night. For years shielded from violence devastating other parts of Mexico, *regiomontanos*, as the people of Monterrey called themselves, found that war was at their doorstep.

"Samara," she said.

"How old are you?"

"Sixteen."

"And your parents?"

"They're upstairs."

It was a lie; two lies, actually. Samara was thirteen and lived alone. Her parents separated soon after she was born, when her father left for Houston and her mother for Fort Worth. They stayed in Texas, formed new families. Samara grew up with her maternal grandmother, who worked long hours, and her teenage aunts, who bullied her. Once a week she'd escape to her father's parents, her *abuelitos*, to the house with the bakery. That was the way things were when she was little and had no say. Now she was independent, trying to make it on her own.

"Órale!" the young man said, without showing whether he believed her. "Would you like to get inside?"

"No," she replied firmly, then turned around and headed back up.

Her apartment afforded a decent view of the neighborhood: an urban mass of bricks-and-concrete sliced up into rectangles and sutured by a cobweb of cables, with a few specks of green here and there. The little money residents could spend on exterior design went into iron fences and window grates. Even by these standards Samara's home was austere. "It was a big apartment, pretty, but it had nothing," she said. There was no stove to cook, no fridge to store food. Samara slept on an air mattress—the single piece of furniture inside. But she didn't complain.

She told herself that living alone had been her choice after all. When she turned eight, Samara's mother called from Fort Worth and invited her to come to the United States. Samara was too upset at her mother for having abandoned her, so she hung up. But a year passed, then another, and the phone kept ringing. Samara's reaction was the same. "Why did she have me if she was going to leave me? Why did she bring me into this world if she was going to go to another place? Why did she make me suffer?" Her grandmother tried to reason with the girl. "You have to give her a chance," she implored. "She is your mother." Slowly, the arguments began to sink in. Samara was doing well at school, was chosen as the *abanderada*—the flag bearer—at official school events, but nobody was there to see her. While other parents came to collect their children's grades and attended performances, the absence of her mother and father nagged at her. Nobody noticed her accomplishments. Maybe her grandmother was right, she thought, maybe she should accept her mother's invitation. Besides, she couldn't stand living with her aunts and this was an opportunity to get away from them. "OK," she finally said.

Samara's first weeks in Fort Worth went well, but the calm didn't last. Her stepfather got locked up because, as far as she understood, the police mistook him for a local gangster. Her mother started working night shifts at the restaurant, on top of her regular hours, but still wasn't earning enough and couldn't pay the rent, so they moved, then moved again. Samara enrolled in school and learned English. In the evenings and on weekends, she did house chores and looked after her younger siblings. When her mother came home from work, exhausted and irritable, Samara shielded her brothers and sisters from her rage, preferring to take the punches alone.

"My grandmother taught me to be strong, not to cry, not to bow my head to anyone," she said. Samara knew how to take care of herself. But, as the months passed, she became more worried about her siblings. With a rotating cast of her mother's boyfriends staying in the apartment, she thought they were not safe there. One time, when Samara was bathing her little sister, she noticed her mother's new partner watching them. She closed and locked the bathroom door, but he began banging, which woke Samara's mother up. "I explained what happened, but she said I was lying," Samara recalled. Her mother dismissed her daughter's accusations against her boyfriend. That night, she beat Samara with her studded belt.

More incidents followed, more lies and beatings, until finally Samara called her father for help. He drove 260 miles to Fort Worth to pick her up and brought her back with him to Houston. But after about a week Samara began feeling that she was a burden to his growing family. Angry at both of her parents, unable to find a place in their new lives in Texas, she made up her mind to go back to Mexico. Her father supported her decision and even helped her with the rent. When after a few months he stopped sending money, Samara found a job attending the cash register and mopping floors at a neighborhood store in San Nicolás. But one day she tripped and got hurt and the woman who managed the store swiftly fired her to avoid legal troubles for employing a teenager. "I was left with nothing. I called my father every day hoping he would pick up," she said. Samara knew she would soon be unable to pay rent for the apartment.

Those weeks after she first ran into the armed guys in the car she was mostly staying home, nothing to lay her eyes on but the action outside. She stood by the window at the same hour day after day and watched the same group return. She avoided them, planning her trips outside only when they were not around.

The holiday season made matters worse. That year was the first time Samara spent Christmas and New Year's without her family. Reluctant to admit failure, she would go days without eating rather than ask her abuelitos for help. "I didn't want them to feel sorry for me," she said. "They would always offer me to eat, but because of pride and because I didn't want them to know I was struggling, I would tell them: I'm good, I've already eaten, thank you." When she visited them at the bakery, she could snatch a pastry or two off the shelves.

One such day on her way back from her grandparents' house she took a different route, which made her walk past a store that served as a meeting point for members of organized crime. Groups of armed men, including the ones she saw coming to the lot in front of her apartment building, would pull up in their trucks and settle their deals there. Samara tried passing them unnoticed, but she heard someone whistle at her and stopped. "How dare you?" she confronted the guy. At the moment she didn't see that he had a gun. "Shut up! You don't know who he is," someone there tried to warn her. "Me vale madre," she said, feeling righteous.

"That's when it all started," she said. She remembered a burst of laughter, then the guy with the gun giving an order—"Pick her up!" Several men grabbed her and shoved her into a truck. Blindfolded, she could not see where they were taking her. The truck made a few stops before someone opened the door and pulled her out. She found herself in a room with other captives: some of them were members of rival gangs, others were people kidnapped for ransom. The men who guarded the room didn't give her anything to eat or to drink. But that wasn't the worst that could have happened. "They didn't touch me. Thank God, they didn't do anything bad to me," she said.

Samara lost track of time, of how many days, how many nights she was there. They moved her from place to place with the other captives. Dead bodies they left behind reminded the ones still alive what would happen to those who were overpriced in this economy of violence, those whose families could not afford to save them. At some point, the guys asked Samara about her parents and she kept to her story, repeating she did not have a family. "My parents are dead," she told them her truth. "I'm on my own."

Perhaps they believed her because they let her go.

Then, a couple of days later, she heard a knock on the door.

"Comandante is waiting for you," the messenger said, and took her to meet the bespectacled young man she talked to that day outside her apartment building. She would learn to call him Comandante Gafudo.

Comandante gave her a 9mm.

"Do you like it?" he asked.

"No," she said.

"*Pues*, you will."

Arming the State

Ciudad de México

"Finally, on August 13, 1521, México-Tenochtitlán is conquered in blood and fire by Spanish weapons," concludes the narrative printed on a plaque inside the hall dedicated to the Mexica (Aztec) Empire at the National Museum of Anthropology in Mexico City. An army officer who was more excited to show me the present and future of Mexico's national weapons industry summarized this early chapter of his country's history by saying, "The Spanish had military technology, while we threw stones at them."

The first firearms came to Mexico in the sixteenth century, aboard the ships of the European invaders, and stayed to enforce colonial order for the next three hundred years. During the Spanish rule, almost all guns protecting the forts and carried by soldiers in the conquered lands were manufactured in the Iberian Peninsula. The colonial administration built mines to extract silver and gold but it wasn't interested in digging iron, which could be brought by ship from the Vizcaya region in Spain.[1] The Crown held a commercial monopoly over the metal and its alloys, and while local production was not prohibited, it was not practical. In times of peace, developing the iron deposits made little sense because it was cheaper to import it from Spain. Only in wartime, when conflicts between European states halted maritime commerce, did this dependence on supplies from the Iberian Peninsula become a problem. Although during one such period of fighting at the end of the eighteenth century an iron ore mine opened in the mountains south of

Guadalajara, production there stopped as soon as ships from Spain resumed their voyages.[2] It wasn't until the last stretch of the colonial era that officials in New Spain began devising a strategy for developing iron mining as a local industry. In a way, controlling the supply of iron helped the Spanish rulers dominate its colonial subjects overseas: lacking primary materials to make European-style weapons, local inhabitants had limited tools to threaten the Crown.

The colonial administration took the matter of guns very seriously. For a long time, firearms in Spanish America were rather scarce. The few harquebuses brought across the Atlantic generally belonged to Spanish soldiers. Indigenous peoples of the conquered lands were not allowed to buy firearms (or horses, for that matter). However, over the years, nations along the northern frontier who were in contact with British and French traders, among them Apaches, Navajos, and Comanches, managed to procure large amounts of guns and ammunition and willingly sold them to others, eventually eroding the military advantage of Spanish colonists.[3] In 1771, as concerns about losing overseas territories to rival powers rose following the Seven Years War, King Carlos III issued a royal decree outlawing all inhabitants of New Spain to manufacture, sell, and use firearms.[4] By then, local artisans had learned how to repair guns, but they were still unable to make them from scratch in their own shops.[5] The Crown also held a monopoly over production and distribution of gunpowder, known as "*estanco de pólvora.*"[6] Because of its high demand in silver and gold mining, gunpowder was made locally: the first munitions factory opened in 1600 in an old flour mill in Chapultepec, about three and a half miles west of the viceregal palace, and another one was built in 1784 farther to the south and west of the capital city in Santa Fe.[7] Though of mediocre quality, local gunpowder was cheaper than its alternative imported from Europe. As with firearms, however, people in New Spain could not procure it by bypassing the state.[8]

What this meant was that Mexicans who answered Miguel Hidalgo's call to arms that started the Mexican War of Independence in 1810 and later defended their country from US and French invasions carried guns made by foreigners, often their enemies. An assortment of these historic guns—muskets, flintlock carbines, rifles—is on display under the tall ceiling inside a government building that houses the Army Museum in Mexico City, which I visited in the fall of 2018. Their stories and significance are briefly noted in accompanying labels: a Tower Model 1760 flintlock pistol from England; a flintlock rifle designed by Isidro

Soler, a renowned harquebusier serving the Spanish king, made in 1804 in Madrid; an 1814 musket manufactured in the Springfield Armory in Massachusetts. Walking counterclockwise through history that begins with the conquest and ends with latest weapons developments, I gazed at dozens of old Winchesters, Remingtons, and Colts and read about their role in the armed struggles that led to Mexico's modern nationhood.

Standing upright on their sleek wooden stocks, their bodies engraved with swirling floral patterns, the rifles in display cases appeared like relics from the past. What could they, so unlike the assault weapons used today, tell me about the making of violence now? I examined the guns slowly, searching for cues. A Colt revolver in one of the glass cases was manufactured in 1860 in New York. I bent over to have a closer look and saw that its handle was decorated with an eagle carrying a serpent—an American gun marked with the Mexican national emblem. A white plaque behind the revolver carried an image of Benito Juárez and the message he delivered while he was the governor of Oaxaca speaking to the state congress in 1852: "Public officials . . . cannot govern at the impulse of capricious will, but subject to the laws." I wondered what those remarks had to do with the weapons surrounding me.

For much of the nineteenth century, Mexico was at war. And in those wars, the new nation-state continued to depend on imported guns, often leftovers from previous conflicts that were no longer used by the countries that manufactured them. When the United States, eager to expand its territory to the south and to the west, invaded Mexico in 1846, Mexican soldiers defending their homeland were equipped with British muskets from the Napoleonic Wars. In those days, the Mexican military was poorly trained, politically divided, and reliant on antiquated foreign firepower, which made stopping the invasion by their northern neighbor an implausible task. Mexico lost about half its territory. Texas, Utah, Nevada, California, and large chunks of what is now Arizona, Colorado, and New Mexico were incorporated into the United States.

The logistics of procuring firearms for Mexican forces fighting against foreign armies were so complicated that successful operations were recounted as adventure stories. Not long after the US invasion, Mexico was plunged into another war, known as the Second French Intervention. Benito Juárez, now Mexico's 26th president, sent agents to Boston, New York, Philadelphia, and other cities around the United States to buy firearms and gunpowder. The American Civil War having just ended, supplies were abundant. President Juárez heard about the "wondrous, unstoppable" Winchester Model 66 and ordered one thousand rifles and half a million rounds of ammunition.[9] Establishing the norm which American gun manufacturers would embrace in conflicts to come, Winchester did not take sides and supplied both warring parties. An order of Winchester rifles had already been shipped to France for Emperor Maximilian's forces when, in 1866, the company's first arms salesman, Thomas Emmett Addis, set out toward Mexico. From the factory in New Haven, Connecticut, he brought the cargo to the border town of Brownsville, Texas, then loaded the guns onto oxcarts, crossed the Rio Grande, and embarked on a 240-mile journey to Monterrey. It was a trip worthy of a movie script: a tale about an American businessman traveling through inhospitable lands, facing danger, outwitting his enemies, and living to tell the story. American guns that Addis brought to Mexico helped Juárez defeat Maximilian's forces, with Winchester rifles responsible for some part of the 50,000 casualties of the war.

Other consequences of Mexico buying American weapons to repel the French took much longer to come to light. Based on archival research in the company's records, historian Pamela Haag argues that the money Juárez paid for the weapons was crucial to balance Winchester's accounts.[10] The demand for guns came at just the right time when a broad consumer market for firearms did not yet exist in the United States. To some degree, Mexico's order of rifles helped US gun manufacturers continue production on a massive scale, creating conditions for the industry's expansion later, which had lasting effects on both US and Mexican societies. Another reason those weapons' sales had significant repercussions was because the Juárez administration, short on cash, exchanged arms for bonds, creating a cycle of credit and debt. In his book *Empire and Revolution*, historian John Hart explained how American investors extended loans for muskets, cannons, and other equipment needed on the front lines without expecting Mexico to be able to pay for them.[11] When the Mexican government failed to redeem its debts, as they predicted would happen, American creditors and arms merchants put pressure on the US authorities to intervene. This way, using arms debt as leverage, US investors gained land concessions to advance railway projects in Mexico. In sum, Mexico got the guns it needed, but did so at the expense of losing control over large sectors of the country's national economy and gaining a potential threat to its sovereignty.

Mexican people who worked for companies owned by US entrepreneurs close to the Mexico-US border experienced the worst consequences of this arrangement. Historian Kelly Lytle Hernández recounts how, in 1906, William C. Greene, the owner of a copper mine in Cananea, Sonora, rushed to Bisbee, Arizona, to buy weapons to suppress a strike by miners who were protesting poor working conditions and pay cuts.[12] Although dozens of people were killed, the Mexican government did not intervene to defend its citizens. After all, Greene was a friend of Mexican President Porfirio Díaz, who allowed US investors to do as they pleased in the large swaths of the country they controlled. US politicians and entrepreneurs even commended Díaz for the "order and progress" he had brought to Mexico during his more than three-decade-long rule.[13] That millions of Mexican peasants were driven off their lands during this time was none of their concern. Not yet anyway.

As I continued my tour of the Army Museum, I stopped in front of another Colt revolver. It was affixed to a square cement stone, like the other guns in the exhibit, but not enclosed in a glass cage. This firearm, too, was made in the United States in the second half of the nineteenth century. The label next to the revolver said that it "was used by the *cuerpos de rurales* during the Porfiriato and subsequently during the Mexican Revolution, by groups in the northern states." A gun that switched sides. Wielded by the rural mounted police patrolling the countryside to brutally enforce Díaz's rule, it landed in the hands of unidentified rebels who turned against the regime. It was just a tool—the gun didn't care what political project its firepower served.

The Mexican Revolution began as a rebellion against Díaz, but soon evolved into a violent decade-long civil conflict over land and power that would remake both Mexico and the United States.[14] As in previous wars, fighters were armed with an eclectic arsenal of guns of various models and calibers. By the beginning of the twentieth century, Mexican gunsmiths had become experts in fixing and modifying weapons and the state was producing munitions, both for artillery and for portable firearms, but not in sufficient quantities to avoid the need to look for guns and ammunition abroad. Various factions vying to overthrow the Díaz regime had been stockpiling weapons in the northern borderlands. Members of the radical rebel movement led by Ricardo Flores Magón collected donations to buy guns and ammunition and then stashed weapons, which they referred to as *dulces y escobas* (candies and brooms), under floorboards in ranch houses belonging to their allies in Douglas, El Paso, Del Rio, and other border towns.[15] In 1910, Francisco Madero, who had been arrested after he challenged Díaz in an election, fled to Texas and began buying guns in preparation for an armed revolt.[16] Gun dealers in the United States, seeing such increased demand for their products, rejoiced.

The beginning of World War I increased global demand for firearms and put an end to the imports of European guns across the Atlantic, which further strengthened the US role as the primary supplier of weapons for various factions of the Mexican Revolution—a role that the US government tried to use to its advantage. In 1912, when Díaz fled into exile and Madero assumed power, US President William Taft declared an embargo on gun exports to Mexico, citing "conditions of domestic violence" south of the border, "promoted by the use of arms or munitions of war procured from the United States."[17] The embargo was to prevent guns from getting into the hands of generals who opposed Madero's moderate government because of its failure to implement the promised agrarian reform: Emiliano Zapata was leading a peasant army fighting for more radical redistribution of land in the south; Pascual Orozco staged a rebellion against the regime in the north; and many other ambitious and disgruntled fighters who had helped oust Díaz were ready to withdraw their support for the new government and take up arms against it. When General Victoriano Huerta staged a coup that overthrew Madero, US President Woodrow Wilson refused to accept the legitimacy of the new regime. In addition to continuing a US arms embargo, he tried to convince European countries and Japan to follow the US lead and stop selling firearms to the Mexican government. Previously wary of rebel generals, now the United States was more inclined to support some of them. US authorities knew that Venustiano Carranza, Pancho Villa, and others fighting against Huerta's regime relied on arms and munitions smuggled across land and sea borders and gave these shipments tacit approval.[18] In 1914, President Wilson even briefly lifted the arms embargo, which particularly benefited the Villa-led Division of the North.[19]

Meddling with the provisions of arms and ammunition was not all the United States did during the Mexican Revolution. In hopes of turning the civil conflict in directions that would spare US interests in the borderlands, on two occasions President Wilson sent US troops to Mexico: in 1914, the US Navy occupied the port of Veracruz, preventing Huerta from receiving a large arms shipment headed there; and in 1916, once the United States decided to back Carranza, thousands of US army soldiers crossed into Chihuahua in a failed military operation aimed at capturing Villa. The Mexican Revolution also affected US domestic affairs. As long as fighting in Mexico continued, US authorities feared that unrest would not stop at the border. These concerns flared upon discovering a manifesto, known as El Plan de San Diego, which called Mexicans and their allies to rise against Anglo-American settlers in the border regions.[20] When in 1915 insurgents in Texas started an uprising, raiding several towns and ranches, destroying railroad tracks and bridges, the US Army violently retaliated against Mexicans and Mexican Americans in the borderlands, killing hundreds, likely thousands.[21]

Despite neutrality laws and restrictions on selling arms to Mexicans and fears that Mexicans could use the guns to take back Texas, American weapons never stopped flowing across the border, often creatively concealed.[22] Guns were hidden in boxes marked as agricultural tools and even in baby carriages.[23] The US government did not do much to intervene, which allowed American gun merchants to profit handsomely.[24] In towns along the border, such as Laredo, Texas, hardware stores could barely keep up with demand for the *treinta-treinta*, as .30–30 Winchester carbines were called, which fighters in Mexico so desired. In his book *Border Contraband*, historian George Díaz recounts how US Customs officers charged with enforcing American neutrality laws watched, their hands tied, as buyers left stores with heaps of guns, then waited until nightfall to take them across the river farther away from town, where customs inspectors didn't go.[25] Even when law enforcement agents amassed evidence against local businessmen involved in arms smuggling, jurors refused to indict them.[26] Contraband fell within the moral economy of the borderlands in those days and remained so for many years.[27]

After a century of wars against enemies both foreign and domestic, the postrevolutionary Mexican government understood that in order to stay in power, it had to do two things. The first was to cut off weapon supplies for rebels who threatened the regime with guns they acquired in the United States, often, at the time, in exchange for whiskey.[28] The second was to build a national arms industry and thereby avoid dependency on the United States for its own military needs. Neither of these would be easy.

Spectators started lining up along the route of the Independence Day parade before sunrise, then waited for hours until the military procession left Zócalo and poured into Paseo de la Reforma. It was September 16, 2018, and I was watching the crowds on TV in my hotel room, its thin walls unable to block the chopping noise of military helicopters as they circled above the rooftops. Having attended military parades before, I knew to stay away. Soldiers in uniforms clutching their rifles, marching in carefully orchestrated columns, to mark events of national significance made me uncomfortable. Memories of my early childhood in Soviet-occupied Lithuania, of Russian tanks crushing the bodies of peaceful protestors defending the country's new freedom the year I started primary school, still haunted me. Watching the parade on television meant I could look away.

The screen on the wall projected military might, showing formation after formation of men and women with animals and machines advancing across Mexico City: sailors in white uniforms with neckerchiefs, snipers in ghillie suits clutching black rifles with scopes, armed marines in green camouflage, trucks and horses and dogs and eagles perched on the gloved hands of military college cadets. More than eighteen thousand members from the army, navy, air force, and federal police were participating in the parade. The presenter's offscreen voice noted that one of those groups marched carrying the new "100% Mexican rifles." Though I could not spot them on the screen, I knew what she was referring to. Formally known as FX-05, the gun had another name, Xiuhcóatl, a Classical Nahuatl word for the "turquoise serpent." The original Xiuhcóatl was a weapon resembling lightning wielded by the deity of war and human sacrifice, Huitzilopochtli. The indigenous rulers of Tenochtitlan decorated their diadems with Xiuhcóatl's tale. Xiuhcóatl the rifle bears the symbols of Xiuhcóatl the serpent: the logo on the side of the firearm depicts a rattlesnake and the transparent magazine clip reveals metal coils that hold 5.56 caliber rounds.[29]

Only two weeks since arriving in Mexico City, I had already encountered Xiuhcóatls twice. It was the last item on display at the Army Museum, the end of the narrative that began with the old Winchesters and Colts from the days of the Porfiriato and the Mexican Revolution. That rifle—long and hefty—was enclosed in a thick case with yellow-greenish lighting which made its black body appear like bronze. The next time I saw Xiuhcóatls, they were dangling on the shoulders of military personnel during a voluntary gun buyback campaign in a colonia on the border between Mexico City and the State of Mexico. "It is too light, made of plastic," said a former Mexican marine turned gun expert for the police, a 9mm Glock on his hip, as we watched three soldiers in camouflage fatigues walk past us armed with FX-05. The man whose job was to know guns said then that he didn't have much confidence in the new 100 percent Mexican rifle. Like others in positions that allowed them to choose, he preferred American and European weapons. Regular soldiers, however, had no say about their guns.

At the end of the Mexican Revolution, when Carranza became president, he was adamant about establishing the country's autonomy over weapons and munitions as a matter of national sovereignty. He saw the dangers of Mexico continuing to depend on the whims of the United States and other countries, which could impose and lift embargoes based on their own interests, thereby exerting influence over the country's internal affairs. He worried that Mexico could not even address its domestic policy issues—the "pacification" of the country—without turning to foreign powers for supplies.[30] American and European guns cost less, but Mexico was paying the price of humiliation, having to explain the purpose each time they wanted to buy firearms.[31] Carranza announced a series of reforms in 1916, laying the foundation for national production of war materials.[32] "We must manufacture our own arms and munitions if we don't want our domestic affairs to be decided by those who procure them for us," he declared.[33]

Although Carranza passed reforms that would make this possible, his aspirations for Mexico to make its own firearms did not become reality right away. It was too expensive an undertaking in the aftermath of the Revolution, when the government had other priorities. And with its northern neighbor emerging from World War I as a major arms producer, Mexico's enterprise would have had to be both efficient and cheap in order to be viable. For all practical purposes, it was still easier and cheaper to buy foreign guns than to make them locally.[34]

But Carranza's warnings about dependency were not forgotten. With some delay and despite the costs, Mexico imported German machinery for manufacturing bolt-action Mauser rifles and carbines and installed it in the national arms factory.[35] The factory began production in the 1930s and, in addition to Mauser rifles, made light machine guns designed by Rafael Mendoza, a veteran of the Mexican Revolution and Villa's former bodyguard.[36] The Mexican military continued to use Mendoza machine guns through the late 1950s and Mauser rifles into the 1960s, but, as other countries switched to automatic and semiautomatic weapons, eventually the time came to find a new standard issue firearm. Besides a traditional repeater system, Mauser rifles contained parts made of wood, which did not fare well in a tropical climate. After initially negotiating with the Belgian company FN Herstal, the Mexican government made an agreement with German Heckler and Koch

(H&K). The company allowed Mexico to produce its own automatic G3 rifles chambered for 7.62 × 51mm cartridges, on the condition that Mexico would not sell them abroad.[37] By the 1980s, Mexico was also manufacturing other firearms based on H&K models, including light machine guns and 9mm semiautomatic pistols. All these weapons were exclusively issued to personnel in the armed forces.

"Germans are tall," said the officer tasked with giving me a tour around the headquarters of the General Directorate of Military Industry that same September of 2018. He raised one arm up above his head, then lowered it. "Mexicans are short, like me," he said, smiling. In his opinion, the G3 assault rifles the army had been using were not adapted for the Mexican physique. As tools, guns were a material extension of both bodies—the national as well as the individual. I followed the officer around the hall dedicated to the centennial exhibit and stopped to read Carranza's famous dictum about the importance of Mexico manufacturing its own arms printed on the wall. Nearly a century after he shared his vision, the plan of a national military industry had at last become reality. Mexico began serial production of the new assault weapon, the FX-05, in 2006. The first batch of new rifles went to the army special forces. A decade later, in January 2016, General Salvador Cienfuegos gave a speech promising to equip every Mexican soldier with FX-05 rifles within a couple more years. The timeline was ambitious, but, once this project was completed, the defense secretary said, "we will be able to avoid dependence on the outside."[38]

In his celebratory remarks, the general did not address the dislike some in the security forces had for the new rifles and did not mention their reluctance to adopt them. The official view was the one I had heard at the headquarters. For the short Mexican military officer, as for the Mexican government, the gun's articulation with the Mexican state was somatic—seen as fitting the body type of Mexican soldiers—as much as it was semantic. Marking it with "made in Mexico" stamps was a matter of national sovereignty. Neither my guide nor General Cienfuegos in his public speech clarified what causes these rifles would be put to use for—those "domestic affairs" Carranza referred to when he made his famous pronouncement about the need for Mexico to have its own military industry.

The Mexican Constitution of 1917 outlined a political philosophy committed to social rights. It laid the foundation for a series of reforms the revolutionaries had been fighting for, which began dismantling old structures of property and power, including expropriating land owned by large haciendas and redistributing it to the peasants, as well as protecting workers, mandating free secular education, and nationalizing oil. Like the earlier version, promulgated in 1857, the new charter of the nation also recognized individual rights, among them the right of citizens to bear arms. As noted in Article 10, "The inhabitants of the United Mexican States have the right to possess arms in their homes for their security and legitimate defense with the exception of those [weapons] prohibited by federal law and those reserved for the exclusive use of the Army, Navy, Air Force, and National Guard."[39] It also said that "Federal law shall determine the cases, conditions, requirements and places [under and] in which the inhabitants may be authorized to bear arms."

Regulating who could own what firearms became the prerogative of the Federal Penal Code enacted in 1931. Carrying pistols and revolvers required a license, which was only issued to people who could prove their need for a weapon and demonstrated records of "honorability and prudence."[40] The law also established the right of public employees to carry arms "needed to perform their duties" and described penalties for persons who "carry, manufacture, import or store, without a legal purpose, instruments that can only be used to attack, and which have no application for work or for recreation." Through these provisions, the Penal Code qualified the constitutional right to bear arms—that right was not unconditional.

But the letter of the law, so neat on paper, corresponded unevenly to the realities on the ground. By the time the Revolution was over, Mexico was swarming with guns. While regulations and license fees limited who could acquire firearms, they became more readily available to Mexican civilians.[41] In Mexico City, where during the Porfiriato few residents had guns, now not only soldiers and policemen, but even congressmen carried high-caliber Colt and Smith & Wesson pistols. According to historian Pablo Piccato, representatives would even bring their firearms to congressional debates, where at least two members of parliament died in fights from gunshot wounds in the 1920s.[42]

As years passed and memories of the Revolution began to fade, Mexico may have looked like a democracy, where people voted in popular elections and their rights were protected by the rule of law, but such appearances were deceiving. Underneath the constitutional veil lurked an authoritarian state. For over seventy years, the Institutional Revolutionary Party (PRI, for its initials in Spanish) never lost power. It controlled society through networks of patronage that were so extensive and profound that more often than not they helped authorities avoid the open use of force. That didn't mean coercion was absent. In the mid-twentieth century, as labor unions raised demands for workers' rights, organizing strikes and engaging in other forms of protest, including land invasions, they were met with violent repression by the government, particularly in the countryside. In Morelos, Guerrero, and elsewhere, campesinos, Indigenous communities, and teacher-led guerilla groups had been resisting the PRI regime for decades, and the government's ruthless response to their organizing only strengthened their resolve. As Alexander Aviña argues in his book *Specters of Revolution*, rather than smothering them, political repression during Mexico's Dirty War further radicalized reformist social movements.[43] What began as "popular acts of armed self-defense in reaction to systematic state-elite violence" developed into guerilla organizations determined to overthrow the regime.[44]

Soon Mexicans living in cities, for decades removed from state terror against rural communities, would get to see what was behind the mask of benevolence their mildly authoritarian government put on for the national media it largely controlled. When thousands of students gathered to a large protest in Mexico City, days before the opening of the 1968 Olympics, the regime dropped all pretense that it was only fighting "criminals." How many were killed when soldiers opened fire at unarmed protestors in what became known as the Tlatelolco Massacre is still unknown, but the death toll was likely in the hundreds.[45] The persecution of protestors led to further escalation of violence, which the government blamed on armed leftist groups and their leaders who allegedly had links with Cuba and the Soviet Union, and who were calling youth to an open rebellion against the regime.[46] Mainstream media in the United States joined the Mexican press to echo fears that Marxist guerilla groups were planning to use force to overthrow the Mexican government. In a story about the Revolutionary Action Movement, the *New York Times* noted that the urban guerilla group behind a spate of bank robberies was "of greater efficiency and sophistication than had been previously imagined" and quoted a Mexican colonel saying that the arms they used were "the most modern and powerful available in the world today."[47]

At the start of the 1970s, Mexicans who began their day by leafing through the newspapers, found in them much to worry about. The situation they saw in those pages seemed dire, made more alarming when events in Mexico were placed in the context of other armed conflicts dominating the global affairs. The US military continued fighting in Vietnam, even though support for the war had diminished and President Richard Nixon began withdrawing troops. In Northern Ireland, violent conflict between Irish nationalist groups and loyalist paramilitaries intensified, drawing in the British Army. Tensions were high in Latin America. Fearing the spillover of the Cuban Revolution, leaders in the region had become more brutal in their repression of Marxist guerillas. In Colombia, the list of movements that had taken up arms against the government continued to grow, with the 19th of April Movement joining the already active FARC, ELN, and EPL.[48] In Chile, President Salvador Allende's bold efforts to nationalize the mining industry, health care, and education, and redistribute land, faced opposition from congress and pressure from the United States, raising questions about whether the country was headed toward civil war. A civil war was already raging in Guatemala, where leftist guerillas were fighting against the US-backed government and their counterinsurgency campaign. Along Mexico's southern border, in Chiapas, the Mexican army occasionally ran into Guatemalan guerillas operating in the Lacandón jungle. Against this global and regional background, news of police raids of guerilla training camps and arrests of students from rural teachers' colleges who were forming alliances with the campesinos and engaging in land invasions in Chihuahua and other parts of the country, served to sow fear among the readers that Mexico, too, could descend into an armed civil conflict, purportedly justifying government's heavy-handed response.[49]

In May 1971, Governor Eduardo Elizondo ordered security forces to take over the Autonomous University of Nuevo León, considered the stronghold of student resistance in Monterrey. In the report they sent to Mexico City, the police warned that skirmishes at the university were particularly dangerous in this region because "heavy caliber weapons are present in every house and people can start using them at any time."[50] As they searched the premises of the university, officers found pistols, knives, Molotov cocktails, as well as typewriters and recordings of Che Guevara. Lists of tools and materials seized during police raids like this circulated in the media as material evidence, as if the objects themselves were metonymic of crimes they could have been—or were planned to be—used for. The state feared both metal and ink as instruments that could undermine its power. When, in support of their peers in Nuevo León, students at the National Autonomous University of

Mexico (UNAM) and National Polytechnic Institute called for a rally in Mexico City, members of the government-trained paramilitary group Los Halcones attacked them with sticks and rifles, killing several dozen protestors and injuring over a hundred more in what is now remembered both as El Halconazo and the Corpus Christi Massacre.

But the more the state resorted to violence, the more active resistance it provoked. Targeted by the government and the paramilitary groups that worked for it, youth activists in cities with large student populations surmised that their only path toward social change—the change of "the socio-economic structure of the country"—was through armed struggle.[51] In Monterrey, students continued their efforts to educate and mobilize workers of the city's industrial plants, but they also began forming the nuclei of urban guerilla groups, preparing to confront the security forces. In need of money to buy firearms, these groups robbed movie theaters, pharmacies, banks, and other businesses.[52] Their firepower was increasing. When in the fall of 1972 the authorities raided a house linked to two student members of the Armed Communists League, the press reported that they found 1 million cartridges, various caliber handguns, sawed-off 12-gauge shotguns, tools to manufacture barrels for submachine guns, medical supplies, typewriters, and calculators; as well as wigs, glasses, mustaches, masks, and other wardrobe items.[53] Guns and disguises were both seen as threats to the government.[54]

It was in this context of civil protests and armed organizing that on October 25, 1971, Mexican President Luis Echeverría sent to the senate the proposal to create a federal law to "meticulously regulate" the conditions and requirements for owning and carrying firearms.[55] He said that this would "guarantee the peace in the country, avoid to the extent possible the spilling of blood and prevent *pistolerismo* (gunfighting) and mishandling of weapons, and ensure respect for the life and the rights of others." The initiative from the president came only a few months after he ordered the brutal suppression of the student demonstration on Corpus Christi Day. Now he was promoting the law as a means to "protect the community from fear of insecurity" and "from those who use firearms for illicit attempts on people's lives and property, causing at times real collective panic." An editorial in the daily *El Informador* celebrated the initiative as an effective means to address "big social problems" that hurt the country, such as armed bank robberies and gangsterism.[56]

The law was precise. In minuscule detail it outlined what types of firearms, how many of them, and which Mexicans under which conditions could own. Semiautomatic pistols were allowed only in calibers that did not exceed .380. Civilians could not own .38 Super and .38 Commander pistols, nor 9mm Mauser, Luger, Parabellum, and similar models. When it came to revolvers, people were permitted to have one with a caliber not bigger than a .38 Special, but not a .357 Magnum.[57] In rural areas, farmworkers and members of agricultural collectives could own a .22 caliber rifle or a shotgun of any caliber, except those with barrels shorter than 635mm and bigger than 12 gauge. People who engaged in hunting or target shooting were allowed to have high-powered repeating or semiautomatic rifles, excluding those with calibers of .223, 7.62, and .30 caliber carbines of any model. The rest—together with machine guns, hand grenades, flame-throwers, and land mines—were designated for the exclusive use by the security forces. The law considered special circumstances, such as permits to own rifles of greater calibers for people who hunted big game abroad as well as authorization for individuals who practiced traditional Mexican horsemanship, known as *charrería*, to have .357 Magnum revolvers as part of their outfit as long as they carried them unloaded. Gun collectors and museums, both public and private, were also allowed to own firearms prohibited by the law, if those firearms had "value" or "cultural, scientific, artistic or historic meaning."

The task of controlling the circulation of firearms in the country fell to the Secretariat of National Defense, which used for this end a newly created federal firearms registry. Clandestine introduction of weapons into the country was defined as a crime, punishable by incarceration between one and fifteen years with a fine between 100 and 100,000 pesos.[58] Business owners who bought guns or ammo without checking the legality of their provenance could spend from six months to six years in prison. Public officials who did not intervene to stop smuggling attempts could lose their jobs.

While the Mexican press described the new law as a necessary measure, major US dailies sounded incredulous. "The ordinary Mexican is not likely to surrender his weapon," wrote the *New York Times*.[59] The article acknowledged the situation of violent crime in Mexico, including bank robberies, as well as guerilla activities, but suggested that "the real problem lies in the attitude of Mexicans toward their weapons." For many Mexicans, the unnamed author claimed, "the quality of masculinity—machismo—means attachment to women, tequila and the pistol."[60] The unsigned article portrayed Mexico as a country where landowners had private bands of armed men to control "dissident peasants," where people in rural areas settled feuds with machetes, and where city dwellers carried weapons in their cars to resolve traffic disputes. "When passed, it will deprive Mexicans of their centuries-old right to carry weapons for self-defense," the anonymous author argued. The *Los Angeles Times* coverage was less vocal in its opposition to the law and avoided such negative characterization of Mexican people, but it, too, noted that Mexican citizens considered the pistol as "standard household hardware."[61] Both newspapers mentioned that Mexico, unlike the United States, had no gun lobby that would oppose such strict legislation. And, indeed, the only disapproval came from Productos Mendoza, the company that had been manufacturing firearms since the Mexican Revolution.[62]

After a brief period of public debates, the representatives approved the law on December 29, 1971, with 171 votes in favor. Seventeen members of congress from the conservative opposition group, the National Action Party (PAN), voted against the law because they disagreed with Article 77, which allowed the authorities to raid a house on suspicion that the owner had failed to register their firearms. "The state has no right to look into whether an individual is behaving one way or another based on suspicion," argued Guillermo Ruiz Vázquez, the article's main critic.[63] He was concerned that an accusation would be sufficient to raid a private residence and that it was therefore unconstitutional. Another member of PAN, Ernesto Velasco Lafraga, challenged articles regulating the possession of firearms by inhabitants of rural areas. He blamed the "climate of violence" on TV shows about cowboys and bandits.[64] Santiago Roel, a member of the ruling PRI representing Nuevo León, rebuffed those opposing the law: "Don't we have a property registry? Don't we have a federal registry of automobiles, of medications?" He was confident about its impending approval. "We, as representatives of the majority, maintain that this firearms law is flawless and definitely constitutional."[65]

The passage of the Federal Law on Firearms and Explosives in 1971 sealed the government's monopoly over the distribution as well as the production of weapons. "Mexico is not a bellicose country," the defense secretary, General Hermenegildo Cuenca Díaz, said when he announced that most of the facilities manufacturing guns and ammunition would close.[66] Only factories producing sports cartridges would be allowed to continue their operations. "These are most used by the peasants and by those who engage in sports, to kill fawn and bunnies on Sundays," the general said. He also said that "every citizen will still be allowed to possess one weapon in his home for the protection of his person and his family."[67] Then added: "But one is enough."

The government estimated that there were over 6 million unregistered guns circulating in Mexico when the new law came into effect in 1972. Within the first six months after its passage, about 150,000 Mexicans had their firearms registered.[68] Those who owned guns that were now designated for the exclusive use of the military—like AK-47 rifles or .30–30 Winchester carbines—were given one year to dispose of them. Records of how many actually complied do not exist. What the government does have is the federal registry, which some fifty years later contains over 3.5 million firearms—about one legal gun for every forty Mexican residents.[69] Adding those that are illicit, the number of firearms circulating in Mexico is likely over four times higher—over 16 million.[70] That is, ten guns for every hundred residents. Even then, it isn't much compared to its northern neighbor. In the United States, there are 120.5 firearms per 100 residents.[71] With a rough estimate of more than 393 million firearms, the United States holds the uncontested world title as the country with most civilian-owned guns. So when people in Mexico wanted a weapon more powerful than what the law allowed them, it was there that they turned to—the store shelves north of the border heaving with handguns and rifles of all models and calibers imaginable.

With a Side of Beans

Monterrey, Nuevo León

Miguel was not the kind of person who gave up easily. When the first truck he sent to San Fernando, in the neighboring state of Tamaulipas, did not make it, he dispatched another one. But it didn't fare any better: the cargo disappeared along the way. The owner of the hardware store who had ordered the merchandise pleaded with Miguel to send him one more shipment. Miguel agreed, but he knew he had to change how he operated. He found an old truck, too shabby to attract attention from armed groups preying on the highway, and, to his relief, the goods reached their destination. On the third try.

Frequent disappearances of cargo along the way was one reason why doing business in the region became costly and dangerous. Goods vanished together with trucks that carried them, no trace left on the road, no police investigations to find out what happened. And that wasn't the worst part. People disappeared too, some abducted off the roads, others from the towns those roads passed through. Miguel owned a construction company and a transportation business that still received regular orders from customers in Tamaulipas, but fulfilling them was getting more difficult. He remembered once the truck driver who was delivering the goods could not even find the man who had ordered them. Miguel had forgotten about the incident when weeks later he got a call from the man's wife. She said that her husband had been kidnapped and she wanted to settle his accounts. Miguel was shocked and refused to take her money. He realized he could not continue working in Tamaulipas.

Not being able to deliver goods to Matamoros or Reynosa was a big loss for the company, but he thought the risks were too high. Until things calmed down, he decided to limit his business to Nuevo León.

Miguel was born in San Pedro Garza García, the wealthiest city in the Monterrey metro area and one of the most affluent in all of Latin America. With Sierra Madre Oriental mountain range to the south and the Santa Catarina River to the north, the strip of land, about a third shorter than Manhattan, has been called an "oasis of prosperity," with residents who could afford shopping at the local Lamborghini and Tesla dealerships.[1] Not everyone was that rich, but for the upper middle class who lived there, the neighborhood offered high quality of life and no reason to leave it, for work or for leisure. High-rise office buildings were flanked by luxury malls and the best restaurants and parks were steps away from upscale condos with mountain views.

As a child, Miguel had spent most of his days at home with his mother and two sisters. He had always loved the outdoors and was jealous of his cousins who put their savings together to buy fishing gear. Since his sisters didn't share his interests, Miguel mostly played alone. Retreated to his room, he once built a city from Legos, complete with a landing strip illuminated by the lights he took off the Christmas tree. He was fascinated with medieval swords, then moved on to firearms. Miguel's grandfather had a gun collection, which intrigued the boy. The grandfather told him stories about their ancestors, among them a lieutenant colonel who fought against the French intervention in the Battle of Puebla, celebrated today as Cinco de Mayo. "All of us here are descendants of generals," he said about the elite of Monterrey.

When Miguel got married, he bought an apartment in the same neighborhood where he had grown up to stay close to his family. Now his daily morning runs took him down memory lane: past the high school he attended back when he dreamt of becoming a surgeon and spent weekends shadowing doctors, past the hospital where his children were later born. As much as he liked traveling—road trips to Las Vegas, vacations in Los Cabos—he never considered moving away from the city that was imbued with so much personal significance. After he graduated, instead of studying medicine as he thought he would, Miguel began assisting his father and his grandmother with running their family business. What had begun as a hardware store, grew into a company that became more difficult for just the two of them to manage. "My father was a workaholic who moved between home and work, home and work, and nothing else," Miguel recalled. "My grandma was the boss of the family," he said affectionately about the ninety-year-old woman who had no wish to retire. Miguel learned from them, but he didn't want to become like them. He would work hard—that was never in question—but he also wanted to have a life outside of the company. He went fishing and rock climbing on weekends, rode dirt bikes and ran 10K races, attended NASCAR events and concerts, singing along with Rush and Chente Fernández and Tigres del Norte.

But his favorite hobby was hunting. When he was little, Miguel had an air rifle, which he used to take outside to shoot at birds around the neighborhood. Later, in his teens, he began joining his cousins on hunting trips in Mexico and across the border in the United States. They shot deer, then boars. He was twenty-four when he killed a mountain lion. After his grandfather passed away, Miguel inherited his gun collection, and firearms became an even more serious obsession. By the time he was in his mid-thirties, when he and I first met, he owned thirty guns and went shooting at his own ranch, about an hour's drive north of Monterrey.

"When violence began, I was ready," Miguel said. As extortion and kidnapping spread from Tamaulipas to Nuevo León, fear of being the next victim motivated some business owners and their families to pack up and move to Texas. Others chose to stay but they no longer ventured outside San Pedro Garza García, the only suburb in the metropolitan area where they felt safe. Counting on the authorities to provide security was out of the question. Police were unqualified and corrupt, while the justice system was so clogged up that impunity for homicides in the country reached over 90 percent.[2] Most property crimes were never even investigated. Many of Miguel's friends in San Pedro armored their homes and their cars. But Miguel was not like his friends. First, he was more thrifty and did not want to spend that much money. But he also didn't like the idea of hiding passively behind closed gates. He decided to learn how to protect himself.

Miguel knew he'd better not fail at this. Escalating violence gave rise to a cruel habit that spread among regiomontanos—that of blaming and stigmatizing its victims. People assumed that those who have been extorted or kidnapped for ransom were not innocent, that they must have been involved in something. "Está metido en algo" ("he is into something") or "por algo le pasó" ("it happened for a reason"), people would say.[3] Blaming the victim was a form of denial, a verbal tactic that residents deployed to refute the possibility that they, too, could be subjected to violence. It was their way of safeguarding themselves—distancing from the kind of people that this happened to.[4] But that was not the sort of protection that Miguel had in mind. He focused on practical things, on what he could do. He avoided luxury cars and accessories that would make him into a potential target for kidnapping. He learned defensive driving. He talked a friend into setting up a system to warn each another if they were in danger: each could send their location data with a tap on the screen and the one who received the alert had to send a text message with the question, "Will you be home for dinner?" If the friend answered yes, all was ok. If it was a no, that was the sign that he was in trouble.

It was around that time, beginning with 2010, that many people Miguel knew flew to Mexico City and returned with brand-new Glocks from the only store that sold them legally back then. Miguel liked to poke fun at their false sense of security: they bought the guns, yet never learned to use them. He, too, carried a handgun, usually his .22 Ruger or the .380 Llama, within easy reach under the seat in his truck, but, unlike his friends, he practiced often and took every opportunity to improve his skills. When instructors from Israel came to train local police, Miguel heard they offered a tactical firearms course to private security personnel and he signed up. From them he learned about guns and ammo that Mexican civilians like him did not even have access to. He knew that to find the best tools for protection he had to look beyond the country's borders. Guns, yes, but also ammunition. Expansive rounds, such as hollow point Hornady "critical defense" cartridges, which reliably penetrated heavy denim clothing and, as the product description explained, left "very large" and "very deep" wound cavities, were prohibited in Mexico. But some of Miguel's relatives and friends, convinced by the company's slogan—"When lives are on the line, only the best will do,"[5]—kept boxes of them in their homes, prepared for the day they wished would never come, and urged him to do the same.

Monterrey was not exceptional.

Residents of Mexican border towns had been experiencing this dynamic—escalating violence and the buildup of private modes of security, both legal and not—since at least the nineties. Take Tijuana. Arturo, who grew up a few blocks away from the Arellano family, when they controlled one of the busiest northbound routes for drugs, remembered that period as "so insecure." In the 1990s, seeing guns in his neighborhood was "normal," he said.[6] His parents refused to do what everyone else was doing—to arm themselves—because "it was not part of their value system." But Arturo didn't have the same reservations. When he was old enough, he began taking classes at a shooting range in San Diego and since then has kept several Glocks, including a 9mm, at his home in Tijuana. In a rough city "es un mal necesario," he said, justifying his reasons. Rather than going to Mexico City, twelve hundred miles away from home, he and many others bought their guns locally, which was faster and cheaper and they didn't have to deal with licensing and registration. This close to the US border, smugglers were abundant and competition among them high, keeping prices low. The black market was so popular that it even developed its own vocabulary—code words that are still used in WhatsApp group chats where sellers offer their merchandise. Bullets were called "frijoles" (beans) or "chicharros" (small mackerel). Guns were known as "juguetes" (toys). A new gun was referred to as "*vegana*" (vegan) because "it hadn't eaten meat," Arturo explained, whereas a used gun was called "carnivora" (carnivore). Sellers would sometimes say they got it "from Roberto" when the gun was "*robado*" (stolen).

As violence further intensified in the late 2000s, people's trust in law enforcement to protect them evaporated and security ballooned into a profitable business with fluid boundaries between state, private, and black markets.[7] In Tijuana, if you wanted to get a handgun without bothering to apply for a license, your best bet was to go through a network operated by police and bodyguards who worked for the city's economic elites. They were well connected and sold more than just guns to Tijuana's residents eager to protect themselves: their inventories included bulletproof vests, scopes, silencers, and other accessories not available for most people in Mexico. But the farther from the border you went, the more difficult it was to buy firearms through unofficial channels. When Arturo moved to Guadalajara, he had to get used to not being able to order the gun and receive it the same day. Through a friend, he had a connection to someone who delivered them all the way down to Jalisco, but the smuggler came only once a week and sometimes had no inventory to sell. Although not impossible, getting a gun there was much more of a hassle than in Tijuana.

According to one study, nearly 2 million Mexican households acquired a firearm between 2012 and 2018, representing just over 5 percent of the 34.1 million households in the country. Increasing interest in buying guns was associated with the rise in perceptions of insecurity in the neighborhood, mistrust in local and state police, and being a victim of a crime.[8] But overall gun ownership rates in urban Mexico still remained low. A 2017 telephone survey conducted in nine cities, including Tijuana,

Guadalajara, Monterrey, Puebla, Veracruz, and others, found that only 3 percent of households reported having a firearm.[9] In Tijuana, only 1 out of 136 respondents said they did; in Monterrey, 1 out of 54. This was likely a gross undercounting: for every seven respondents contacted by the research firm, only one agreed to participate. Residents who owned unregistered firearms were probably more reluctant to speak and admit they had a gun. The fact that a quarter (25 percent) of those surveyed said they knew someone (neighbor, friend, or relative) who owned a gun indicates that firearm possession was more widespread than the data suggested. Over half of the guns (57 percent) were reported to be handguns, and the majority said they kept them for self-defense (58 percent). A quarter of the respondents who owned guns had a rifle or a shotgun and about that many cited hunting as the reason for possessing a firearm. These numbers would undoubtedly be higher in rural areas, where many people kept rifles that were passed down in families for generations. After all, that was how Miguel got his first guns.

Miguel insisted we meet at a Starbucks in the shopping plaza off Avenida Eugenio Garza Sada Sur, near the campus of Tec de Monterrey. "You will recognize me from a white water bottle," I texted him. Then I waited. I was used to waiting. When setting up interviews, sometimes hours went by before I heard back; other times I waited for days, followed up, waited more, until I would finally give up. But when I first got in touch with Miguel, his number shared by a friend of a friend, he wrote, "Of course, it will be a pleasure." He suggested we meet a quarter to eight in the morning, to make sure we had enough time to talk before an important event with the mayor-elect that he had to attend before noon. "I am worried we may run out of time," he texted. It seemed too good to be true.

I arrived at the café early, as always, and scanned the customers in line and seated at the tables. None of the people there resembled what I imagined Miguel looked like. I waited inside, my back to the wall, my gaze fixed on the door, and when a young man in dark sunglasses and slicked back hair, wearing a down vest over a blue checkered shirt, walked in, I knew instantly it was him.

That morning, as we sat at a table in an otherwise empty coffee shop, Miguel walked me through a stack of documents he brought with him neatly arranged in a folder: his gun club membership card, copies of his hunting license, birth certificate, proof of completed military service, receipts from the federal arms registry, certificates of purchase, permit to transport firearms, and more. He had to carry all these with him whenever he moved the guns, always locked in a safe in the back of his truck, whether he was driving to his ranch or going on a hunting trip. "We are in the pigeon season," he said, when I asked him what animals he hunted. "It will be followed by ducks and then geese." He also hunted deer, bobcats, and coyotes, he said, and I asked him about the kinds of rifles he used to kill each.

I asked him many more questions—about the ethics of trophy hunting, about gun clubs around Monterrey, and about laws regulating firearm ownership in Mexico—before I breached the topic of smuggling. Unfazed, Miguel pulled out his smartphone and showed me a thread on a WhatsApp group with photos of guns for sale. "Nobody asks where they are from," he said. Many of the firearms offered to group members were "armas registrables"—the types of firearms permitted for civilian use, so they could potentially be registered even when bought on the black market. But there were also weapons on the message thread that common Mexican citizens were not allowed to own. As he scrolled down, I saw what appeared like an Uzi submachine gun. Miguel said he had recently seen a Desert Eagle—a big, heavy semiautomatic pistol known as the "bad-guy star gun," the one Arnold Schwarzenegger carried in *Red Heat* and Agent Smith in *The Matrix*. It uses a very large cartridge and is enormously powerful. "I don't think it's very reliable to have at home," Miguel said. "You'd need to be a good shooter and have beefy arms to control it."

Although he was part of the group, Miguel didn't order guns through WhatsApp himself. He preferred to drive to Reynosa, two to three hours away from Monterrey, cross the border, and meet up with his cousin in McAllen, where they'd purchase guns together. Since his cousin lived in Texas, he could help out with paperwork if need be. Pawn shops were generally easier than sporting goods stores. Last time Miguel had been at a pawn shop, nobody raised their eyebrows that he was Mexican and nobody said anything when he carried the boxes with two Browning rifles they sold him, a .270 and .300, to a car with Mexican plates. Miguel said he noticed two men watching him as he was leaving the store and he feared they worked for law enforcement, but nothing happened. He handed the boxes over to the *chivero*—a person who, for a few hundred dollars, would smuggle them into Mexico—and collected the rifles across the border in Reynosa.

The problem with this plan was that going to Texas required traveling through Tamaulipas. State and federal security forces were now patrolling the highways, but there were stretches of the road where, more than a decade since the region began experiencing high levels of violent crime, kidnappings continued. To be safe, some of Miguel's friends in Monterrey bought what they referred to as the "full package": they paid someone to take care of everything, from buying the firearm in Texas to smuggling it across the border and then delivering it to a rendezvous spot close to Monterrey. The full package was the least risky for the buyer, but it cost significantly more than just paying the chivero. In this sense, Monterrey was different from Tijuana, where a few years ago smugglers charged $300 US dollars, if that, to bring a firearm over from San Diego. With the smuggler's fee, Mexicans in Baja California paid about double what a cheap handgun cost in US stores. In contrast, by the time it reached Monterrey, a handgun from McAllen could end up costing three or even four times more than its retail price in Texas: the person who purchased the gun could ask for an equivalent of its value, while the chivero could take double that for smuggling it across the border and then transporting it past military and police checkpoints on the highway.[10] With a price tag this high, it would be more economical to just buy handguns legally from the army store in Mexico City.

"But the difference is that here you can choose what you want," Miguel said about Texas. Stores in the United States offered a staggering variety of guns compared to what was available in Mexico. In McAllen, you could pick a firearm that met the model and caliber requirements allowed for civilian ownership in Mexico. Even when they were not in the inventory at the store in Mexico City, officers at the army base in Monterrey would usually ask no questions and register them. But the stores in Texas also sold guns that were restricted in Mexico, such as AR-15 models chambered for .223 or 5.56 cartridges, AK-47 variants, made in the United States or imported from Romania or Serbia, and .50 caliber sniper rifles. Miguel had little interest in those kinds of guns—they were of no practical use to him. He understood, however, that those were precisely the sorts of weapons sought by people who stole the goods from the trucks he used to send to Tamaulipas, the reason he could no longer do that.

I hadn't seen Miguel for a while when one scorching day in late July of 2019 we decided to go out for lunch and catch up. He arrived in a white SUV with a cracked windshield, not the one I had been used to, so I didn't recognize him at first. "My wife's car," he explained as I got in.

"We switched because the child seats are still in my truck." Miguel was wearing his usual checkered shirt and a crimson baseball cap with Browning company logos. They had just returned from a long family vacation in "*La Isla*," as people in Monterrey called South Padre Island. The Texas beach resort has been attracting tourists from Nuevo León's capital since the 1980s, when spending Easter and summer holidays there was a symbol of distinction for the elite.[11] Now full of hotels, the destination had become more affordable to Mexicans, but still only for those who had resources to cross the border.

"I bought a new gun," he said as soon as we ordered coffee. "A Smith & Wesson .380." Miguel pulled out his phone and showed me a picture. "With a short barrel like that you must be close to the person to shoot," he said.

"How did you get it?" I asked, not even attempting to hide my interest in the process over the product.

Even when he paid a chivero, Miguel already took more risks than his friends by driving to Texas—risks posed by organized crime groups operating on the highways as well as risks of getting caught by any one of the law enforcement agencies in the United States or in Mexico. But sometimes he ventured even more. I knew that at least once he had smuggled a gun across the border in his own car.

"I had been trying to get in touch with my chivero, Alex," he began. After a while of not hearing anything, Miguel said he learned that his smuggler had been arrested in Texas. "I hope you had nothing to do with that," he said now, looking me in the eyes, and smiling wryly.

Without Alex, Miguel said, he had to either abandon the gun he had just bought in Texas or cross it himself. He weighed his options. He knew that at the end of the holiday season, whether it was around Christmas or Semana Santa, southbound lanes at border crossings were swarmed by Mexican travelers returning from trips to the United States. When the lines of vehicles waiting for inspection became too long, officers generally waved them through without stopping. That had been Miguel's experience the previous time he smuggled a gun into Mexico. Although this was the middle of summer and his trip to La Isla did not coincide with any holiday, he was counting on that happening again.

It started off well. American agents in McAllen didn't flag him. He stopped at the booth to pay the bridge toll and proceeded south across the river. But when he got to the other side, the light at the Mexican customs turned red, sending him to the inspection's area. Miguel tried to act cool as officers approached the vehicle. After all, he was with his family and he thought he could pass as a vacationer. "I had a nice tan from lying on the beach for days," he said. Whether the agents who searched the car believed the show he put on or they were not thorough enough, they didn't notice the firearm he had covered up with clothes and medications. He was lucky, but it was a close call. Miguel swore not to do it ever again.

"It was the last time," he said, taking a long sip of his coffee. I didn't know whether to believe him and said nothing.

Per Article 84 of the federal firearms law, clandestinely bringing into Mexico a gun that was otherwise permitted for civilian ownership, such as this Smith & Wesson .380 caliber pistol, was punishable by three to ten years of imprisonment. Had Miguel been caught, he could be in jail now. But he knew the odds were low.

Just how low I would understand later, when the information on gun seizures at the border that I requested from both US and Mexican customs authorities arrived in my inbox the following winter. In 2019, Mexican customs agents in Reynosa who stopped Miguel that summer caught only eighteen people attempting to smuggle firearms or ammunition from Texas, each seizure of contraband recorded in their log:

January 12: 120 cartridges

January 20: 1 firearm and 1 magazine

January 25: 29 cartridges

January 25: 5 pistols, 1 revolver, and 2 magazines

January 28: 50 magazines

February 13: 2 magazines

March 25: 29 cartridges

May 18: 100 cartridges

May 22: 1 shotgun, 1 rifle, and 1 magazine

June 23: 1 pistol and 6 cartridges

June 26: 558 cartridges

July 2: 8 magazines, 1 telescopic sight, and 5 grips

July 20: 1 pistol, 1 magazine, and 6 cartridges

July 23: 1 firearm and 100 cartridges

August 2: 1 rifle

September 10: 1 Barrett rifle, 1 empty magazine, 40 cartridges

September 25: 60 boxes × 20 cartridges

Gun seizures all along the border, by agents on both sides, did not amount to much that year. Mexican customs confiscated 122 firearms, about half of them in Tamaulipas.[12] US Customs and Border Protection captured another 226. A total of 348 guns prevented from crossing the border south.[13]

Collateral Damage

On November 20, 2009, Mexican soldiers in Naco, Sonora, stopped a twenty-one-year-old woman driving a truck with a .50 caliber Beowulf rifle and forty-one AK-47s. She said she was transporting the guns to Sinaloa. A few weeks later, over three hundred miles west, in the border town of Mexicali, Baja California, the army seized another arsenal of forty-one AK-47s, one AR-15, and one FN 5.7, and detained twelve people, all of them from Sinaloa, some of them identified as members of an organized crime group. By the end of February 2010, US federal agents in Phoenix counted more than one thousand weapons confiscated before or after they crossed the border with Mexico. Most were semiautomatic rifles, primarily AK-47s.

Colloquially called *cuernos de chivo*, or goat's horns, AK-47 style rifles have been popular among organized crime groups in Mexico, immortalized in *narcocorridos* the leaders commissioned about themselves.[1] But rank-and-file gunmen didn't have the luxury of caring about style and took whatever weapons were given to them. In general, the choice of the group's arsenal had more to do with practicality than with symbolism, even though disentangling the two is not that simple. The preference of one style of assault rifle over another has been wrapped up with national politics and symbolic narratives that spread around the world. For the AK-47, it all began in the late 1940s, at the start of the Cold War, when a Red Army sergeant, Mikhail Kalashnikov, designed what became the standard issue rifle for soldiers in the Soviet Union.

Soon factories manufacturing AK-47s opened in other Warsaw Pact countries—East Germany, Bulgaria, Hungary, Poland, Romania—and the Soviet government built an arsenal of 3 million guns hidden in the underground tunnels of a salt mine in Ukraine, in preparation for potential war with the West.[2] China, Egypt, Iraq, North Korea, and other countries began making similar models. They manufactured and stockpiled the guns as tools to defend the state and keep power in the hands of repressive regimes who were prepared to use violence to maintain control. But in a twist of history, this product and instrument of state violence also became the symbol of rebels and revolutionaries. When Salvador Allende was elected president of Chile, Fidel Castro presented him with a Kalashnikov with an inscription on a golden plate: "To my good friend Salvador from Fidel, who by different means tries to achieve the same goals."[3]

The gun served various and contradictory purposes. "The Kalashnikov marks the guerilla, the terrorist, the child soldier, the dictator, and the thug—all of whom have found it to be a ready equalizer against morally or materially superior foes," writes journalist and former US Marine C. J. Chivers in *The Gun*, his seminal book about the history of the AK-47.[4] The properties of the rifle—rugged, light to carry, easy to use—made it the ideal "everyman's gun."[5] Assembled from bulky loose-fitting parts, it worked even when soaked in muddy water and coated with sand. It might have been less accurate, but it was a trade-off for reliability. Sixteen-year-old students in Soviet schools competed at assembling and disassembling AK rifles; some could do it in fewer than thirty seconds.[6] After the collapse of the Soviet Union, the rifles from the arsenals in Eastern Europe supplied the expanding global black market of weapons.[7] It became the instrument of terror, implicated in gruesome acts of political violence. Its name and image accompanied stories of hijackings, kidnappings, assassinations, and executions.

The United States, however, in part due to Cold War rivalry, refused to recognize the value of the Soviet-made gun.[8] Before adopting the M16 as the general-issue rifle in 1969, defense secretary Robert S. McNamara had ordered the army to look into the "relative effectiveness" of three firearms: the heavy and long M14 which American soldiers carried to Vietnam; the AK-47, used by the Viet Cong and the North Vietnamese Army;[9] and the AR-15, designed by ArmaLite and then manufactured by Colt, which was being pushed as the new all-purpose American rifle. To determine their utility for war, evaluators subjected the guns to a series of tests that measured their accuracy, reliability, durability, and other aspects of performance. Among them were lethality tests, an affair so disturbing that the authors appealed to national security to cover up the study and avoid public scrutiny. Some documents, now declassified, provide shocking details of experiments carried out at the army's Biophysics Division at the Aberdeen Proving Ground in Maryland, where ballistics experts fired into live Texas Angora goats, measuring the volume of blood loss and the time it took for the heartbeat to stop; into human legs, amputated from frozen and then thawed human cadavers; and into decapitated and processed human heads, filled with gelatin, that had been shipped from India. Writing about these experiments, Chivers called the lethality tests "forensic absurdity."[10] All heads shattered when struck by bullets fired from military-style rifles. The differences in damages, in the fragmentation of the skull upon impact, were meaningless in practical terms. Although the other tests, done in a rush, also failed to provide conclusive evidence, the AK-47 was dismissed as "inferior" to the two US-made weapons. With some hesitation, despite evidence that the AR-15 was prone to malfunctioning, the military accepted the prototype as the standard service rifle. It became known as M16A1. But in the battlefield, frustrated by jamming and corrosion, some Marines opted to arm themselves with the AK-47s they snatched from the hands of their dead enemies.

Over the years, US forces deployed to wars and military interventions abroad captured more AK-47s from their opponents and brought them back to use for training purposes. Firearms dealers began noticing that American soldiers returned home with a new appreciation for the gun and by the 1980s were ordering semiautomatic AK-47s from China and later from Eastern Europe to sell them to American consumers.[11] In 1989, concerned about the "dramatic increase in the number of these weapons being imported and police reports of their use in violent crime," the administration of President George H. W. Bush banned the importation of guns lacking a "sporting purpose," such as "semiautomatic assault rifles" that possessed a "military configuration," which applied to all AK-47 variants.[12] But the ban had limited effect: foreign gunmakers and importers learned to modify their rifles by removing some prohibited features, such as folding stocks, or bypassing restrictions by assembling them from parts in the United States.[13]

The guns sold well and not only among US military veterans and other gun enthusiasts. Demand for them was increasing south of the border. For organized crime groups in Mexico, the availability of ammunition was perhaps as important as reliability of the rifle. The AK-47 used 7.62 × 39mm cartridges, which were widely available on the black market fed by leftover stocks from the civil wars in Central America. It made sense logistically for armed groups to buy the same style rifles for their arsenals rather than mixing them with firearms of different calibers. If every gunman could use 7.62 rounds, they didn't have to look for other types of ammo. This is not to say that the symbolic power of the Kalashnikov was irrelevant, only that it mattered to the select few who could act on their desires. For the rest, cuernos were popular because they were both practical and abundant.

Tracing the AKs seized in Sonora and Baja California was the task of the US Bureau of Alcohol, Tobacco, Firearms and Explosives. The agency, better known by its acronym ATF, was initially part of the US Department of the Treasury, where its main mandate was enforcing federal alcohol and tobacco tax laws. In 1968, following the assassination of Dr. Martin Luther King, President Lyndon B. Johnson formed the National Commission on the Causes and Prevention of Violence, whose recommendations led to the passage of the Gun Control Act.[14] Soon after, ATF began overseeing violations of federal laws involving firearms and explosives, including arson and bombings. However, it wasn't until the reorganization of US federal agencies following the 9/11 attacks in 2001, when ATF was moved to the Department of Justice (DOJ), that illegal use and trafficking of guns became its priority.

Gun tracing is a critical part of this work. Still analogue in the largely digitized world, it is a time-consuming process, which relies on phone calls and paper records instead of searchable databases. To trace a gun, the agent has to submit a request to the personnel at the National Tracing Center in West Virginia, providing a description of the gun and its serial number. Then, people at the tracing center begin making calls: first, they call the manufacturer or, if the gun is foreign-made, its importer, dictate the serial number, and ask which wholesale distributor the gun went to; next, they call the distributor and ask for the name of the dealer that ordered the gun; then they call the dealer. But the dealers don't keep electronic records either, so when they get a call from the tracing center, the manager has to look through file boxes to find the right firearm transaction record (it's known as ATF Form 4473), which lists the person who bought the gun from the store—their name, date, and place of birth, address, and sometimes their social security number. This process, from beginning to end, takes about a week for each gun and may require as many as seventy calls.[15] When the request is urgent, the National Tracing Center can turn it around in twenty-four hours.

ATF agents in Phoenix who reviewed the tracing reports of guns confiscated in northern Mexico in late 2009, could have skipped this process. By then, they already knew about the handful of men purchasing large quantities of high-caliber weapons in a handful of stores in Arizona. One firearms dealer who had for years voluntarily informed ATF about sales he found suspicious contacted the office in Phoenix on October 31, a few weeks before the seizures in Naco and Mexicali, and told them about four young men who had purchased nineteen AK-47 style rifles.[16] Following that conversation, an agent reviewed the firearms transaction records the dealer provided, including one documenting a sale of six identical AK-47 rifles to a man who had also bought several FN Herstal 5.7 caliber pistols. Over the next few weeks agents gathered more 4473s from Phoenix-area gun stores and conducted background checks and surveillance. They established connections between the individuals making these large purchases and merged their cases into a single investigation.

Coordinated by the ATF's Phoenix Field Division, the operation was conducted under the auspices of Project Gunrunner, a nationwide initiative launched in Laredo, Texas, in 2005, which sought to reduce the smuggling of firearms across the US southern border. But while the primary tactic of Gunrunner was the interdiction of buyers and sellers who were violating the laws, the agents in Phoenix had other plans. They wanted to see where the guns went if they were allowed to cross the border—to follow the small fish until they caught bigger ones. The men buying AK-47 style rifles in bulk used an auto body shop as one of the stash houses, so agents named their operation "Fast and Furious," after the popular movie about car racing.

In law enforcement lingo, what the agents did is known as *gunwalking*. "It's like saying that gangsters run guns, but governments walk guns," journalist Ioan Grillo said, noting the irony, in his book *Blood Gun Money*.[17] The speed of movement has nothing to do with it. The logistics are the same. The difference is in law only: gunrunning is a crime, while gunwalking receives the government's authorization. The tactic's formal name is "controlled delivery," defined in Article 2(i) of the United Nations Organized Crime Convention as "the technique of allowing illicit or suspect consignments to pass out of, through or into the territory of one or more States, with the knowledge and under the supervision of their competent authorities, with a view to the investigation of an offence and the identification of persons involved in the commission of the offence."[18] The tactic is often used by agents pursuing the

trafficking of drugs, wildlife, and counterfeit products. Following minor
buyers and smugglers until they deliver the goods allows law enforcement officers to learn about the transit routes and destinations, map
criminal schemes, and understand the structures of organized crime.[19]

ATF agents in Arizona had been using controlled delivery for decades. The most recent precedent was Operation Wide Receiver, run
out of their Tucson office in 2006 and 2007, under President George
W. Bush's administration. Then, too, agents watched hundreds of
weapons—AR-15 and AK-47 style rifles and Colt .38 Super pistols—
being sold to "straw purchasers." These were men and women hired for
the job who went to retail stores and gun shops to buy the firearms,
who passed the background checks and signed the forms and, once they
left the stores, handed the weapons over to others who smuggled them
across the border through ports of entry. Then, too, ATF hoped to build
a bigger case against an arms trafficking network. But after years of
delay the prosecutors ended up charging only low-level buyers, mostly
for committing paperwork violations. Only 64 of the 474 firearms sold
during the operation have been recovered.[20] Mike Detty, a licensed firearms dealer who served as a confidential informant for the ATF, was so
upset by how the agents handled the operation that he poured his outrage into a book.[21] Despite failures, agents continued using this tactic in
other cases, sending weapons to Mexico, where they lost track of many
of them.[22] They allowed people who were known to law enforcement
for being involved in selling and smuggling drugs and guns to continue
their activities. They could have stopped the men who procured some of
the firearms the Zetas used to kill ICE agent Jaime Zapata and wound
his partner Victor Avila during an ambush of their armored SUV in the
Mexican state of San Luis Potosí, but they did not.[23]

Fast and Furious was a reiteration of these earlier schemes, and a
repetition of their failures. Over a year and a half, between September
2009 and December 2010, a joint task force comprised of federal officials from ATF, FBI, DEA, and ICE, working under the US Attorney's
Office for the District of Arizona, let over two thousand guns "walk" to
Mexico. Instead of arresting suspects as soon as they identified them,
agents waited. Straw purchasing cases were "hard to pursue," wrote
William Newell, special agent in charge of the Phoenix division, in the
memo he sent to the ATF headquarters in DC. Their approach in this
case was to "further establish the structure of the organization and
establish illegal acts before proceeding to an overt phase."[24]

Not everyone involved in the operation thought it was a good idea.

Some gun dealers and ATF agents they cooperated with became concerned when they saw the same buyers return to purchase large quantities of weapons: Alfredo Celis bought 133 AK-47 style rifles and one .50 caliber weapon in the span of one year; Joshua David Moore, a former member of the US Marine Reserves, acquired 138 AK-47s and two .50 caliber rifles, all in just five months; Uriel Patino bought a total of 723 guns.[25] But supervisors instructed those who raised concerns to keep watching and waiting. Special agent John Dodson recalled the time the owner of the Lone Wolf Trading Company tipped them off that a straw buyer they had already identified in the case was about to purchase more weapons.[26] The agents hurried to the store and saw a man walk out with more than a dozen AK-47 style rifles, load them into a car, and drive off. They followed him, expecting an order from their superiors to intercept the vehicle. But the order never came. Rather than receiving authorization to intervene, they were told to return to the office. "We've got it handled,"[27] Newell assured ATF leadership.

Some on his own team doubted it.

"What are we doing here? I don't know. What the hell is the purpose of this? I have no idea. This went on every day," Agent Dodson later told congressional investigators.[28] "Every day being out here watching a guy go into the same gun store buying another 15 or 20 AK-47s or variants . . . , guys that don't have a job, and he is walking in here spending $27,000 for three Barrett .50 calibers . . . and you are sitting there every day and you can't do anything," he recalled his frustration. "I cannot see anyone who has one iota of concern for human life being okay with this."

Special agent Lawrence Alt, who had been a police officer before he joined ATF, was also worried: "Prior to my coming to Phoenix, Arizona, I had never witnessed . . . a situation where there wasn't at least an attempt to interdict or take the firearm at some point."[29] During eleven years he had spent with the ATF, Agent Alt worked with cases which involved illegally purchased guns. "Follow the gun was also the motto, follow the gun, stay with the gun." Sometimes "people would sit on houses all night long, days on end, waiting for the guns to go so that they could then follow it, satisfy the requirements of the investigation." He'd never been in a situation where he was told to do nothing. "Something bad was going to happen," he said.

"On our first visit to the home, just hours after the massacre had occurred, we'd seen the bloodstains on the walls, the sneaker prints stamped in dried blood. The blood that had not yet been mopped had run down the driveway in rivulets and had caked on the tires of parked cars, including our SUV,"[30] wrote journalist Alfredo Corchado about what he and his companions saw when they arrived at Villas de Salvárcar, a working-class neighborhood of small cinder block homes in the southern part of Ciudad Juárez, Chihuahua. Corchado had returned to Texas after years at the *Wall Street Journal* and still dressed like a business correspondent, pairing shirts and blazers with blue jeans. Having grown up in a family of migrant farmworkers, who left Durango for California and then settled down in El Paso, he felt at home on the border.[31] As a reporter for a major regional daily, the *Dallas Morning News*, he had been writing about communities on both sides, including the murders of women in Juárez. But even his experience of routinely covering violent organized crime couldn't prepare him for what he saw on that winter day in 2010.

The previous night, on January 30, the small house on Calle Villa de Portal was packed with high school and college students celebrating the eighteenth birthday of Jesús Enríquez. They were watching a soccer game when around midnight several trucks with tinted windows pulled up in front of the residence where the party was taking place. Inside the vehicles were members of La Línea, a gang that served as enforcers for the Juárez cartel.[32] They disembarked, entered the house, and opened fire, killing fifteen people, injuring fourteen others. No police or ambulances arrived when witnesses called emergency services. Parents had to drive their children to the hospital on their own. More than a hundred 7.62 caliber bullet casings were found at the scene.[33] Three of the weapons used in the attack were later traced to Fast and Furious.[34]

When Corchado asked a father whose son had been killed what he wanted readers in Mexico and the United States to understand about the massacre, the man said: "I want them to feel my pain."[35] The residents had been calling for police to come to their neighborhood for years, but now that the armed officers finally arrived people were ambivalent, even apprehensive.[36] In his comments to the press, Mexican President Felipe Calderón said that the massacre may have been due to the rivalry between youth groups and could be related to gangs.[37] His words hurt grieving families and caused an outrage in the community. Decades-long neglect by the government could not be quickly remedied by heavy militarization. Since his election in 2006, Calderón had embraced a hard-line approach toward organized crime—what everyone soon began calling the "drug war." Under Joint Operation Chihuahua, the government dispatched more than two thousand soldiers and federal police officers to the border state in 2008. But with the arrival of federal forces in Ciudad Juárez, homicide rates only continued to rise. People in the border city knew that more militarization would result in more violence and that this violence would disproportionately affect poorer, marginalized communities.[38]

This strategy of combatting crime was supported and partially funded by the United States. Soon after Calderón took office, Mexico and the United States signed a bilateral security cooperation agreement known as the Mérida Initiative, aimed at dismantling criminal organizations, strengthening border controls, reforming the justice system, and building "resilient communities."[39] Mexico significantly increased police and military spending, while the United States provided training and equipment, which, among other things, included drug-sniffing dogs and Black Hawk helicopters.[40] Although the agreement called for "institutionalizing the rule of law while protecting human rights," law enforcement operations—"combatting transnational criminal organizations"—were given precedence.[41] Those operations led to an increase in grave human rights violations: excessive use of force, torture, extrajudicial executions. Murdered civilians were routinely labeled "presumed criminals" without anyone bothering to investigate their transgressions. When Calderón prematurely said that the young people killed in the massacre may have been involved with gangs, he merely repeated the government's script which consisted of blaming the victims.

In Villas de Salvárcar, residents didn't wait for the government's apologies. They began organizing their own programs addressing drug addiction and promoting sports. "We're building community with the blood of our children," another father whose child had been killed told Corchado.[42]

Villas de Salvárcar was just one particularly brutal crime scene where weapons from Fast and Furious were found. The firearms sold to straw buyers in Arizona kept turning up in violent encounters around Mexico.[43] One was linked to an attempted assassination of the state police chief in Tijuana, Baja California, on February 25, 2010. Another was recovered after a shootout in Tubutama, Sonora, on July 1, 2010. Two were used by suspects who kidnapped, tortured, and murdered the brother of former Chihuahua state attorney general Patricia González Rodríguez on November 14, 2010. Three were seized after an organized crime group fired at a Mexican army helicopter in Jalisco on May 27, 2011. Forty associated firearms were found in the home of Jose Antonio Torres Marrufo, an enforcer for the Sinaloa cartel in Ciudad Juárez on April 30, 2011.[44] Two were recovered in Rancho del Sol, Michoacán, following a raid by the Mexican federal police on a rural ranch believed to be controlled by Jalisco New Generation Cartel (CJNG) and an extended gun battle which left forty-two suspects and one police officer dead on May 22, 2015.[45] One was in an abandoned vehicle in Parral, Chihuahua, where law enforcement found three bodies riddled by bullets on August 7, 2015. Most of these were AK-47 variants. But not all. When the military entered the home of Joaquin Guzmán Loera, better known as El Chapo, or The Shorty, in Los Mochis, Sinaloa, on January 11, 2016, one of the firearms they seized was a .50 caliber also bought by someone linked to the Fast and Furious operation.

Some of these crimes in Mexico, like the Villas de Salvárcar massacre, made it to the news in the United States, mostly through efforts by El Paso–based journalists like Alfredo Corchado, Angela Kocherga, and others who reported from the Texas borderlands. But the murder that made the flawed operation public and political in the United States was of an American citizen on US soil: the killing of US Border Patrol agent Brian Terry northwest of Nogales, Arizona, on December 14, 2010. Terry died from a single gunshot wound to his lower back, fired from an AK-47.[46] Though the investigators could not identify the specific gun that fired the bullet, two AK-47 style WASR-10 rifles were recovered at the scene. Both were traced to the Lone Wolf Trading Company in Glendale, Arizona, where they had been sold to Jaime Avila Jr., one of the straw purchasers the agents were monitoring under the Fast and Furious operation. During a seven-month period Avila bought fifty-two guns, including seventeen AK-47 style rifles, two AR-15 variants, and two .50 caliber weapons.[47]

Terry's murder precipitated a scandal about Fast and Furious that fueled several conspiracy theories about the operation.[48] According to one of the theories, better known in Mexico, it was a deliberate attempt by the United States to weaken and control its southern neighbor. Additionally, there were whispers that since most of the guns went to the Sinaloa cartel, it was proof that the US government had made a deal with this organized crime group and supported them against their rivals. In the United States, the most popular conspiracy theory saw Fast and Furious as a plot by President Barack Obama's administration to reinstate an assault rifle ban and implement new gun control measures. Some said that Arizona was specifically chosen for this plot because it had lax gun laws which could easily be made the culprit. But, as Grillo put it, this theory is oblivious to the fact that "gun deaths in Mexico don't swing politics in the United States."[49] Violence south of the border is more likely to increase the budget of the Border Patrol and investments in building walls and surveillance towers to prevent it from "spilling over." It is more likely to result in paramilitary groups gathering for private spring break "operations" in southern states—men bringing their tactical gear, radios, and AR-15s to "protect" the country by "hunting" Mexicans.[50] In other words, deaths in Mexico, rather than being a liability, are profitable to the US gun industry. ATF agents have made horrible mistakes with Fast and Furious and the gunwalking operations that preceded it, but it was not because the agency was part of some plot to strengthen gun control laws in the United States.

ATF agents who shared their experiences during interviews conducted by a congressional committee admitted they knew that the only way they would learn the whereabouts of the guns they let go would be when Mexican law enforcement recovered them at crime scenes. "Most of the Mexican recoveries are related to an act of violence," Agent Alt said.[51] "You can't allow thousands of guns to go south of the border without an expectation that they are going to be recovered eventually in crimes and people are going to die." ATF agents stationed in Mexico, who were not aware of the operation when they began noticing that a large number of weapons seized were traced to the same Phoenix stores, said they were told that the situation was under control. "Never in my wildest dreams ever would I have thought that this was a technique. Never. Ever. It just, it is inconceivable to me," said Carlos Canino, ATF's deputy attaché to Mexico.[52] "You don't lose guns. You don't walk guns. You don't let guns get out of your sight."

When the investigators questioned special agent Olindo Casa, an eighteen-year veteran of ATF who had previously worked firearms trafficking cases in California, Florida, and Illinois, he confirmed that violence in Mexico was an expected outcome of what they were doing:

Interviewer: It was a likely consequence of the policy of walking guns that some of those guns would wind up at crime scenes in Mexico?

Agent Casa: Yeah.

Interviewer: And is it fair to say that some, if not many, of these crime scenes would be where people would be seriously injured or possibly killed?

Agent Casa: Of course.

Interviewer: So is it a fair, predictable outcome of the policy that there would be essentially collateral damage in terms of human lives?

Agent Casa: Sure.[53]

This collateral damage was not only anticipated, but read as an indication that the plan was working. In an email that the supervisor of the Phoenix group sent to his team on April 2, 2010, he cited worsening homicide statistics in Mexico: 842 killed in December 2009, 937 killed in January 2010, 958 killed in March 2010.[54] Next to "March 2010" he added a comment: "most violent month since 2005." The email continued: "Our subjects purchased 359 firearms during the month of March alone, to include numerous Barrett .50 caliber rifles." He asked the group for patience: "I believe we are righteous in our plan to dismantle this entire organization and to rush in to arrest any one person without taking in to account the entire scope of the conspiracy would be ill advised to the overall good of the mission." In other words, US officials continued watching how people working with organized crime groups bought powerful weapons and smuggled them to Mexico, where violence was getting worse every month, and they lauded this as their operation's success.

Fast and Furious ended like most firearms trafficking cases did. Nineteen men and one woman were indicted, many of them on counts of "making a false statement in connection with the acquisition of firearms," that is, for noting on Form 4473 that they were buying the firearms for their own use, not on behalf of others. Some of them were also charged with "conspiracy," "dealing in firearms without a license," and "money laundering."[55] Jaime Avila Jr., who bought dozens of guns, including the two AK-47 style rifles found at the scene of Terry's murder, pleaded guilty to what the judge called running "weapons of war," and was sentenced to fifty-seven months in prison.[56] In addition, the nearly five-hundred-page report released by the Office of the Inspector General cited fourteen individuals, ranging from senior ATF officials in Washington, DC, to line agents and prosecutors in Arizona, who "bore a share of responsibility for ATF's knowing failure in both these operations [Wide Receiver and Fast and Furious] to interdict firearms illegally destined for Mexico, and for doing so without adequately taking into account the danger to public safety that flowed from this risky strategy."[57]

News that the guns found in Mexico were part of the US government's scheme caused outrage in Mexico. José Carlos Ramírez Marín, president of the chamber of deputies, called the US government an accomplice in a serious international crime committed against Mexico, "a crime perpetrated by the government of another country in the Mexican territory."[58] Marisela Morales, Mexico's attorney general, told the

Los Angeles Times, "it is an attack on the safety of Mexicans."[59] "At no time did we know or were we made aware that there might have been arms trafficking permitted," she said. "In no way would we have allowed it." It remains unclear who in Mexico knew and who didn't know about the operation, who was informed of what and when. Congressional hearings at the US House of Representatives revealed that in 2007 US attorney general Michael Mukasey briefed Mexican attorney general Eduardo Medina Mora on ATF's gunwalking operations.[60] At least back then, the United States was working jointly with Mexico. But publicly Mexican officials denied their complicity in controlled delivery of firearms and turned their anger squarely toward the United States. In December 2012, Mexico's chamber of deputies approved an agreement to send a rebuff to the US government condemning its operations in Mexico as a violation of the country's sovereignty and an insult to its dignity. Marcos Carlos Cruz Martínez, from the Party of the Democratic Revolution (PRD), summed up the discontent that he and his colleagues felt: "This attitude of the US government can be considered interventionist and destabilizing, because it has contributed to increasing the firepower of criminal groups that in some regions have exceeded that of the Mexican state."[61]

Others considered legal recourse. One lawyer who had worked at the Nuevo León attorney general's office in Monterrey wanted to sue ATF over the damages Fast and Furious caused to Mexican citizens. In 2012, she told the press that she was looking for more victims' families to come forward to build the case.[62] But there was no lawsuit. With tens of thousands disappeared in Mexico at the time, many families did not even know what had happened to their missing relatives, much less what kind of guns were involved or where they had come from. Suing the US government officials for enabling the supply of weapons to organized crime groups was something only US citizens considered within reach: Both Brian Terry's and Jaime Zapata's relatives filed lawsuits for the agents' wrongful deaths.[63]

Two years after the massacre in Villas de Salvárcar, his term ending, President Calderón flew to Ciudad Juárez to unveil a north-facing billboard, its message written in English, directed at the audience across the border: "NO MORE WEAPONS." The letters were molded from firearms, mostly American, recovered from crime scenes by the Mexican military. He called gun trafficking "inhumane." Standing in front of the sign, the man who had welcomed US assistance to militarize public security through the Mérida Initiative said, "One of the main factors that allows criminals to strengthen themselves is the unlimited access to high-powered weapons, which are sold freely, and also indiscriminately, in the United States of America."[64]

The billboard was taken down in 2015, an effort by Juárez's mayor to rebrand the city's violent image and welcome American tourists back. But the consequences of Fast and Furious are felt to this day, as weapons that could have been stopped from crossing the border continue to wound Mexican citizens and the anger at the US government for their recklessness keeps reigniting. "The destruction of Mexican society is in part coming from the American society," said the governor of Nuevo León, Jaime Rodríguez Calderón, in 2017, when hundreds of guns traced to Fast and Furious were destroyed in a public ceremony in front of the government palace in Monterrey.[65]

Hundreds of others are still out there.

Ghost Highway

La Ribereña, Tamaulipas—Nuevo León—Coahuila

The road unfurled toward the west, stretching for hundreds of miles ahead of us. In the beginning, right after the last colonias of Nuevo Laredo faded from the rearview mirrors, the two-lane highway was crowded with trucks hauling heavy cargo and fuel tankers racing on the narrow strip of asphalt with no breakdown lanes. But soon they scattered and, once we crossed into Coahuila, their sightings on the road became more sporadic.

The grey sky dimmed the already monotonous colors of the winter landscape—a sea of shrubs and grass parted by *brechas*, those rutted paths that zigzagged through the backcountry, forming shortcuts between towns and ranches that only those who lived here could navigate. We passed a lone horse standing in the middle of the highway and, sometime later, a burnt carcass of a car. A falcon glided low across the road and disappeared in the direction of the river. I couldn't see it through the window, but the map on my phone, still catching the signal from cell towers on the other side, showed us moving parallel to a squiggly blue line marked as Rio Grande.

"There it is," Juan said, and I lifted my eyes from the screen to focus on the distant shapes on the hill ahead of us.

"A checkpoint?" I asked, my heart beating faster.

"Yes," he said. "This one run by the crimen organizado institucionalizado."

I turned to look at Juan and saw he wasn't smiling.

"What are they?"

"Coahuila state police. A special tactical unit," he said. "Those are filled with cement," he added, as I snapped a photo of the piles of rubber tires painted olive green that were supposed to shield the officers from the bullets.

I had heard that the checkpoint was frequently attacked by what the government and the media nowadays called "armed civilians." But it was still the safest place for them to be. Less risky than in the brechas. A few months ago, patrolling a dirt road that ran parallel to the highway somewhere near here, the police stumbled upon a convoy of thirty trucks with armed men who were trying to cross from Nuevo León into Coahuila avoiding the checkpoint.[1] In the shootout that ensued, the gunmen injured three police officers and torched a patrol vehicle before fleeing into the backcountry. In another recent encounter, the military came to assist the police, killing nine armed men and seizing their armored truck and a .50 caliber Barrett rifle.[2] But the military wasn't always helping the police. Sometimes because the police didn't want them to.

"These are the dangerous ones," Juan said, just in case his earlier comments had confounded me.

By now, I knew that the police in Coahuila had been working for the Zetas. They would stop cars and question drivers in order to pass that information to the comandantes.[3] Other times they would detain people on behalf of them. But these men we would soon meet were not just any police—some of them were the former GATES, members of the elite specialized weapons and tactics group created by previous Coahuila governor Humberto Moreira. Moreira had been taking bribes from the Zetas, but their agreement broke down when, in 2012, they murdered his son.[4] The state's complicity and cooperation with the organized crime group began to rupture then.[5] Violence became even more erratic, the sides harder to tell apart. GATES held an abysmal human rights record. As well-armed and feared as the criminal groups they pursued, the state police threatened, robbed, kidnapped, and murdered with impunity. They were involved in numerous disappearances and Mexico's National Human Rights Commission recorded multiple complaints of torture to frame people for crimes they did not commit.[6]

As we got closer to the roadblock, my attention turned to the black tactical vehicle armored like a tank. "El Miura," it was called, after the Spanish fighting bull; the most menacing of the trucks parked facing the road in the fortified outpost looming in front of us. I noticed the letters PAR, for Policía de Ataque Rápido, on one of the vehicles. Another had

"Agencia de Investigación Criminal"—AIC, for its initials—written on its side. There were others, all new units with new names, an attempt by the new government to rebrand the old Coahuila state police. As if the old names had been the problem.

"It is a war zone," Juan said, slipping into the lexicon of the government. Even for journalists it was hard to talk about anything without falling back into the traps of the vocabulary we had gotten so used to, repeating the official story of the conflict that the authorities on both sides of the border endorsed.

"What should I tell them? What if they have questions?" I asked, alarmed that we hadn't discussed this.

"Don't say anything. I'll handle it."

Juan pressed on the brakes and rolled down the windows. The men were dressed in black, with bulletproof helmets and vests, automatic rifles slung on their shoulders. I tried not to look at their faces, avoiding their eyes meeting mine. Tried pretending that passing through checkpoints was a nuisance that was routine.

The policemen didn't care about us enough to interrupt what they were doing. An officer sitting in the driver's seat of a truck, slouched over a phone in his palm, threw us a lazy glance and turned back to the screen. Three others, standing in a semicircle, tinfoil wrapped sandwiches in their hands, their breakfast and their conversation momentarily on hold, were looking in the direction of our car, but said nothing. We waited. Ten seconds, fifteen at most, though it felt like minutes. At last, someone with authority, a lieutenant or a shift commander perhaps, appeared from behind one of the tactical vehicles, greeted us without approaching, and gestured that we could proceed.

Route 2 is a narrow stretch of federal highway that runs along the southern bank of the river that people in Mexico call Río Bravo. It is like a cement spine of the borderlands, extending from Playa Bagdad in the Gulf of Mexico to the Amistad Reservoir, just past the twin cities of Ciudad Acuña, Coahuila, and Del Rio, Texas, about seventy miles west of Uvalde and about twice as far from San Antonio. The road connects the towns of Matamoros, Reynosa, Nuevo Laredo, and Piedras Negras, and strings together smaller municipalities in between, with names like Gustavo Díaz Ordaz, Guerrero, and Jiménez. The road and the region it traverses is called La Ribereña.

News reports sometimes referred to Route 2 as the "ghost highway" or the "Bermuda triangle," with articles about the road accompanied by photographs of dozens of vehicles torched and left on the wayside, like the one we passed that morning. There were stories about scores of people who had been disappeared. Family members would tell journalists about men and women who left on a bus or in a car one day and never returned. Witnesses spoke of convoys of as many as a hundred trucks—Hummers, Suburbans, GMCs, Ford Lobos—with armed men speeding along the desert highway. The letters painted across their hoods and doors—"CDG" or "Z" and now "CDN"—helped identify the groups, but the distinction made little difference to residents whom they threatened, kidnapped, and killed.

We passed a small San Judas chapel on the side of the road and Juan recalled dozens of Santa Muerte shrines that used to speck the highway. The skeletal deity personifying death was increasingly worshipped all over Mexico by all sorts of people, but the Señora de la Noche, as she was sometimes called, was particularly popular among those who faced dangers working at night: taxi drivers, sex workers, soldiers, and police officers asked her for safe passage and for protection against assaults and violent death.[7] In the media, however, she was often associated with drug traffickers and criminality, which goaded public officials into doing something about the multiplying shrines. "The military destroyed them," Juan said. The municipality of Nuevo Laredo also participated, sending workers to demolish the shrines at the entrance to the city. According to them, it was merely a matter of road safety: the shrines were in disrepair and posed a danger to drivers. "We respect all religious beliefs," the mayor said, maintaining the official story that their removal had nothing to do with the kind of devotees who worshipped her.[8] Ominous skeletal deities with scythes in their hands were gone. The benign green-clad figure of San Judas, the saint of lost causes, was allowed to stay.

Juan was speeding and, when we switched, so did I. We had to be back in Nuevo Laredo before nightfall. Later in the evening, the road would no longer be safe. Under the cover of the night, those "armed civilians" the police and the military fought in shootouts erected their own checkpoints. Drivers who disobeyed the tacit curfew and dared to be on the road past sundown could be mistaken for the rivals attempting to take over the plaza, and find their vehicles sprayed with bullets before anyone would bother asking questions. Robbery and kidnapping were other possibilities. For now, this stretch of La Ribereña was relatively quiet because the plaza was under the reign of a single group. But they were young, many still in their teens, and they were violent, rattled by rumors of their old rivals from the east encroaching on their territory, and alarmed by occasional sightings of newcomers from Jalisco in the border region. That made them unpredictable.

The night before, as I lay on the bed in my hotel room in Laredo, listening to the signals of the freight trains and the hum of traffic heading in both directions of I-35, I opened the pages of *El Mañana*. I wanted to know more about the city south of the border where I was going to meet with Juan—not the panic-stricken travel advisories that both the US government and my university shared with me, which cautioned against traveling to Tamaulipas "due to crime and kidnapping" and warned that "heavily armed members of criminal groups" patrol the area and "operate with impunity," while "law enforcement has limited capacity to respond." According to the latest travel advisory, "gun battles, murder, armed robbery, carjacking, kidnapping, forced disappearances, extortion, and sexual assault" were common. The advisories were not wrong. It was not a safe place. But the list of warnings read like a label on a bottle of prescription pills: if any of this happens, don't say that we didn't warn you. Yet people were commuting between the two Laredos every day. From the park down by the river earlier that afternoon, I watched small figures move across the bridge. They weren't many, but the border had just reopened after the pandemic.[9]

I didn't see anything that made me worried. Still, I picked up my phone and found the number of the one person who could tell me what I most needed to know. I hadn't seen Alfredo since Covid-19 paused my fieldwork, but we occasionally talked about the stories he did about migrants stranded on the border. I knew he had been to Laredo and understood this place better than I did. On one of his visits back in 2005, when he was writing about Americans kidnapped on the other side, a man came up to him at a bar and told him what would happen to those who asked questions about the Zetas. That was not the first nor the last threat he received while covering organized crime. He knew how to recognize the ones to be taken seriously, how to overcome that natural response—denial. I had been threatened once before, and that evening in Laredo, standing by the window looking out over the vast empty parking lot in front of the hotel, I remembered how unreal it had felt when it happened, years ago, how I thought it was just my paranoia. I knew better now.

We didn't dwell on "what ifs." I asked Alfredo about the basic stuff, like which of the bridges was the safest to walk across at sunrise. "Puente uno," he said, referring to the main pedestrian bridge that started at the outlet mall in Laredo—an enormous building with "Coach" and "Puma" and other brand signs affixed to the faded yellow facade turned toward Mexico—and ended in the populated shopping district in downtown Nuevo Laredo. "There will be *halcones*," he said, referring to the lookouts, but their presence was ubiquitous. It was what would happen after I crossed that Alfredo was more concerned about. "Keep me posted. And careful out there," he texted after we hung up.

"A plaza is a city . . . where you establish control over the municipal police, over the federal police, and other law enforcement agents, where you pay a monthly fee so you can do whatever drug business or whatever other crimes you want to commit," was how someone who knew it very well explained the nature of the Zetas' power in the region.[10] I remembered this definition almost word-for-word because I had read the transcripts of José Treviño Morales's trial just days earlier, on the plane from Boston. It was common knowledge that the plaza of Nuevo Laredo now belonged to the Northeast Cartel, a group formed by one faction of the remaining Zetas. They tagged their name using an acronym, CDN, for Cártel del Noreste, which recently began appearing as far as Monterrey, and they had an armed branch called "*Tropa de Infierno*." As the busiest commercial truck port between Mexico and the United States, Nuevo Laredo was particularly well suited for trafficking drugs and extorting businesses. I found an article about CDN burning eight passenger buses belonging to a company that didn't pay their quota. Evening folded into night, but I kept reading, as if the more knowledge I could cram into my head, the less room there would be left for unease. I read an article about the time they shot at an army helicopter that was hovering above a colonia on the west side of the city. And another, about three members of the organization arrested here, in Texas, with half a million dollars they wanted to spend on military-style rifles, machine guns, and grenades. I don't know how late it was when I finally fell asleep.

I woke up in the early hours of the morning and kept checking my phone for news from Juan. He was going to drive north from Monterrey on Route 85, another highway marked by horror. Over seventy people disappeared there, in an area contested between CDN and their rivals, last year. As I knew from my late-night reading spree, that section of the road was now called "*tramo de terror*" (branch of terror) or "*hoyo negro*" (a black hole).[11] Most of the disappeared were men, drivers of passenger buses or ride shares. But there were women and children, too, Mexican and US citizens. Various searches were carried out around KM 26, but no bodies had been found. I worried about Juan, even though he knew what he was doing.

Perhaps anticipating my concerns, he called me before sunrise, as he was leaving Monterrey, and told me he was traveling in tandem with another journalist headed to Reynosa. Next time he called, two hours later, he was already approaching Nuevo Laredo and separating from his colleague who would continue east. It was time for me to go, too. The sky was overcast, the last drops of winter rain were gently tapping the sage green waters of the river below, as I walked across the bridge and past the Mexican customs agents to the street corner we had agreed on. There I stood and watched the cars pass by, waiting.

A grey Yaris blinked its headlights before it stopped in front of me. I jumped inside and hugged Juan. Then I gave him the box with the apple pie I had promised to bring from Texas and he reached back to put it on the empty seat behind me. With a scruffy stubble and black curls tinged with more silver than when I had last seen him, Juan looked frazzled. The denim jacket and pair of round sunglasses he was wearing on this gloomy morning gave an impression of a classic rock fan hungover from a late night concert, not a seasoned organized crime reporter. I surmised it was intentional. Having been writing about the Zetas and their ties to the government for almost two decades—"submerged in the world of the narco," as he put it to me once—visiting places where few of his colleagues dared to go, he knew better when to display his media credentials and when it was better not to. Appearances could save lives.

Juan hadn't planned on becoming a journalist and even less on dedicating himself to organized crime. In the eighties, he went to Mexico City to study history, but returned to Monterrey a few years later without having finished his degree. A friend from high school, who was a section editor at the conservative daily *El Porvenir*, offered him a job covering business. Monterrey is a major industrial center and economic news is as important there as politics, maybe more. That was Juan's beat for years, even after he moved on to the national business newspaper *El Financiero*, then to a major Mexican daily *El Universal*. But by the mid-aughts, violence replaced business as the main news story in Monterrey. Soon, all journalists, regardless of whether they had any experience with security issues, began covering it, Juan included. "It was a new topic, attractive, despite the dangers," he said. In 2009, he started writing for the weekly magazine *Proceso*, focusing exclusively on drug trafficking and organized crime. "I descended into this world and, unfortunately, I haven't been able to leave it ever since," he told me.

Juan shifted into gear and we pulled away from the curb and merged into traffic. A small black device which resembled a walkie talkie lay on the center console, next to a triangle of a sandwich left over from Juan's breakfast on the road. "*Mecanismo*," he said when he noticed me glancing at it. The government had placed Juan under the federal program for journalists and human rights workers known as "*el mecanismo de protección.*"[12] That device was a special phone with the panic button he carried around. But when he did more risky assignments, like this trip, he asked for additional monitoring. Every three hours someone called him to check in. Juan used code words when he spoke with them, certain phrases they had agreed on that signaled his condition without anyone else being able to make sense of it. If Juan didn't answer when they called, the system would alert the authorities about his latest GPS location and ask to dispatch a police unit to look for him. The plan was better than nothing, but it was full of lacunae. Skeptical about its use, some reporters called the phone "a moral support button." It was a piece of plastic, not a shield from bullets. And it only worked if the area had cell coverage and if local authorities were willing to send out the patrols. When threats to journalists came directly from the police—which was often the case—the plan was a cruel joke.[13]

We stopped for gas and were about to turn onto the street that would take us out of Nuevo Laredo and onto Route 2, when Juan's phone rang. It was the journalist from Mexico City who was driving to Reynosa. He told Juan that he stopped to take some footage of the area where people had been disappearing and that, as soon as he pulled out his camera and set it up with the drone, he was approached by a pickup truck, an acronym CDN painted in white across its side. The men in the truck didn't say anything and left, but, as soon as they were gone, the police showed up and the officers told him he couldn't film there. He understood it as a warning, packed up and sped away. Juan pressed him for details: Where exactly did this happen, who was there, and what else did they say? He asked the reporter to call him again in a few hours to check in. This was how they operated in this region—through informal networks, sharing information and locations, so somebody would know if things went wrong and would be able to tell the last time and place the other was still alive. This system seemed more trustworthy than the mecanismo, though I was glad we had both. I, too, had promised Alfredo I would text him throughout the day with updates, but it was still early and I decided to wait until we reached Coahuila.

I rested my eyes on the landscape, which hadn't changed much in the last hour that we had been following the thin grey thread of Route 2, my thoughts drifting to the forms of violence in the region I still didn't know well. My arrival in northeast Mexico in early 2019 coincided with the height of the federal government's clampdown of fuel theft colloquially known as *huachicoleo*.[14] For years, organized crime groups had been siphoning off oil from the state-owned oil company PEMEX through schemes that flawlessly fused government and criminal structures. In 2018, leftist politician Andrés Manuel López Obrador, who campaigned on promises to fight institutional corruption, was elected Mexico's sixty-fifth president. One of the first things López Obrador did after taking office was to turn off the pipelines to dry the supply for huachicoleros. Some gas stations stood empty the week I landed in Monterrey, the absence of fuel and cars at the pumps evidence that they had depended on illicit suppliers. That, too, was violence, but to see it you had to know how to recognize it, to draw the connection between an empty fuel station and organized crime groups engaged in stealing oil. You had to imagine the underground tunnels lined with pipes and hoses through which gasoline was siphoned off to tankers—the subterranean theft invisible to the security forces patrolling on foot and military drones surveilling the area from the sky. PEMEX's chief of security once told the press that hydrocarbons gave off intense odor and it was often the smell that led them to discover these criminal operations.[15] The authorities had to literally sniff out the crime they couldn't see.

Huachicoleo was the main reason the government placed Juan under the protection of the mecanismo. He wrote an article about how the Zetas brought engineers to divert the pipeline near Cadereyta and, with the help of union members, sold the fuel to the public transport authority in Monterrey. Juan asked the editors not to add his byline to the story, but they refused, and, as soon as the article came out, Juan started receiving threats. He knew it would happen. After all, it was a story of how the Zetas stole from the state and then sold it back to the state; a story of the dissolving boundary between the state and organized crime. But that's presuming one ever existed. Historian and sociologist Charles Tilly's observation that states were "quintessential protection rackets with the advantage of legitimacy" seemed more apt.[16] Strip away legitimacy, and the difference between the state and organized crime was no longer clear.

The road we were taking ran across this grey zone, where recognizing perils was a skill one acquired from experience.

"Another checkpoint," Juan announced a barricade on the road before I even noticed, in shades of light and dark green, fusing with the drab tones of the landscape. This one was manned by the military. They, too, had piles of tires for soldiers to hide behind during shootouts and a makeshift shed with black drapes that offered some cover from the sun. Since seven soldiers died and one was wounded in a recent gunfight, army checkpoints in Coahuila were now reinforced with .50 caliber weapons.

We slowed down, opened the windows, nodded to the heavily armed soldiers. Like the state police before, they didn't say anything and didn't ask us any questions. The soldiers nodded back and that meant we could go.

Between this and the next, larger, military checkpoint, we took a left turn onto a narrow road. At the first town we drove through, we saw a man and stopped to ask him for directions. When we reached the second village farther west, its streets were eerily quiet—no people, no vehicles, no dogs. The silence felt strange. Looking right and left, we didn't notice the speed bumps that were the same grey color as the road, and the car jumped up and down loudly. Local residents didn't even have to peek through their windows to see Nuevo León plates—as soon as they heard loud clunks on the road, they knew we were strangers. In the third town, we sat down at an empty restaurant and ordered tacos and tequila.

It was already early afternoon when we passed the fields of black walnut trees and then a pink cross in front of a gate, closed and overgrown with shrubs. We turned around and drove slowly for several hundred yards, looking for anything resembling a rutted path, until we came across a patch of gravel and sand and two lines the width of car tires trailing off into the distance. Any foreboding I had hours ago, when we set out west on Route 2, had been pushed aside by the more immediate task of finding the way. The way in, but also the way out.

The thick grasses scraped the bottom of the Yaris as Juan carefully pressed forward. The car flattened some anthills, its roof barely cleared gnarly branches of lone trees. It went like this for a while, and we began to doubt whether this was the right place after all. The scratching sounds from the undercarriage made me wince. If the car broke down here, we would be in trouble. It was not safe to poke around a crime scene that local authorities had helped cover up. Trying not to show my unease to Juan, I stared at the blue dot on my phone moving slowly in the middle of blank space. We'd gone too far to turn around now.

Then the dirt path curved and in front of us the horizon appeared smudged, as if a few extra brushstrokes were messing up the clean shapes of the grassland. Maybe an orchard. Or an old barn. As we got closer, the blotches sharpened into ruins of a ranch, carcasses of houses emerging from behind the trees.

"This is it," Juan said, relieved.

He had been here before, years ago, the first journalist to report about the massacre at the Garza ranch, traveling disguised as a tourist, pretending he got lost and ended up in the wrong place, naively unaware of what had happened. Witnesses were too afraid to talk back then, so he didn't interview anyone on the record. Taking photographs was out of the question. Even signing his name under the article, which his editors insisted he do, could have been a death sentence. Now I watched Juan reach for his camera, hidden under clothes in the backseat, so I didn't even know he had brought it when he picked me up in Nuevo Laredo. It was the old one, which left dark spots on the images from the dust and dirt stuck to the sensor, the one he was less concerned to part with should they smash it against the ground.

We didn't talk as we wandered from building to building. In a warehouse that had no doors and no roof, I stepped carefully on the shards of ceramic tiles that grated under the soles of my shoes. Skulls with crossbones sprayed in red paint covered the concrete walls, riddled with bullet holes, some as big as a fist. Juan started shooting, pointing his camera at the initials P.E.C. The only group we knew using that acronym was one of the special Coahuila state police units.

Clouds had parted and the sun, bright and warm, brought back some color to the blanched land. There was no wind, as if we were standing in a still photograph. Juan kept taking pictures. Every few minutes I scanned the horizon to check whether anyone was watching us. It was better if we saw them first, if we had a moment to compose ourselves before explaining who we were and why we were here, in hopes they would listen. But there was no movement and, when I stood still, there was no sound.

When the forensic investigators arrived at the ranch in 2014, they were accompanied by the army and the marines—part of a large multiagency operation with over two hundred people, led by the state's deputy attorney's office for the investigation and search of missing persons. They collected the drums and cans of fuel and dug up the teeth and bone fragments from the mass grave. Juan showed me the site: now a ditch full of weeds.

As I wandered away from him, I looked down at the dry cracked ground and noticed something red—a shotgun shell. Then I saw another, and another, until they were all around me. Shotgun shells and brass bullet casings glinting in the sun. I realized the field I was standing in was full of spent ammunition. I picked a few of them up, one by one, and read the markings: 223 Rem, 9mm Luger, 762. As I turned them in my fingers sand spilled out on my sneakers.

"What is it?" Juan asked when he saw me examining something in my palm.

"A spent bullet casing from an AK-47. There are AR-15 rounds too. And these are 12-gauge shotgun shells," I said as I held one up to show him, pleased that I knew something useful.

Most of the spent bullet casings were of cartridges that were not allowed for civilian use in Mexico. They belonged either to the security forces or, more likely, to an organized crime group, probably the one that aptly called themselves "Tropa de Infierno." The same guys that Juan's colleague saw earlier this morning. The same that used to be the Zetas.

In one of the buildings, which still had a roof, we found Tecate and Corona cans that faintly smelled of beer. The locals had been avoiding this place after the massacre, both out of respect for the murdered and out of fear of the murderers. But not everybody had such reservations. Whoever these people were, they had been coming to the ruins of the ranch to drink and do target practice.

"We should go now," Juan said.

I collected a handful of bullet casings and put them into my pocket.

The Last Letter

We don't know when the Zetas were founded. There is no official date marking the beginning of their story. Around the turn of the millennium, the group emerged from the seam where state violence and organized crime came so close together that it was difficult to tell them apart. Nobody disputes that the first Zetas were deserters from an elite unit of the Mexican army who became the bodyguards and hitmen working for the Gulf Cartel. Until their violent split, the two groups operated as La Compañía. Trained in military tactics and equipped with assault weapons, former soldiers imposed a reign of terror unseen before in Mexico. Fear helped them consolidate control over parts of the country, where local governments, unable to compete with their firepower, had to tell residents to stay off the roads after sunset. La Compañía owned the night, and it owned people's nightmares.

The details, however, are not so easy to pin down. Doubts over the identities and life trajectories of the Zetas leaders are exacerbated by the government's refusal to release information that could potentially implicate the security forces. Multiple names and nicknames adopted by some commanders add further confusion about who is who, or rather who was who, since many of the founding members of the organization have since been killed. But not even death can bring certainty about their identity. Speculation over faked or forged deaths adds twists to a narrative already so macabre that anything seems plausible. The story of the Zetas is steeped in rumor and myth, denying the comfort of a solid boundary between the real and the imaginary, between fact and fiction, as if this blurring was the only way to make sense of their brutality, to understand what appeared to be beyond comprehension, like chopping off people's limbs so that the bodies would fit into metal barrels, dousing them with fuel to set them ablaze, and dissolving what's left—bones, teeth—in acid. This is but a tentative outline of what happened and of how people were making sense of what made so little sense.

This story starts in the northeastern Mexican state of Tamaulipas. Sharing a 230-mile border with Texas, Tamaulipas has long been a strategic location for profiteering from different laws in neighboring countries and thus a fertile ground for criminal enterprise. During the Prohibition Era in the United States, in the 1920s and early 1930s, smugglers crossed over from Mexico to supply thirsty American consumers with whiskey, rum, and tequila. Demand was so high that it enabled one Mexican man to build a business empire. Juan Nepomuceno Guerra, who grew up working at his father's ranch in Matamoros and was passionate about racehorses, started with bootleg alcohol, before extending his operations to contraband cigarettes, prostitution, gambling, and car theft.[1] Aided by ties with mayors, governors, police and customs officers, and other government officials that he patiently tended to, his organization grew steadily over the decades and Guerra solidified his position as the patriarch of a criminal dynasty. He became a legend, the godfather of the borderland mafia, but his business was still a local affair, a smuggling enterprise entangled with the regional economy that did not reach far beyond the two sides of the Río Bravo/Rio Grande. It was Guerra's nephew, Juan García Ábrego, who would later see and seize an opportunity presented by events unfolding far from their home state and, by doing so, change the nature of organized crime in the area.

Until the 1980s, the main route for bringing cocaine from Colombia to the United States was across the Caribbean, by boat or by plane, or a combination of the two.[2] But political hysteria about the cocaine and crack epidemic in the United States led to a rigorous enforcement campaign along Florida's coastline. Colombian traffickers who supplied American consumers sought alternative routes to the United States and those routes cut across Mexico. In the beginning, they used the Mexicans as contractors, paying them a fee to handle the logistics of their cargo bound farther north. The Colombians worked with various Mexican crime bosses who controlled smuggling routes across the border— men who sometimes formed alliances, and other times violently competed for power and plazas: first, Miguel Ángel Félix Gallardo and his associates, many of them from Sinaloa, who formed a network of family-based organizations that the US media and government later came to call the "Guadalajara Cartel";[3] then, after this loose alliance disintegrated, with the Arellano Félix brothers in Tijuana, Joaquín Guzmán Loera in Baja California and Sonora, and Pablo Acosta and Amado Carillo Fuentes in Chihuahua. Over time, these crime bosses outgrew their roles as middlemen for Colombian traffickers and demanded a more substantial share in the cocaine business. García Ábrego, who continued on the path that his uncle had started—maintaining their organization's independence from Félix Gallardo and his partners—formed a separate agreement with the Cali Cartel, guaranteeing their cocaine would be delivered to the United States in exchange for half of each load. This deal helped the CDG, or Cártel del Golfo (known as the Gulf Cartel in the United States), to become one of the first major drug trafficking organizations in Mexico and led to García Ábrego being placed, in 1995, on the FBI's Top Ten Most Wanted List, the first Mexican drug trafficker to receive such recognition from the US government. Except it wasn't an honor to be celebrated: García Ábrego's days relishing wealth and notoriety were coming to an end. Nine months later, he was arrested on his ranch near Monterrey, extradited to the United States, and sentenced to eleven consecutive life terms.

His successor at the helm of CDG was a former mechanic from Matamoros, who, for a time, worked for the Federal Judicial Police.[4] His name was Osiel Cárdenas Guillén and, because he assumed the leadership of the organization by assassinating a friend, he became known by the nickname El Mata Amigos, the Friend Killer. Once in power, Cárdenas Guillén hired infantry corporal Arturo Guzmán Decena and asked him to assemble a trustworthy team to protect El Mata Amigos from the fate he decided for his rivals. As far as qualifications go, Cárdenas Guillén could not have chosen anyone better prepared for the job. Decena was a member of the Mexican Airborne Special Forces Group, known by its initials GAFE, and had five years of experience serving in the military, where he trained in heavy weapons, urban guerilla warfare, and wilderness survival. Decena arrived in Tamaulipas in early 1997, as part of the government's experimental new approach to combat drug trafficking. Based on advice they received from the United States, Mexican authorities began integrating military officers into the structure of the Federal Judicial Police. PJF, as the agency was referred to in Mexico, had been mired in allegations of corruption and those responsible for the operation must have thought that populating it with soldiers would restore its credibility. Army officers assigned to the judicial police were divided into groups and each received an identification key comprised of the letter representing their unit followed by a number. Decena became Z-1.[5]

Decena's redacted military file shows that on September 30, 1997, less than a year since he came to Tamaulipas, he deserted the army. On the run, he dedicated himself to the task Cárdenas Guillén had entrusted him with: creating the enforcer wing for the Gulf Cartel. The initial group consisted of his pals—fourteen elite soldiers, trained in the use of military equipment and counterinsurgency operations, who, like Decena, were sent to Tamaulipas to integrate with the Federal Judicial Police. Their military files, full of black censor bars over their dates of birth and other key details of their biographies, repeat nearly identical stories.[6] Heriberto Lazcano Lazcano: finished sixth grade; enlisted as an infantry soldier in Pachuca, Hidalgo, in 1991; promoted to corporal in 1993; assigned to GAFE; requested leave in 1998 due to "family problems." Jaime González Durán: born in San Luis Potosì; enlisted in the military in Nuevo León in 1991 as an engineer in signals and communications; promoted to corporal in 1992; became a member of GAFE; declared on the run from military justice in 2000. Jesús Enrique Rejón Aguilar: born in 1976; joined the army in his home state of Campeche in 1993; promoted to corporal and assigned to GAFE in 1996; sent to Tamaulipas and then Coahuila; defected in 1999. Luis Reyes Enríquez: sent to Tamaulipas to join the Federal Judicial Police in 1998; left the army the following year. And so on.

Recruitment to the mercenary army went smoothly. Public ads targeted members of the military and police, offering them a salary in dollars, brand-new trucks, life insurance, and houses for their families. A banner hung on a pedestrian bridge in Nuevo Laredo in April 2008 announced: "Operative group 'Los Zetas' wants you, soldier or ex-soldier. We offer a good salary, food and benefits for your family. Don't suffer any more mistreatment and hunger. We won't feed you instant noodles."[7] The message included a telephone number to call if interested. Another banner, signed by the Gulf Cartel, appeared later that month near Tamaulipas Autonomous University in Tampico. It, too, hailed those wearing government uniforms, telling them to "stop suffering."[8] The compensation and other benefits lured chronically underpaid and poorly equipped Mexican soldiers and police officers to switch sides. Whatever discomfort they may have felt for betraying their legal and moral obligations, it dissipated when they weighed their duty to serve the government against the safety and well-being of their families. Back then, joining the enemy could have seemed like a better option to increase their odds of surviving the "drug war." "Tamaulipas, México, United States and the whole world: Territory of the Gulf Cartel," one of the banners boldly declared.

This recruitment campaign extended beyond Mexican territory. Pirate radios in El Petén, the northernmost department of Guatemala, broadcast announcements addressed to Kaibiles—the elite members of the Guatemalan armed forces—recruiting them to transport and protect "merchandise" in vehicles headed north.[9] Kaibiles signed up. Mexican military personnel did too. The country's defense secretary, General Gerardo Clemente Vega García, admitted that more than a hundred thousand soldiers had deserted from the military in the six years of President Vicente Fox's administration.[10] That came down to an average of forty-nine desertions per day. One thousand and twenty-three of those who left before 2003 held officer ranks. Nine were lieutenant colonels. Between 1985 and 2006, the army, navy, and air force lost 347,055 soldiers to desertion.[11] There is no way of knowing how many of them joined organized crime groups, but the numbers are likely in the thousands, possibly tens of thousands. Following this embarrassing news, SEDENA urged the Mexican Congress to declare "betrayal of the army" to be a serious crime and prosecute deserters in martial court.[12]

For about a decade, the Zetas continued working for and with the Gulf Cartel. Their own name did not immediately draw public attention. When it was uttered, the last letter was but a whisper, too elusive to leave a trace. According to one journalist's account, around midnight on January 27, 2002, a convoy of a dozen or more Suburbans entered Nuevo Laredo and parked in front of the Santo Niño parish church.[13] When municipal police officers approached the vehicles, the occupants told them not to interfere in the operation. Those who tuned in to the police radio frequencies that night could hear the men in the convoy identify themselves by the letter Z followed by a number. That same year, on November 21, Z-1 was killed. It happened in Matamoros, where Decena went to visit his girlfriend. Her family owned a small restaurant—a one-story cement establishment with three plastic tables and red chairs branded with Coca Cola logos. Decena was washing his hands when a group of armed men in black uniforms, members of a special unit for combatting organized crime, found him there, dragged him outside, and shot him on the spot.[14] According to a popular account, several weeks later a funeral wreath appeared at the site where he died with a note that read: "You will always be in our hearts. From your family Los Zetas." But those who were on scene say that the only signature on the wreath was that of the family and that the Zetas were not mentioned. All I could find on the web was a low-resolution photograph of a cross with a wooden plaque that spells out Decena's full name, his date of birth, and the date of his death. News reports about his killing referred to him as "the presumed chief of security" for Osiel Cárdenas Guillén, not as the leader of the Zetas.[15]

After Decena's death, the name of the Zetas began appearing in the mainstream Mexican press more often, usually in the news about their members being arrested or escaping from prison. In those early articles, the Zetas were described as "cells" of the Gulf Cartel, then as a "gang," until the media settled on referring to them as "a group of sicarios" who were the armed branch of the CDG.[16] They were called "loyal gunmen" working for Cárdenas Guillén.[17] One story reported how forty members of "grupo de sicarios Los Zetas," dressed in black uniforms, simulated a police operation and stormed a maximum security prison in Matamoros to free four men affiliated with the Gulf Cartel.[18] Later, their name started to come up in the news of a "war of assassins" over the plaza of Nuevo Laredo, which erupted in 2003, when Joaquín Guzmán Loera and the Beltrán Leyva brothers sent their crews to take over the border town seen as strategic for crossing drugs into the United States.[19] The Zetas fought to defend CDG's territory and that fight was gruesome. The streets smelled of "gunpowder and death," wrote journalist Francisco Gómez in his report for *El Universal*, describing black-clad heavily armed hitmen riding in trucks and convoys, noting that the community "was being held hostage."[20] This was the beginning of a decade-long turf war about to spread beyond Tamaulipas: west, to Coahuila and Nuevo León; southeast, to Veracruz and Chiapas; and southwest, to Guerrero and Michoacán, where the Zetas would fight against an organization that matched their level of brutality, known as La Familia. As the Zetas moved into new plazas, their name gained recognition. Through repetition, it became synonymous with terror.

The defense of Nuevo Laredo was entrusted to Heriberto Lazcano Lazcano, Z-3, who had become one of the leaders of the group. A former infantry corporal, he completed special operations and wilderness survival courses in the jungle of Quintana Roo, the mountains of Durango, and the deserts of Sonora, and possibly trained in Fort Bragg and Fort Benning in the United States.[21] After deserting and switching sides, Z-3 earned the nickname El Verdugo, the Executioner.

Terror tactics that the Zetas introduced to Mexico resemble the instructions listed in counterinsurgency manuals that the US military used to teach in the School of the Americas. It is therefore widely believed and often taken for granted that the original Zetas who deserted from the Mexican army, including Lazcano, received training in torture techniques from instructors north of the border. Whether it was true or whether the connection with US counterinsurgency training helped the myth of the Zetas as elite mercenaries capable of ruthlessness that had previously been unimaginable among drug smugglers remains an open question. Mexican journalist Ricardo Raphael, in his book *Hijo de la guerra*, tells the story of the man he met in prison who claimed to be Galdino Mellado Cruz, known as Z-9. This man, one of the founding members of the organization, recounted how he and other Mexican soldiers sent for training in the United States in the nineties—a group that allegedly included Decena and Lazcano—were taught to kill slowly, extending the victim's suffering for as long as possible.[22] In the scene in Raphael's book, they practiced on a wild pig they caught in the forest, starting the ordeal with the hoofs, which they pulled out using pincers, then poured vinegar and ashes on the wounds to seal them; then they dismembered the animal, according to a schedule that would not allow it to die for hours. Every forty-five minutes they cut a piece of the body—ears, tusks, legs. The pig had to be dismembered, but still breathing, when their instructor returned to check on their work in the morning. Whether this really happened or whether it was an imaginative leap into the horror story the Zetas aroused—and whether this exaggeration was the work of the person who claimed he was a former Zeta or the journalist who was writing a fictionalized narrative about the man he could not trust, or both—the elements it was comprised of were not untrue.

There was no doubt the Zetas were dismembering and then burning their victims. When called to testify in a US court, witnesses who had seen how Zetas hacked people to death by using axes noted the repetitiveness of the process: "First the knee, then this part here, then an arm, and then the other side likewise; the knee, the same, the arm. And at the end, they beheaded him. . . . All of them, the majority of them, they cut them the same way."[23] The Zetas' signature method of disposing of their victims, known as "*cocinar*" (to cook) or making a "*guiso*" (stew), entailed throwing body parts in a steel drum, pouring in fuel, and setting it on fire.[24] In some cases, they finished by dissolving the bones and teeth in chemicals. There was nothing left when they dumped the ashes into mass graves.

But even the other parts of the story—the role of the US military and their use of animals for torture practice—are plausible. The US government has a long history of training elite soldiers from various Latin American countries in torture and interrogation techniques, which they did at the School of the Americas in Panama and later in Fort Benning, Georgia, where the institution, now called the Western Hemisphere Institute for Security Cooperation, was relocated in 1984.[25] Several hundred members of the Mexican special forces, the GAFEs, trained in the United States in the 1990s.[26] Even though the US government denied that any of the founding Zetas commanders were among them—at least not since 1996, when the US Embassy in Mexico City began keeping electronic records of Mexican military sent to the United States for training—they could have learned the curriculum from other special forces officers who did go north and then passed their knowledge onto future Zetas upon their return to Mexico. Finally, and still true to this day, the US military does use pigs (as well as goats) as surrogates for human bodies, shooting and stabbing them, amputating their limbs, and otherwise mutilating animals to inflict injuries, so that soldiers could practice trauma care they would need in the battlefield.[27] Put all of these together and the story about Mexican soldiers learning from the Americans to slowly kill the wild pig as a proxy for a human being no longer seems unthinkable.

Torture invoked terror and terror was an anticipatory tactic to weaken resistance. In Raphael's book, the man claiming to be Z-9 said that in the early days, "the goal was not to control territory but to sow terror among the adversaries."[28] Excessive violence was meant as a message to scare their rivals and thus make conquest easier. Once the Zetas instilled fear, there would be no need to use force. The possibility of violence would suffice, imagination filling blank spaces with details people gleaned from rumors and scraps of news. Like the one that appeared in *El Universal* on June 29, 2005, about barrels with burnt human remains that the army's special forces found at a property along the highway connecting Nuevo Laredo with Monterrey.[29] It wasn't clear how many people had been killed nor who they were, but it was presumed that they were executed by the Zetas. Other times, the perpetrators were their rivals. After all, it was a contest. In 2005, four members of the Zetas who were sent to Acapulco, Guerrero, to kidnap and kill La Barbie—an important figure in the Beltrán Leyva organization allied with the Sinaloa cartel—were captured and tortured in front of a camera. The video documenting their suffering was sent to the media and circulated widely, premiering a new genre in Mexico called *narco-video*.[30] People watched in horror. Others refused to watch. The videos kept coming.

Violence turned into a spectacle, fodder for the tabloids and narco blogs that published images of bodies—tied up, bruised, decapitated—without censoring content. Human flesh became the parchment for sending messages. At first it still made news headlines, as when the letter "Z" was carved into the torso of a man, his arms and legs tied, his severed head found in a bag in the city hall of Acapulco.[31] Many of those headless bodies were dressed in police uniforms.[32] Many of the messages left with the corpses were addressed to the government, warning the authorities that "heads will keep rolling" until they stopped protecting their rivals.[33] This brutality got a name, too—*narcoviolencia*—and the media adopted a new vocabulary to report on the evolving story, one replete with *narcopolicías, narcoprotestas, narcofosas, narcomensajes, narcocuotas, narcoabogados, narcoalcaldes*. A story of *narcoguerra*. This language has survived to this day: during the Covid-19 pandemic, organized crime groups were giving out packages of food and other supplies to people in some communities, a practice which the press quickly labeled "narco despensas."[34]

In Monterrey, the largest Mexican city closest to the US border, assassinations of police chiefs and public officials became ordinary. In September 2006, the Zetas killed Marcelo Garza y Garza, the director of the state investigative agency. At a press conference held hours before the attack, the man put in charge of the most important law enforcement agency in Nuevo León announced dramatic personnel changes in what was previously known as the state judicial police, including the removal of dozens of high-ranking officers alleged to have ties with organized crime.[35] Although he had received threats, Garza y Garza did not surround himself with bodyguards. That early September evening he was alone, walking across a plaza in San Pedro to meet his wife and daughters and attend a cultural event. His cell phone rang and, when he picked up, a man approached from behind and shot Garza y Garza twice in the nape of the neck. The gun was a five-seven—a pistol that used 5.7 caliber cartridges and was called a "matapolicías" or "cop killer" because of its ability to penetrate body armor, likely bought in the United States.[36] Two months later, armed men in a black Cherokee truck with Tamaulipas plates assassinated the police chief of San Nicolás, Humberto Chávez Varero, just a few days after he coordinated an arrest of three members of the Zetas.[37] The list of public officials killed in Nuevo León grew longer, new names added nearly every day. It included the head of police in San Pedro, the secretary of public security in Santa Catalina, and a federal agent from the attorney general's office, among many others, shot to death on the streets outside their homes, in parking lots in front of their offices, while drinking coffee at an Oxxo, by assailants presumably linked to one or the other rival group.

President Calderón began his first year in office by signing the extradition orders for several important leaders of criminal organizations sought by the US government, among them Osiel Cárdenas Guillén and Héctor Palma. He deployed the military to confront organized crime groups, first in Michoacán, then in other parts of the country. In January 2007, he sent over two thousand soldiers to Nuevo León and Tamaulipas.[38] But that did not end ferocious turf wars. To the contrary, this move further fueled the conflict between those groups and the government. Protestors demanding that the military leave blocked the streets in Monterrey, closed a highway in Ciudad Victoria, and shut off the international bridges in Matamoros and Nuevo Laredo.[39] Many of those wielding the signs "Fuera el Ejército!" were women and children. Some covered their faces with handkerchiefs. A few admitted they had been offered bus rides and received money to shout slogans against the soldiers. It was widely believed that these blockades—*narcoprotestas*, as they were known—were orchestrated by organized crime groups.[40]

Mexican officials were not their only targets. Around midnight on October 13, 2008, two attackers threw a grenade at the US consulate in Monterrey and fired at the compound with a .45 caliber pistol.[41] The grenade failed to explode, which Mexican authorities interpreted as a sign that it had nothing to do with organized crime. "Had it been organized crime," the state secretary of public security said, "I believe they would have activated the grenade and would have fired with a different type of gun."[42] It turned out he was wrong. Several weeks later, masked men launched a grenade and fired at the Televisa news station in Monterrey.[43] Both of these attacks were linked, attributed to Sigifredo Nájera Talamantes, known as El Canicón, an important member of the Zetas active in Nuevo León and Coahuila.[44] In a public announcement on March 20, 2009, President Calderón said that El Canicón was responsible for kidnapping, torturing, and beheading police officers and soldiers whose corpses were found in various locations across metropolitan Monterrey.

Confrontations between organized crime groups and Mexican security forces escalated and it was not clear who had the upper hand. Every victory the government announced was followed by a heavy blow. Such was the assassination of General Brigadier Juan Arturo Esparza, former chief of security for President Fox. Days after he was appointed as chief of police in the city of García, northwest of Monterrey, ten trucks surrounded his unarmored vehicle at an intersection and fired from all sides. Crime scene investigators recovered the general's body behind the truck. Four men in his security detail were dead.[45] At the scene, they counted over two hundred spent cartridges, mostly from AK-47 and AR-15 rifles. Mexico was descending into what political scientist Guadalupe Correa-Cabrera compared to a "modern civil war"—an unconventional armed conflict, in which paramilitary-style criminal groups fought one another and the security forces for the control of territory.[46] The war was over the plazas.[47] Whoever controlled the plaza, made money from shipping drugs, kidnapping and extorting northbound migrants, exacting tribute through protection rackets, as well as profiting from the sale of natural resources, such as oil, coal, and gold. As Correa-Cabrera argues in her book *Los Zetas Inc.*, the Zetas and other criminal syndicates that followed their model "have waged war in order to loot and have looted to be able to wage war."[48]

Waging this war required weapons that were not for sale in Mexico. Four days after the attack on the US Consulate, Mexican federal agents recovered fifty-five grenades from a bodega and a house southeast of Monterrey. According to ATF, these grenades, as well as the one that was launched at the consulate and failed to explode, were made in South Korea and got into the hands of the Zetas either when they were stolen from the Mexican army (which the Mexican authorities denied) or when they were purchased on the black market in Central America.[49] Around then, crime scene investigators began recovering all kinds of high-caliber weapons manufactured for use exclusively on the battlefront, including RPG-7 grenade launchers and M72 anti-tank missiles.[50] Some of those weapons and ammunition undoubtedly came from the south—remnants of the civil wars in Guatemala, El Salvador, and Nicaragua. But most of their firearms for everyday operations, like AK-47s, AR-15s, .45 caliber pistols, and the coveted matapolicías, the Zetas got from across Mexico's northern, not its southern, border.

The Camp

Nuevo Laredo, Tamaulipas

"Only men are *sicarios*," El Zombie objected.

About a week had passed since Comandante Gafudo handed Samara a gun and invited her to ride along in a pickup truck with four armed men. Known as *estacas*, these mobile units—assemblages of engine-, man-, and firepower—constituted the basic operational element in the Zetas' structure.[1] Comandante usually rode in the front, next to another seasoned member of the group.[2] Two or three soldiers sat in the back. They wore bulletproof vests and, in addition to pistols, carried military-style rifles and grenades. Some of the trucks were equipped with machine guns. From her back seat, Samara observed what the guys in her estaca were doing. She didn't talk and didn't ask questions. She was taking it all in.

"She's cool. She's smart. We'll train her. It will be good for us," Gafudo reasoned with the man Samara did not yet know but already disliked. No wonder they called him El Zombie. "He was nauseating, ugly, bad," she said.

El Zombie didn't budge to Gafudo's arguments. He didn't want to have anything to do with the girl. But her comandante persisted.

"Try her out," he held on. "Take her to La Ribereña. Take her to the war."

When the Zetas captured Samara, *narcoviolencia* had become the new normal in San Nicolás and other parts of Monterrey. Gunfights between soldiers and armed men affiliated with organized crime groups happened frequently and lasted for hours, leaving injured on both sides. With the military in tow and their ranks depleting due to deaths and arrests, the Zetas needed to replenish their manpower. They broke into prisons and detention centers to free their own. But that wasn't enough. They had to train new foot soldiers, new "recruits"—some lured with promises of a better life, others violently abducted during their conquest of cities and towns across the northeast—and teach them how to use the radio and how to load a gun. Zombie agreed to send Samara to the camp: a training facility where members of urban gangs joined poorly paid municipal police officers, former enemies now learning side-by-side to become proficient killers. Some boys were as young as she was, the only girl in their group. Together, they spent weeks going through physical conditioning and education in weapons. But for the absence of marching, it was just like a military boot camp. A process meant to break you down as a civilian and build you up as a soldier.

In an organization formed by army deserters, training camps were seen as a necessary rite of passage for recruits who did not have a military background. The Zetas had a number of these camps in Tamaulipas, Nuevo León, and Coahuila.[3] Some doubled as execution sites, where the organization disposed of their enemies' bodies. Like the one Samara went to, they were often located on ranches and equipped with shooting ranges and vast arsenals of guns.[4] When federal agents raided one such ranch in Tamaulipas, about six miles south of the US border, they discovered the largest cache of weapons seized from an organized crime group in two decades, including Galil and Colt rifles, 12-gauge shotguns, a Browning machine gun, and two P90 submachine guns, the same kind used by the US Secret Service and military and police special forces worldwide.[5] Some of the weapons recovered at the ranch carried the markings "SDN," indicating that they had passed through SEDENA and the hands of Mexican security personnel.

Although recruits learned various skills, such as radio communications, the core of the curriculum revolved around guns: shooting at targets with AK-47s and AR-15s, aiming for the head.[6] To help them train the recruits, the Zetas enlisted the Kaibiles, who brought with them their experience in the Guatemalan special forces and knowledge of counterinsurgency tactics.[7] These boot camps could last from several weeks to a couple of months. There are stories of recruits drowning from exhaustion during swimming practice, of executions for insubordination, of suicides from fear.[8] But it is difficult to know how much of that is just rumor, feeding the public image of the Zetas as tough and brutal. What we do know from testimonies in Texas courts was that recruitment to the Zetas was often forced. If they knocked on your door or picked you up in a truck, your only option was to do as they said and start working for them. Those who refused—for in the beginning there were some who thought that was possible—were shot in front of the others and those others learned fast not to say no.[9] Recruits were handed guns, assigned to estacas, and given orders. Some were charged with protecting bosses. Some guarded kidnapped people. Others were tasked with fighting the military and rival groups. Even boys in their early teens were put to work, as scouts or mules or drivers taking loads of drugs across the border.[10] Kids were useful for the Zetas because once caught, and even if locked up, they were quickly released. They didn't have to languish for years in US or Mexican prisons before they could be back at work.

Samara was fourteen when she arrived at the camp. She found combat training arduous. "There were *puros hombres*," she recalled. "They hit me. When I didn't do things right, they punished me. I didn't like to be bossed around. I didn't like being beaten, being tied up, or being left alone *en el monte*," she told me. Yet she didn't protest. Not wanting to appear weak, she did what she was told, trying to learn fast and be smart about it. "When they showed me two ways of doing something, I learned three," she said. "I didn't want others to find out how much I knew."

From the camp, Samara was sent to Montemorelos and General Terán, where the Zetas were fighting a turf war over control of Nuevo León, then to the border towns of Piedras Negras and Nuevo Laredo, for more of the same. By the time she arrived in La Ribereña, she had adjusted to her new life: always armed, always on the move. Her crew spent most of their days patrolling in their trucks. Ever since they pushed out their rivals from Sinaloa, preventing them from taking over the plaza of Nuevo Laredo, their main opponents, besides the Mexican military, was the group that used to be their allies—the CDG, or "los Golfos," as the Zetas referred to them. On some days, Samara skirted death. Others were dull, as they waited, hiding in brechas or in safe houses, surviving on canned tuna and instant ramen.

It was not Samara's first time in the borderlands. It felt like ages ago, yet not even two years had passed since she crossed the Río Bravo somewhere to the east of Nuevo Laredo on her way to reunite with her mother in Texas. Samara did not know the exact route they took that summer, only that the river was broader and deeper in that place. She was twelve. Her grandma was over seventy. They were fortunate to make it to Texas unscathed. The measures the US government took to stop irregular migration in the 1990s and then in the name of homeland security following 9/11 had made crossing increasingly dangerous. Redirected to travel on foot through remote deserts and vast private ranches—which the architects of border security called "hostile terrain"—migrants succumbed to heat and cold, the sun persistently depleting their bodies of water, few people around to offer help.[11]

The whole region had become a cemetery. Nobody even knows how many migrants have died attempting the trip that Samara and her grandmother made. Official numbers are in the thousands: between 1998 and 2020, more than eight thousand migrant deaths were recorded along the entire Mexico-US border.[12] But this is an underestimate. Statistics only include those human remains that have been found and assigned to the right jurisdiction. It is possible that the actual death toll is several times higher. Hundreds of unidentified remains from this stretch of the border lie in drawers in the forensic lab at Texas State University: Case 0377 carried a hollow cross with a single grain of rice; case 0435 had a MacGregor baseball in his backpack; case 0519 was found with pages on Psalms and Revelation torn from the Bible.[13] Samara's life could have been reduced to a case number and a brief description of the things she carried. She may have even lost her name.

To lower the risk of anything happening to them on this perilous trip, Samara's parents hired an experienced, expensive guide. She referred to him as "*coyote élite*." They crossed the river together, Samara and her grandmother. "We were taken through a ranch owned by some *malandros*, a ranch with cattle, and we walked among the cows," Samara recalled. "I felt like I had been walking for days," she said about the fifteen or so hours they spent on that leg of the journey. At some point her grandmother could not go on any further. Samara remembered her father's warning: "When they run, don't fall behind. They will leave you in the desert." Seeing that the men were moving on ahead of them and afraid of being abandoned, Samara turned to her grandmother: "Abuela, run!" she urged the old woman. But her grandmother was too weak. "She had not been drinking enough water," Samara said. "You run. If they leave me, I'll find someone to take me back. But you run," Samara recalled her grandmother telling her. "No, you are crazy," Samara objected. She wrapped her grandmother's arm around her neck and helped her walk and somehow they made it the rest of the way, eventually reaching Fort Worth where Samara's mother had been waiting for them.

Although the threat of violence had accompanied Samara most of her life, the stakes for disobeying orders from the comandantes were different. It was no longer her aunt's hurtful remarks or her mother's studded belt or being dropped off in the middle of a large Texas city with no cash for bus fare and no idea how to walk home that she had to be concerned about. Here, defiance could mean a death sentence. But to comply she had to use force. Those were the only alternatives. Samara learned this lesson during an ambush soon after she arrived in Nuevo Laredo. "We were in a convoy of ten trucks when we reached a brecha full of soldiers. It was my first shootout and I ducked because I was too afraid," she recalled. Then the comandante put a gun to her head and said: "If you are no use as a soldier, we don't need you. Either you confront them or you die like them."

The job of a Zetas soldier entailed driving into towns and villages to fight their rivals whom they simply called "*los contra.*" Their orders were "to shoot them, to kill them." It was easier back then because there were only two sides: you either worked for the Zetas or for the CDG. Lookouts on the streets were paid weekly or monthly for alerting the comandantes whenever they spotted los contra selling drugs at the spots the Zetas claimed as theirs. "There were *chavos* and *señores* who were hanging out on the streets," Samara recalled. Taxi drivers, truckers, and deliverymen who supplied milk and potato chips to local stores and kiosks—all of them informed. "They had our phones and they would call and say, listen, an armed truck just arrived and it is not one of yours." Police were on the Zetas' payroll too: they stopped and searched vehicles to find drug shipments that belonged to their rivals, alerted them about the presence of unknown individuals in town, and kept an eye on their safe houses.[14] "There were many people who told us where and when," Samara said. Although that often led to gunfights, it wasn't the only scenario. The Zetas soldiers also caught their rivals, disarmed them, beat them, questioned them, and, quite often, arranged for them to be sent south to Monterrey. Border towns were small and the territory highly contested, but in Monterrey the Zetas had paid off enough authorities to know that their rivals would be locked up and would not return to the battlefront. Sometimes, when the Zetas brought their captives to the city, they placed guns into their hands and then turned them over to the police. Charged with carrying weapons restricted for the exclusive use of the military, los contra disappeared behind bars.

As months went by, Samara got used to the rough lifestyle on the front lines. "In La Ribereña, people have orchards of large orange trees and we'd go there, pull our trucks into the groves," she remembered. Afraid that flames and smoke in the sky would give them up, they would wait until sunrise to start a fire to cook their meals. Supplies came by an auxiliary vehicle: water bottles, toilet paper, soap, shampoo, bread, cans of tuna and beans, cookies, juice. Once in a while, the comandante would even ask the police under their payroll to get them takeout tacos or fried chicken. "The police went and bought us food, enough for forty or fifty, then come up to the hills. We descended a little to meet them and paid them." Other times, when their supplies ran out and they were staying too far away from any town, they would hunt. "Rabbits were good," Samara recalled. But when her famished companions started killing rats and lizards, she didn't join them. "I preferred not eating anything. I stayed hungry."

Those nights in the orange groves she slept in a truck, clutching her rifle. "It's not comfortable, but you get used to it," she said.

When Samara told me about her time in La Ribereña, she said, "I was taught to be a Zetas soldier." She said "soldado," not "soldada." Whenever she spoke about the boot camp and Nuevo Laredo, she talked about herself as a combatant first, a girl second. The dominant narrative of the "drug war" in Mexico afforded women few active roles. As anthropologist Shaylih Muehlmann notes in her book *When I Wear My Alligator Boots*, most women who lived in proximity to the drug trade in northern Mexico experienced organized crime through the care and loss of men who were involved in the illicit business.[15] Although some, inspired by famous characters popularized through narco novelas, aspired to a better life by seeking romantic relationships with drug traffickers, few succeeded at the pursuit of this upward mobility. And although some were directly involved in smuggling—carrying drugs through checkpoints and customs, often on or inside their bodies—not many climbed the ranks to become more powerful drug traffickers.[16]

Like the military and insurgent movements, organized crime groups generally took the masculinity of their members for granted.[17] As did society at large: after all, gunmen and hit men are all "men." Most women affiliated with the Zetas either did accounting or engaged in sex work. But some had other roles. A group known as "Las Panteras," composed only of women, was accused of everything from bribing the police and government officials to extortion, kidnapping, and human trafficking.[18] It appeared that some of them received paramilitary training and knew how to use guns. However, the media was more fascinated with the women as a spectacle, printing photos of them in black leather pants and jackets, masks over their faces, gold and silver plated AK-47 rifles in their hands.[19] News coverage emphasized their looks and their ingenious use of makeup and hair styles, which they presumably changed to adapt to the circumstances of the crimes they committed. They were seen as a glamorous accessory of the Zetas, not as violence workers to be taken seriously.

Even when women committed violence, which was seen as rare, exceptional, their stories were often bound to a social identity of victimhood and survival.[20] This emphasis is not wrong—*feminicidio*, or depriving women of life for "gendered reasons,"[21] is so ubiquitous in Mexico that federal law classifies it as a separate crime from homicide. Its pervasiveness has given rise to an ardent resistance movement. In November 2019, thousands of women gathered in Mexico City to stage a popular feminist performance that had spread across the streets and squares of Latin America that year, chanting, "El estado opresor es un macho violador."[22] But this agency, too, is derived from women being victims of gender-based violence, subjected to state neglect and cover-up.

Samara did not see it that way. "No woman deserved what they had done to me," she told me years later, admitting that not everyone regarded her as a comrade, but not dwelling on the details. She refused to identify with the other women she'd encountered among the Zetas, looked at the roles they took on with disdain. She was not somebody's girlfriend. She did not engage in sex work. And she was adamant that she was not a victim. She was a soldier among soldiers. A soldier who carried a gun. A perpetrator of violence. "I felt like a monster," she said.

By the time Samara arrived in Nuevo Laredo, she had lived through a lot. So when she saw El Zombie again, when she heard him shout in her face, "What is this *burra* doing here? Women are good for only two things: to cook and to fuck," Samara felt a surge of anger. She no longer was the same powerless person she had been back in Monterrey. "I had grown up," she said. She would not wait for men to decide her fate. "He wanted to abuse me," she said, "and I killed him. I put a bullet in his head."

She said it so matter-of-factly, without pausing to explain, that at first I thought she was exaggerating. Samara had told me about the shootouts, about their daily confrontations with their rivals, which left many dead and wounded, but this was the first time she admitted to killing an individual. And he was not a member of los golfos, not an army soldier or police officer, but her comrade. Perhaps that's why she remembered it so clearly, I thought when she told me. Or maybe it had more to do with what happened next.

What Samara did—refuse to obey the command of a superior, standing up for herself by means of violence, using language they all understood—earned her respect from her peers. But it turned out that El Zombie wasn't just anybody. He was related to Miguel Ángel Treviño Morales, better known to his soldiers as Comandante Cuarenta and to the public as Z-40, one of the top bosses of the organization. A native of Nuevo Laredo, Treviño Morales did not have the military background shared by other founding members and leaders of the Zetas, like Decena and Lazcano. He began his career in crime by selling drugs in his home-town, where he also engaged in kidnapping and disappearing people and executing those who did not pay their ransom.[23] After the death of Z-1 in 2002, Miguel Treviño rose through the ranks quickly, compensating for the lack of military credentials with brutality, becoming known as "the most savage" and "bloodthirsty" among the main protagonists of Mexican organized crime.[24] It is said that of all the ways to kill his enemies, which included stabbing them with a knife, beheading them, and burning them alive, he particularly liked "cooking": watching the bodies simmer in drums filled with fuel until the flesh disintegrated.[25] When the Zetas took over Coahuila and Nuevo León, Treviño Morales oversaw the supply of weapons and the training of soldiers in the region.[26] His reputation of cruelty commanded fear among those who fought against him as well as those who fought for him.

When Comandante Cuarenta called her to a meeting, Samara knew she might not return alive.

"Do you know what you've just done?" she recalled Miguel Treviño asking her and her replying, "Yes, I know."

"Do you know who you've just killed?"

"Yes, *un cabrón* who tried to rape me, *un cabrón* who thought that your mother was only good for two things."

"My mother?"

"Yes, your mother, since he was talking about women in general and you were not born from a rock, so I believe he was also referring to your mother when he said, 'Women are good for only two things: to cook and to fuck.'"

"Do you realize how you are talking to me?" Z-40 asked, startled by her confidence.

"Yes, I know, but I don't care. If you are going to kill me, do it. I came here with no rancor, no zeal, I came here to do my job, to do what you taught me to do."

Treviño Morales ordered his men to tie her up and throw her in a truck. It was just like that first time they held her captive in San Nicolás. But she had come a long way since then. "I hid a penknife inside my blouse in case someone tried to do something to me," she said. "I survived a shootout. I saw kidnapped people. I saw a woman who begged me to help her. I saw dead bodies loaded into the truck next to me. I slept on a seat soaked with blood from a person they killed." The smell made her sick, she said. "It was the most horrible week of my life," Samara told me.

Some days later—time had lost all reference points—Treviño Morales had her brought to him again. He put a gun to Samara's head, the metal rim of the barrel sharp against her temple.

"I won't kill you, you know?" he finally said.

"Whatever you want . . . just kill me. This is the worst punishment anyone can get," she implored.

"You are just a child, but I recognize your courage and I respect you," Comandante Cuarenta told her. "Go take a shower and I'll be waiting for you here in an hour."

When she returned, Samara saw several trucks packed with a few dozen armed men waiting for her.

"You are their leader now," Z-40 told her. "You'll answer to me. You'll take care of me. If something happens to me, the same will happen to your family. If something happens to my family, yours will suffer twice. You'll protect me. You'll be my eyes, my ears, and my hands." It wasn't an offer. It was a lifeline.

On the eve of her fifteenth birthday, with an armed crew under her command, Samara was ordered to go back to Monterrey.

The Player

Nogales, Arizona

Almost there. Before the rising sun set the edges of the valley ablaze, you couldn't make out the shapes of the hills that the desert road snaked through. But Ricky knew that Mexico was right there, right behind the bright lights illuminating the border checkpoint.

It was the day before Thanksgiving and agents had just taken their seats in the booths.[1] The port of entry opened only minutes earlier and they could already tell it would be a full day with few breaks. Although there was another crossing downtown that operated 24/7, it was here, on the west side of Nogales, that all the commercial trucks hauling fresh fruits and vegetables, automobile parts, and raw materials had to pass through, forming lines that sometimes seemed to have no end. Built in the early 1970s to handle some four hundred trucks per day, the Mariposa port of entry had recently undergone a large-scale renovation which more than doubled its capacity.[2] "The jewel of the Southwest border," was how the mayor of Nogales called the port of entry during the ribbon-cutting ceremony in October 2014. With eight truck and twelve passenger vehicle lanes, it consistently ranked as one of the busiest land crossings along the US-Mexico border. Over three hundred thousand trucks passed through it each year.

The agents anticipated that traffic would soon back up on the Mexican side. Sipping lukewarm sugary coffee from Styrofoam cups that they stopped to get from Pilot or Circle K on their way in, they began asking early commuters to show their IDs, then letting them through, one by one. For many locals who lived on either side of the border, either in Nogales, Sonora, or Nogales, Arizona, this was routine, a ritual they were used to, as they crossed back and forth to go to work, shop, see doctors, visit relatives. With a holiday coming up, there would be family reunions and those required preparations and decisions: Is it turkey or carne asada this year? Pumpkin pie or *chocoflan*? Why not both?

Every person entering the United States had to stop and wait until CBP agents checked their documents. Some were reported to secondary inspection, where their vehicles were more carefully searched for contraband, sometimes using scanners or dogs or both. This started at six a.m. and would go on until ten p.m., when the Mariposa port of entry closed for the day. But outbound lanes were a different matter. US authorities did not stop most vehicles leaving the country no matter when they crossed. Sometimes they would get an alert to look for a specific car. Usually, though, they just stood there eyeing drivers about to leave the country to see whether any of them acted suspiciously. But that wouldn't start until later. During the first hour of operations agents would not pay outbound lanes any attention and they often walked away from them about half an hour before the end of shift as they prepared to shut down the port for the night. Their priority was inbound inspections, not catching people on their way out. Once travelers entered Mexico, it was up to chance whether they would be referred to customs inspection over there. For vehicles driving into Mexico, a green light meant you could go—no need to stop, no need to show any papers. A red light meant that you had to pull to the side and the Mexican customs agents would ask you to open the trunk and they would peek inside the car.

Ricky was familiar with how it worked. He had crossed the border hundreds of times before. Born on the Sonoran side of Nogales, he held a Mexican passport, but he had been coming to the United States regularly since he was little. His family belonged to the working class, living on the salary his father brought home from his job as a backhoe operator, while his mother stayed home and took care of the chores. Ricky had dreams of something more. He began playing baseball and it turned out he was good at it. As a ten-year-old, he joined a team in Nogales, Arizona. When he graduated from high school at the age of seventeen, the Seattle Mariners scouted him for the pitcher position and flew him out to the cool and rainy American Northwest. A professional baseball player—for a moment, it seemed that he had made it. But soon shoulder and elbow injuries put his career on hold. The Mariners didn't renew his contract and Ricky returned to the borderlands. After a while, he resumed playing baseball with a team in Hermosillo, Sonora's capital, about 170 miles south of the US-Mexico border. He got to travel, but he wasn't making enough money. Then one day at a baseball game in Culiacán, Sinaloa, someone asked Ricky whether he'd be interested in transporting "things" from the United States.

That November morning in 2015, on Thanksgiving Day's eve, Ricky was at the port early and expected to get through in a matter of minutes. Once on the other side, someone would retrieve the bags. Last time, two men came in two separate vehicles and each took one duffel bag. He wasn't sure who he would be meeting today. The details were none of his concern. All he knew was that Poncho would bring him the money. Poncho was his brother's best friend. The two went to high school together. Since his injury brought him back to Nogales, Ricky began tagging along when his brother went to see Poncho. Poncho and Ricky went running together and spent afternoons hanging around Poncho's trucks. When Ricky traveled for a game in South America, he brought Poncho some Bolivian currency. They became friends. By then Ricky knew Poncho had connections in Sinaloa. This was his opportunity. Twenty years old, his baseball career derailed, Ricky was looking for a way to make more money. He will later tell the court that he got involved because he was desperate.

Crossing the border was the last thing he had to do. He was exhausted from the day before, when he spent three hours on a shuttle bus to Phoenix and three more on the way back. He knew the drill by now. Once he got to Phoenix, the champagne-colored Tahoe was waiting for him at the shuttle stop. They rode to the store and Ricky bought what he was told to. Then they packed the purchases into suitcases they got at Walmart and Ricky hopped on the bus back to Nogales. Here, he loaded the bags into the Chevy Impala that was conveniently parked in the nearby lot. Despite the hassle of waiting overnight until the port opened, everything was going according to the plan. The clock on the dashboard reassured him that he was doing well with time. Inspections on southbound lanes would not begin for at least another hour.

Agents Jackson Reid and Alex Gibson had to connect many dots before they set their eyes on the Impala. They'd been working on the investigation for over a month, since the day an ATF intelligence specialist showed Alex the trace report for four firearms Mexican authorities recovered on the highway between Nogales and Hermosillo in September of 2015.

Three of the weapons seized were 7.62 × 39mm AK-47 rifles, purchased just days earlier near Phoenix. The unusually short time-to-crime—the term ATF used to refer to the number of days from the date the gun was purchased to the date of its recovery—caught his attention.

By then, Alex had been investigating violations of federal firearms laws for close to half a decade. A University of Arizona graduate who looked like he was plucked from a Norman Rockwell painting, he once had ambitions to go into politics. "Quintessential all-American guy, solid moral compass, patriotic to the core," was how his partner described him. Instead, Alex took a job in immigration adjudications first, then stumbled into ATF. The academy at the Federal Law Enforcement Training Center in Brunswick, Georgia, lasted twenty-seven weeks. After recruits learned the fundamentals of conducting criminal investigations, they did special agent basic training, which, for Alex, included firearms and ammunition identification, interviewing, and tactical and undercover techniques. In 2008, Alex moved into the ATF office in Tucson, located on the second floor of a nondescript building off West Ina Road and North La Cholla Boulevard, to begin working on firearms trafficking. His desk was in a cubicle positioned diagonally across from that of his partner Jackson's.

Jackson was a US Air Force vet who liked guns, pit bulls, and Harleys. "Saoirse nó bás"—liberty or death—was tattooed on his muscular right hand. Enlisted when he was seventeen, he had spent most of his career as a helicopter gunner on combat rescue missions overseas. He did nine years active duty, six years in the reserve, and eleven years in the Air National Guard. Between his deployments in the Gulf and the Balkans, he and his wife cobbled together a domestic life of sorts, moving from one military base to another. In the late 1990s, they returned to the United States and Jackson looked for civilian jobs. He joined the Border Patrol and, to make ends meet, worked behind the gun counter at a sporting goods store. But this home phase didn't last long. After 9/11, he went back to the Air Force and served two tours in Afghanistan doing special operations under "Enduring Freedom."

Once he settled down in the United States again, this time for good, Jackson applied for a job at the US Customs Service. It took a while for the appointment to go through because of hiring freezes, and by the time he got the call, there had been a massive governmental restructuring. Customs had been merged with immigration, becoming Immigration and Customs Enforcement (ICE), now under the auspices of the newly created Department of Homeland Security (DHS). For the first five years with the agency's investigative branch—Homeland Security Investigations (HSI)—Jackson was assigned to a gang task force in San Francisco, where he mostly worked on cases involving MS-13.[3] After that, he did narcotics investigations in southern Arizona. He liked Tucson and wanted his family to stay there, so when an opportunity came to join the local HSI's Border Enforcement Security Task Force, he took it.[4] His unit focused on drugs, money, and guns.

US federal agencies in charge of border security are like nested dolls. HSI is housed under ICE, which, together with CBP, falls under DHS. DHS competes for power and resources with the DOJ, which oversees DEA, FBI, and ATF. Each agency ferociously protects their jurisdictions and budgets, which means multiple officers from different institutions may be working on the same case without sharing information and sometimes without even knowing of parallel investigations. The slightly different mandates of ATF ("the gun police") and HSI ("the smuggling police") means that both pursue firearms trafficking, but each has a blind spot: if a firearm is seized in the United States, even when it is about to be smuggled to Mexico, ATF doesn't count it in its trafficking statistics; on the other hand, if the gun sold in the United States is recovered in Mexico, HSI may never find out about it and would not include it in its smuggling reports.[5] Each agency has partial knowledge. One provisional solution to this counterproductive arrangement at the federal level was to assign HSI intelligence analysts to local ATF offices, where they would have access to trace records and could help build gun smuggling cases.

It was this initiative—an experimental collaboration between HSI and ATF in Tucson—that had Jackson move into the ATF office as a full-time partner in 2015. He decorated the partition walls of his cubicle with patches from his Air Force uniforms and other mementoes—engraved lighters, grenades, and a figurine of Mr. Incredible. Jackson also brought his experience with guns, from .50 calibers he fired from the Pave Hawk during his deployments oversees to 9mm pistols preferred by gangs he worked with while undercover on the West Coast. Before moving in with the ATF, he had already investigated one significant gun smuggling case in Arizona, which involved firearms from Phoenix taken across the border through Lukeville. Now, in this office, weapons and ammunition trafficking would become his only preoccupation.

Their group consisted of ten to a dozen agents, each in their own cubicle. "It reminded me of Meerkat Manor," Jackson said, describing their floor, as agents were always standing up and talking to each other over the walls. Alex's desk was in front and to the right of Jackson's. Soon after Jackson moved in, the two became inseparable. Both shared a strong work ethic and, though they had rather different styles, these differences proved useful. Alex was the more organized of the two, did everything by the book, and asked pointed questions during interviews. "He could cite criminal elements and statutes in a very authoritative way," Jackson said about his partner. Jackson, who was ten years older than Alex, had more experience from working undercover and more street cred, and got along with some of the men they met on a "hey, bro" level. They had their method of interviewing people nailed down, each playing their role: Alex would comment on the severity of their situation and the charges they were facing. Alarmed, they would turn to Jackson, who appeared less intimidating ("lying in wait," is how he called it). Both agents would then home in on "inconsistencies" in the stories they heard. They would back off after that and give people the chance to try again, to talk more honestly. This back-and-forth helped them "break" those who were reluctant to talk.

Alex and Jackson were already in the middle of one complex weapons case together—it focused on two men who were shipping guns, silencers, and ammunition from Arizona to Hong Kong—when they learned about the four rifles seized across the border in Mexico.

The name on that ATF trace report—the only document they had to go off at first—was Oscar Morales. ATF agents are not alerted when people go store to store and purchase one gun at a time from licensed dealers. Although the buyer fills out Form 4473 and the dealer contacts the FBI to check whether that person is allowed by law to purchase a firearm (it's called NICS, for National Instant Criminal Background Check System), there is no federal database where an agent could type in a name and know who owns what gun. Ordinarily. There are some red flags—for example, when someone buys two or more handguns from the same dealer in a five-day period. In states along the southwest border—California, Arizona, New Mexico, and Texas—dealers must also report to ATF when, within five business days, someone buys two or more semiautomatic rifles that have a caliber larger than .22 and can accept detachable magazines. Information in these reports of multiple sales is limited: it tells them about the manufacturer, the dealer and the person who filled out the ATF form when buying the guns. Not much. But it was something the agents could start from.

Oscar, as they soon learned, was an eighteen-year-old high school student who lived in Rio Rico, Arizona, just one highway exit north of Nogales. They also learned that he had bought eight rifles in less than a month, all of them cheaper varieties of AK-47.[6] This was significant to Alex. "It would be if someone wanted to go out and buy eight Ford cars that are all similar sedans." Unusual, in other words, unless the plan was to sell or give them away. Another detail that stood out was that Oscar often drove to stores up in the Phoenix area, over 150 miles from his home, bypassing Tucson, which was closer and had plenty of gun shops. According to the ATF records, there were 215 federal firearms licensees (FFLs) in Tucson in 2015, 146 of them registered as dealers or pawnbrokers. Per every three square miles of the city, there were two places selling firearms.[7] Gun owners could get anything they needed in Tucson without driving to Phoenix. But going to Phoenix could make sense. Phoenix metro area had nearly seven hundred FFLs, which meant there were more guns and dealers offered them at slightly lower prices. Alex reached out to the stores that sold Oscar the rifles and learned that other members of the Morales family also bought similar weapons from some of the same dealers during the same month. Oscar's cousin Pilar bought eight AK-47s, his cousin Fabio also bought a few, and his sister Vilma bought an AK-47 rifle and a pistol.

While Alex was calling gun stores, Jackson consulted records from the Nogales port of entry and learned that many of the same people who were buying AK-47 style rifles were also frequently crossing the border. He found that Oscar usually drove into Mexico on the same day that he purchased the guns and that he often traveled together with others, mostly family members, who also bought semiautomatic rifles. He noted vehicles that appeared again and again, going outbound to Mexico and inbound to the United States. Some of these vehicles were seen parked in front of gun stores where the Morales family bought the guns. There was a pattern.

One of the stores that members of the Morales family visited was AJI Sporting Goods in Apache Junction, east of Phoenix. It took about three hours to get there from Nogales or Rio Rico. Driving from Tucson, the agents made it in less than two. Once they turned on East Apache Trail, a green GUNS sign was visible from a few blocks away. The store was across the street from a mobile home park, a self-storage facility, and a strip mall with Big Lots and Big 5, surrounded by RV resorts. As they approached, they could see coils of razor wire on the roof and grates on the windows of the one-story white brick building.

The wall above the entrance displayed a mural populated by US soldiers, their uniforms and their rifles changing with the times: from the American Revolution on the far left side through the Civil War, two world wars, Vietnam, and, finally, the "war on terror" on the right, the desert landscape representing Iraq or Afghanistan, or both. The family-owned store had a gunsmith on-site and offered a variety of new and used firearms, including AR-15 and AK-47 rifles. The manager welcomed the agents and gave them the footage from the surveillance cameras they asked for.

Watching the videos from AJI Sporting Goods, Jackson and Alex noticed that another person was often in the store with members of the Morales family when they were buying the guns—Oscar's older brother Darius. In the footage from September 23, the day Oscar bought two AK-47 style rifles, one Romarm and the other Zastava, both of which later turned up on the highway to Hermosillo, they saw that it was Darius, not Oscar, who walked out with the guns and put them into his car. But Darius had a record: an earlier felony conviction for a drug offense, which prohibited him from owning firearms. This was enough. Two weeks into the investigation, the agents decided to go after Darius. They had sufficient evidence that he had committed a crime and asked the judge for an arrest warrant and permission to search Darius's and Oscar's homes.

The plan was to hit both residences at the same time. On the morning of October 21, the first group of agents exited I-19 in Rio Rico and followed a cobweb of roads spreading farther east into the receding desert. By 2015, it was becoming a residential neighborhood, but homes were still scattered at distances allowing for privacy. The one-story beige brick house where Oscar and his parents lived was tucked away deep in the folds of rolling hills. An unfinished concrete block wall surrounded two desert palm trees in the courtyard out front. The agents didn't see anything noteworthy when they went inside, but behind the house they found some advertising from a gun dealer and empty cardboard boxes with Century Arms and Inter Ordnance logos. Oscar will later claim that he had been assaulted and the rifles he bought had been taken away from him, insisting he didn't give them to Darius.

Darius lived in an older construction mobile home with vanilla-colored walls located farther south off I-19, in the maze of roads next to Potrero Creek. The second group of agents executing the search warrant there didn't see any guns either. Darius was at home when the agents knocked, and they questioned him and his wife Rita. They found an old sales receipt for the purchase of bulk ammunition from a store up in Phoenix. The cost for one thousand rounds of 7.62 caliber ammo, five hundred rounds of .223, and two thousand rounds of 5.7 was approximately $3,800, and the sum was paid in cash. They collected the evidence—the sales receipt, cell phones, and documents related to vehicle registrations. Darius was arrested, and they drove him north for the initial appearance in court scheduled for the following day. Before the agents turned him in that evening, Darius led them to a large mobile park in Chandler, a suburb southeast of Phoenix, and pointed out a residence with a manicured lawn. The agents noted the address.

Next morning, with less than an hour to go before Darius's court hearing, Alex and Jackson returned to Chandler. They parked about a hundred yards from the house on South Arizona Avenue that Darius had showed them the previous night. Something was going on. They saw people, and a commotion on the front porch. Jackson took out his binoculars. Alex took out his phone and began filming. Among the many vehicles in front of the house they recognized a red Dodge Ram pickup with a vanity plate CHXSIN. The defense lawyer will later argue that it could belong to a pastor, that the letters could stand for "checks sin." But the agents were certain that the plate referred to Choix, Sinaloa, a town some family members of the organization they were investigating hailed from. One thing they knew for sure: the owner of the truck, Gustavo, was no pastor. Several months earlier, in June, he was stopped traveling eastbound on I-10 near Phoenix in a Saturn Ion loaded with eighteen weapons, most of them 7.62 caliber rifles. Gustavo was not charged and the car was not seized, only the guns were taken, since the agents had reasons to believe that they were going to be smuggled into Mexico. By law, ATF can seize a vehicle if they find drugs, contraband cigarettes, machine guns, or silencers, but not for a pile of semiautomatic rifles. But ATF agents were not even there when Gustavo was stopped. In fact, Alex didn't know about that incident until later in their investigation. Once agents reviewed records from the port, they saw that the truck with CHXSIN plates had crossed the border in tandem with some of the other vehicles they were watching. They also learned that after the incident on the highway, the Saturn Ion was taken to Mexico and did not reappear until a few months later, driven back and forth by different people, among them Alfonso, who was Gustavo's brother-in-law and who, as far as they could tell, lived in this mobile home with the manicured lawn in Chandler that they were surveilling. Besides the Dodge Ram, they saw a black PT Cruiser that was registered to Darius and Oscar's mother, who they later identified among the people crowded on the porch at a gathering which also included Darius's sister Vilma and his wife Rita.

The web thickened. More leads, more names Jackson ran through the crossing records database. They learned that it was Rita who a couple of days after Gustavo's encounter with law enforcement drove the Saturn Ion to Mexico, where it stayed until mid-fall, when, as Alex will later testify in court, it was brought "back in play." They scoured over the data—photos of outbound vehicles, records of entries—trying to understand the connections and see the bigger picture. They noticed the pattern of some people taking the vehicles outbound and others driving them inbound. They already had some idea of straw purchasers—that was what the Morales family usually did. Now they began adding the names of individuals who drove empty cars to Arizona, and those who drove them across to Mexico with loads. In addition to the Saturn Ion, a white Chevy Aveo caught their attention: in the last twelve months, twenty-five different people had driven it across the border, including some they were already familiar with: Oscar, Darius, Vilma, Gustavo, and Alfonso. They saw them in various pairs crossing back and forth, often early in the morning or late in the evening, when the agents at the port did not perform outbound inspections.

The agents realized that vehicles were being staged. They called this "dead-dropping." Somebody would drive the car from Mexico late in the evening, park it close to the shuttle stop near the DeConcini port of entry, and leave, often walking back to Mexico on foot. Overnight, the car would be loaded with bags or boxes containing guns or ammunition, and the following morning somebody else would drive it across. They saw how one time a man crossed from Mexico on foot through DeConcini port of entry downtown, got inside the staged vehicle, drove to the Mariposa port of entry, about ten minutes away, and crossed into Mexico, all in only twenty-four minutes. They understood that the people who were engaging in this activity were smart and well organized. They used tandem vehicles—one was bringing the load, the other, either in front or behind it, served as a spotter. They rotated the cars—used some for a while and let them "cool off" when they got "hot." They knew what they were doing.

Alex and Jackson kept looking for more evidence. They noticed that some of the vehicles were re-plated over and over—one went through eleven temporary registration plates in six months—which was another trick to confound law enforcement because outbound plate readers at the port did not react to paper plates and didn't trigger the cameras. They saw a photo that captured Alfonso, driving the Saturn Ion, positioning the visor and raising his hand to obscure his face from the cameras on the outbound lane. They heard from another agent who was following Alfonso's pickup truck, a red Chevy Cheyenne, in Chandler, that when Alfonso realized he had a tail, he started jumping lanes of traffic, making U-turns, going down cul-de-sacs and dead-ends. As they continued mining the data they saw a record of Alfonso driving his pickup inbound to the United States on the same day that Oscar and Darius purchased several firearms that were recovered by the Mexican authorities on the highway in Sonora. Next to him in the car sat a young man whose name was Ricky. The agents saw another photo, taken four hours later, which showed the two of them crossing outbound into Mexico together in the Chevy Aveo, just nine minutes before the closing of the port. They also saw Ricky drive another car they had been following, a grey PT Cruiser.

The agents felt they were always a few steps behind, trying to catch up. They knew that during the time it took them to follow the threads and build the case, which they did from records of events in the past, smuggling continued. Sometimes they found out about the weapons only when they were recovered in Mexico. But whenever they learned about an impending load, they did what they could to stop it. They would not repeat the errors of Fast and Furious. In these attempts to prevent guns and ammunition from crossing the border, the port was their last-ditch effort.

That day before Thanksgiving in November 2015, their eyes were on the Impala. They had been suspecting this car of being involved in the operations they were trying to understand and had been watching it parked in Nogales when Ricky got inside. Everything was happening so quickly that Jackson sent an alert to the port telling the officers they should stop the vehicle before it reached Mexican soil. These attempts didn't always go well. Sometimes drivers refused instructions to stop and instead accelerated, trying to make their way across the border.[8] But Ricky complied when CBP officers ordered him to stop for a secondary inspection. He didn't object when the agents opened the trunk and saw the suitcases. Inside the suitcases they found metal containers. Inside the metal containers there were 10,800 rounds of 7.62×39mm ammunition, the type used in AK-47 rifles. On the back seat, they also found three hundred rounds of .380 ACP cartridges stuffed in a duffel bag with Seattle Mariners logo.

After they arrested Ricky, the agents browsed through the photos on his cell phone—hundreds of images of him playing baseball, pictures of people he was close to—family, girlfriends. They saved a photo of a stack of money in $100 bills. Three pictures in particular piqued their interest. One was of Darius and his wife Rita, who turned out to be Alfonso's sister. Another showed Alfonso buffing his pickup truck. A third was of Alfonso holding a rifle, which could have been an M4 or an AR-15—expert opinions differed. They also browsed through the contact list and found the name "Poncho" and two Mexican phone numbers linked to him. The call history showed 126 calls between Ricky and Poncho in the past sixteen days. They knew that "Poncho" was Alfonso's nickname. They arrested him a few months later, on the morning of St. Patrick's Day, crossing the border in Nogales in his red pickup truck.

Ricky cooperated with the investigation. He said he knew what he was doing was against the law and pleaded guilty. While Darius, who was supposed to testify against Alfonso in court, fled, Ricky took the witness stand and gave curt replies to the prosecuting attorney's questions.

> *US Attorney:* Do you remember, did you try to hide the ammunition in the vehicle?
>
> *Ricky:* Yes.
>
> *US Attorney:* Do you remember where you put it?
>
> *Ricky:* Half in the trunk and half in the back seat.
>
> *US Attorney:* And were you hoping that it wouldn't—that the officers at the port of entry wouldn't see it?
>
> *Ricky:* Uh-huh, yes.

Ricky claimed he knew very little about the organization that was held responsible for conspiring to smuggle over seventy firearms and more than seventy-five thousand rounds of ammunition for the Sinaloa cartel, which, the prosecuting attorney admitted, was a fraction of the weapons that crossed the border that the government will never find out about. Ricky said he did it for the money at first, but later felt pressured to continue. Another defendant in the case said that the man Ricky worked for had beaten up other people for losing the organization's money. The lawyers acknowledged how difficult it was to testify against organized crime groups, how witnesses preferred to go to jail rather than be accused of snitching. Agents confirmed this, saying they met people who thought the men they worked for were "significantly bad folks" and were scared to even talk, much less testify.

Because of his cooperation in the investigation, Ricky's attorneys argued for a reduced sentencing. They said that Ricky "had no knowledge of the scope of this offense"; that he didn't know for whom the people who hired him worked; that he didn't know where in Mexico the ammunition was headed.[9] The attorneys claimed that he "had no decision-making authority and did not recruit others" and "he simply followed instructions." Ricky, they wrote, "has now spent almost 10% of his young life (22 months of 22 years) in custody for this matter. He has lost his Work Visa and his ability to play professional baseball in this country. He is now a convicted felon with the consequences attendant to that status."[10] The public defender asked for a sentence of time served followed by three years of supervised release: "reasonableness and common sense make clear that grossly expensive and unnecessary incarceration for 24 additional months in this case serves no one, not even the Government and people of the United States."[11]

There was no federal law against gun trafficking in the United States at the time. Most often, the charges were for paperwork violations (such as "false statements in connection with acquisition of firearm") or the smuggling of goods from the United States, which, as Angela Woolridge, Assistant US Attorney for the District of Arizona, who prosecuted the case, once put it to me, didn't differentiate "between avocados and grenades." State laws varied. Of those bordering Mexico, California was the most restrictive, with a state-level assault weapons ban and legislative initiatives to regulate high-capacity magazines. But Arizona held the top spot in the annual ranking by *Guns & Ammo* magazine as the best state for gun owners and, concurrently, received an F from the Giffords Law Center to Prevent Gun Violence.[12] The state had no required licensing, no background checks for private sales, and any twenty-one-year-old here could carry any gun they legally possessed, openly or concealed.

In addition to "conspiracy" (Class D Felony), Ricky pleaded guilty to "smuggling goods from the United States" and "possession of ammunition by non-immigrant alien" (both Class C Felony offenses). The last two counts could be confusing. The prosecutor wanted the jury to understand how come someone could be guilty of owning ammunition in a country where people were able to buy all the firearms they wanted and could afford. Smuggling was also a crime usually committed by others, who are bringing drugs or guiding people across the border into the United States, not those going in the opposite direction. How could someone be guilty of smuggling a commodity that was legal in the United States?

US Attorney: Ammunition itself is not illegal, is it?

ATF Agent: Can I—in the United States, not necessarily it's not.

US Attorney: We mentioned that in this case an individual could be prohibited from possessing ammunition, correct?

ATF Agent: If they are prohibited, correct.

US Attorney: What is it about—so why would—why is there concern for inspection for ammunitions or firearms at the port of entry between the United States and Mexico? Is there some sort of violation there?

ATF Agent: Yes, there could be a violation if a person either is attempting to smuggle it contrary to law or they don't have a license from the State Department to be able to take firearms or ammunition from one country, from the United States to a different country. They have to have permission to do so.

US Attorney: So can anyone take—can I take ammunition from the United States into Mexico?

ATF Agent: If you had a permit, you could.

US Attorney: How about firearms?

ATF Agent: If you had a permit, but that's on the US side. It would depend also in consideration of what the Mexican laws are.

US Attorney: Just focusing on the US laws, because that's why we're here.

US residents in Arizona were allowed to buy unlimited rounds without as much as passing a background check. As one ATF agent explained during his testimony in court, "if somebody wanted to purchase ammunition, whether it would be one round of ammunition or a semitruck full of ammunition, there's no paperwork that's required to fill out." But Ricky was a Mexican national. His immigration status—he had a work visa—prohibited him from owning firearms and ammunition in the United States. Neither did he have a permit from state or commerce departments. US firearms manufacturers that have export licenses send tons of weapons to Mexico every year, legally.[13] But since Ricky did not have an export license, what he did qualified as "smuggling." He was sentenced to twenty-seven months in prison, with credit for time served, and three years' supervised release.

The trial made it clear that the laws and the people that the court was concerned about were those of the United States, not Mexico. What happened when the weapons crossed the border was none of the court's business. Agents admitted that they had no way of knowing what was going on when the people they followed were on the other side. They could not send anyone to continue surveillance. Their jurisdiction ended at the line.

Poisoned City

Monterrey, Nuevo León

Some they found on the stairs, collapsed within an arm's reach of the door they didn't know was there because they couldn't see through the smoke. Many more were on the floors in the bathrooms and between rows of slot machines, a labyrinth they found no way out of. Firefighters arrived in less than five minutes, but they didn't have enough manpower and equipment.[1] It took them too long to get inside the building, which lacked emergency exits. When at last, using mallets and heavy construction machinery, they punched holes into the cement walls to reach the victims, they carried a few bodies outside before they even realized those people were no longer alive.[2] The fire chief described the scene as "dantesque."[3]

That day Rubén had shown up early for his first shift as a waiter at Casino Royale. Born in the state of Querétaro, in central Mexico, Rubén had come to Monterrey with his father.[4] Nineteen years old and about to finish school, he dreamt of going to Spain and becoming a sommelier. But he couldn't leave just yet: his father had been recently diagnosed with an illness and Rubén felt he had obligations to his family. They lived in San Nicolás, so Rubén left home an hour before he was due to start, just in case he got stuck in traffic. After a year at Papa Bill's, he already had experience working at restaurants, but the casino had higher expectations for its personnel—they had to do everything to make the guests feel good, stay long, and return often. Rubén wasn't going to disappoint his employers.

Opened in 2007, Casino Royale had become a place for regiomontanos to socialize, to meet friends, to have fun playing slot machines or watch sports games. Food and drinks helped create a welcoming atmosphere. At the buffet, guests could choose from a variety of salads, stews, and deserts, such as churros, flan, and arroz con leche.[5] Popcorn and sodas were free, as was menudo for those who stayed overnight, playing roulette or bingo, betting on horse racing or on baseball. There was a cart selling hot dogs, and plenty of cold beer and nachos with cheese. By the time Rubén changed into his uniform to start his shift at the restaurant, lunch guests were finishing their rib eyes and red snappers and paying their bills. Among those getting ready to leave were Dora and Rómulo, her husband of nearly thirty-five years who was a professor of medicine.[6] Before they headed out, Dora went looking for a restroom. The one on the first floor was out of service, so she climbed upstairs.

With rain in the forecast that hot August afternoon, heavy clouds were assembling over the city, but the mood at the casino was buoyant. More than three hundred people were enjoying food and games inside, when at 3:48 p.m. four cars pulled up in front of the entrance on Avenida San Jerónimo: a blue GMC Sonoma, followed by a Mini Cooper, a Chevy Equinox, and a Volkswagen Beetle.[7] Surveillance cameras recorded armed men getting out of the vehicles and heading for the door, carrying fuel containers. Two minutes and thirty seconds later the video footage shows them leave and then people begin spilling out of the building, chased by black smoke.

Survivors recall the men entering, drawing their weapons, and pointing them at the people inside. They remember hearing conflicting commands. Some of the men shouted: "Get down!" Others yelled "Run! Go!" They watched the assailants pour gasoline on carpets, chairs, game machines, food carts. One of the armed men hit an employee at a desk by the entrance with his gun and she fell to the floor, unconscious.[8] Everybody tried to get out at the same time, causing a stampede. People running toward the main entrance toppled the metal detector, which fell, trapping several guests. Others headed in the opposite direction, deeper into the smoke-filled maze of slot machines. "We are being attacked. I hid in the bathroom," one of the guests at the casino, Laura, told her husband on the phone.[9] A fuel tank attached to a hot dog cart exploded, making those who were not witnessing what was going on think they heard gunfire. It was the smoke that made Laura realize she had been wrong. "It's not an attack. The casino is burning. Call firefighters." Laura didn't hang up, but all her husband could hear afterwards were the emergency sirens.

Like Laura, Dora was in the restroom when a group of women entered shouting that something had happened. She tried to go back down to find her husband, but the crowd was pushing her upstairs. Black smoke enveloped them. She tripped and fell, sprained her ankle, but people didn't stop to help her, climbing over her trying to escape. Rubén, who was close to an emergency exit, dropped to his knees and bent over so that the women could step onto his back to reach it. Dora was the last one to get out.

Rubén's father found his body at the university hospital.

The coroner's record for August 25, 2011, contained fifty-two names. Ten men and forty-two women. Most of them died from smoke inhalation.[10] The bodies of seven women were so badly burned that they could not be immediately identified.

As violence in northeastern Mexico intensified, deaths and arrests of plaza bosses began affecting the Zetas' revenue from drug trafficking, so they ramped up extortion rackets. The owner of Casino Royale had refused to pay a protection fee of approximately 130,000 pesos.[11] The attack was a punishment and a warning to others.

With the nation's attention on Monterrey, the authorities scrambled to identify the perpetrators of what President Calderón called an "abhorrent act of terror and barbarism."[12] A series of arrests ensued. An eighteen-year-old known as El Colitas, recognized as one of the men carrying an AR-15 inside the casino, was charged as the "material author" of the crime.[13] Over the following months, the government captured foot soldiers as well as "principal suspects"—various leaders of the Zetas allegedly responsible for planning the attack: El Toruño, referred to as "one of the *cabecillas*" of a Zeta cell; El Mataperros, The Dogslayer, who was said to have ordered the attack; and La Rana, The Frog, called "presumed boss of the Zetas cartel" in the states of Coahuila, Nuevo León, and Tamaulipas, accused of being the mastermind of the fire.[14] Another man implicated in the attack, who was known as El Quemado, The Burnt One—a nickname he got after a grenade explosion during an earlier confrontation with the security forces caused serious burn injuries to his face and arms—was killed in a shootout with the Mexican military on Route 2 between Nuevo Laredo and Piedras Negras, in April 2012.[15] Among those the attorney general's office arrested was a policeman who had been a lookout for the Zetas. Hours after his name was announced in the press, his father, stepmother, and stepbrother were murdered.[16] Some of the accused confessed. So far, only three have been sentenced.

Families of the victims refused to believe that this was the whole story. They demanded justice, insisting on learning the extent of corruption that enabled government officials responsible for civil protection to ignore safety violations at the casino.[17] The attorney general's office did not share with the families information about the leaders of organized crime involved in the attack. "Even though we know it was the Zetas who carried out this monstrous act," one mother told me. A decade would pass and the survivors and the families of the dead would still be waiting for answers and for compensation. And the suspects would be waiting too. A dozen cases remained open in 2020, the accused alleging they had been subjected to torture and human rights violations during their arrests and interrogations.[18] In 2021, the company hired to demolish the two-story casino building removed the memorial with fifty-two crosses that family members created at the site.[19] In 2022, Colitas hanged himself in his prison cell.[20]

When the Zetas attacked Casino Royale, the war in Monterrey had been going on for over a year. The Zetas announced their arrival in a handwritten message in black and red on a banner they hung from the statue of José María Morelos in front of the government headquarters in February 2010.[21] However, violence did not begin just then. It had crept up slowly. After the extradition of Cárdenas Guillén in 2007, the Zetas began operating more independently from the CDG. Although in 2009 the media still described them as the armed branch of the Gulf Cartel, there were hints that the organization was breaking apart; the CDG continued to traffic drugs, while the Zetas diversified their predatory activities and, in addition to selling drugs, widely engaged in kidnapping, extortion, and murder. The Zetas had been suspecting that Cárdenas Guillén was providing intelligence to the US government.[22] News of his closed sentencing after a plea deal in February of 2010 confirmed their misgivings. Angry about the betrayal, they split from the CDG and moved to take over Monterrey.

Regiomontanos watched with alarm and disbelief as their city began to change. "Organized gang violence has spread into Nuevo Leon from neighboring border areas," wrote US Consul General in Monterrey, Bruce Williamson, in a confidential cable.[23] He noted that Monterrey was experiencing record numbers of carjackings of SUVs, many of them Chevy Tahoes, and that banners appearing in public places claimed, "the Zetas were as widespread as McDonald's." The one affixed to the statue in front of the state government building warned: "hay biene el mostruo Z."[24] But the Gulf Cartel had no intention to leave the city to the Zetas. Messages scrawled on banners they hung from overpasses warned their rivals—and the people of Monterrey—of what was coming: "you fight venom with venom."[25] Soon, it wasn't just the banners anymore. Bodies began appearing too, some still alive when ropes were put around their necks, left hanging in the dark above still empty streets of Mexico's major city, awaiting morning traffic.

Back in Monterrey, Samara's routine stayed very much the same as in the contested borderlands she had returned from: not that of a civilian, but that of a soldier. She rode in a truck with four armed men under her command, wore camouflage pants and black boots, a .22 or a 9mm holstered to her leg, an AK-47 strapped across her chest. "Cuerno was more malleable, better for defense. AR-15 jammed a lot," she said, explaining her preference. Samara's main responsibility was bribing local authorities to get their permission for the Zetas to sell drugs at bars and nightclubs. To do that, she arranged meetings with police in various neighborhoods, introducing herself and her group. "We are here to distribute our drugs. We don't want any trouble. We don't want any killings," she would tell them.

To keep track of all the officials on their payroll, the group recorded their names on what became known as "narcolistas." When in early 2009 the Mexican army detained five suspected members of the organization in the Bosques de Anáhuac neighborhood of San Nicolás, they found two plastic boxes with lists of names of public officials, money deposit slips, and empty paper envelopes.[26] The names of the officials on the lists were not made public, but it was believed that most were state and municipal police.

"Everyone had a price," Samara said. "When you arrived in a municipality, you had to speak with the mayor and threaten him, tell him, 'You do your job and I will do mine. Get your police out of the way. I'll pay them.' You write them a check with many zeroes and that's it, the municipio is yours," she explained. Not everyone complied right away. When one mayor declined to come to a meeting at a restaurant that she had called him to, Samara and her armed companions went to the town hall, ordered officers to the floor, grabbed the mayor, and dragged him to the truck. "I'll show you what this girl can do," she said, offended by what she described as his refusal to "bow to a girl." She said they drove

the mayor around the city and he got so scared that "he wet his pants."
Then Samara wrote him a check. "I gave it to him: 'Here's your check.
Do you have any more questions?' 'No, it's all yours.'"

Arming the Zetas in Monterrey was a complex operation. Some of the
older weapons, like grenade launchers and machine guns, they bought or
stole from the arsenals in Guatemala. They also purchased some newer
firearms from the security forces in Honduras.[27] The rest—the majority—
were procured directly from the bountiful consumer market in Texas.[28]
"All the weapons are bought in the United States," Rejón Aguilar, Z-7,
told the police interrogator in 2011.[29] The supply chain was well organized. Plaza bosses would tell those controlling drug shipments on the
border how many guns they wanted each of them to get, imposing a sort
of a weekly or monthly quota on everyone who was moving drugs across.
Traffickers in charge of distributing cocaine and collecting the money on
the US side were also asked to get guns. Firearms and ammunition were
smuggled across the river and over the bridges, in passenger vehicles and
cargo trucks, in ones and twos and by dozens.

One of the main supply routes went through Eagle Pass and Piedras
Negras.[30] Here, like in other border towns, the men who coordinated
the shipments of marijuana north were in charge of organizing the
delivery of guns south. A member of the Zetas who went by the nickname La Tripa (which could either mean "tummy" or "guts") and his
associates, including one they called Cochi, didn't smuggle anything
themselves, but recruited others and assigned them to different roles
within the operation. Those who handled the money did not buy the
guns; those who bought guns did not store them; those who stored them
did not transport them. With rare exceptions, different people took care
of different tasks, doing what Cochi and La Tripa told them.

Jose was in charge of getting the guns. He was in his mid 20s and had
been bouncing from job to job—restaurants, landscaping, oilfields—
when his sister's boyfriend introduced him to La Tripa and La Tripa
asked him to buy weapons. The person who sold the Zetas' cocaine and
marijuana in San Antonio—Jose knew him as Primo—gave him the
money for the guns. Then Jose found people to do the buying: his
brother Marco, his friend Gordo, Gordo's girlfriend Flaca, some others.
All in all about twenty people were going to stores in San Antonio, Dallas, Fort Worth, and Austin, filling out ATF forms and walking out with
the guns they were told to buy, usually ARs and AKs. Primo collected
these guns and took them to Chilango. Chilango's task was providing

temporary storage for the goods—stashing bags of marijuana coming from the Zetas and stockpiling guns they had paid for. Once Chilango had enough weapons ready, maybe twenty or forty, he dispatched a load to Piedras Negras. Occasionally, he made the 140-mile journey to the border himself, with rifles hidden inside the door panels and a scout behind him to distract the police if it came to that.[31] More often, he helped load the guns into trucks and let others do the driving.

Julio was one of those drivers. The twenty-year-old had quit his job as a teller at a bank in Eagle Pass and began hanging out at parties in Piedras Negras, where one day he met Cochi. Cochi convinced him to make some money driving trucks loaded with guns. The first time, when Julio took a Ford Ranger to a house in Eagle Pass, helped hide seven assault rifles under the back seats, and returned across the bridge to Piedras Negras, he made $700. A few weeks later Cochi asked him to drive a Ford F-250 with an auxiliary gas tank all the way to San Antonio. Once there, Julio reached out to Chilango, then waited several days hanging out at his uncle's house. When the guns were finally loaded, he took the truck back to Eagle Pass and crossed the bridge to Mexico. Cochi paid him $2,500.

Sarai also drove. Born and raised in Eagle Pass, she had just finished college, when she started dating Daniel, who lived south of the border, in Piedras Negras. After they had been going out for a few months, Daniel asked her to transport money. Then he added guns to her cargo. She drove to San Antonio, Austin, Dallas, Houston. Sometimes she met people who put the bags or boxes in the trunk and sent her back on her way immediately. Other times, she stayed overnight, waiting for them to load the vehicle with guns. It became a routine: she would park the car, leave the keys on the gas cap, text the number Daniel gave her, check into a hotel, and wait. When the vehicle was returned to the lot, she drove it back to Eagle Pass and would either leave it there, at somebody's house, or take it across the bridge to Piedras Negras herself. She didn't ask questions about what she was transporting or where the stuff was hidden. The door panels could usually hold two or three AK-47 or AR-15 style rifles. A few more could fit under the back seat. An auxiliary diesel tank in the bed of the F-250 that both Sarai and Julio drove carried more than forty semiautomatic rifles. Submerged in fuel, they didn't show up on mobile X-ray scans.[32]

Crossing the guns in pickup trucks was convenient, but it wasn't the only way. Smugglers working with the Zetas also concealed weapons in trailers, where dozens of rifles could be easily disguised within stacks of sheetrock. To lower the odds of large loads being caught, the Zetas paid off Mexican customs agents to look the other way when vehicles carrying guns rolled past inspections. Driving across bridges was their preferred route for smuggling guns—easy, fast. But occasionally, they also hired "mules"—the same people who hauled marijuana to the north shore of the river—to take duffel bags packed with guns and ammo and bring them across on inflatable rafts or inner tubes as they waded back across the Rio Grande.

Backed up with US guns, the economy of extortion in Monterrey spread to every sort of trade.[33] The Zetas not only collected *cobro de piso* or *cuotas* (extortion fees) from bars and night clubs, but also sent local gangs to gas stations, pharmacies, restaurants, hotels. They took over scrap metal businesses as well as auto body shops and used car dealerships. Those who resisted saw the consequences of disobeying— beatings, kidnappings, death. People saw what happened to José Víctor Ramos Salinas, owner of a meat packing company, who fought his captors when they tried to shove him into the truck—they shot him twice in the head.[34] Few dared risking their life like that. The default option was to comply and pay the fees. At some point, collecting protection money became so simple that fake "Zetas" proliferated. A few kids with a gun could draw on the fear of violence that merely pronouncing the last letter generated among regiomontanos. Pretending to be the Zetas, any group could scare their chosen victims into submission.[35]

For the Zetas, extortion was not a side gig. Italian sociologist Diego Gambetta, who studied organized crime in Italy, argued that protection is the Mafia's main commodity.[36] Although they sell drugs and profit from other illicit goods, theirs is first and foremost an industry which deals in private security. Gambetta proposed this idea based on his analysis of the Sicilian Mafia, but it equally applies to organized crime in Mexico. Their business is not in the use of violence, but in the threat of violence and the withholding of that violence. The more spectacular the violence could be, the more readily everyone paid for protection. Word of the Zetas' cruelty made violence less necessary. This explains why co-opting the police was important for the racket: the state, like the Mafia, offers protection; if the two join forces, extortion fees could be doubled. People had nowhere else to turn to for safety. If business owners couldn't pay, their stores and warehouses and restaurants went up in flames.

The wealthiest city in Mexico, nicknamed *La Sultana del Norte*, was on the verge of surrendering to organized crime. "If Monterrey falls, Mexico falls," a news article by Reuters warned.[37] The attack on Casino Royale was only one incident among many that scared local residents who had earlier thought that "drug war" violence didn't concern them, that it happened elsewhere—in Tijuana, Juárez, Nuevo Laredo. Regiomontanos were witnessing their social world contract with each new day. Their sense of security had already been fraying when on March 19, 2010, Mexican soldiers killed two students from Tec de Monterrey, then planted weapons on them, and claimed the youths worked for organized crime, a lie that the military would admit and apologize for years later.[38] Soon familiar places that people used to go to, such as restaurants and bars, would no longer feel safe, nor did the streets they would have to take to get there. It was like living under siege. Armed men blocked highways around the city with trucks and buses to prevent army operations. Gunfights in public spaces were common. The atmosphere was tense. At a *norteño* music concert in the city of Guadalupe, southeast of Monterrey, the sound of gunfire caused panic and five people died in the ensuing stampede.[39] Four people were killed during an attack on Café Iguana, a popular music venue in Monterrey's Barrio Antiguo. Less than two months later, armed men fired at Bar Sabino Gordo, leaving twenty-two people dead.[40] It went on and on: the announcements of new attacks in public spaces, the counting of the injured and the dead, the recovery of firearms and spent bullet casings.

Weapons of war distorted the face of the city, altering "the physiognomy of the streets,"[41] wrote Juan Cedillo about those years in Monterrey. Urban space became a canvas for spray-painted messages declaring or contesting the rule of "Loz Z." Building facades displayed bullet holes and cracks from grenade explosions. After the CDG attacked the Los Ramones municipal police station east of Monterrey, firing nonstop for half an hour, the building's white walls looked like Swiss cheese. More than a thousand spent casings of high-caliber cartridges were found at the site. But what this firepower did to the built environment paled in comparison to how it ravaged human bodies. Emergency physicians who had almost no experience of treating wounds caused by assault-style weapons and even less from grenade explosions looked for guidance from colleagues who had military background. Among them was a cardiologist who specialized in heart surgery, but still remembered how to manage traumatic injuries from the time he served with the US forces in Vietnam.

Journalists who reported on these events and the media they worked for in Nuevo León and Tamaulipas became frequent targets. In August

2010, a car bomb exploded outside Televisa studio in Ciudad Victoria and grenades were launched at their offices in Matamoros and in the vicinity of the TV station in Monterrey.[42] In September 2011, the editor of *Primera Hora* newspaper in Nuevo Laredo, Marisol Macías, was decapitated.[43] In July 2012, attackers threw grenades into buildings that belonged to *El Norte* newspaper and later that month masked men set fire to the lobby of the headquarters. Press workers were threatened and disappeared. Many news organizations began protecting journalists and editors by publishing pieces about crime without identifying their authors. By default, most stories were *"por redacción,"* responsibility for the content spread to the editorial collective. Many newsrooms, aware that organized crime groups were using press coverage of their brutal acts to send messages to their rivals, stopped naming the organizations too, blending the Zetas with the rest, all of them an indistinguishable category of "organized crime" or merely "gunmen." At the lowest point, even covering traffic accidents became a risky affair because the police were controlled by the Zetas and anything related to them was off limits.[44] Other newspapers, those that were too small and operated in towns taken over by organized crime groups, like *El Mañana* in Nuevo Laredo, stopped writing about crime altogether.[45]

In 2011, led by two major Mexican TV stations, Televisa and TV Azteca, representatives of hundreds of media outlets gathered at the National Museum of Anthropology to sign an agreement on media coverage of organized crime, pledging to stop being spokespeople for rival groups, to stop "using their language," and to cease interfering in their affairs by disseminating their propaganda.[46] Their intentions were good: abstain from spreading terror and avoid the killing of journalists. But not everyone was on board. Even those who agreed to sign did so with some reservations. *Milenio* made fun of the new vocabulary that would be needed to write about violence, by noting that, instead of a "narco," one should perhaps say an "alternative, underground farmer," and a "shoot-out between the army and the assassins" could be replaced with a "blind date between the two who love each other with crazy passion."[47] The following day after the media outlets signed the agreement, members of the CDG kidnapped and killed José Luis Cerda Meléndez, a TV show host on Televisa Monterrey, and two men—Cerda's cousin and a young photographer from Coahuila who had come to Nuevo León for an interview with Cerda—unlucky to be in the same car that evening.

The material impacts of gun violence—bullet holes on building facades, penetrating and explosive injuries on human bodies, redacted and suppressed news stories—had profound effects on Mexican society, fracturing the local and national social fabric. "A culture of fear is evident," wrote the *Los Angeles Times* reporter based in Mexico City during a visit to Monterrey in 2012.[48] People compared the situation they found themselves in to living in a war zone. By 2011, 80 percent of regiomontanos said they felt insecure, a steep increase from 30 percent a decade earlier.[49] People retreated from public spaces and enclosed themselves in their homes, choosing a self-imposed curfew, staying behind fences and window bars and under the watch of security cameras. Many didn't dare to be out after dark.

"Monterrey residents retreated and lived increasingly compartmentalized lives with their nuclear families due to fear," noted Ana Villarreal, observing how her neighbors in San Pedro Garza García reorganized their work and leisure in response to insecurity.[50] While social bonds between residents of greater Monterrey were fraying, the fear tightened the affluent community. It "generated specific spaces of sociability," Villarreal wrote, and created feelings of trust and solidarity. Too afraid to go out downtown, residents of San Pedro opened their own nightclubs and yoga studios and on weekends came out together to walk on closed streets. They could afford armoring their vehicles and erecting walls around their homes and hired private security for their families and their neighborhoods.

But that was not the case for the rest of the residents of the metropolitan area—less wealthy, less powerful, and more readily disposable. As the "drug war" raged on, more of them ended up living surrounded by fences and armed security guards too, but under radically different conditions.

Fallen Sovereigns

Monterrey, Nuevo León

"I want you to meet someone," Consuelo wrote in a message. "Bring your ID. Some money. Comfortable shoes. Don't wear black."

April hadn't ended yet, but one glance at the sun melting all over the sky foretold the beginning of a scorching day. A windy one, too. I had been waiting on the sidewalk for ten, maybe fifteen minutes when I saw a car pull up to the curb and recognized the man with the salt-and-pepper goatee and biker sunglasses behind the wheel: Gabo.

It was usually him. A few months earlier, a local journalist told me she knew of a woman who had been visiting people incarcerated in various state prisons. "I don't know how, but she goes inside," the journalist said, scrolling through the contact list on her phone. "Consuelo Bañuelos," she said, and gave me her number. Consuelo squeezed me into her tight schedule and let me accompany her to the TV studio for an interview about plans to close one of Monterrey's largest prisons. Wearing blue jeans, sparkly flip flops, and large hoops in her ears she spoke to the cameras the way she did preparing tea in her kitchen: in a calm, measured tone that was unexpectedly blunt. Afterwards, over breakfast, she told me about her work with the incarcerated. She had been doing it for about two decades and had seen injustice and suffering from up close but also witnessed human resilience. As I got to know her better, I began to understand what this kind of work demanded of her. She counted years as men and women waited, neither guilty nor innocent, for their cases to move through the legal system; celebrated as they became parents; watched them complete their sentences and leave, get jobs at call centers and shopping malls and as security guards at the airport. When they returned behind bars, for one offense or another, she was there waiting for them. Walking along the hallways still wet with blood after riots and massacres, she prayed for those who died.

Consuelo was raised by a grandmother whose faith guided her to open their doors to feed the hungry. Her grandma was so committed that, if Consuelo was not back from school by 1 p.m., she had to ask the cook to set aside a plate for her to eat later. Otherwise, at 1:30 p.m., all the leftover food was given away. Her grandma's example set her on a path to help others. She began working in prisons through the archdiocese. But their rigid adherence to religious doctrine, like the refusal to bring condoms to events on HIV/AIDS prevention, disappointed her. In 2011, she founded her own organization which had a single goal—empowering "people deprived of freedom." She never called them *presos* (prisoners) or *reos* (convicts), the way many reporters did. She named the organization "Promoción de Paz."

Promoción de Paz occupied several rooms with baby blue walls on the first floor of a building located across a busy street from the largest prison in Monterrey. Inside those rooms, a small team of employees, volunteers, and former inmates completing mandatory community service were planning logotherapy workshops and other activities to engage the men, women, and children locked up in Nuevo León's correctional facilities. Their work required making difficult compromises. Access to prisons was contingent on the whims of officials who held the keys to the cells. To be allowed inside, Consuelo had to limit criticism of those in power, leaving that task to human rights advocates. And she had to meet with government officials, to attend their public events, participate in this and that roundtable. She visited people in prisons nearly every day, but her schedule, already packed, would fill up with tasks she could not postpone or delegate. When that happened, she would ask Gabo to go with me.

Heading northwest on the highway toward Apodaca, we passed a column of black smoke, too far in the distance to see what was burning. With gusty winds ruffling the flames, fire on a day like this could devour a warehouse, or even a city block. Gabo listened to me talk about fighting fires in the past. I listened to him talk about the times he'd been locked up. Outside, patches of dry land not yet weighed down under concrete houses and storage facilities on either side of the road crumpled into dust that swirled and slapped onto the windshield.

More than half an hour later we turned off Route 85, which continued on to Nuevo Laredo, and proceeded toward the security checkpoint manned by the Fuerza Civil. Gabo stopped the car and greeted the officer who, in a polite, even friendly tone, asked him to open the trunk, peeked inside, and allowed us to move on. At the far end of the parking lot, we put all our possessions in the trunk: cell phones, watches, sunglasses. I squinted as the light bounced off metal roofs of cars. Heat clung ferociously to the skin under my shirt. With hesitation, I let go of my water bottle—it, too, had to stay in the car.

"Can I take this?" I showed Gabo my notebook, and he nodded.

The massive one-story building we were walking toward was long and flat, with several antennas and a watchtower rising above its grey walls. A large colorful coat of arms representing the state of Nuevo León hung next to white block letters announcing the purpose of the place: CENTRO DE REINSERCION SOCIAL APODACA. "Perhaps the government was engaging in wishful thinking," I said to Gabo, perplexed why it decided to call a facility that some of those inside would never leave "a center for social reintegration." This was where the armed men who survived the gunfights with the security forces—the ones designated as the government's enemies in the "drug war"—ended up, charged with engaging in organized crime and, very often, possession of weapons reserved for the military.

I followed Gabo, copied what he did, taking my spot behind him in a short line of visitors under a canopy, where a German shepherd unenthusiastically sniffed us for drugs. Once cleared, we headed for the entrance. As many as five thousand people stepped inside this prison on busy days, most of them family members of over a thousand inmates who lived there. It could take hours to get past security. But families wouldn't start arriving until later in the morning. At registration, I handed over my Massachusetts driver's license in exchange for a visitor's badge. The woman who checked me in brushed the inside of my forearm with some transparent liquid. "Y eso?" I asked, looking at Gabo quizzically as we approached the turnstiles. "It's for the scanners," he explained. "The proof of admission. And our ticket out."

After the turnstiles, we passed through a metal detector, then parted ways: Gabo went right, with the men; I turned left, with the women. A female officer patted me down. Wives and girlfriends who came to visit their partners brought food and other necessities for the incarcerated that the authorities should have but often failed to provide.[1] Women also smuggled in phones, drugs, and guns that the men asked for. Standing there, my hands raised, I doubted anyone would be able to bring a firearm through security, unless the officers let them do it. I was allowed to keep my notebook and my pen. Once reunited, Gabo and I stepped into a long outdoor corridor that connected the reception area to other prison buildings. Chain-link fences separated our path from those parallel to it, where inmates and corrections officers were moving in one direction or another, like in a two-way multilane highway, but one designed for people kept in cages. As soon as we passed, metal doors clinked behind us.

The last time I had been in a Mexican prison was shortly after the latest riot. Security in Topo Chico was still hyped up that day, with heavily armed personnel crowded in the yard. Three weeks earlier, hundreds of police officers and soldiers came inside to move "high risk" inmates to the federal facilities in Coahuila and Durango, prompting protests and unrest, in which thirty people were injured and one was killed.[2] During an inspection of the prison following the transfer, officers lifted a metal drain bin filled with wastewater and found a hidden vault storing buckets of drugs, alcohol, cell phones, rifles, handguns, ammunition, and a bulletproof vest.[3] The discovery led to further violence and injuries. Despite that, the authorities considered the operation a success, which could have been the reason why they let me in: to show that they had the situation under control. For my own sake, I wanted to believe they were right.

But the feeling of being a spectator of a show I couldn't understand disoriented me that day. The officer in charge of my visit looked as if someone had plucked her from a telenovela stage: dyed blond hair; pink lipstick and matching nails; a golden pendant with the first letter of her name on her neck; golden platform shoes. It seemed as if she had been mistakenly dropped in the bleak set of film noir. Or a horror movie.[4] But prison reality could be even more uncanny than fiction. In 2010, Topo Chico's chief of security was kidnapped, cut into pieces, and his remains left in a plastic box in a car parked in front of the gate with a message from an organized crime group. The authors of the crime blamed the chief of security for allowing the abduction of a female inmate, former leader of a band engaged in express kidnappings, nicknamed La Pelirroja, The Redhead, whose half-naked body was later found hanging from a pedestrian overpass on the northern side of the city.

It wouldn't be until later that I saw the parts of the prison my guide didn't show me that day when the cells were still occupied by men too dangerous for us to approach. Only once they were gone, transferred to Apodaca or elsewhere, were we able to read the messages they left to the living and the dead on the walls of their quarters. In a red-painted cell, a page torn from a magazine with a photo of a naked woman, her glistening thigh turned toward the camera, was taped above the cement cot marked with the word "ZETAS." Another was decorated with black silhouettes of trees, weeds, and mushrooms reaching toward the black and yellow squared ceiling. A gothic drawing of a clock partly hidden by a dead king seated on the throne. A picture of Santa Muerte, her skeletal hands clutching a scythe and a red rose. Another, posing as Virgen de Guadalupe, against a burst of golden rays, a pile of skulls beneath her feet. Every flat surface covered in letters, acronyms, signatures, declaring ownership and allegiance. "Old School" written in English under a drawing of a hand making a sign of the horns.

"I don't know how I got out of there intact, in one piece," said Ivan, when he told me that some of those drawings were his. Consuelo introduced us two days after he walked free from the prison, where he had spent twelve years—more than a third of his life. He hadn't been inside for long when fighting for the plaza of Monterrey began and the cells of Topo Chico swelled with members of the Zetas. Other inmates were forced to pay quotas to the leaders, who lived in private luxury cells equipped with stereos and television sets. Sometimes they had to work for them selling drugs or engaging in extortion or doing other favors, such as fighting on their behalf.[5] There were *riñas*—violent confrontations between two groups of inmates. And there were *motines*—riots against prison authorities like the one before my visit.[6] Everyone knew that power inside Topo Chico belonged to inmates affiliated with organized crime. *Autogobierno* was not even a public secret. Mexico's National Human Rights Commission reported that in about half of the country's prisons—74 out of 165—inmates either held authority or participated in governance.[7] Crime bosses, when detained, continued running their operations and giving orders from the inside.[8] Some prison areas were off limits to penitentiary officials.[9]

"It was a different world," Ivan said about his time in Topo Chico. Despite the show that the authorities put on during the day, when government representatives and human rights groups and social workers would visit, it was "esos gentes" (those people), as Ivan referred to them, who held the power after dark. "Those people lived at night because they could do all they wanted." They brought in weapons and whiskey. They threw parties and invited women. The walls were porous to them. Sometimes, those people would leave the prison at night. Other times, men from outside were brought to them for torture. People disappeared in Topo Chico, their remains not found until later, in clandestine graves, if at all.

Ivan was not affiliated with either group and treaded carefully. He got used to being woken up at early hours and asked to draw portraits, as gifts for birthdays or other occasions. As long as he complied, he had their protection and they did not mess with him.

"Were you afraid?" I asked him.

"Fear is natural," he said. "You make it your friend. You use it to survive."

By 2019, the Apodaca prison that Gabo and I had entered was heralded as a success story—the facility where violence had abated. Or at least it was considered better than Topo Chico. But memories of what happened there a few years earlier did not wash away so easily. In 2012, this was the site of what was back then the deadliest prison massacre in Mexico's history. On a Sunday in February, two hours past midnight, with the nod from the warden, custodial staff unlocked the doors and let thirty-seven inmates, including a high-ranking leader of the Zetas known as La Araña, The Spider, escape.[10] To cover up the jailbreak, other members of the Zetas were allowed to enter the block holding their rivals. The attackers used pipes, sticks, bricks, and rocks to bludgeon their victims to death. They stabbed them with knives and improvised weapons, such as broken CDs, leaving them to bleed out. Almost three hours had passed before federal agents looked at the video monitors and saw bodies lying on the ground. When they finally arrived to reestablish control, those who perpetrated the violence had retreated back into their cells. At least forty-three people associated with the Gulf Cartel were murdered that night, though some speculate the number of those killed was as high as seventy. In autopsy reports prepared by the state attorney general's office, causes of death for victims V2 through V44 alternate between severe head trauma and variations of "hypovolemic shock secondary to stabbing wounds from a sharp object to the neck, chest, and abdomen." V1 was found hanged with a piece of blanket tied around his neck on the bars of his cell, making the official count of the dead that night to be reported as forty-four.

But it didn't end there. When two days later federal police officers, clad in black uniforms and bulletproof vests and heavily armed, came to transfer four inmates to a different prison, they encountered resistance.

Men set their mattresses on fire and attacked the officers with Molotov cocktails. The officers drew their guns and began shooting, wounding at least twelve inmates. They ordered the rest to undress, rounded them up in the yard, told them to lie face down on the ground, and beat them.[11] When personnel from the National Human Rights Commission arrived to investigate, they found cellblock walls ridden with bullets, windows shattered. The investigators collected sixty shell casings and obtained the records from the medical staff who attended to the injured. The count continued, expanding the list of victims from the earlier night: V45 had "three gunshot wounds to the abdomen and hip region"; V48 had "wounds from a projectile from a firearm that enters through the right buttock and exits from the same region and involves soft tissue injury to the lower inside quadrant of the right buttock"; V53 had "a gunshot wound of approx. 3 cm to the left upper lip." And so on. Officers from the Secretariat of Public Security tried to argue that these penetrating injuries were caused by small caliber cartridges, not the type of ammunition that the federal and state agents carried during the operation. But the spent shell casings investigators found at the scene contradicted this official version: they were of calibers .223 and .308, the very kind that the police used to feed their Panther, Bushmaster, and Galil rifles.[12]

That spring day seven years later, the prison was still overcrowded, with up to sixteen men sharing cells built for twelve, some having to sleep on the floor. It still had rules imposed by the most powerful inmates who were still the Zetas. "To survive, you need to learn about the jungle," I recalled Ivan's words, "to know who to associate with, who to avoid." I trusted Gabo and wanted to believe he had the kind of status that made us both safe. I tried not to think about all the gates that separated us from the outside nor check my forearm for the mark I couldn't see, the promised ticket home.

We were headed to the *talleres*, or workshops, in the section of the prison through which the Zetas escaped the night of the massacre. On the second floor, we entered a classroom with walls the same blue color as the offices of Promoción de Paz, and I recognized two art instructors I had met before at a public event for civil society organizations. About a dozen men were sitting in a semicircle, working on lyrics for a song in which they had to use words scribbled on large white boards: vivir, camino, esperanza, valor . . . They stopped briefly when Gabo and I walked in and we all went around the room introducing ourselves. Then they got back to their assignment, putting together nouns and verbs to create hope.

I had no watch, but it appeared to be past noon when we headed downstairs to the prison yard. People packed inside the large dining hall under the roof. Outside, in the heat, was less crowded. Some visitors brought homemade meals to share with their loved ones. Others waited in line to purchase tacos. Next to the food stalls, one vendor was selling toys. Families sat around picnic tables in the shade, children ran around playing, couples held hands. I saw no corrections officers. If the authorities were watching, they were doing so discreetly. We pushed two plastic tables together to make room for everyone Consuelo had invited for lunch, her "protegidos," who came wearing light grey pants and white shirts made of thin material suitable for hot summers that Promoción de Paz gave those who attended their workshops. The waiters brought us flour tortillas and several plates with refried beans, rice, meat, and sausage mixed with cheese, and everyone took small portions, making sure there was enough for the rest before reaching for more.

A boy of maybe six or seven walked past our table carrying a brightly colored toy rifle, but none of the men looked up. Some of them had only been inside for a few years, while others had lived in prison for over a decade. Some only knew Apodaca; others were transferred here from Topo Chico. All of them were here because of guns. One man had already spent seventeen years inside for a murder and, because of firearm charges, did not qualify for parole. Another, a youth still in his teens, was serving a twenty-plus-year sentence for an armed robbery. The older ones said that it used to be difficult to get firearms, that back in the day they broke into ranches to steal hunting rifles. Someone with a .38 Magnum would be revered in the neighborhood. But all that started to change when "the mafias" arrived. They began hearing the rattle of gunshots more often, recognized the shapes of AK-47s in the hands of men riding pickup trucks around the colonias. By 2012, the city was awash in weapons. Some said they had buried their guns before they got arrested, hoping to find them once they were released. But, they also said, a lot of those firearms were probably not there anymore because comandantes questioned new inmates about where they had hidden their guns and sent others to dig them up and put them back in circulation.

A little girl in a pink dress and two long ponytails was playing with a green kite, running on the lawn enclosed by a cement wall with two watch towers that only partially blocked the view of the mountains farther away. Suddenly the wind picked up and caught the kite, which got stuck in the coils of razor wire. Another girl, probably her elder sister, came to help free the kite, but she couldn't reach it. The little girl left and returned carrying a chair and her sister stood on top of it, her hands flailing in the air still unable to reach the kite. The men at our table were watching them, but nobody stood up, not even when the taller girl nearly fell off the chair. At last, she grabbed the kite's tail and pulled it down. But with its fabric ripped by razor wire, the kite could no longer fly.

I was still keeping my eyes on the girls and the drama with the kite, when the man sitting to my left asked to borrow my pen. I didn't know whether that was allowed. In the maximum security state prison in Florida that I used to visit with my students, giving anything to an inmate would have had us expelled, or worse. But here I didn't want to make a big deal out of this. Besides, he had already done me a favor. Forgetting Consuelo's instructions, I had left my cash with all the other stuff in Gabo's car. The man who was asking me for a pen had bought me a roll of toilet paper—nothing in prison was free—and neither he nor anyone else at the table laughed at my embarrassment about the incident. I handed him my pen. He tore a piece of toilet paper from the leftover roll and drew what looked like a plank, then added three small circles in the center. "Very thick, so it won't break, with holes for the air," he said, describing the instrument, usually made of pine wood. He said that many people associated this torture technique, known as the *tableada*, with the Zetas, but it was also widely used by the prison authorities. Perhaps they even learned it from the Zetas. "Getting one of these is enough," my neighbor said. Inmates could be punished with thirty, sometimes fifty. "One time, I got seventy," he said in a tone that was more proud than sorry.

A scar on his head, tattoos covering both forearms, the name of his gang etched across the fingers of his left hand—David was the reason Consuelo wanted me to come to Apodaca that day, the person she wanted me to meet. Gabo pulled some chairs away from the others and the three of us sat down. He did not leave me alone with David. Gabo knew prisons too well and, unlike me, he trusted no one.

"My first weapon was a compass," David said, referring to the tool students use to draw arcs in a geometry class. "It had a sharp steel tip good for stabbing," he explained, then swung his hand mimicking a circular strike. Davíd was small when he was a kid and, growing up in San Nicolás, he was an easy target for bullies from the local gangs. He had to learn to protect himself. By the time he was twelve, the neighborhood boys began fighting with knives, so Davíd took one from his mother's kitchen and carried it every time he left home, to go to school or to the grocery store down the street. Soon he did what everyone around him seemed to be doing—he formed his own gang, asked older guys to teach him about the drug business, and began selling. In those days he was still too young to raise suspicion, so the police didn't stop him. At fourteen, Davíd was already committed to the street and to his gang. "Being a gangster is a lifestyle," he said. "Drugs and money give you power." But to be able to sell drugs, his gang needed guns. A friend with a legal job and a credit card helped them buy a .22 caliber rifle. Then, another friend brought a .38 Magnum he found in his father's drawer. "It was a point of no return," Davíd said, about carrying the revolver around. With a handgun, he no longer needed a company of a dozen pandilleros every time he crossed the territory of another gang just to get some tacos. He could invite his girlfriend out to the main street to eat corn on the cob.

That's how things were until the Zetas began recruiting local gangs. Davíd's business was tiny. He exchanged joints to get bullets. Meanwhile, the Zetas offered youths weekly salary and supplied them with drugs, guns, and ammo. With the mafias came corrupt police who were notifying gangs allied with the Zetas of impending raids in the neighborhood. "Se les quitó la ley," Davíd said about his rivals who no longer had to fear law enforcement. For a while, his gang resisted. They did not immediately realize that the rules of the game had changed. "We thought we were still fighting with the other *pandilla*, like before," he said. Davíd's gang maintained a low profile in the neighborhood, only selling drugs to buyers they already knew. When they saw caravans of Suburbans and Cherokees cruising up and down the streets, they clambered onto the rooftops to hide.

But then his cousin Carlos returned from Atlanta after completing a six-year prison sentence for drug trafficking and got a job at a telemarketing firm in San Pedro Garza García. Davíd strung along with him and used his cousin's connections to begin selling drugs farther away from his old neighborhood, now dominated by the Zetas. He dressed nicely to better fit in with white-collar workers and stashed the drugs in Sabritas bags he carried in the backpack, next to his gun. If police stopped him, Davíd passed them a two-hundred-peso bill, so they wouldn't search him. He knew he was taking risks. Unlike the rest of Monterrey, which belonged to the Zetas, San Pedro was controlled by the Beltrán Leyva organization, which meant that going back home to San Nicolás or to his cousin's place in Escobedo required crossing the boundary between the realms of two warring groups. One time, when he and Carlos were driving through the center of Monterrey, just past Barrio Antiguo, they heard the sirens of transit police. The officers who pulled them over told Carlos to step out of the car and Davíd saw the terror in his cousin's face. He decided to try the one thing that he thought may save them. "Que chingados quieren?" Davíd asked the officers, sounding annoyed. Acting assertively, he got out of the car and showed them a hand sign that he heard the Zetas used when stopped by police. To his surprise—and relief—it worked. The police let them go.

But Carlos, accustomed to the old days and the old ways of drug dealing, didn't understand that, during the time he was locked up in Georgia, the situation in his hometown had changed. In his aunt's house in Escobedo, Davíd came across ten thousand pesos worth of marijuana, which his cousin said he planned to send to the United States. "If the Zetas learn about this, nobody will find our bodies, not even a piece," Davíd warned Carlos. "This is Mexico. Monterrey already has *un dueño*," he tried to explain that the mafias were serious. But his cousin didn't listen. Later that year he disappeared. "Lo levantaron," was how Davíd put it. There was no investigation and no body for the family to bury.

By then Davíd was already in prison, sentenced to fifty years for killing two people. At first, some members of his gang would come visit him in Topo Chico, where he spent eight years before they transferred him to Apodaca. But very soon Davíd learned that there were rules he had to follow inside, too. "Nobody can move a finger without *their* authorization," he said. By "them" he meant the Zetas, a name barely audible in his voice, lest someone overheard us. It was just the two of us talking now—Gabo had walked away, though I could still see him. Davíd said that, just like in his neighborhood earlier, here too he had to lie low to survive among those whom he and his gang had disobeyed. He worked at the prison factory, both to pass time and earn some cash for the life inside. To defend himself, he fashioned a weapon out of scrap metal and a hand plane used for shaving wood. When another riña broke out, this makeshift weapon could save his life.

Blurred Lines

Monterrey, Nuevo León

Every morning, I rode the elevator downstairs to the hotel lobby with floor-to-ceiling windows and mirrors framed in golden imitations of wood, and sat down in front of the glass table covered with neatly folded newspapers. I picked one up, not sure whether I wanted to know or dreaded what I might learn. Recently, there was the news of vehicles torched in the lot a few blocks away and many more articles about extortions and murders in the colonias. Every morning I read the papers and left the hotel unsure whether I was in the same city that I read about in those articles.

Take, for instance, the story about the coolers. On Monday morning the police found two Styrofoam containers with red Oxxo logos that someone left near the prison in Apodaca. According to the newspapers, each of them had a human foot protruding from under the lid, held in place by hastily wrapped tape. Handwritten messages were addressed to inmates, warning that those who associated with the management were taking a risk.[1] That same morning, coolers containing human remains were also left close to the prison of Topo Chico and next to the building of the state investigative agency. It was believed that the body parts in all the coolers belonged to one individual, who was only identified as a man with multiple tattoos. There were threatening messages signed by CDN accusing the police and Fuerza Civil of working with their rivals. "Don't mess around with those assholes anymore" and "déjense de mamadas," one of them said.[2] Without naming them, the state secretary

of security attributed violence to the territorial dispute between organized crime groups.[3] Two months earlier, similar containers with human
remains—head, torso, limbs—were found near all three state prisons
and that time the dismembered body belonged to an old leader of the
Zetas, Luis Reyes Enríquez, known as El Rex or Z-12.[4] His corpse was
stolen from a funeral parlor, then decapitated and dismembered.[5]

As I read them, horrified, these stories seemed like shadows from the
past, something that may have been possible a decade ago. The official
line was that such violence in Monterrey had ended. I thought about
Davíd, wondering whether he knew about the coolers and the messages,
wondering whether he was safe.

The roundabout at the entrance to the hotel was clogged by taxis, valets
helping guests who were arriving or departing, and no parking was
allowed on the side streets around the shopping complex. Stopping on
the four-lane Avenida Lázaro Cárdenas in front was out of the question. Perhaps this difficulty to drive up to the hotel protected it from
potential attackers, but this was also very confusing for visitors. Miguel
circled around the hotel, bemused, and then sent me a WhatsApp message with a link showing his live location. I followed the dot on my
phone until it stopped right in front of the lobby. Walking in his direction, I saw an attendant gesturing to Miguel that he could not park
there. But Miguel didn't care about rules like that.

He was grinning when I hopped in. By then I recognized this look on
his face: he had something exciting to share and it probably involved
guns.

"You know the construction project I am overseeing near the airport
in Apodaca?" he asked. I nodded. He said that workers had been com-
plaining about flooding at the site, so he went to check what was wrong.
He arrived in the evening, after everyone had left. Golden shafts of late
midsummer sun fell through the gaps in the concrete wall that surrounded the construction area. Miguel was sitting in his truck talking to
a friend on the phone when he noticed a taxi drive by on the other side
of the wall. His eyes absentmindedly followed the trajectory of the vehicle, expecting it to appear through the next gap. But it didn't. The taxi
must have stopped behind the wall where he couldn't see it. A few
moments later, he noticed two men emerge through the opening and
start walking toward him.

"One of them was wearing an orange safety vest, typical for construction workers. The other looked like from the Mara Salvatrucha,"

Miguel recalled. He had only seen images of Central American gangsters online, but this person reminded him of them. "He was skinny, bald, and had tattoos on his face."

Miguel watched a construction vehicle approach the two men. He was too far to hear the conversation, but from their gestures he surmised the men were telling the driver to leave. "But how would these strangers know the truck was not supposed to be here?" Miguel thought, his suspicion soaring. Once the construction truck was gone, the two men continued advancing toward Miguel's car. Miguel asked his friend to remain on the line and placed the phone on the dashboard.

"Who are you looking for?" he asked the men through the window that he opened halfway when they were close enough to talk. The skinny one with tattoos on his face remained silent and appeared nervous. His companion, the one in an orange vest, said, "We are from the *sindicato*."

Miguel found it odd, because he had already made arrangements with the union. "I have been working with so and so," he said he told them, picking the first name that came to his mind. The man nodded, pretending to know this person Miguel had just invented. At that point, Miguel had no more doubts that the two were not who they said they were. Carefully, so as not to draw their attention, he shifted the gear into drive mode, then slowly reached for his gun, which lay under a dust mask on the passenger seat. He slid the gun over to his lap, keeping it low, so the men wouldn't be able to see it. They were still talking about the union and what not, but Miguel had stopped listening to them, his attention focused on their body language. As soon as he noticed the man in an orange vest lift his right hand toward his waist, Miguel pulled the gun and pointed it at his face. The men ducked. Miguel slammed the gas pedal and didn't look back.

"The gun was not loaded," he told me, smiling.

I knew which gun he was talking about: a Spanish Llama .380 ACP 1911 semiautomatic pistol. He allowed me to practice with it once at the range. Its smooth metal skin, smeared by time and use, felt cold against my hand when I lifted it. The gun was forged in the Basque Country, but the markings on its steel body had no date. The first Llama models appeared just before the Spanish Civil War, but this was more likely made in the 1970s. Nobody knows who carried this Llama across the ocean nor how many lives it saved—and ruined—before Miguel paid a few hundred dollars to the smuggler and the gun became his. These days he carried it in his car, not locked in a safe box in the trunk, as the law required, but on the passenger seat, under a hoodie or whatever else he had with him, to hide it from soldiers or police should they stop him on the road.

I was glad Miguel got away unscathed. His tactical driving and firearms lessons had finally paid off, but only because he risked being caught with a gun. He didn't have a permit to carry a pistol. As of 2019, only 3,243 individuals in all of Mexico had such licenses.[6] I remembered what other gun owners had told me about police encounters. "Normally, you bribe and go on your way," Arturo said about his experiences in Tijuana. But sometimes that didn't work. A friend of a friend was once pulled over and detained for twenty-four hours because the officers found an unregistered gun in his car. Since it was a .380, the type of caliber permitted for civilian ownership, and it was his first offense, he got away with a large fine and no jail time.

"What would happen if you were caught?" I asked Miguel, genuinely concerned.

"It would cost me *lana*," he said. He was aware of the risk, but it dimmed when compared to the danger of not having a gun on him when he needed it. The encounter in Apodaca only strengthened his resolve to always be armed.

We left San Pedro and headed south on Route 85. The sky was overcast, just a few tones lighter than the asphalt road. Traffic barely inching forward clogged northbound lanes. "All those people are coming to work. Every day it is like this," Miguel said. "They can't afford to live in San Pedro, so they commute." I couldn't tell whether he was sorry for the commuters or blamed them for congestion. Miguel liked people who worked hard. But I had also heard him complain about workers he hired for construction jobs, calling people who came from other parts of Mexico and those of Indigenous background "incompetent." I didn't want to go back to our last conversation about the "*indios*" and so I said nothing.

Miguel kept talking about Monterrey's urban sprawl, its contours visible on both sides of the highway. "Nuevo León has a strong economy," he said. "There is business. There is industry: cement, steel. But our taxes go to other parts of the country," he lamented. "We are subsidizing other states." That argument was also familiar to me, repeated by nearly every business owner I knew in Monterrey. Most of them voted conservative, wanted small government, and not infrequently confessed they liked Trump. Miguel was no different.

We passed shopping malls, glass office buildings, car dealerships, gas stations, and hotels—miles and miles of commerce, occasionally speckled with trees—gradually replaced by white condos and private houses that climbed the hills hugging the road. It took almost half an hour before the city was at last behind us. Then it was ranchos and haciendas, locked behind fences and gates. In the 1990s, when Miguel was growing up, residents of Monterrey would spend weekends in the country farms scattered between Santiago and Montemorelos. They came to relax here, gathering friends and relatives for a barbecue. But violence had put an end to all that. Some owners stayed away from their ranches temporarily, waiting out the worst years secluded in San Pedro. Others, concerned about insecurity, afraid of kidnappings, left for good, fleeing Nuevo León for a new life, moving, if they could afford it, to Texas. With this retreat, the value of land and property in the area fell sharply.[7] Abandoned ranches were turned into safe houses, where organized crime groups hid drugs, guns, and people. Things had improved for the better since, and some residents have returned to their weekend homes. But if Miguel's friends were coming down here, it was for a different reason. In this stretch of the highway, flanked by semitrailer rentals, repair shops, and parking lots, they picked up the firearms that drivers of freight trucks brought from across the border. The guns came wrapped in aluminum foil, then covered in cellophane, and smelled of gasoline, which is why some of Miguel's friends thought they were carried inside fuel tanks.

"I told them you wanted to talk to them about their guns," he said, turning to me.

"What did they say?" I asked.

"What's she like?" he said.

"What did you say?"

"*Buena.*"

Once we reached Montemorelos, Miguel followed the directions he received and we parked in front of an austere looking one-story building that housed the police station. He said he knew the man who took over as the chief and he wanted me to meet him. But the chief was not in and an officer Miguel approached told us to come back later. We drove around town, past the square, where seven years earlier the CDG had left the dismembered bodies of several men and one woman they claimed were the Zetas. Their heads, legs, and arms were piled just steps away from the Montemorelos town hall and later a video of the killings was circulated online. The town we looked at through the windows of Miguel's car that morning stoically guarded those memories of violence, the scars now too faint for us to read. We went to a nearby restaurant with white-and-red checkered tablecloths and ordered chilaquiles.

When we returned to the station an hour later, we found the chief waiting for us. He greeted us politely, though without much enthusiasm, and invited us to follow him into his office, a desolate room just slightly bigger than his desk. The few things in there—a black desktop computer, a white telephone, a grey filing cabinet in the corner—appeared like props set up to stage police work, not to carry it out. There were no papers piled on the desk, no photographs or diplomas on the walls. It was as if the chief did not want to leave his mark. The assignment in Montemorelos was the opposite of a promotion.

We sat down on the chairs facing the desk. Miguel spoke with the chief casually, as with an old acquaintance, which he was, but the official maintained distance, his reactions subdued, often just nods in between the long sips of tea he took from a large mug. After a few jokes that failed to warm up the atmosphere in the room, Miguel got to the point and introduced me. By then it was clear that I should not ask to record the conversation, so I took out my notebook and opened it to a blank page. I also knew I had to ask specific questions if I expected the chief to talk. So I asked about the types of guns the police carried (AR-15s and 9mm, he said) and about the rule of leaving service weapons at work at the end of the shift (unless they had a private license for a .22 for home defense, police officers were unarmed when they were not on duty). I also asked him about the kinds of guns that organized crime groups used and he said that here "malandros" preferred *cuernos* and Galiles (the modernized and more expensive AK-style assault weapons manufactured in Israel). Since Miguel had told me the chief used to oversee the gun buyback program in San Pedro, I asked what weapons they collected, and he said people brought all kinds of guns, including mortars and grenade launchers. His every answer was succinct. Not a word slipped from his mouth without his weighing it carefully first. Miguel had warned me that talking to the men in charge of security wouldn't be easy. But he had a good relationship with the chief who once held an important position in the region's military command and thought it was at least worth a try.

During the worst years of violence in Monterrey, the police were of little help to the people they were purportedly protecting. Even if they had been serious about it, over two thousand officers who worked for the state of Nuevo León were too few to maintain law and order. But they barely made an effort. When the plaza "heated up," police officers were among the first to begin receiving threats and two years later many of those who survived had been co-opted, enmeshed with the criminal groups they were supposed to be investigating and dismantling. The Zetas delegated enforcing the protection rackets in their plazas to the police, which obfuscated the line between organized crime and the state. "Delincuentes con uniforme" was how some regiomontanos described officers who threatened residents, participated in kidnappings, protected drug loads and safe houses.[8] Not only did the institution responsible for citizen safety fail to fulfill its duty, but it became the conduit of violence.

US diplomatic representatives were aware of the situation. In September 2009, the US consul general in Monterrey reported hearing from the mayor-elect of San Pedro, Mauricio Fernandez, that "all of the region's police forces are controlled by organized crime."[9] In Nuevo León, only half of the officers on the state police payroll reported for work and half the patrol cars were missing.[10] Even in San Pedro, which was spared the most brutal violence destroying other parts of the metropolitan area, only one of twenty-four roads leading into the city had camera surveillance and a number of police radios had disappeared, compromising the secure network. The rest of the police forces in the area first answered to the Gulf Cartel and then to the Zetas. Police officers were underpaid and undertrained and their work was extremely dangerous. No wonder they had trouble recruiting. Few regiomontanos wanted to risk their lives working for an institution that held no respect and no trust.

And it wasn't just the rank and file. Heads of police and security agencies continued to receive threats as well. In early 2011, with the assistance of several state police officers, the Zetas kidnapped and executed the director of Nuevo León's command center for security and intelligence operations, known as C5. On a Sunday night in February, Homero Guillermo Salcido Treviño's body was found inside an armored vehicle in the center of Monterrey, charred from a grenade explosion.[11] The headquarters of C5—a bleak concrete building with curved walls set on the edge of Federal Highway 85, south of the city—had withstood rifle fire and several grenade attacks.[12] But the safety the bunker's walls offered those working inside was temporary. As soon as they left the fortress, they became targets.

At first, President Calderón's strategy was to deal with organized crime by bypassing the police and going straight to the military. Operation Tamaulipas-Nuevo León, launched in 2007 and soon renamed Operation Northeast, was carried out by soldiers who were not there to look for "suspects" but to fight "enemies." Armed civilians were presumed to be criminals and were treated as such, their involvement in outlawed activities rarely investigated, the narrative of the "drug war" purportedly justifying extrajudicial measures. Residents often referred to the suspects as "malos" or "malitos"—the bad ones, the little devils.[13] If they died, it was because they had been involved in something nefarious. In the villages of northeast Mexico it was not uncommon to hear people call them "cockroaches."[14] Unlike humans, cockroaches could be exterminated. Witnesses recounted how the military killed armed men instead of attempting to arrest them, how they covered up the evidence of gunfights, how they used water hoses to wash away the blood from the roads, how they removed the corpses.[15]

But President Calderón couldn't rely on the military forever. He had to do something about the police. In 2008, he announced federal police reform aimed to improve law enforcement institutions and disentangle them from connections to the drug trade. The governor of Nuevo León, Rodrigo Medina, tagged onto this initiative. Working closely with Monterrey's business leaders and the academic community through a public-private partnership called Alliance for Security, Medina approved the creation of a specialized state police force.[16] Entrepreneurs who participated in this initiative knew the significance of branding and hired a marketing firm to do an image makeover for the institution, which they proposed calling Fuerza Civil—a civil force—meant to be "for the people and by the people." Their slogan was "*La Fuerza de Todos.*" Salaries for Fuerza Civil members were much higher compared to what the old state police earned. Officers received pensions, health care, life insurance, and scholarships to support their children's education. They were even offered housing in gated communities built for them and their families, to protect them from retaliation by organized crime groups. But these rewards required hard work and a clean background. No officers who had served in the old state police were allowed to apply. Recruits completed six months of rigorous training, including a month-long physical and tactical boot camp run by the military. Some of the funding for preparing police instructors and for training them in crime scene investigations, collection of evidence, and intelligence gathering came from the United States through the Mérida Initiative.[17] The plan was to hire over ten thousand new officers, doubling the size of the police force in Nuevo León by 2012. Although that didn't happen, the new institution attracted hundreds of recruits, many of them from out of state, and began the slow process of rebuilding people's trust in law enforcement.[18]

Residents of San Pedro accepted Fuerza Civil, but doubts over whether the government could protect the neighborhoods they lived in did not vanish. Those who had the right family names still appealed directly to the armed forces, avoiding civilian institutions. Miguel and his friends, whenever they needed information or reassurances on matters of security, rather than calling the police, dialed the personal number of the general or his second in command. This personal connection had to be maintained through reciprocity. When the military organized a gun buyback program, Miguel and other business owners collected thousands of pesos to buy games for children who came to swap their toy guns. None of them, of course, had even considered exchanging their own firearms for some coupons to buy domestic appliances.

After the peak of violence between 2009 and 2012, Monterrey entered a few years of relative calm, with homicides decreasing and fear no longer orchestrating daily routines. Still, security remained a major political issue. When Aldo Fasci ran as an independent candidate in Monterrey's mayoral elections in 2018, a campaign billboard above a busy avenue showed him being held at gunpoint next to a question in bold green letters: "Quires seguir así?"[19] A lawyer by training, Fasci had already served in various positions in the government apparatus, including a stint as the deputy attorney general. "Iron prosecutor, with fingers of a pianist," was how a feature story in *El Norte* described Fasci's interests in both law enforcement and music.[20] Fasci ended up withdrawing his candidacy from the mayoral elections and instead assumed the role of Nuevo León's secretary of public security. The job was familiar to him—the same appointment he had held a decade ago. Back then, Fasci projected an image of a young, determined public official. Even US diplomats repeatedly used the words "ambitious" to describe him and his efforts to reform the police.[21] But he was also speaking the language of the "drug war" that dehumanized a sizable portion of the population. After a state police officer was killed on a street near Fasci's house, Fasci refused to accept that the location of the execution had been a coincidence, that it was just a settling of scores between the Zetas and the CDG. "So are we going to believe the words of a presumed criminal?" he asked, adding, "How credible is the version of a sociopath?"[22]

In 2019, half a year after he was appointed the secretary of security, Fasci said that he found violence and rising homicides in Nuevo León "nauseating." "We could have Superman as the secretary [of security] and it wouldn't be better," he added.[23] It was this blunt style that many people in Monterrey liked about the man in charge of their safety.

Mexican sociologist Luis Astorga astutely observed that those who are authorized to fight the "war on drugs," are invested in it never ending.[24] The war is self-perpetuating, and so is the feeling of insecurity. This situation benefits both government agencies and the business sector. Companies that offer private security services—providing bodyguards, protecting goods, patrolling properties, installing alarms, and monitoring surveillance cameras—have proliferated in Mexico. In 2017, Monterrey had the second largest number of these businesses in the country, after the capital city.[25] According to a 2018 report, employees in Mexico's private security sector outnumbered police officers.[26] But boundaries between public and private security were not that clear, as law enforcement and military personnel were routinely lured to work in the booming private industry.[27] The move was attractive to both the rank and file and those officers in higher positions. Unlike the majority of private security guards who had to lock up their guns in a safe box when off duty, retired army officers were allowed to keep and carry their weapons at all times, which was reassuring to those who hired them. The direct experience ex-military had with assault rifles and machine guns—and their access to these weapons—also proved useful for another slice of the security business profiting from fear, that of armoring vehicles and homes.

Once, when we were visiting Miguel's uncle Efraín, who lived in a house in a quiet residential neighborhood in San Pedro, our host invited us to see a panic room he was building for himself. I had heard about these from news stories about American survivalists preparing for the end of the world, but only ever saw them online and on TV. "It is almost finished," Efraín said, escorting us to a section in the middle of the building, a windowless room with walls that were reinforced with ballistic steel. There was some furniture in there already, but it didn't look like a place where one would want to hang out. It was like those rooms in art museums where the most famous paintings are stored away from daylight and fluctuating temperatures. Secure like a tomb.

"Five hundred is the thickest and best for walls," Efraín said, going over the properties of ballistic steel. He knew this because it was his job—he owned a business selling automatic gates and security doors. "Seven hundred is the thinnest, often used for armoring vehicles," he explained. According to the association of Mexican companies that specialize in bulletproofing vehicles, most commonly attackers use 9mm caliber pistols.[28] This type of weapon was involved in 20 percent of the incidents. The most frequently used long guns were AK-47 rifles, implicated in 10 percent of the attacks against armored vehicles, closely followed by AR-15s. The remaining incidents involved a variety of weapons, from 12-gauge shotguns to fragmentation grenades. There was no similar survey about the kinds of weapons used to attack homes. From what people saw on the news, they assumed the attackers would wield military-style rifles.

Efraín picked up his smartphone and showed us a video he recorded when testing the strength of a 6mm ballistic plate. The cartridges he used—.308 with a full metal jacket—were of the same diameter as the 7.62 × 39mm. If the target could withstand an impact from a .308, he reasoned, then slower rounds from an AK-47 would surely not be able to penetrate it. In the video we watched on his phone, Efraín aimed the rifle at a circle he had drawn on a metal plate some distance away, then fired three times: two impacts for the eyes and one for the nose, followed by a series of shots to make a smile. "Eight shots. Zero penetration of the steel. Excellent material!" He shot a second time at one of the spots, where an earlier bullet had left a whitish abrasion upon impact, then a third, but the bullets didn't go through, and the metal plate with the smiley face remained intact. "With this steel we can be certain," he said from behind the camera. Efraín had tested the steel plates with an AK-47, too, just to be sure, and the steel withstood the shots. He said he borrowed the rifle from a friend who was a colonel in the military.

In addition to installing a panic room and wiring his house in San Pedro with an elaborate surveillance system, Efraín also equipped his ranch in the countryside. It now had two different power backups, armored walls, and windows with holes to position firearms without having to crack them open. He even stuffed the pockets of a jacket full of ammunition and hung it on the bedroom door, to have everything ready. I could see that Miguel admired his uncle's foresight, his meticulous planning. "We need to be prepared to hold on for forty-five minutes," Efraín said. "That's how long it would take for help to get there."

It could still be too late. Everyone knew what happened to Don Alejo. Monterrey's elite may have bypassed civilian police, tapping directly into the military for their security needs; they may have covered their houses and their vehicles with bulletproof plates and bought guns and ammunition on the black market to match the firepower of criminal groups. But even this excess of security was not enough once they left their armored neighborhoods. To them, Alejo Garza Tamez's story was both an inspiration and a warning. Don Alejo was a successful businessman, who owned a trailer line and a lumberyard, and whose family had a ranch in Padilla, Tamaulipas, with three thousand hectares of land, where they raised cattle, horses, sheep, geese, and peacocks. While other regiomontanos, concerned about robberies and kidnappings, stopped going to the countryside, Don Alejo was not deterred. In his seventies by then, he continued the routine he had for decades, visiting his ranch every weekend. When people warned him about violence, he would say, "Before they take my watch or my truck, I'll take down three or four of them."[29]

In the video footage of Rancho San José, its walls, windows, even blinds are riddled with bullet holes. Journalist Diego Osorno called his documentary "El Valiente ve la muerte solo una vez." In November 2010, Mexican marines found Don Alejo's body in the bathroom, in his pajamas, with gunshot wounds to the head and the chest, two rifles and a pistol on the floor next to him. Spent casings littered the house. Four attackers were dead and two injured. After the news broke, rumors started circulating that Don Alejo had received a threat, that he had been told to give over his ranch within twenty-four hours, and that he refused. That he let his employees go home and prepared to defend the ranch alone, placing rifles around the house. The attackers arrived early on a Sunday morning and, according to the popular account of that night's events, shot into the air—the last warning for Don Alejo to leave. But he responded by picking up a rifle and firing at the attackers. The men threw grenades at the house and got inside, where they killed Don Alejo and fled with his Rolex, his ring, and his gold chain.

More than a decade had passed and still nobody knows what happened that night on the ranch. Family members later said they weren't aware of the threats and didn't believe Don Alejo had been preparing for a gunfight. But the popular story of a brave family man who died defending his home from the bad guys has made Don Alejo into a hero in the "war against the narcos."[30] He stood up to the enemies alone to protect what he had spent his life building. He did not look to the government and its security forces for help.

The day I watched the cut of Osorno's film about Don Alejo, in January 2019, the opinion page of *El Norte* published a cartoon depicting two hands with warped fingers protruding from scruffy black sleeves and grabbing a purple car. The car had letters NL, for Nuevo León. Written over one of the hands was VIOLENCE. "And the year is just beginning," someone inside the car was saying. In the first twelve days of January, the state registered thirty-five homicides, most of them by firearm, the worst figures in half a decade. The paper warned of the "red wave of blood." While the authorities blamed this on organized crime groups fighting over the plaza, the author of the piece accused the government, noting that this was happening in the aftermath of the elections, as the new administration started pulling back the army and the navy. With the military scaling down its operations, a vacuum of power was opening, the article implied, and the police, despite the reforms, were not ready to step in.

The lines between the police and the mafias remained blurred. All over Mexico, police agencies were "losing" firearms. Often, they simply sold the guns and then reported them stolen. In 2015, fifty firearms from a shipment from SEDENA, including AR-15 rifles and 9mm handguns, disappeared from Nuevo León's public security agency.[31] Every time investigators recovered weapons marked with SDN, these inscriptions were proof of diversion, confirming the continuity between state institutions and criminal groups. Too often it was still impossible to say which side violence professionals worked for. Some of them worked for both. That same year when Miguel and I went to Montemorelos to talk to the police chief, one of his former bodyguards, a member of an elite unit in San Pedro, was detained and charged with involvement in organized crime. According to the attorney general's office, a group of police officers that included the former bodyguard responded to a call about loud noise at an apartment in downtown San Pedro and, when they arrived, they kidnapped an American man and three of his friends who were inside.[32] The group demanded a two-million-peso ransom from the American's family. After three days in captivity, he managed to escape, and his family contacted the FBI. Nuevo León's attorney general's office arrested eleven police officers who allegedly participated in the kidnapping. If found guilty, the officers could be sentenced to between fifty and one hundred years in prison.[33]

Back at the hotel after our trip to Montemorelos that winter evening, I took the elevator up to my room on the seventeenth floor and stood by a large window overlooking the city in twilight: skeletal frames of high-rises under construction, the jagged silhouettes of the mountains in the distance, a ribbon of white and red lights unspooling along Avenida Lázaro Cárdenas. I noticed flashing overheads on the roofs of patrol cars haphazardly parked in front of the steak house across the street, too far to make out the details of what was happening. I couldn't push aside a question bothering me since Miguel dropped me off: If those men in Apodaca, instead of having orange vests and face tattoos, wore police badges, would he have drawn his gun?

Brothers

Tucson, Arizona

As soon as the grey PT Cruiser crossed the border, at 5:53 p.m., Jackson got an email notification.[1] It was December 22, 2015. He hadn't seen the car for about a month, since they arrested Ricky and Ricky told them the vehicle was used for smuggling. If the PT Cruiser was now in Nogales, odds were it would be loaded with guns and somebody would drive it back to Mexico before the Mariposa port of entry closed later that same evening. Jackson called Alex and they decided to leave for Nogales at once.

Jackson lived north of Alex, so whenever they went to Phoenix, Alex would pick up Jackson on the way. When they went to Nogales, it was Jackson's turn to take his car and stop by Alex's place to get his partner for the ride south. It made sense to use one vehicle. During the months they were doing this investigation, they drove to Phoenix and Nogales so often that it became routine and they didn't have to negotiate each time. They had settled on other ground rules, too, such as tuning in to '90s rock on the radio. Alex would always adjust the volume up whenever Weezer came on, despite Jackson making fun of him. They had learned how to be good partners, which was important since they were spending more time with each other than at home with their families.

The journey from Tucson to Nogales is a straight drive south on I-19. The agents were there in about an hour, but by then it had gotten dark and they still had to find the PT Cruiser. They drove from one parking lot to another, looking for the vehicle. On the Arizona side,

Nogales is not as big as its sister city in Mexico, but it is an important node in cross-border commerce and parking lots abound, some close to the ports of entry or scattered along North Grand Avenue, more in the shopping area on West Mariposa Road. When the agents finally located the PT Cruiser parked in a paid lot close to the DeConcini port of entry, it was already past midnight. They were relieved the car hadn't been moved, that they weren't too late. Since the vehicle was still in Nogales, they suspected the plan was to cross it early in the morning. The Mariposa port of entry opened at six a.m., which meant they had at least five hours left, so they drove to Circle K to get snacks and drinks to last them through the night. Then they returned to the lot, parked at a distance from the PT Cruiser, and waited, not taking their eyes off the vehicle.

Nogales was empty and quiet like an airport terminal after the departure of the last flight. When the stores shut their doors and the Mariposa port of entry stopped inspections, the rumble of diesel engines and Union Pacific trains faded, letting the city sleep. Founded in the 1880s as a customs outpost on the side of the railroad that connected Arizona with Mexico, it was inseparable from its double: Nogales, Sonora. The two are known as Ambos Nogales, entangled by more than the incessant commercial traffic between the maquiladoras and the mines down south and the warehouses and grocery stores up north—people here share blood and water, and memories.[2] But an ugly border fence, which got taller and longer over the years, sliced the city in two, separating families and blocking rivers and doing nothing to stop smuggling. On the contrary, the more the border was fortified, the more security cameras and checkpoints were put in place, the more profitable it became to move goods and people across. This obsession with security also benefited US federal agencies and contractors—border security made political and corporate and blue-collar careers. Those were largely built on intercepting the northbound traffic of drugs and people and, for the most part, ignoring the fact that neither that many drugs nor that number of people would be crossing the border if it weren't for the guns. Intercepting gun traffickers was not a high priority for the US government. But for Alex and Jackson, it was what kept them awake that night.

They waited, but nothing happened. Nobody approached the vehicle to put anything in the trunk. Then, at 7:02 a.m., the same man who had dropped the vehicle off in the evening and then walked back to Mexico, reappeared, crossing the border into the United States on foot, and got inside the PT Cruiser. His name was Ramiro and the agents had met him before. He had even served as an informant for the CBP, but that didn't go so well and the agency cut him off. Now the partners, tired after sitting all night in their car, perked up. This was going to be the smuggling event they had been anticipating. They had already alerted other units and multiple agents were lined up to follow the vehicle. They expected Ramiro would head straight toward Mariposa and then attempt to drive outbound to Mexico, which is when they planned to stop him.

Instead, Ramiro got onto the I-19 and headed north, not south. This surprised the agents, but they went along with him. As Ramiro was passing Sahuarita, a state patrol officer pulled him over for a traffic violation, and Alex, worried this would compromise their operation, called DPS and asked them to let the driver go. Despite this stroke of luck, Ramiro didn't suspect anything unusual and continued northbound. He left the highway in South Tucson, passed Stofft Armory, which served as the quarters of the Arizona National Guard, and arrived at Pueblo Gardens neighborhood. There, he turned on South Campbell Avenue and drove up to a beige one-story duplex with chain link fence, still unaware that he was being followed by plainclothes agents in unmarked cars.

Kevin was asleep when Ramiro walked into his room and woke him up. It was his day off from his job at Walmart, where Kevin worked since he quit school after tenth grade. School wasn't for him. He preferred to make money and was saving to buy a car. "Do you want to go to Cabela's?" Ramiro asked Kevin, though he already knew the answer. Kevin looked forward to his brother's visits. They were close, but now Ramiro, six years older than Kevin, lived in Nogales, had a family there, was a father of a baby boy, and didn't come up that often. Kevin had long been eager to go to the huge sporting goods store up in the Phoenix area. Ramiro's invitation perked him up.

The brothers stopped at a gas station for drinks, then hit I-10 north. Two hours later they were in Phoenix, pulling up in front of El Güero Canelo on West McDowell. But they didn't get any Sonoran-style hot dogs that the restaurant was well known for. When they parked, a man approached the car and got into the back seat. He took out a stash of bills, counted to $3,000, and handed the money over to Ramiro. The whole transaction took less than two minutes. Since the car had the child lock on, Kevin got out and opened the back door from outside to let the man go. Through the window of the truck parked farther away from the PT Cruiser, Jackson took pictures of Kevin briefly stepping out of the vehicle and of the man walking back inside the restaurant.

Then Ramiro drove to Staples. With Kevin waiting in the car, he got out and approached a red Toyota Prius parked nearby, then got inside. Kevin didn't pay attention to what his brother was doing. He was bored and was checking his friends' posts on Facebook. When Ramiro got back to his car, he threw a large white cardboard box in the back seat. It opened and Kevin saw there was a gun inside, an AK-47, with a pink stock and foregrip.

"Cabela's is close from here," Kevin said to his brother. He was looking at the map on his phone, ready to guide Ramiro if he needed directions. Even though he was careful not to say anything to criticize his brother, Kevin was getting impatient.

They headed west and about fifteen minutes later Ramiro pulled into the enormous parking lot in front of Cabela's. This time both brothers got out of the car and went inside. Kevin wanted to check out camouflage gear, so first they went through clothing for hunters, then looked at fishing rods. When they got to the gun counter, they glanced at firearms there and then stopped in front of large boxes of bulk shotgun shells. "This is just shotgun shit. We want rifle," Ramiro said and they moved on to the cases containing .223 rounds used for AR-15 style weapons. They didn't buy anything, just talked as they walked around. At 160,000 square feet, the store was massive, bigger than a New York City block, with trophy animals, indoor archery area, large aquariums, a boat shop, and the famed Santa's Wonderland, as busy as it gets two days before Christmas. Kevin wanted to stay longer to browse the aisles, but Ramiro said they had to go, that he had other business. Kevin was disappointed— they had come all the way here and didn't even spend half an hour inside the famed store—but he went along with his brother.

Back in the car, Ramiro drove to the far end of the parking lot, got out, and spoke to another man who had arrived in a white Chevy Trailblazer. When he returned, Kevin saw him put another gun in the back seat, this time a Petronov AK-47, though Kevin couldn't tell the difference between the brands. After that, they got onto the highway and headed back to Tucson.

A little while after they left Phoenix, Ramiro thought he saw a car following them, so he got off and then back on I-10, hoping to lose the tail. Having dealt with federal agents before, he was suspicious, but he also knew that what he did was not against the law: he could buy as many AKs as he wanted and, if he did it through private sales, there was no paperwork involved. In Tucson, right after he exited the freeway, he made a stop at the AMPM on Speedway and, after he filled up the gas tank and Kevin paid the teller, Ramiro drove behind the building. There was another man waiting for him in a brown Chevy Silverado and Ramiro walked up to him and came back with a third rifle, which he put next to the others on the back seat.

By this time, Ramiro was certain they were being watched. The agents used unmarked cars, but they had been following the PT Cruiser for hours and eventually Ramiro noticed. He tried to get rid of them again, driving through neighborhoods in circles. He stopped at Fry's and went inside to buy some groceries to take home to Nogales, then made another stop at an auto loan repayment office in South Tucson, and finally at a taco stand, before he pulled into the unpaved driveway next to their mother's house on South Campbell. There, he said good-bye to Kevin, loaded the car with Christmas gifts, toys, and clothes for his family, and continued on to Nogales. That's all Jackson and Alex could see from where they were parked, on the opposite side of the road, across a wide median planted over with mesquite and ocotillos. But even if they had stayed on the narrow lane next to the house, they wouldn't have been able to make out what was going on around the building. An agent in the helicopter who was recording the scene from above relayed to the team on the ground that, before he left, Ramiro threw something over the fence into the neighbor's yard. When they were sure he would not return, one of the agents went to retrieve it: the box of the pink Lady AK rifle.

Jackson and Alex were dog-tired. They left home for work in the morning of December 22 and now it was already the afternoon of December 23 and they were still at it. They missed a night of sleep keeping their eyes on the PT Cruiser and then followed Ramiro all day, from Nogales to Tucson to Phoenix and back again—more than four hundred miles. Twenty units were involved in the surveillance operation throughout the day, including a Border Patrol helicopter. They were determined not to let that car out of their sight, not to let it cross into Mexico with the guns. So when they saw Ramiro drop the vehicle in the parking lot in downtown Nogales and leave, they had to decide what to do next. Dusk was falling and they knew that continuing surveillance after dark would be difficult. The CBP helicopter had already returned to the headquarters and, though they still had several units on the team, they had to consider how much longer they could ask their colleagues to stay watching the vehicle. Their fatigue didn't help either: Jackson and Alex were facing a second sleepless night. Alex didn't want to call his wife and say goodnight to his girls over the phone again. They both wanted to go home. With the court already closed and the next day being Christmas Eve, it was impossible to get the warrant to search the car right away. The agents decided to seize the vehicle and wait until after the holidays to see what's inside. The PT Cruiser was sealed up, put on a flatbed, and towed to the garage at the HSI office in Rio Rico.

When six days later, on December 29, the search warrant finally came through, Alex and Jackson drove down to Nogales. They had rested during the holidays and were in good mood. Using their contacts at the CBP, they convinced Ramiro to cross over from Mexico with the keys to unlock the car, so they wouldn't have to break the windows to get inside. Ramiro met them at the McDonald's parking lot by the DeConcini port of entry and they gave him a ride to Rio Rico. "Why do you think you're here?" Alex asked Ramiro when they took him to the PT Cruiser. "Because you guys are thinking that you caught me slipping," he said. Ramiro acted cool. "Way too cool," Jackson would later recall. He didn't seem concerned about the situation and this attitude troubled the agents. "Suddenly, I had a bad feeling about the guns," Jackson said. Ramiro unlocked the car and they searched inside and opened the trunk, but all they found were some boxes of clothes and blankets and children's toys. There was a Paw Patrol trailer and a small bike with training wheels. There were no guns.

"We hit the panic button," Jackson later said. They knew Ramiro bought several guns and put them inside the car. "What did we miss? How could this have possibly happened?" Alex was incredulous. The agents immediately returned to Tucson, where they picked up the CBP aerial surveillance video and, reviewing the footage from December 23 on a laptop, they could now see what the helicopter crew didn't notice on the small screen they were watching while they were filming: when Ramiro dropped off Kevin at his mother's house, he took the guns out of the car and, one by one, carried them to the back of the building, carefully positioning each under his right arm and close to his body, so that if someone was watching from the street, they would not be able to see the rifle blended with Ramiro's silhouette.

As soon as they finished watching the video, the agents rushed to the house on South Campbell Avenue, praying the guns would still be there. When Ramiro and Kevin's grandmother, who opened the door, called their mother, Ms. Castillo, and Ms. Castillo returned from work, she allowed them to search the house. The women didn't approve of guns and said they didn't allow any firearms in their house. The agents looked but didn't find anything. Later that evening, when Kevin's dad brought him home from work, Kevin said to the agents: "He sold them." Then Kevin told them more: about how Ramiro brought the firearms around the house and handed them over to him through the bathroom window, about how Kevin then wrapped them in plastic bags and put them in a duffel bag and left them in his closet, where they stayed over the holidays. He told them about the two men in a white Chevy Silverado with mufflers and custom wheels who looked as if they had come "straight from Mexico" when they picked up the rifles. He said they were here the previous night. The agents were too late. The guns were gone.

When Alex and Jackson began this investigation back in October, the people they looked into, like the Morales family, were buying guns in stores. But after the arrests of Darius and Ricky, the organization changed their tactics. Now they were procuring the weapons through private sales. No more need to fill out 4473s, no more surveillance cameras at the dealerships. The Lady AK rifle that Ramiro bought at the parking lot in front of Staples was advertised on Backpage—an online store that worked something like Craigslist for weapons, which was popular among gun sellers in southern Arizona at the time. The person who posted the ad, Tom, already had over a dozen firearms, including long guns, in his collection, so when a family member gave him the pink rifle as a gift, he didn't care for it and decided to sell. Ramiro sent him an email saying he was interested. They exchanged a few text messages and arranged a time and place to meet. Ramiro bought the rifle for $650. The other AK-47, the Polish 1968 model known as Circle 11 built by Petronov Arms, which Ramiro purchased for $700 in the parking lot at Cabela's, was also sold through Backpage. Bill, a commercial driver by occupation, had been selling furniture and other stuff online, so when he decided he no longer needed the rifle he had bought a year earlier, he posted an ad on the site and soon heard from Ramiro. The agents never found out how Ramiro arranged to buy the third gun nor what kind of gun it was because nobody witnessed the transaction behind the AMPM and nobody took note of the license plate of the truck the seller had arrived in. Even if or when this gun is recovered in Mexico and traced to its last buyer from a federal firearms dealer, they may never tie it to Ramiro because private sales in parking lots usually left no records.

With the organization switching to private sales, it also took agents longer to investigate the chain of transactions between sellers and buyers that would lead them to the last owner of the gun. "You follow the path of this gun from manufacturer to distributor to however many retailers it was before it gets to the final gun dealer," Alex explained the gun tracing process. That alone can take a week and dozens of calls. But that's only the beginning. After that, the agents will have to start knocking on doors and asking whether the person who purchased the gun still has it and, if not, then whom they sold it to. And since private sellers are not required to fill out any forms and keep any records, the more weeks, months, or years that pass after an individual sells the gun, the less likely they'd remember any details.

Some people improvise and keep handwritten receipts, just a piece of paper with the gun's serial number and the buyer's ID or license plate. "Just in case it came back to bite me, I wanted to make sure I covered my rear end," a military vet who owned about a hundred guns explained why he saved the messages and the receipt from the only time he sold an assault rifle through Facebook. "A firearm can hurt people," he said. He met the buyer in the Fry's parking lot in Phoenix one evening in late December 2015 and asked him to sign a handwritten receipt. The receipt was for an AK-47, sold for $500. Like the vet who was selling the gun, the man who was buying it carried a military ID. He leaned onto the trunk lid of the vet's car and scribbled his name, Hugo.

Revenge

Allende, Coahuila

I picked up my phone and noticed I had new messages on WhatsApp from Juan. He often shared the news before it was the news. "Now near Allende," his text read, followed by three forwarded videos. I hit play to watch the first: the camera is directed at a street in a neighborhood of one-story houses, black smoke is rising from behind a red building, the sound of heavy gunfire. I watched the next one, which is silent, counting six pickup trucks—black, red, white, black, black, white—with armed men standing in the back, turning a street corner; at least one of the trucks has the letters "CDN" on the side. The third video, which was filmed from the porch of a house, has more intense firing, more smoke, dogs barking.

"Are you there????? What is going on?" I texted back.

"This happened a few hours ago," Juan replied. "So only the players know what is happening."

Later that evening more photos appeared on my screen. I swiped through them, looking for answers about what those armed men were up to. One showed a black truck with a ripped front tire, machine gun on top, its doors flung open, military personnel pulling stuff out. In another, there is a bunch of clothes. Then a pack of .50 caliber cartridges wrapped in cellophane. More boxes of ammo. And then a man in black boots, green camouflage pants, a bulletproof vest with the CDN logo, an assault rifle by his left side, his head blown off. I dropped my phone. Wish I hadn't seen that. The image of blood stuck with me, soaking through everything I set my eyes on, like a filter: magazines spread out on the table, the open page on my computer screen. I remembered once asking Juan how he carried on when he was seeing this day after day. His answer: "Listening to Mozart, reading Shakespeare, looking at Rembrandt."

Soon explanations of what happened in Villa Unión started to emerge. We learned that at a quarter to noon on November 30, a convoy of over twenty armored trucks carrying more than one hundred members of CDN arrived at the small town about 30 miles from the Mexico-US border. The men headed to the town hall, attached to the police station, and opened fire. According to the *Houston Chronicle*, the town's mayor dove for cover to hide from bullets that perforated the walls and smashed the windows of the two-floor building.[1] The men had brought drums of gasoline, allegedly planning to set the town hall on fire.[2] When the Mexican federal security forces showed up, battles between them and the attackers lasted into the following day. A government helicopter was hit and had to do an emergency landing.[3] Some of the attackers tried to run away and, because they were not from around there, they kidnapped several residents to guide them through the brechas. By the time it was over, more than twenty people had died: most of them were the young men affiliated with CDN, four were police officers, and two were local firefighters abducted by the attackers.

The authorities informed that they seized twenty-two vehicles and recovered over two dozen military-style weapons, including six .50 caliber rifles, plus bulletproof helmets and vests.[4] One of those guns, a belt-fed .50 caliber M2 rifle from JnC Manufacturing, was sold less than two weeks earlier at a gun store called Zeroed In Armory, located near Houston. The man who bought it, Israel Chapa Jr., purchased over one hundred assault rifles, including one more .50 caliber rifle, over a six-month period from July to December.[5] He then handed them over to another man, Victor Camacho, who regularly crossed the border. It was a mere coincidence that a sheriff's deputy, Danny Tandera, stopped Camacho for speeding, going at seventy-four in a fifty-five-mile-an-hour zone, on US 59 South, the highway connecting Houston to Laredo. Tandera had a service dog with him and the dog alerted the officer that there was something inside the vehicle. When he searched it, he found a .50 caliber rifle with an obliterated serial number and about one hundred rounds of .50 caliber ammo in the trunk.[6]

When I flew to Monterrey a few weeks later, I brought Juan a heavy book of Brueghel's paintings. I stumbled upon it while browsing basement shelves at my neighborhood bookstore. The vivid, chaotic scenes depicting village life in sixteenth-century Belgium appeared oddly familiar and I wanted to know whether Juan would agree. We met for lunch at La Nacional, which was still empty at that early hour, barely half past noon, and Juan thanked me for the gift. He said that Brueghel's *The Triumph of Death*—an apocalyptic panorama showing an army of skeletons advancing on the living, who put up a weak, futile resistance before being slaughtered in one of myriad ways, from beheadings to drownings to the gallows, all against the background of distant fires and a sea full of shipwrecks—was his favorite painting. We ordered drinks.

Juan was having arguments with his editors again. He complained that the magazine refused to publish his latest story about the "Tropa de Infierno" in Nuevo Laredo. He had gone to visit his relatives on the border and used it as an opportunity to report on what was happening in the city, but nobody he approached to interview wanted to speak on the record. That was one problem. Another was that Juan's editors wanted him to publish the story under his name, not anonymously, which would have been safer for him. This was not the first time they had a disagreement at the magazine, though they had more of them these days. Juan was already in the government's protection program, but he knew that was not enough. He was thinking of buying a gun.

We left the restaurant and drove to the neighborhood of narrow labyrinthine streets in Barrio Antiguo where he lived. Recently, he began noticing strange vehicles and people waiting outside. One time he was returning home when he spotted four trucks parked in front of his building, with armed men in the first two vehicles facing forward, those in the rear facing back. When he saw them, he thought they had come for him. The driver of the truck that was closest to him appeared confused, lost in the urban maze of stone and concrete. "They were not from around here," Juan said. He waited until the men left before he approached the door. Another time, when he was leaving the building, a car blocked him in and the driver called someone on the radio, then took pictures of his home and his vehicle. Juan complained to the federal protection program and asked state police to investigate. "I was puzzled," he told me. "I hope it was something insignificant."

The old city around us bore the scars of violence. The deep blue walls of Cafe Iguana we drove past were still riddled with bullet holes from the attack almost a decade ago. Juan liked sharing memories about the bars that the Zetas owned and attended in those days, the bars where his path and theirs crossed. He recalled the summer night when he got a call about the shootout at Sabino Gordo. It took him five minutes to get from his home to the scene and join other photojournalists aiming cameras at a poorly lit area where personnel of the forensic examiner's office were carrying the bodies and loading them into their vehicles. Twelve of the dead had worked at the bar, where the Zetas packaged drugs for distribution. The armed men who attacked them were said to be from the Gulf Cartel. They came with AK-47s and, besides the employees, killed the security guard and a hot dog vendor who may have been a lookout. Six other victims just happened to be in the wrong place at the wrong time. That night in 2011, twenty-two people died in what the officials described as a settlement of scores. But Juan didn't take the government's narrative for granted, not then, not now. He always found his own sources.

"The waitresses were the best. They saw and knew everything," he said. Serving drinks while the men talked about their business, some sleeping with them, they had information that nobody else did. Juan had been a regular at the bars and night clubs in the old town before the Zetas arrived, so the staff was comfortable with having him around. One waitress confided in him how once she was serving drinks to a group of armed men when an army truck pulled up in front of the bar. She thought it was the end and anxiously scanned the room for a place to hide during the gunfight that could start any moment. But when the soldiers came in, they cordially greeted the armed men. Waitresses showed Juan just how blurry the lines between violence workers, legitimate and not, had become. He knew that stories about the attacks and the shootouts were seldom as straightforward as the news headlines made them appear.

Every street downtown triggered memories. We drove past a funeral parlor and Juan said that the Zetas used it to return the bodies of their members to their families. Here, the armed men received the "official" cause of death that was more acceptable to their relatives—something other than being killed in gunfights with security forces. He recalled the time he was with other journalists reporting from a crime scene nearby when suddenly gunfire erupted and without trying to understand who was shooting and from where, he dropped to the ground. "Not as fast as my colleagues," he said, laughing. Despite the risks that came with covering organized crime, Juan was too submerged in it to think about changing subjects. He knew it had affected him on a deeper level and he found temporary reprieve by writing books about the history of the Second World War. But there was something that attracted him to criminal violence, something darker. As if he had become addicted to poison. At some point, he started collecting keepsakes from the crime scenes he went to, perhaps to prove to himself and to others that what he saw really happened: a bingo chip from Casino Royale in Monterrey; a DVD cover for a movie starring Brad Pitt from Lazcano's ranch in Coahuila; half a kilo worth of spent bullet casings from the days before the police began cordoning off the press, out of concern that scouts working for the Zetas or the CDG were mingling with the reporters and could see the faces and name tags of the investigators.

Among those keepsakes Juan brought home was a tiny cross made from flowers that had already wilted when he found it outside an abandoned warehouse in Tamaulipas. He had to toss it out because it spoiled, but he still had the photographs he took that day which he wanted me to see: heavily armed soldiers on Route 101; charred bodies of vehicles left along a dirt road; a makeshift cross decorated with purple satin ribbons lying on the grass; a green sign with white letters "Bienvenidos San Fernando, Tamaulipas," barely visible in gathering darkness, the last picture he took before he had to leave.

Juan and other journalists would not have even gone there if not for a young migrant from Ecuador, Luis Freddy Lala, who was shot in the neck and managed to survive.[7] One day in late August 2010, Lala walked up to a military checkpoint about a hundred miles south of Matamoros, Tamaulipas, and told the soldiers that the Zetas had kidnapped him and other migrants he had been traveling with on their journey to the United States, that they took them to a warehouse in a nearby ranch, and killed them, one by one, after they refused to work for the group.[8] He said he pretended to be dead and waited until they left before he attempted to escape. The soldiers didn't believe Lala at first. But when the military went to that ranch to check it out, they had to fight their way in. One marine was killed in the operation. Once there, they discovered seventy-two bodies of men and women: blindfolded, hands fastened with zip ties, dead from gunshot wounds to the backs of their heads. And that wasn't all. More reports about disappeared people soon followed, leading the authorities to mass graves and horrific stories, including about the Zetas erecting a fake military checkpoint on Route 101, where they hijacked buses and kidnapped passengers, raping the women and making the men fight for their lives in gladiator-style combat. In the span of a few weeks, the investigators found more than forty mass graves and nearly two hundred human remains.[9] After that, Juan said, they got a call from the state capital telling them to stop counting the bodies publicly.

Journalist Marcela Turati, who accompanied Juan to San Fernando, recalled hundreds of people waiting in line to find out whether their missing relatives could be there, among the bodies being loaded onto the trailer. One woman asked Marcela: "You are a journalist? And why are you here? For months we have been saying that people disappear on these roads but nobody cared. It seemed we were speaking from the bottom of the sea."[10] Over eighty people were arrested following the discovery of the mass graves, including a Zetas leader known as El Wache, and several dozen local police officers who were helping the Zetas kidnap people off the roads. But a decade later, not a single person has been convicted for the murders. Nine of the bodies found at the ranch remain unidentified, and some of the families are not even sure whether the bones in the coffins that the government sent them really belonged to their children, their siblings, or their parents.[11] Their distrust of the Mexican government runs deep.

And then there was Allende. When Juan went to Allende in 2012, a year and nine months after the events that nobody yet talked about, he found its streets quiet and its residents mute, living in fear, lest the perpetrators, who were still nearby, learned they dared speaking to a journalist.[12] He didn't even bring a camera. A web of spies still kept watch over the entrance to the town and swiftly reported anything unusual. Trucks with armed men still drove along the main roads. This, despite the army and the marines, hundreds of them, patrolling the federal highway leading to Allende and making rounds inside the town. The sophisticated machines with gamma rays installed at military checkpoints on the highway scanning vehicles to detect guns were too little, too late. At the time of the massacre, the only presence of the federal forces was a checkpoint on Route 57, a highway connecting Piedras Negras to Monclova, a few kilometers from Allende.[13] When people's calls to the local police went unanswered, that was where they headed to tell someone— anyone who had the power to help them—what was happening. But to no avail. Even the military stood back.[14] It took the government another year after Juan's report to start an investigation that began revealing a horror story without a clear beginning or a certain end.

Three days and two nights somewhere in the middle of that horror story is what we know most about. Before sunset on March 18, 2011, a caravan of forty-two trucks carrying Zetas soldiers and escorted by municipal police arrived in the picturesque ranching town in Coahuila, close to the border with Texas. The gunmen came there with orders to kill everyone with the family names of Garza and Moreno—a retribution for a betrayal. Several weeks earlier, DEA agents pressured a cocaine distributor in the Dallas area, who worked for the Zetas, into cooperating with the agency. His name was José Vásquez Jr. The agents asked Vásquez to provide the trackable identification numbers of Blackberry phones used by Miguel Ángel Treviño Morales, Z-40, and his brother Omar, Z-42. American officials then shared this intelligence with a Mexican federal police unit, without considering what would happen if the information leaked. Someone inside the Mexican government alerted the Treviño Morales brothers, who knew that, except for the top Zetas commanders, only three people had access to the PINs of their cell phones. Z-40 and Z-42 didn't even need to ask for names before they sent armed men on a mission to find Alfonso Cuéllar, Héctor Moreno, and José Luis Garza Gaytán.[15]

All these men—Vásquez, Cuéllar, Moreno, and Garza—were associated with the Zetas, but were not Zetas themselves, even if the distinction may seem fuzzy. Another person involved in their trafficking scheme explained it this way: "the ones that we called Zetas, they're the ones who were armed in pickup trucks, in bulletproof vests, . . . they were the ones who were patrolling the city. They were the ones with weapons."[16] In other words, the Zetas were the ones who killed. The fact that Vásquez organized the smuggling of hundreds of kilos of cocaine into the United States and, on orders from the regional commanders, brought them hundreds of AK-47s and AR-15s from Texas in return did not make him part of the Zetas. He was not one of "them." Nor were Garza, Moreno, and Cuéllar. They had been smuggling drugs through Piedras Negras and Eagle Pass before the Zetas arrived and left them no choice but to work for them if they wanted to continue. Cuéllar and Moreno knew what would happen to them once Z-40 and Z-42 learned about the leak and their cooperation with the DEA, so they fled, crossing into the United States, where they later became protected witnesses. Vásquez, too, remained in Texas after he pleaded guilty to charges of conspiring to distribute cocaine and was sentenced to over thirteen years in prison.[17] Their extended family members and employees, however, were left behind in Coahuila, not suspecting what was coming for them.

"Things began happening in the evening," Martín Márquez, a hot dog vendor, told Ginger Thompson and the team of reporters from *ProPublica* and *National Geographic* who visited Allende five years after the massacre to collect testimonies of residents, local officials, and others who witnessed what unfolded that day.[18] "Armed men began arriving. They were going house to house, looking for the people who had done them wrong," Márquez told the journalists. They grabbed everyone they found inside and took them away. Around 7:30 p.m., firefighters received reports of a blaze at the ranch that belonged to the Garza family and rushed to the scene. A small building was burning and they saw lots of trucks and lots of people. In their statements to the Coahuila state prosecutors during the investigation in 2014, firefighters claimed that when they arrived at the ranch that evening, among multiple police vehicles guarding the entrance, they recognized the police chief and other senior officials. They also recognized some of the locals who worked for the Zetas beating men and women and leading them inside a bodega. They saw large drums of gasoline unloaded from a truck. "When the Zetas became aware of our presence, and that we were there to put out the fire, they said to us: "You guys get the fuck out of here! A chingar a su madre! Or do you want the same thing to happen to you and your family?" And they also told us that we were prohibited from going out to any reports."[19] The firefighters were ordered not to respond to any further calls about fires.

Allende firefighters had been a nuisance to the Zetas for some time. Unlike the police, they had refused to cooperate. When the plaza boss came to the station and offered the fire chief a wad of money—"tengan para que se alivianen," he reportedly told the chief—the chief declined to take the cash, so armed men directed the firefighters to take off their pants and beat them with a wooden plank.[20] The tableada didn't change their stance against working with the Zetas but that made them an exception. That evening in March 2011, as the firefighters stood by the entrance to the ranch, seeing that the police were on the side of the Zetas, they realized that unless they left, they would end up in the same bodega to which gunmen were leading their neighbors. "We couldn't fight bullets with water,"[21] the fire chief later said. Firefighters returned to the station and shut themselves inside for a week.

One resident who spoke to Thompson recalled, "The town was completely deserted." By 11 p.m. at night there was no traffic on the streets. There was no movement of any kind. The next morning, armed men told residents in the neighborhood that they could take whatever was left inside the buildings they had emptied of people before they demolished them using heavy machinery. Although the condemned homes and businesses were close to local government offices—the house that belonged to Moreno's father was on the corner of the main plaza, facing the city hall—and despite over two hundred emergency calls from people reporting fires, looting, and other disorders, pleading for help, nobody responded. When members of the Garza family went to the municipal police station to ask for help finding people who had been taken by the armed men, officers told them they had neither personnel, nor firepower to do anything.[22] Local government officials also did nothing. In a written affidavit requested by Coahuila's attorney general's office, the mayor of Allende claimed that he did not see what happened and did not receive any formal complaints.[23] But witness testimonies tell a different story. Multiple police officers recalled a meeting three days earlier, in which their chief told them that he and the mayor had met with the Zetas, that in this meeting they were told that "things were going to get hot," and that they agreed to "turn a blind eye."[24] Armed men stayed in Allende for three days, killing and burning, and nobody intervened. Over thirty houses were turned to ruins. Two ranches became extermination camps. The bodega was set on fire, with the people inside.

How many people were killed or disappeared that weekend is not known. At first, by official count, there were fewer than thirty. After years of investigations, the National Human Rights Commission identified more than forty. But organizations working with the families of the victims estimate there could be over three hundred.[25] Few people were formally reported missing. Their family members feared law enforcement just as much as they feared organized crime. Even before the massacre, everyone in Allende knew that the police were on the Zetas' payroll, some by choice, others through coercion. In their declarations, firefighters recalled that municipal police officers had Nextel radios and a private channel to communicate with the Zetas.[26] According to the case files that Mexican journalist and human rights activist Sergio Aguayo and the team of researchers he worked with obtained from the state attorney general's office, eleven out of twenty municipal police officers actively collaborated with the Zetas, receiving monthly payments in exchange for ignoring residents' complaints, serving as lookouts, providing information about the movements of the military, letting the Zetas inside the prison to do what they liked with the incarcerated, collecting extortion fees from local businesses, and participating in kidnappings.[27] That weekend in March 2011, municipal police officers had orders to "not go on patrol and not respond to calls for help," to "detain anyone whose family name was Garza," and hand them over to the Zetas.[28]

Despite threats, some residents went to the authorities and complained that entire families they knew had been disappeared. They said they heard rumors about bodies being burned on the ranch. Still nobody did anything until two years and ten months after the events, when at the end of January 2014, scores of soldiers, marines, public functionaries, and crime scene detectives came to Allende and the surrounding region to investigate what had happened in those demolished houses and abandoned lots.[29] The team found piles of empty fuel containers and tires burnt to facilitate combustion. They collected ashes and what remained of clothes from the barrels where the victims were incinerated.[30] A lone forensic investigator sent to the Garza ranch was in charge of gathering the human remains. According to the forensic analysis report prepared by the federal police, the evidence from the ranch consisted of "66 bone fragments and 68 teeth fragments characteristic of the human species."[31] There was no information in the documents that Aguayo and his team obtained on whether anyone attempted to identify the people that these bones and teeth once belonged to.

More than a decade later, Juan was still trying to account for the victims, to find out once and for all how many people had disappeared in Allende and nearby towns between 2010 and 2014, while the region was under the reign of terror imposed by the Zetas with the complicity of the state. Those forty-nine hours were only an episode in a much longer history of violence in the region. In 2012, a group of armed men working together with the police forcibly disappeared four more members of the Garza family: a couple and their two children, a six-year-old boy and an infant.[32] People were killed all over the region of Cinco Manantiales, not only in Allende, but also in the municipalities of Nava, Guerrero, Zaragoza, and Piedras Negras. Juan's count had now increased to fifty-seven victims.[33] But he suspected there were more. For the most part, media stopped covering the story, so Juan continued this work on his own time, with his own money.

In July 2016, he drove to San Antonio to attend the trial of Marciano Millan Vasquez, known by his nickname Chano, who had been the Zetas' boss in Piedras Negras. The trial lasted eleven days, but Juan could only afford to stay for three. He was not in the courtroom when the jury delivered a unanimous verdict:

> Which victim or victims did you unanimously find the defendant Marciano Millan Vasquez guilty of killing or counseling, commanding, inducing, procuring, or causing the intentional killing of while engaged in drug trafficking offenses, or aiding and abetting the killing of various individuals while engaged in drug trafficking offenses beyond a reasonable doubt?
> Answer yes or no next to each name.

Rodolfo Reyes, Jr.—Yes

Severino Abascal—Yes

Vaneli Luna—Yes

Cesar Sanchez—Yes

Victor Cruz—Yes

Victor Cruz's wife, Brenda Saluda—Yes

Victor Cruz's son (1)—Yes

Victor Cruz's son (2)—Yes

Domingo Sanchez-Garza's grandson—Yes

An unknown military PGR commandante—Yes

An unknown male killed by chopping off his limbs and head (1)—Yes

An unknown male killed by chopping off his limbs and head (2)—Yes

An unknown male killed by chopping off his limbs and head (3)—Yes

An unknown male killed by chopping off his limbs and head (4)—Yes

An unknown female killed by chopping off her limbs and head—Yes

An unknown adult male killed on knees near the Rio Escondito—Yes

An unknown adult male, possibly a second captain in the Mexican military, killed on knees near the Rio Escondito—Yes

An unknown adult female killed on knees near the Rio Escondito—Yes

An unknown adult male killed by chopping of his limbs and burning the body near the Cereso Prison—Yes

An unknown young girl killed in front of her parents—Yes

Her mother—Yes

Her father—Yes

Newspaper boy killed at junkyard (1)—Yes

Newspaper boy killed at junkyard (2)—Yes

Newspaper boy killed at junkyard (3)—Yes

Newspaper boy killed at junkyard (4)—Yes

Miguel Uribe—Yes

Mauricio Uribe—Yes

Francisco Villarreal—Yes

The Allende murders (an unknown number of persons)—Yes[34]

Chano was sentenced to seven life terms.

In March 2018, Mexico's National Human Rights Commission published a report detailing how various state institutions had failed the residents of Allende, from municipal police arbitrarily detaining and forcefully disappearing people on the orders of the Zetas and watching how their homes were looted and destroyed, to the federal security forces ignoring pleas for help, to government officials denying the survivors and their families the right to truth and the right to justice.[35] Following the commission's recommendation, in June 2019, officials from the federal and state governments came to Allende to offer a public apology for what had happened there. Speaking on behalf of the Mexican state, the secretary of the interior, Olga Sánchez Cordero, asked the victims for forgiveness and for help "reconstituting the social fabric" and "healing the fracture" that the massacre had opened in the country.[36] But once the officials left town, the families of the killed and the disappeared continued to wait for what they were promised: truth, justice, and reparations.

Sometimes, when I asked Juan a question, usually about the Zetas and the fusion between the Mexican state and organized crime, he would answer with a phrase like "Yes, San Fernando." Or "Remember Allende." As if the names of these places sufficed as indexes of reality so gnarled that it resisted a simplified explanation. As if he wouldn't even know where to start. And neither did I. So I nodded and wrote "San Fernando" and, even more often, "Allende" in my notebook. Underlined those names. Wrote them down again next time he mentioned one or the other. Then one day, perhaps tired of my questions, Juan said we could go to Allende. The ten-year anniversary of what happened there had come and gone, but there were still no answers: not how many people were killed, not who in the government was responsible, nor would they ever face justice. Allende remained an open wound. Juan said what I both wanted and dreaded to hear: "We could make it there and back in one day."

On a sunny Saturday in the winter of 2022—eleven years after the massacre and eight since the investigation[37]—we followed Allende's quiet one-way streets set in a grid-like pattern looking for the main plaza. Juan was driving. I was looking at Google Maps on my phone and giving him directions. We parked next to Oxxo. Heavily armed soldiers in camouflage fatigues stood at the steps of the city hall and, as we passed them, we nodded and uttered barely audible hellos. I followed Juan upstairs. He had called the mayor's office ahead of the trip and was expecting a meeting, but an employee now informed us that the mayor was away and nobody knew if he would be coming in. Juan didn't insist. It seemed he wasn't that interested in talking to the mayor after all. Contacting him and requesting a meeting was more of a necessary gesture.

A couple of blocks from the city hall, we stopped in front of a peach-colored house built in Spanish mission style. Or rather in front of what used to be a house, for it was now a ruined structure with huge gaping holes in the walls. In a sworn statement, a member of the Zetas who went by the nickname El Pájaro, The Bird, recounted the evening when they kidnapped the owners of the house: "We arrived and forced our way in firing shots, from there we took [Víctor Garza], his wife [Alma Patricia Pérez], and their youngest son, I think that [his name was Julio Garza]. With the help of these same police, we put them in the patrol vehicle. Later we took these people to the Garza ranch . . . where we put them in the same house where we had the others."[38] The three were murdered later that night, together with many others that the Zetas forced into the bodega.

The excavators and other heavy machinery the Zetas brought from around the region to demolish the houses in 2011 were never located. It was too late for that when the investigators finally showed up. Now the peach-colored house stood apart from other buildings up and down the street: simple rectangular structures painted yellow and pink and beige, grates on their windows, their walls intact. People who lived in those homes saw the cement carcass every day—a reminder, a warning. Two men working on an electrical pole nearby glanced at us but said nothing when Juan and I got out of the car and approached the house. We stepped inside through a jagged hole, avoiding red and black cables protruding from the sides. Treading carefully on sharp-edged fragments of ceramic tile grinding under our feet we went from room to room, no longer covered by a roof. The markings, spray-painted on the walls, told us that this place, too, now had new owners: "CDN rifa putos."

50 BMG

The way he likes it told, when recounting the company's history, it begins on the first day of 1982 with him standing on the shore of the Stones River near Nashville, Tennessee, pointing his camera at a gunboat, and pressing the shutter. About to turn twenty-eight, Ronnie Barrett owned a photography studio and his pictures won awards from the state's professional photographers association. He took many shots of the boat on the river that day and one picture in particular—the one in which you can see two Browning machine guns mounted on the deck—changed the direction of his life. Not only his, in fact, but those of many others far away from Tennessee.

Ronnie Barrett grew up in a family that owned guns for protection as well as recreation.[1] As a teenager, he liked hunting and later became an expert marksman and, although he pursued a career in photography, he would spend hours tinkering with firearms in his garage, as a hobby. After he took those photographs of the river patrol boat, he became interested in the Browning machine guns he saw that day. They used .50 caliber ammunition, technically known as .50 BMG rounds, where the number .50 referred to the inside diameter of the bore of the barrel and the outside diameter of the projectile, in inches, and BMG stood for Browning machine gun. Back then, such rifles were only manufactured for the military, primarily used against armored vehicles and aircraft, and no commercial version existed. A small group of civilians organized into the Fifty Caliber Shooters Association, Inc., based in Utah, had been experimenting with shoulder-fired rifles that could handle the pressure of the .50 BMG cartridge, but most of these guns were single-shot, bolt-action design.[2] Ronnie Barrett wanted something different. With no background in engineering, he dove into books on firearm design. He fancied to build a semiautomatic rifle firing .50 BMG rounds.

The shops he approached with the sketches were skeptical about the feasibility of his designs, but he refused to abandon the idea until a friend of a friend who ran a hobby machine shop in his garage agreed to help. The gun they made, the Barrett Model 82A1/M107 rifle, will become "the stuff of legends," to quote *Rolling Stone*.[3] The company's first government contract was a sale to the Swedish army in 1989. The following year, the US government ordered a batch of them for the Marine Corps for use as long-range sniper rifles. Soon the US Army's combat engineers and explosive ordnance disposal units adopted Barrett rifles, as did the Navy SEALs. Soldiers took them to Iraq during the Gulf War and deployed them in operations Desert Shield and Desert Storm. Prizes and recognition followed. At the Barrett factory near Mursfreesboro, Tennessee, engineers developed other models capable of firing .50 caliber ammunition, including a lightweight tactical rifle known as the Model 99–1, marketed for law enforcement.[4] The company's website announces that it is good for disabling vehicles and for penetrating barricades.

The original Barrett M82A1, which the manufacturer calls "an American icon," is a recoil operated semiautomatic rifle that weighs 32.7 pounds without scopes and ammo (about the same as a cinder block) and is fifty-seven inches long—approximately the width of a queen-size mattress.[5] Just its barrel, which is made from chrome moly steel, weighs eight pounds and is twenty-nine inches long. The rifle has a ten-round magazine and is accurate at ranges that exceed one thousand yards—that's ten football fields. As an article published in *The Small Arms Review* about ArmaLite's AR-50, a cheaper .50 caliber rifle designed "for the masses," noted: "It turned out that hitting something at 1000 yards was not the challenge. The real challenge was finding a place to safely shoot at a target 1000 yards away."[6] A trained shooter can hit a target that is nearly twice that far. A piece in the *American Rifleman* cited the US Army's report from Operation Iraqi Freedom: "The Barrett .50-cal. Sniper Rifle may have been the most useful piece of equipment for the urban fight . . . Soldiers not only appreciated the range and accuracy but also the target effect . . . a combat multiplier due to the psychological impact on other combatants that viewed the destruction of the target."[7] Violence Policy Center calls Barrett "the super gun" and describes it as "a devil's blend of long range and massive power."[8] At closer distances and depending on the type of ammunition, it can blast through nine inches of concrete wall, perforate light armored vehicles, ignite fuel tanks, and shoot down helicopters.

The company makes about six thousand rifles per year.[9] Only California, Illinois, New Jersey, and Washington, DC, ban the ownership of .50 caliber weapons; several other states prohibit machine guns. But the rest have almost no state-level regulation.[10] There, you can buy a Barrett in cash and own as many as you like. The 2020 catalog offered four colors: black, flat dark earth, tungsten grey, and burnt bronze. Sportsman's Warehouse, Gunbroker.com, GrabAGun.com, and other auction websites promised to ship the guns to the nearest dealer, though buyers were advised that they may not be legal in every state. "Complete your purchase within the law," one listing warned.[11] Some sellers even offered ninety-day, interest-free financing, which was understandable considering that a Barrett M82, with accessories, could cost over $11,000. Ammunition for the rifles, including armor-piercing incendiary rounds, was sold online and through mail order catalogs. A 50 BMG cartridge is about the length of a Sharpie marker.

In 2016, the Barrett Model M82 became Tennessee's official rifle. State Representative Micah Van Huss, former Marine sniper who carried the gun during his deployments in Iraq, introduced the resolution to add the firearm to the list of state symbols, next to the mockingbird and honeybee. Van Huss praised Barrett for "changing battlefield tactics." Some other states have recently adopted official firearms, but they are mostly historical: the Colt single action army revolver in Arizona, the Kentucky Long Rifle in Kentucky, the Grouseland rifle in Indiana. Speaking in support of the resolution, Republican Senator Bill Ketron said that no other products made in Tennessee, "have saved lives like this rifle has on the battle lines."[12] The senator's argument resonated with the narrative about guns saving lives that has a long history. A century and a half earlier, the man who invented the first prototype of the machine gun used a very similar reasoning. Richard J. Gatling, a medical school graduate who saw the remains of Union soldiers return in caskets from the American Civil War, realized that most of them did not die from trauma but from disease, as their wounds got infected. He decided that making the killing more efficient would shorten the war and that would spare more men. "It occurred to me that if I could invent a machine—a gun—that would by its rapidity of fire enable one man to do as much battle duty as a hundred, that it would to a great extent, supersede the necessity of large armies, and consequently exposure to battle and disease would be greatly diminished."[13] This noble cause behind the machine gun became part of the origin myth that Gatling repeated throughout his life—one which survived to this day and became incorporated into Barrett's story.

After its debut in war zones abroad, Barrett M82 has left the hands of the military and the battlefields of conventional war and began changing the value of life in places and in ways that its proponents, if they were not oblivious to it, at least chose to ignore. In 1999, about two decades before Barrett was honored by being named Tennessee's official rifle, the Government Accountability Office submitted a briefing paper titled ".50 Caliber Rifle Crime." It read: ".50 caliber semiautomatic rifles have been linked to domestic and international criminal activity" that included "terrorist groups, outlaw motorcycle gangs, international drug cartels, domestic drug dealers, religious cults, militia groups, potential assassins, and violent criminals."[14] The tracing records GAO obtained from the ATF concerning .50 caliber rifles connected them to an alleged plot to assassinate Fidel Castro; a doomsday cult that built underground bunkers in Montana; a religious sect in Texas; tax protesters in Georgia; and militia groups in Canada and West Virginia. There was also a case on "Mexican Drug Cartel Multiple Homicide," which was summarized as follows: "The Los Angeles Police Department, at the request of Mexican authorities, requested that ATF trace a .50 caliber semiautomatic rifle in October 1996. It was determined that the weapon was purchased legally in Wyoming. The weapon, along with over 100 AK-47s, was recovered by Mexican authorities at the scene of a multiple homicide involving a shootout with drug cartel members in Sinaloa, Mexico."[15] A single .50 caliber gun found in Mexico was still a novelty in the 1990s. Back then, the US government was most worried about .50 caliber rifles being used in domestic terrorism in the United States.

In 2019, the Mexican military recovered seventy-two Barrett .50 caliber rifles. Forty-eight of the firearms—two-thirds of them—were captured in the state of Tamaulipas, nine were confiscated in Michoacán, five in Sonora, and three in Sinaloa.[16] In previous years, between 2010 and 2018, the military had already confiscated 554 weapons that used .50 caliber ammunition, about three-fifths of them in Tamaulipas. According to *The Trace*, an independent nonprofit news site dedicated to covering gun violence, nearly half of these rifles (227) were manufactured by Barrett in Tennessee and it is known that 104 other firearms (whose make could not be identified because their serial numbers and brand names had been erased) were made in the United States.[17] We don't know much more about them, but it is likely that their journey to Mexico took a similar trajectory to those that came before—the fifty-six .50 caliber guns that the Mexican authorities asked the ATF to trace between 2006 and 2010.[18] Of the twenty-one rifles traced to Arizona, two were sold at Cabela's in Glendale. Others came from Yuma, Phoenix, Mesa, and Scottsdale. Nineteen of those weapons were traced to locations in Texas: El Paso, Mission, Dallas, Fort Worth, Garland, Laredo, and other places. Only one was sold in New Mexico and none in California, which has a ban on manufacture, importation, possession, and sale of .50 caliber rifles. The remaining guns were bought in states farther away from the border: A Barrett fired by the Zetas in Rancho La Cebolla in Durango was purchased in Van Burren, Arkansas; two others—one of which was found on Route 2 in Tamaulipas and linked to the CDG, and the other recovered from a Zetas training camp in Nuevo León—were both sold by Kramers Guns & Supplies in Spring Valley, Illinois; the rest came from Nevada, Utah, Oklahoma, Florida. The majority were Barrett Model 82, though the list also included two M93 Black Arrow rifles made by Zastava Arms in Serbia, which were imported by a company based in Cocoa, Florida, sold by a dealer in Roma, Texas, and recovered over a year later, in Matamoros, Tamaulipas, in the hands of the Zetas.

These guns were associated with various crimes, including "firing weapon," "kickback-receiving," and "willful killing of a public official."[19] But the majority were simply logged in as "possession of weapon." That alone was sufficient to initiate prosecution: only the security forces were allowed to have .50 caliber rifles in Mexico. Civilians caught with one faced two to twelve years in prison for possession, four to fifteen years for carrying. According to Mexico's attorney general's office, over a period of sixteen years, from 2006 to 2021, only 603 people were charged with violating Article 84 of the federal firearms law, which prohibits "clandestine introduction into the national territory" of firearms, ammunition and other materials designated for the exclusive use of the military.[20] Guanajuato (145) and Sonora (117) surpassed the other states with the most charges, followed by Chihuahua (84), Baja California (55), and Coahuila (33). Although it is not clear what portion of those Article 84 violations involved .50 caliber rifles, the use of these powerful weapons had particularly deep social effects.

In a video circulating on social media, a man in a blue medical mask presses his back against the wall in a garage, his face turned toward the street, where darkness is beginning to peel off the edges of the sky. The man listens to what sounds like gunfire. At first, the shots are distinct, then they begin pouring and the man with the mask drops to the ground and looks for shelter behind a grey Volkswagen; the other man, the one who has been filming, follows. His phone camera continues recording, though all we can see is the underside of the car the witnesses hope will protect them from whatever is happening down the street.

Early in the morning on June 26, 2020, Mexico City's secretary of security, Omar García Harfuch, was sitting in the front passenger seat, reviewing documents while on his way to the daily cabinet meeting, when he saw a truck overtake their SUV. "At that moment, I knew we were ambushed," he later told newspaper *El País*.[21] As soon as he heard the first bullet hit the glass, Harfuch drew his handgun and fired back. "From then on, there was a rain of hits and deafening noise." A total of 414 shots were fired at the vehicle the security chief was in during a shootout that lasted about twenty minutes.[22] Although his armored Chevy Suburban was reinforced with thick ballistic steel, which could protect the occupants from several shots from an AR-15 or an AK-47, it could not withstand multiple rounds.[23] Bullets hit Harfuch in the shoulder, clavicle, and knee. Had it taken thirty seconds more for the backup to arrive, "they would have probably hit me in some vital organ," he later said.[24] A helicopter flew Harfuch to the hospital, where he underwent surgery, then broke the news himself with a post on Twitter from his hospital bed: "Two companions and friends of mine lost their lives, I have been hit by three bullets and shrapnel." Two experienced police officers who served as Harfuch's bodyguards were killed in the attack, as was Gabriela Gómez, a young woman from an Indigenous community in the municipality of Xalatlaco in the state of Mexico, who was on her way to sell tlacoyos when the car she was riding in got caught in the crossfire.[25]

A photo of the black armored Chevy Suburban that Harfuch was riding in along Paseo de la Reforma in a prestigious tree-lined colonia Lomas de Chapultepec showed its metallic body pierced by bullets, tires flat. Another photo that circulated that morning displayed several assault-style rifles left in the back of a truck that the assailants abandoned after the operation. And then there were two black-and-white videos from the city's security cameras with time stamps indicating the footage was taken just after 6:38 a.m. They showed a group of armed men in a large stake bed truck with fake logos of a construction company getting ready for the attack. They have hoods on, so we don't see their faces. Some are picking up weapons. One is gesturing with his gloved hand, giving directions. They disembark. Twenty-eight people participated in the assassination attempt, Mexican officials said. That same day, they announced having detained twelve suspects, whose mug shots were circulated to the media. Some were from Mexico City; others had come from Guadalajara, Nayarit, Chihuahua, and Michoacán; one was Colombian. They confessed that they had been hired for the job three weeks earlier. By the following day, nineteen suspects were in custody, including the leader of CJNG in Jalisco, who, the government said, was the intellectual mastermind behind the assassination attempt. The judge, at least initially, did not charge him and his accomplices with homicide. They were sent to preventive prison on charges of bribery, crime against health, and carrying weapons that are designated for the exclusive use of the military.

The arsenal used in the attack was impressive. The spokesperson to the Mexico City attorney general's office said that security officers seized one grenade launcher, 34 rifles, including M16s and Barretts, 8 handguns, 7 fragmentation grenades, 39 vests, 51 Molotov cocktails, 96 magazines, and 2,805 cartridges.[26] Over four hundred spent bullet casings were recovered at the scene. Security analysts who saw the photos of the seized guns suggested that, besides Barrett, the hitmen used an FN SCAR 17S made by FN Herstal in Belgium, a civilian variant of a combat assault rifle adopted, among other agencies, by US Special Operations Command, Los Angeles police SWAT teams, the Japanese special forces counterterrorist group, and the military police of the state of São Paulo in Brazil.[27] The firearms were brand-new and some experts speculated that the men had no experience with them.[28] The assassination attempt failed because they didn't know how to wield their tremendous firepower.

Immediately, the role of the United States in supplying these arms became part of the conversation. An article in *Milenio* called the Barrett M82A1, five of which were seized from the assailants, an "icon of the United States."[29] Even though it wasn't clear whether the men used those rifles to attack Harfuch or merely had them in their arsenal for backup, Barrett guns had been showing up regularly at critical events with profound consequences for Mexican society. Less than a year had passed since October 17, 2019, when Mexican security forces were sent to

Culiacán, Sinaloa, with orders to arrest Ovidio Guzmán, the son of the group's former leader, El Chapo.[30] But the operation was a spectacular failure. Footage shared on social media showed heavily armed men riding in convoys of pickup trucks, streets blocked with burning vehicles, and panicked residents fleeing for safety at the sound of gunfire. Plumes of black smoke filled the sky. Armed men broke into the jail and released inmates. They took soldiers hostage and, according to officials, fired at an apartment complex that housed military families.[31] After four hours of fighting, the government ordered security forces to retreat. At least eight people were dead, according to official figures, but those who counted the bodies in the morgues following the confrontation say there were four or five times as many victims. Mexico's defense secretary, Luis Cresencio Sandoval, explained that the army and the National Guard could not compete with the group's firepower—their military-grade arsenal included armored vehicles, .50-caliber machine guns, and rocket launchers that hit a helicopter. The decision to back down was justified as the way to avoid further civilian casualties.[32] In the press conference the following morning, President López Obrador, said, "You cannot fight fire with fire. We do not want deaths. We do not want war."[33] His security strategy was summed up by a popular slogan "abrazos no balazos" (hugs not bullets). Early in López Obrador's presidency, this stance was hailed as an important reversal of the militarized approach to fighting organized crime that his predecessors, Presidents Calderón and Peña Nieto, embraced. But organized crime groups had no intentions to give up their power.

That time in Culiacán, the fighting was not over yet when analyses of what had gone wrong began. Media coverage highlighted two issues. The first was the "surrender" of the Mexican state to organized crime.[34] In the past, this "failed state" narrative was used in the United States to justify sending more American military aid to Mexico, as happened with the Mérida Initiative. More recently, however, it has prompted threats of US military intervention.[35] Meanwhile, in Mexico, this narrative was embraced by López Obrador's opponents, as evidence of his failure to address violence. The other matter—not unrelated to the state's surrender to organized crime—was the fact that .50 caliber Barrett rifles that the gunmen used came to Mexico from the United States.[36] In other words, the failure of the Mexican state, which both US and Mexican politicians denounced, has been, at least in part, made in the USA.

Attitude

Monterrey, Nuevo León

Miguel showed me how to hold the rifle and handed it to me. Awkwardly, I molded my body around the gun and aimed at the metallic silhouettes in the distance. But steel chickens slipped from sight, up and down, right and left. I switched the gun from my right hand to my left and leaned over the sights again. I located the target, slowly exhaled, then held my breath to stop my hands from shaking and my eyes from losing sight of the chickens. Then I pressed the trigger: Plink. Again: Plink, plink. I hit some. I missed many.

"Don't pause," Miguel said. "Keep your finger on the trigger. Ta-ta-ta-ta-ta," he prompted me.

I couldn't. I looked up at the floor-to-ceiling windows of the luxury condo building towering over the range, imagining what it was like living up there, going about your day to the routine soundtrack of gunfire.

When I paused shooting, I could hear men in parallel lanes hit metallic silhouettes. They had arrived in nice cars to enjoy the last hours of a short winter day with their favorite weapons. Some were hunters. Others were competitive shooters practicing for national and international tournaments. Located across the river from San Pedro, Club Deportivo de Cazadores was the oldest and most prestigious gun club in Monterrey, with a shooting range occupying an elongated rectangular terrain that curled at the edge of a mountain. It was founded nearly a century ago when the city was maybe a sixth of its current size. Today, the entrance gate—the only gap in the grey brick wall with sections of barbed wire that surrounded the club—opened to a busy four-lane street, less than a few blocks from an H.E.B. supermarket and Colegio Euroamericano. Proximity gave it an advantage: gun owners had other clubs to choose from within an hour's drive from San Pedro, but they could reach Cazadores in under ten minutes. The club had about a thousand members and anyone wanting to join needed recommendations from two current *socios*.[1] More than a shooting range, Cazadores was an exclusive social club.

When I asked Miguel what I could bring for the evening with his friends, he said: "Attitude." So that's all I had when earlier that afternoon Uber dropped me off in front of the security booth at the gate. Tomás met me there and gave me a ride up to the range, where we found Miguel unloading his truck. After greeting me, Miguel passed me a pair of earmuffs, then picked up two gun cases and told me to follow him. At the range, he opened the first case and pulled out a rifle, all black, with a quad rail and tactical scopes. I recognized it as an AR-15, the gun whose silhouette was too familiar from video footage and photos Americans had been seeing. The one that wasn't even popular twenty years ago but has since become the best-selling weapon manufactured by every major gunmaker in the United States.[2] It was used in ten out of the seventeen deadliest mass shootings in the last decade, including at schools in Newtown, Parkland, and Uvalde. No longer, if ever, just a tool, the gun was a symbol, a political statement.

Miguel had already told me how he bought this Smith & Wesson M&P15 at Academy Sports in McAllen and smuggled it across the border. Because it used .22 caliber rounds, permitted in Mexico, instead of the more powerful ammunition of other Smith & Wesson models, the rifle was not exactly illegal. Miguel could register it with SEDENA. But despite its compliance with the law, the branding of the model irked Mexican authorities—M&P stood for "Military and Police." Lawyers representing the Mexican government in the lawsuit against US gunmakers claimed that Smith & Wesson marketed this firearm in ways that appealed to "civilians wanting to carry out unlawful military-style combat missions."[3] Miguel had no plans to do anything of that sort, though. He bought the rifle to take it to the range to shoot metallic silhouettes shaped like chickens.

Now he took the M&P15 from me and leaned it against the barrier separating us from other shooters. I could tell he was disappointed I didn't follow his instructions, that I didn't spray the targets with bullets. Without saying anything, he opened the other, smaller, gun case and handed me his Ruger pistol. I didn't want to practice anymore, but

Miguel wasn't listening. "Where is your attitude?" he asked, sounding irritated. He brought me here to shoot and I had a sinking feeling that he would not be inviting me again. I raised the pistol, took a few deep breaths, and pressed the trigger, repeatedly, fast, emptying the magazine, then another, until we were out of ammo.

It was almost dark when we joined Miguel's friends hanging out by the grill, holding paper plates greasy from carne asada. I had already met Tomás. Now Miguel introduced me to the rest: Tomás's brother Rafael, along with Esteban, Mateo, and Javier. Except for Javier, who was slightly older than the others, they were about the same age as Miguel, in their early to mid-thirties, with successful careers and family lives that they had come here for a few hours to forget. Back at home, firearms were a taboo for some of them—acquiescing to their wives, they kept their guns in their offices or locked up in garages where their children would not find them. Here, the conversation that began with Sonoran meat swiftly turned to American guns: comparing the advantages of different calibers, sharing news on good deals for accessories, praising the latest additions to their arsenals.

"Look at this!" Rafael pulled up a photo of a .45 Colt with a small diamond heart on the grip and passed his phone around for us to gawk.

"I bought it from a *judicial*," he said, referring to an officer from the judicial police. "And he gave me a second .45 for free, as a bonus."

Nobody said anything about the gun of this caliber being illegal in Mexico. Instead, they said, "Está bien padre!" and "Qué chido!"

Rafael and Tomás did not grow up around guns. Their parents forbade firearms in their home. They discovered the club through serendipity. Tomás worked in one of the office buildings in the neighborhood and one day he decided to follow the sound of gunfire he was hearing in the afternoons to see where it was coming from. A peek inside Cazadores and he signed up as a member and signed his brother up too. In one year since they joined the club, Rafael had already purchased fifteen firearms. The new hobby was expensive, but he didn't mind splurging on guns. He showed me a picture of a pricey old revolver, which the others had already seen, one of four handguns he now owned. Then he walked over to his car and returned carrying a box with a Browning 7 Magnum with Leica scopes—a beautiful hunting rifle with a walnut stock that elicited more compliments from his friends. If they sounded less enthusiastic than when they saw the picture of the diamond-crusted Colt, it may be because their reserves of praise for Rafael's fancy new possessions were depleted for the night.

Rafael bought most of his guns through smugglers who procured them in the United States and delivered them to the trailer parks along Route 85 south of Monterrey. All he had to do, once he made a deal for a purchase on WhatsApp, was to get the cash and, when they told him the gun was here, go pick it up. Though others were more circumspect about sharing the details, most of them got their guns in similar ways. But not Javier. He was the only one of the bunch who took the legal route—made an appointment at the *armería*, as gun owners often called the army store in Mexico City, flew to the capital, and bought half a dozen firearms in one go. To return to Monterrey, Javier had to ask the federal police at the airport for permission to take the guns on board. Buying legally cost him less than he would have had to pay smugglers, but it did take time and involved a ton of paperwork.

The armería, located inside the three-story cement building on Avenida Industria Militar in Mexico City's Lomas de Sotelo neighborhood, was for decades the only store in the country authorized to sell weapons. SEDENA maintained that most Mexican people had no need for guns, legal or illegal. Colonel Eduardo Téllez Moreno, who oversaw the Directorate of Commercialization of Arms and Munitions (DCAM), compared owning firearms at home to "having a match close to a fire."[4] "It's an obligation of the state to provide security to the people who live in the country, not for you to take justice into your own hands," he said.[5] And yet people did come to buy guns. From 2006 to 2018, the store sold 276,348 handguns and 237,102 rifles and shotguns.[6] Many of those were bought by organizations that held collective licenses—public and private security companies. But regular citizens also came to purchase guns here. In 2018 alone, SEDENA registered over ten thousand requests for firearm permits.[7] Still, even though sales had been increasing, the single gun store in Mexico was only selling an average of thirty-eight guns a day.[8]

I told Javier that I had been to the armería. The official letter from the Secretariat of National Defense, authorizing my visit, noted I had to arrive at DCAM at 9 a.m. I recalled that I was half an hour late, that my bag set off the metal detector, but Colonel Téllez Moreno waved me through security and led me into the lobby, where about two dozen men sat in chairs facing several counters, waiting for their turn, as if they were at a motor vehicle registry. On their laps they had leather briefcases and paper folders, which, the colonel explained, contained documents that were required to get a permit: a birth certificate, a copy of a government-issued ID proving they were Mexican citizens and were at least eighteen years old, a letter from their employer that demonstrated a source of income, evidence of a clean criminal record obtained from the attorney general's office of the applicant's home state, and, if they were subject to military service, proof of completion. Behind their backs, guns lay quietly in wooden display cases, under glass, like dormant snakes in a serpentarium: wood stocked Beretta rifles popular with hunters; .380 Brownings sold for self-defense; Trejo pistols and Mendoza rifles representing the Mexican gun industry. There were black Glock and Sig Sauer pistols, and the colonel said, "When it comes to firearms, Sig Sauer is like a Ferrari." He showed me a 5.56 × 45mm Norinco CQ, the Chinese variant of the M16 rifle, which cost $4,877.80 USD, in a case facing the display of American weapons; and an Israeli Galil Sniper S.A. 7.62 × 51mm with telescopic lens and a price tag of $12,235.10 USD, the most expensive gun in the store. Many of the firearms we looked at could only be sold to police agencies.[9]

I remember asking Colonel Téllez Moreno whether it made sense for someone who lived in Nuevo León or in Sonora to travel this far and pay more for a firearm that they could buy for less on the black market back home. "As a matter of principle, we don't recognize that black market exists," he said. Someone who lived in Monterrey and wanted a gun could buy it from a neighbor or an acquaintance and then go to the regional military zone to register it. That was not illegal. But such arrangements mostly worked for older, used weapons, not for what gun aficionados like Miguel and his friends wanted. "It would make sense to follow the law," the colonel said.

Getting ammunition without leaving Monterrey was less of an ordeal. Miguel sometimes went to a store on Francisco Madero Avenue downtown and one weekday in January he brought me along. As we entered, Miguel greeted the owner, Marco, whose father founded the store two decades ago and had since left the business to his son. We were the only customers, and I walked around looking at hunting and fishing gear: backpacks and vests in camouflage patterns, Swiss pocket knives, insulated bags and cookware, pepper spray. Marco didn't deal in firearms, but a permit from SEDENA allowed him to sell ammunition. Supplies, however, were low. Marco hadn't restocked since before the Christmas holidays, when customers nearly emptied the store.

The majority of the boxes stacked on the shelves behind the cashier were marked .22, the most frequently used caliber. There were also some boxes of .32 and 12-gauge shotgun shells for sporting clays. The law permitted individuals to buy one thousand pieces of 12- or 20-gauge, five hundred pieces of .22, and two hundred pieces of other caliber ammunition per month. A red bullet-shaped logo with the head of an eagle decorated many of the boxes with the brand name Aguila— Mexican ammunition that Marco ordered directly from the factory in Cuernavaca, in the state of Morelos, one of only two places in the country that manufactured cartridges. He had to request higher caliber ammunition from the army store in Mexico City and its inventory fluctuated, depending on supplies from abroad.

"I haven't been able to buy .270 for two years," Miguel complained, glancing at the available ammo on the shelves.

"They are available on the black market," Marco said, hinting that, if Miguel wanted, he could get some. Miguel told him that he already knew about that option.

The store had no .308 caliber cartridges either. Long range shooting was becoming popular in Mexico, Marco explained, but without this caliber available at the store, regiomontanos had to either fly to Mexico City or learn to handload their own ammo.

"Isn't that illegal?" I asked, still a bit confused about the law.

"It's illegal but not enforced," Marco said frankly.

We were standing with our backs to the entrance while talking to Marco, so when I heard the door open, I turned and saw three Fuerza Civil officers in full armored gear enter the store. They wore black bulletproof vests and Kevlar helmets, their faces, except for their eyes, covered by balaclavas. Strapped to their chests were AR-15s, their barrels pointing down. Fuerza Civil had been in the news nearly every day because of repeated attacks against its personnel. That very morning the front-page story in *Milenio* informed that overnight assailants fired at a Fuerza Civil outpost in one of the cities surrounding Monterrey and injured two police officers on duty in another.

While I stood there stunned by the presence of heavily armed officers, Miguel approached them and started chatting, allowing the rest of us in the store to exhale. One officer said they came to buy ammunition. The Secretariat of Public Security did not issue them enough rounds for practice, so they learned to improvise: buy the cheap .22 caliber cartridges and use a converter to fire them from their 9mm handguns. Miguel didn't ask about the rounds for their AR-15s, which I kept staring at, unable to tell whether they were Colt or Bushmaster. Even though I knew they used different ammo, they looked to me just like the M&P15 Miguel taught me to shoot.

Once the Fuerza Civil officers left, it was time for us to go too. The store was out of .380 caliber cartridges that Miguel needed for his Llama, but not to return empty-handed, he asked for a box of .22 Interceptor rounds from Aguila. Miguel could use those both in his Ruger and the M&P15, at least for target practice, when the quality of ammunition mattered less. The cashier did not want to see his gun permit or his registration—the documents listing which types of ammunition he was allowed to purchase. She took down his name and gave him a handwritten receipt. Once we returned to the truck, Miguel said, "They should have asked me for my papers. They didn't because I acted as if I knew Marco." He wanted me to understand that in Monterrey rules did not apply evenly.

In fact, Miguel would have had no problem showing the cashier his paperwork. He had all the documents in order: printed, signed, stamped, and organized in a folder. He knew the law well, even better than the law enforcement agents from Fuerza Civil who once stopped him on the way back from his ranch. When he told them he was transporting firearms, they didn't even know what to do with that information, so he had to walk them through the steps of asking for his permit and verifying his ID. During the hunting season, the army also erected checkpoints on roads in rural areas to inspect licenses. So did the rural police, whose jurisdiction covered illegal hunting and wildlife trafficking. "They make you nervous," Miguel said about the *rurales*. "They are very strict. When they stop you, you know you'll be there for a while." But police in and around Monterrey, including Fuerza Civil, had less experience with hunters. They were trained to deal with organized crime groups and saw all armed men as potentially dangerous. Interactions with them could be tense.

Hunters like Miguel and his friends and others who hung out at Cazadores were not against law enforcement, but they thought the regulations were too stringent and found ways around the rules they didn't like. One morning in winter we had coffee with a relative of Miguel's in a room filled with taxidermied trophies from his hunting trips, including a large brown bear from Kamchatka and a tiger he killed on a private reserve in Mexico. "Ieva, every species that is not hunted will be extinct," he said, perhaps sensing my discomfort sitting at a table laid with cookies in the middle of a zoo of dead animals. Before I could ask why, he added: "Because they don't have value." Counterintuitively, putting a price on killing animals made them profitable to keep. Hunters helped save the deer population in the region, he said, but the government wasn't helping them. On the contrary. The problem, he said, was that the government didn't understand that ten firearms were not enough. "You need different firearms for various activities," he explained: A small rifle, like a .243, for coyotes or wild pigs; a 7mm Magnum or a .300 for deer; two types of .22, one for the silhouettes and one for hunting; and two shotguns, one for skeet shooting and another for geese. You also needed a .22 pistol for coup de grace, or to defend against snakes. And you needed two .380 handguns for protection, one for your home and one for the office. "But that's the bare minimum," he said. Many hunters wanted additional models of each caliber and the only way they could legally have more firearms than ten was by obtaining a collector's permit. There was further paperwork involved, but the permit was valid for life. A collector's permit even allowed civilians to own restricted firearms, as long as they removed certain components to make the guns nonoperational. Everyone knew nobody followed up to check that they didn't put those back on.

Since Miguel had over thirty guns and no collector's permit, he had to choose which ten to put on the list each year when he renewed his registration. Personnel at the registry never looked into discrepancies between the guns he entered on the form in consecutive years. Registering different firearms was not necessarily suspicious since private citizens were allowed to sell their guns and buy new ones. Although, in theory, the Secretariat of National Defense should have the records of all these transactions, they didn't bother checking them to look for violations. Gun owners speculated that the government found it more important to have the firearms registered and didn't want to do anything that would discourage people from doing that. As long as they could put the gun on the books legally, they asked no questions. That was Miguel's experience at the military base in Monterrey. Soldiers never inquired where he got the guns from. One time he witnessed how a man tried to register a .45 caliber pistol, like the Colt that Rafael was showing us at the club, and overheard soldiers tell him the gun was illegal and therefore they couldn't register it. Still, they gave the gun back to the man and he left with the outlawed weapon.

The next time I returned to Cazadores, on a grey winter afternoon, the parking lot in front of the shooting range was empty. I could barely recognize the clubhouse from what I had seen in the evenings. Just the night before dozens of people were packed inside and I had to say "perdón" and "gracias" to make my way squeezing between men's backs. It was a hunting tournament and men brought in antlers of the deer they had killed. Before vanishing in the crowd, Miguel introduced me to Tito, a taxidermist who served as the head of the jury, and I spent the evening observing how he, measuring tape in one hand and a pen in the other, inspected the antlers and filled out score sheets. The mood was festive. Fathers brought their sons. A boy not older than ten was holding a pair of smaller antlers, proud to be participating in the competition, beaming from the compliments he received. All night, I didn't see a single woman.

The next day was no different. I came to the club with the surgeon and his engineer friend. The surgeon opened the trunk and showed me a handgun he brought—"in case you wanted to do target practice," he said, but I said I didn't, so he closed the gun case and instead gave me a stack of old *Safari International* magazines he kept in the car. With the magazines in my hand, I followed the men inside the clubhouse and we joined a few socios hanging out around at a wobbly plastic table. Discussion turned to the new rules requiring gun owners to present proof of a clean criminal record when registering their firearms. Since the state of Nuevo León didn't issue such letters, the request would have to be routed through SEDENA in Mexico City. These senior club members laughed that now people their age were also being asked to prove they had completed military service. They, like many gun owners I met at the club in 2019, attributed stricter requirements to the change in government. In November 2018, General Luis Cresencio Sandoval, who had been overseeing the 4th military region, which included Nuevo León, Tamaulipas, and San Luis Potosí, was called to Mexico City to take over as the secretary of defense in López Obrador's cabinet and regional command passed to General Jens Pedro Lohmann Iturburu. Although neither this change of military leadership nor that of the country's president had anything to do with gun regulations (requirements to present criminal records when buying a firearm predated the elections), the new government was an easy scapegoat, especially since few members of the gun club were López Obrador's supporters. "It is in the interest of the government to have firearms registered, so why are they making it more complicated?" was the question I heard repeatedly. But they did not complain publicly, weary of drawing attention to themselves.

Their fears were justified, some club members told me, because of incidents like the one that became known as the .30–30 case. It involved a man named Noé Elizondo Moya who owned a shop in Guadalupe, where he sold stainless steel appliances for restaurants. Originally from

General Terán, Elizondo Moya inherited a .30–30 carbine from his grandfather. It was an old gun, a Winchester 1894 model, the most popular rifle during the Mexican Revolution.[10] In 2006, Elizondo Moya went to the ranch to get the carbine because he wanted to exchange it for vouchers through a gun buyback program. But the program had ended by the time he returned to Guadalupe, so he decided to post an ad in the newspaper, hoping someone would buy the gun. When three people who came to his home pretending to be buyers turned out to be federal agents, he was perplexed because he didn't know that selling this gun was against the law. The agents arrested Elizondo Moya and sent him to prison for owning a gun prohibited under Section C of Article 11 of the Federal Law of Firearms and Explosives, which restricted .30 caliber carbines for the exclusive use of the army, navy, and air force. His case was not the first time someone was charged for possessing this type of firearm. In 1999, a bricklayer in Hualahuises, a small town over sixty miles southeast of Monterrey, close to Nuevo León's border with Tamaulipas, tried to go hunting with a .30–30 carbine he had inherited from his grandfather and was arrested for possessing a military weapon. He stayed in Topo Chico for two years and fifty-five days, until ballistics experts determined that the caliber of the gun was a few millimeters off from 7.62 and the man was let go with a fine.[11] In another case, a rancher in Reynosa, charged with carrying a .30–30 in 2001, was sentenced to eight years, one month, and fifteen days in prison.

Elizondo Moya's case drew a lot of public attention. An expert in firearm ballistics argued that his Winchester carbine did not have the characteristics of firearms restricted for military use and instead fell under the category of guns for sports and hunting. Although Section C of Article 11 prohibited civilians from owning .30 caliber carbines, according to the expert, the designation of .30–30 as such was no longer accurate. The original firearm, the historical Winchester .30–30, had a barrel that measured .30 inches in diameter and used thirty grains of gunpowder, but the later versions of the .30–30 carbine had barrels that measured .308 inches in diameter and varied in the amount of gunpowder. "The inner diameter of the barrel measuring .308 inches is equivalent to 7.8232 millimeters, which the law does not designate as being for exclusive use of the army," the expert argued.[12] Elizondo Moya also spoke up: "There are people who have done many bad things that truly should be here (in prison), but speaking about my case, I think it is not just that I am here," he told a reporter from *El Norte*.[13] He said that the agents "set up a large operation to arrest someone who is really not worth it," when more important crimes, "like the murder of police chiefs," went unpunished. Elizondo Moya ended up spending fifty days in Topo Chico before the judge ordered his release.

Thirteen years later, gun owners in Monterrey still talked about the .30–30 case as proof that the law was absurd. An anonymous author of an opinion piece summarized what he called the "perverse" situation many regiomontanos were denouncing in private conversations at gun clubs: Elizondo Moya had been "a victim of the totally flawed federal justice system," which is "torturously persecuting innocent citizens" but is "freeing dozens of narco gunmen," who carry "extremely dangerous weapons like Uzi, AK-47 and M15."[14]

In the summer of 2019, the Secretariat of National Defense announced plans to open the country's second gun store to be located in Monterrey. During a public ceremony of laying the cornerstone of the future building inside the military zone in Apodaca, General Lohmann Iturburu said that demand for firearms had been rising in Mexico and the choice to open the store in Monterrey made sense: it was estimated that up to eighteen thousand residents of Nuevo León belonged to recreational shooting and hunting clubs and the sport was popular in neighboring Coahuila and Tamaulipas. "This will be the first step in decentralizing sales in the national territory. It's practically an experiment," the general said.[15] "Sometimes we only see guns as a symbol of violence," he noted, adding, "Shooting is also a family activity." He spoke about healthy competition. Perhaps most importantly, however, the officials expected that the second store would reduce crimes related to trafficking and unlicensed possession of firearms—if there was a place that sold guns legally, there would be fewer incentives to break the law.

The announcement received mixed reactions. "Congratulations to compañeros in Monterrey!" someone from Jalisco left a comment in the virtual discussion forum hosted by México Armado, a popular online platform dedicated to guns.[16] Someone else, also from Jalisco, whose profile picture was of a soldier in camouflage uniform with a machine gun and a necklace of ammo, expressed a similar sentiment: "Excellent news, let's hope they open one in Guadalajara soon." Others called for further decentralization with stores in Puebla, Hermosillo, Culiacán, as well as the southern part of the country. One suggested that decentralizing the sale of firearms would prove lucrative for SEDENA and agreed with the general about new stores reducing "coyotaje." But a couple of people who commented on the site were more skeptical. One wrote:

"With this, the sales of legal guns will increase. Let's hope that the inventory of brands and models also increases." A byline below his comment stated: "Only an authoritarian government denies legal carry of firearms."

Gun owners in Monterrey were reluctant to celebrate the news. "We are nervous," Miguel told me when I asked him about the new gun store. He feared he would not be able to register firearms he bought on the black market because doing paperwork for a gun not purchased from the army store would begin to raise suspicion. It was one thing with ammo—they didn't have to register cartridges, which made it reasonable to look for other than legal ways to procure them: they could reload or they could buy them in Texas, placing orders via the WhatsApp group or stocking up themselves when they made trips across the border. Although bringing any kind of ammunition into Mexico was prohibited, once they were here, they passed checkpoint inspections by transporting cartridges of outlawed calibers in boxes of permitted ammo, hiding .45s under a layer of .22s, for example. They had perfected the ways to dodge law enforcement. With the army store in town, they'd have to adjust their tactics.

"If you have a 9mm, I'd advise you to bury it in your backyard," a relative told Miguel.

Caged

Monterrey, Nuevo León

"She was furious, aggressive," Consuelo said, recalling the teenage girl she saw in the grainy video one day when she was visiting the youth detention facility. "She looked like she was about to have a panic attack." About half a dozen custodians on duty were too busy keeping their eyes on the monitor connected to the surveillance camera to even care that the boys upstairs were smoking weed. All of them were watching this one girl, alone in her cell. Nobody told Consuelo how she ended up in detention. But Consuelo had been working with incarcerated people long enough to understand that the boundary between perpetrator and victim of violence was fluid, that one could be both, that in fact this was often the case. She knew that all the girls she was meeting in the facility had been or would be abused, often raped, by the uniformed personnel representing the state and the rule of law. The question was not if, but rather when and how often.

That Mexican security forces engaged in torture was no secret. The police and military personnel habitually detained individuals without arrest warrants, then took them to military bases or illegal detention sites and kept them there, for hours or even days, denying them access to attorneys, trying to extract information and obtain confessions, before they would hand them over to civilian prosecutors.[1] An Amnesty International study carried out in 2014 found Mexico to be among the five countries in the world where torture by state institutions was most systematic and widespread.[2] With the government's fight against organized crime heavily militarized, it was getting worse. Mexico's National Human Rights Commission reported that between 2006 and 2012 there was a significant increase in practices of torture and cruel, inhuman, or degrading treatment.[3] A similar conclusion was made by Amnesty International, which claimed that in the span of a decade the number of complaints of torture and ill-treatment in Mexico rose 600 percent.[4] More than sixty-four thousand people incarcerated in municipal, state, and federal prisons all over the country participated in the National Survey of Detained Persons in 2016, and the results were alarming: 76 percent reported experiencing psychological violence; 64 percent said they were subjected to physical violence during arrest; 59 percent were hit or kicked; 49 percent were held in isolation; 46 percent were undressed; 40 percent were tied up; 39 percent were blindfolded; 36 percent were choked, smothered, or held underwater; 19 percent received electrical shocks; 6.5 percent reported burns; and 4.5 percent experienced sexual abuse.[5] Studies found that almost three-quarters of women who were imprisoned in Mexico were subjected to sexual violence during arrests or interrogations.[6] When a delegation of the United Nations Subcommittee on Prevention of Torture and Other Cruel, Inhuman, or Degrading Treatment or Punishment visited Mexico in 2008, several prison wardens admitted to them that many women had arrived at their facilities "with evidence of numerous blows and visible injuries on various parts of their bodies."[7]

Samara could check off a number of boxes on those lists. "Soldiers raped me, they hung me from my feet. They pulled my nails. They pulled out one tooth. They cut my hair and burnt it with gasoline," she said. Before bringing her in, they drove her around the city asking to identify locations, to give up names. But she refused to turn anyone in. When they finally took her to the juvenile detention center, the striped blouse she was wearing did little to cover up the wounds on her body. "I came to the juvie bleeding," she told me. In the photo I found in the news report about her arrest, Samara's face was bruised, black circles were around her eyes, her mascara was smudged, and her lush black hair was reduced to clumps.

Capture had been outside of her imagination. Samara knew she could die. As a soldier in the war between the Zetas and their rivals, and between all of them—multiple armed groups wrapped under the label of organized crime—and the Mexican government, supported by military aid from the United States, death was within the realm of possibility, even a likelihood. Her group took precautions. As the leader of a cell, Samara was a potential target, so she was rarely left alone. All day she rode in the truck with her heavily armed crew. When she needed to use a restroom, they waited outside. When she stepped into a store to buy clothes, her escorts would stay at the door. Only at night would she let them go. "I sent them away—*váyanse!*—and walked, so nobody would know where I stayed," she recalled. "I didn't trust anyone." Samara moved from San Nicolás to Escobedo to Apodaca to the center of Monterrey. "I had to live *brincando*," she said, bouncing around safe houses. Alone, she would try to get some sleep, but that was not a luxury she enjoyed every night.

This had been her routine until the day her crew ran into a group of soldiers and Samara got injured in the gunfight. Her arm hurt from a bullet wound, but worse was her hip. She had been standing behind the Barrett, when their truck crashed, and upon impact she dislocated her leg. The doctor at the university hospital realigned the bones—pulled and twisted her leg "like you do to a doll," she described to me—and told her that she would need months to heal. Samara was taken to her aunt's house. The same aunt who had once told Samara that she owed the woman her life for "not throwing her out in the trash when she was little." Samara had no other choice but to stay there while she recovered. At first, she lay in bed, unable to sit, and had to bathe standing in the tub. Patience had never been her virtue, so as soon as she could, Samara started walking around the house leaning on a stick. Each day she went a little farther, back and forth between her bedroom and the kitchen. A couple of weeks went by like that until she decided it was time. "When my aunt left, I got out through the window," she said. Locked doors didn't stop her.

Samara went straight to her comandante. Surprised to see her, he said that she didn't owe them anything anymore, that she was free to go and do what she liked with her life. The comandante even suggested paying her aunt for taking care of Samara. It was her chance to leave the Zetas. But Samara was resolute. "You think that I really want 120,000 pesos to stay with her and be happy? I want my job, I want my soldiers, I want my gear, I want my truck," she said. "Are you sure?" the comandante asked, not yet convinced. "Yes," she said. "Believe me, I'm sure. I belong more to this world than to the other. I have nobody," she said, making it clear that she wanted him to let her back in. The Zetas were more than family to her. "They protected me, they gave me what my family had never given me," she said. She insisted until the comandante gave in.

Later that summer, not long after her return to work, Samara was with her crew when they got word that the man they had been looking for was spotted at a car wash in San Nicolás. They headed there right away and saw that he was not alone. Worse still, the second man was a police lieutenant. Instead of backing off, they picked them both up and took them to a baseball field nearby. While they stayed there, waiting for the comandante to come and take over the captured men, a witness who saw the abduction at the car wash alerted the security forces. The military launched a rapid rescue operation, inundating the neighborhood with soldiers and sending a helicopter for backup. Samara's crew fought back, but they were outnumbered. The soldiers found the police lieutenant alive, albeit with signs of torture. They took Samara alive too.

Charges against her included possession and the carrying of firearms reserved for military use, engagement in organized crime, kidnapping of a police officer, and first-degree murder. "If a soldier said that she had killed and kidnapped and carried ten firearms and had ten trucks, the judge believed him," Samara said. "*Pues*, maybe it was true," she told me, "But at that moment they didn't catch me with anything else but the guns." Guns were enough though: their physical presence at the scene was material evidence of criminal activity that was irrefutable, with penalties for possessing them clearly outlined in the law. The other charges—engaging in organized crime and committing murder—required opening an investigation. But deaths of people associated with the Zetas or other groups were the government's last priority. In the country where impunity for murder was over 90 percent, such cases were on the bottom of the pile. Many never even made it to the paperwork stage. There were easier and faster and often illegal ways to lock up suspects the soldiers brought in. One of them involved coerced confessions.[8] Samara said the soldiers made her sign one. When they brought her to the judge, all beaten up, there was no more need for a trial. The judge gave her three years.[9] The officer who reviewed and deleted the photos on her cell phone as he checked the fifteen-year-old girl into juvie said she did not deserve to live.

The Detention and Reintegration Center for Young Offenders, or CIAAI for its Spanish initials, was a two-story olive-green building located on the six-lane Avenida Constituyentes in Monterrey.[10] Pegged to the juvenile court, the site was formally for pretrial detention. Kids stayed there while they waited for the judge to decide whether what they had done qualified as a minor offense and they could be sent home on supervised release or whether it was grave enough to warrant convicting and confining them, in which case they would be transferred to another facility in Escobedo to complete their sentence. That was the system for the boys. All girls, regardless of the severity of their crimes and whether they had been sentenced or still awaiting trial, stayed at CIAAI. In the past, they used to live in a separate building, with dormitories on ground floor and rooms for workshops on the second. But in 2006, when the Mexican juvenile justice system was at last formally aligned with the international conventions protecting the rights of the child, many girls and young women who had been confined for low-level offenses were released and the few who remained fit into two rooms with a shared bathroom located on the first floor of the main building.[11]

The living conditions inside the facility were abysmal. Members of the delegation from the UN Subcommittee on Prevention of Torture were horrified by what they saw and heard when they visited the CIAAI in 2008:

> The delegation can only rate the treatment received by minors in this facility as cruel, inhuman or degrading. They were locked into cage-like enclosures all day, with no opportunity to engage in any kind of physical, educational or cultural activity. They were allowed out for only 15 minutes a day and they had no programme of activities. The guards took away the mattresses at 5 a.m. and they were left without even a place to sit. They had no chairs or other furniture and no libraries or books. They could receive visits from their families for an hour and a half per week. While the conditions in the facility left a strong impression on the members of the delegation, their interviews with the inmates had an even greater impact. These young people told the delegation that the guards constantly reminded them of the offences or infractions for which they had been sent to the centre and that they were threatened daily. They also said that there were daily fights between inmates and some said that they lived in constant fear and that they were sometimes beaten, not only by the guards but also by other inmates, often for reasons of discrimination. The delegation was informed that one young man had committed suicide at the centre.[12]

The report noted a complaint by one young woman who suffered a miscarriage, followed by a serious infection, because the custodians ignored her pleas to take her to the hospital. Hers was just one story. "The delegation members were truly disturbed by what they heard from all the young people interviewed at this facility. The delegation was told that kids were not allowed to keep any personal belongings, not even pictures of their families. One of the boys recounted how the guards had taken away a photo he had of his mother."

The Mexican government was shamed into action. The following year, in May 2009, a new director took over the CIAAI. Víctor Castelán Alonso was a criminologist by training and had founded the detoxification clinic at the prison in Apodaca, the first in the nation focused on helping incarcerated people experiencing addiction. He had big plans for the juvenile detention center: create a more comprehensive treatment program, invite nongovernmental organizations to occupy youth during afternoon hours, provide more extensive vocational programs, and hire psychologists who were young and could better relate with the boys and girls they counseled. But he had barely started in his new job when the parameters of his work radically changed.

For several years, the detention and reintegration center in Monterrey had only been housing youth who had committed *delitos de fuero común*—crimes that fell under the jurisdiction of the state of Nuevo León, such as robbery or homicide. Since the judge allowed most kids to complete their sentences for low-level offenses at home, there weren't that many of them living in the facility. Only several dozen boys and four girls stayed in the CIAAI in 2009, the more serious cases. Youths charged with federal crimes, like *narcomenudeo* (drug trade) or violation of federal firearms law, fell outside the scope of state courts and, after being held for thirty-six to forty-eight hours, they would be released. But in December 2010, the federal authorities and the state made a deal, which gave power to the courts of Nuevo León to oversee all juvenile captives. This happened at a time when the Mexican government's fervent pursuit of organized crime groups was at its peak and the numbers of captured youth soon skyrocketed.

Kids were disposable like "cannonball meat," the director of CIAAI said about boys and girls in the war between the Zetas, the CDG, and the Mexican security forces. Over a period of about a year, the population of incarcerated youth in the two facilities in Nuevo León grew from sixty to four hundred. The building in Monterrey, which was suitable for about eighty boys and fewer than ten girls, crammed in more than three times that many teenagers. "The infrastructure wasn't prepared for them," Castelán said, looking back. The numbers weren't the only issue. The profile of the detainees had changed as well. Kids were locked up together regardless of whether they were charged with stealing a cell phone or throwing a grenade at a police station. Most new inmates were members of organized crime groups that were fighting with each other. "It was a time bomb," Castelán said.

Tensions at the juvenile detention center had been simmering for years, but disagreements, even when they turned into brawls, were usually over minor things. One time, what began as a fight over socks escalated when the custodians intervened to break it up: locked in their cells, the boys started launching pieces of concrete through the windows above a busy street, which prompted the police to temporarily close Avenida Constituyentes to traffic.[13] Another time, when custodial staff inspecting the cells found and confiscated some prohibited items—these were usually cell phones or battery chargers, but sometimes larger objects like floor fans and TVs—the boys set their mattresses on fire to protest.[14] There were escape attempts and successful escapes, sometimes with the help from the staff. The script for subduing rebellious youth was usually the same: evacuating the personnel, calling in police forces to surround the perimeter of the facility, sending in an antiriot unit, and eventually restraining those who had been causing trouble. But as 2010 folded into 2011, disturbances that used to make the news became routine. When incarcerated kids heard that members of organized crime groups would be transferred to their facility, they shouted slogans and hung banners on the buildings that said: "We don't want the Z."[15] But it was not up to them to decide.

With hundreds of new detainees in state custody, the director had to revamp the old system for classifying and separating them. Youths were still split into three age groups, but also divided by the level of danger they posed to others and by their affiliation with organized crime. In Escobedo, boys from the Zetas and those from the CDG were living in two separate buildings. In Monterrey, close to 90 percent of the youth belonged to the Zetas, so they didn't have to worry about isolating one group from the other. But they had plenty of other troubles. Unlike in an adult prison, the staff at the juvenile detention center didn't carry firearms, only tear gas and clubs. The boys broke ceramic tiles lining the bathrooms and fashioned weapons as sharp as knives, threatening each other and making the custodians—sometimes as few as six of them overseeing twenty or thirty times as many youths—too fearful to intervene. The director's Nextel phone kept getting hacked and he and his staff glanced warily at the trucks parked in front of the main entrance of the CIAAI, the "outside support" for the associates of the Zetas they held inside. Some of the corrections officers themselves were on double payroll, earning salaries from the government and taking bribes from organized crime groups. The director installed closed-circuit security cameras in the facility and replaced the hollow core wood doors serving as the main entrance to the center with reinforced steel that could withstand a bazooka attack. "It was exhausting," Castelán said, "a very difficult period."

Samara was locked up in a cell on the first floor with other girls from the Zetas, in a room measuring approximately thirteen by nineteen feet, with two bunk beds, and a wooden icon of Virgen de Guadalupe mounted on a pale pink wall. The windows were painted over in layers of black and dark green, not letting sunlight or fresh air seep through. Next to the girls' quarters were several individual cells where the director placed youth who were at the greatest risk: usually transgender and nonbinary kids or sometimes boys who were slight for their age and were subjected to bullying and abuse. The rest of the boys lived upstairs. Cage-like chain-link fences that had shocked the UN Subcommittee on Prevention of Torture had been removed and now their cells were separated by gridded Plexiglas walls. "When the boys came down to eat or wash their clothes, the girls had to stay locked in their rooms, not allowed to leave for anything, not even to use a toilet until all the boys had returned to their quarters," Samara recalled. Farther down the corridor, with all white tile and off-white walls, there was a small multipurpose room, to be used in better times for various vocational activities; the dining hall, where they celebrated mass; and the kitchen. In front of the kitchen, there was a room designated for schoolwork and another for doing laundry. Adjacent to it was a tiny custodial closet. "We called it *un cuarto de castigo*," Samara said. "That's where they punished you. It was super-hot because it was next to the laundry room with gigantic dryers."

Not long after her arrival at the CIAAI, the comandante told Samara that she had to carry on with her duties. She was beginning to like it inside. "I could sleep in my own bed every night, I could take a shower every day," she recalled. "Wow! I want to stay here for many years!" she said, remembering those early days. But one of the custodians brought her a cell phone and the voice on the other end summoned her back to work. The comandante asked her what she needed for protection, how much drugs they could send her to distribute inside. "It's not a question. You decided to stay, so you follow orders," he told her. Since Samara had kept silent and didn't give anyone up during interrogations, her loyalty earned her trust and status in the organization. But it also meant she had to continue what she did before she was caught.

"She was very strong, had a lot of power," the director said, remembering Samara back then. "She wanted control inside." Many custodians were afraid of her because they knew the kind of people Samara associated with on the outside. She maintained contacts with the police in San Nicolás and with members of the Zetas locked up in Topo Chico. When they started tracing calls between the prison and the juvenile detention center, special teams from the Fuerza Civil came to search Samara's room for cell phones. She always had one or two and replaced them as soon as the police left. They came again, swept the cell again, confiscated what they could find. It made no difference.

During that time, due to overcrowding and chaos at the facility, all programs were cut back, and only youths who could walk around the facility without stirring up trouble were able to continue limited activities.[16] Samara was not among them. "She fought with everyone," the director said, and she "started threatening and intimidating those around her as soon as she left her cell." He did not allow her to go outside to the small courtyard where more compliant kids could play ball or run loops. Trying to ease tensions, he decided to move several dozen girls charged with minor offenses to another building, leaving Samara in a cell of her own. But even that didn't calm her down, at least not at first. Samara started pounding on the sheetrock door of her cell and kept at it for hours. The door had a single latch, so the staff reinforced it. They watched her through the surveillance monitors in the director's office, waiting for her to quit fighting. "She became a myth," Consuelo said, recalling those months when Samara would not yet speak to her.

While confined at the CIAAI, young people were not supposed to be idle: they were expected to do schoolwork, play sports, learn practical skills that prepared them for the job market. A disciplinary team should have been monitoring their progress and sending monthly reports to the judge. But reality didn't live up to what was on paper. With the facility severely overcrowded, individual psychotherapy sessions were halted, nongovernmental organizations suspended their visits, and vocational training was interrupted. A handful of attorneys representing the youths could not keep up with hundreds of cases, losing track of who had completed their goals and qualified for privileges, such as more time outdoors or an earlier release.

"Nobody was paying attention to me," Samara said. As weeks went by, she became depressed. She stopped relentlessly banging on the door of her cell and was spending her days lying on the bed, gloomy, alternating between sleeping and crying. With a hip still healing after the crash, she needed regular exercise, but she was locked up in her cell all day and her leg pain got worse. The doctor who worked at the CIAAI noticed her deteriorating condition and told the director that he had to allow Samara take walks in the yard. He acquiesced. When they finally let Samara outside, she followed all the rules. She didn't argue with the custodians and didn't fight with other girls. "When I saw the sun, I ran. I ran around the field, I did maybe twenty laps," she recalled. For the first time in many weeks she felt happy. From then on, the director permitted Samara to go outside for thirty minutes to exercise. It wasn't much, but it was something.

The Magistrate of the Superior Court of Justice reduced Samara's sentence for the kidnapping of the police officer to two years, and in the early summer of 2013 the judge let her go. "They had already been waiting for me," she said about her old crew. Back in her neighborhood, she gathered up a team of youths and picked up where she had left off. But eight weeks later Samara was captured again. The police of San Nicolás arrested her together with five others in a car with an AK-47 and thousands of pesos in cash. She said she wanted to be caught, that she had made a deal to give herself up. When she was brought to the judge, he charged her with engagement in organized crime and with an additional count of homicide.

But her second time at the CIAAI was different. "That's where I started recovering," Samara said. The facility was less crowded by then, a semblance of order had been restored inside, and Samara moved into the girls' building, to a cell with four bunk beds. She still fought with everyone over minor things—food, toothpaste, toilet paper, sanitary napkins. "I was very *peleonera*," she admitted. Having been inside before, she also had experience and little patience with those who were new. "Girls were very emotional when they came. They arrived screaming, and my job was to discipline them," Samara said. She slapped them on the face and, shocked more than hurt, they cooled off. One time, however, Samara went beyond her usual means and beat a girl up. She was in the bathroom when she overheard someone shout "Calm down! Calm down!" and, when she walked to the hallway and saw that a new girl was hitting an elderly custodian, Samara grabbed the girl and dragged her down to the floor. "Many custodians are old," she explained. "That woman was over seventy, she was tiny, and they sent her alone among people who had committed crimes, who were from dysfunctional families and didn't mind beating their own fathers and mothers." Samara kept punching and slapping the girl until other custodians pulled her away. They cuffed Samara and locked her up as punishment. But she didn't mind. When she spoke about the incident years later, she laughed.

Though still impulsive, Samara was set on a new path. "I asked myself: If I don't take care of myself, then who will?" When the comandante asked her again whether she wanted to work with them, she finally said no. "Ok, if you don't mess with us, we'll not mess with you," he told her. Together with another girl in her cell, Samara began taking high school classes. "She was very smart, much more advanced than the others," Consuelo recalled. By then, Samara had gotten to know Consuelo and became involved in the activities Promoción de Paz provided to the incarcerated youth. A young female psychologist visited her several times a week and brought her photocopied materials to read. Samara annotated the Mexican constitution. She learned about the rights of juvenile detainees—her rights—and complained when what they were offered fell short of what the law had promised them. She became versed in the law.

Her routine had never been so regimented: rising at five o'clock to take a shower, followed by breakfast and cleaning up, then spending the rest of the day completing various tasks and assignments—the goals that juvenile detainees had to accomplish, designed to lead them toward "social reintegration." Besides meeting with psychologists and social workers, they listened to motivational talks by religious groups and nongovernmental organizations. The girls were also offered various craft lessons, learning knitting and embroidery. Samara started making bags and shoes that the woman who taught them sold outside and she used her earnings to buy toiletries. There were cooking classes and beautician and secretary courses. During their downtime, the girls watched Mexican music programs on TV—neither news nor telenovelas were allowed. On weekend afternoons they had family visits. "My aunt visited me nearly every Sunday," she said. Her grandmother came too. But not her parents, who remained in Texas.

By the time she was up for release, Samara had finished high school and multiple vocational training programs, collecting a stack of certificates to prove her knowledge and her skills. "I believe it served me to be there," she told me years later, reflecting on this period of her life. "Otherwise, I would have continued with my *pendejadas*." But she didn't hang her diplomas and the certificates she earned on the walls. She didn't want to show them to anyone. "They all have the name and the stamp of the CIAAI," she said. She wanted a clean start. "If I don't do this for myself, nobody will do it for me."

When I asked her how, she said, "I will find a way."

Homefront

Phoenix, Arizona

The trail of evidence that would eventually lead them to Hugo began on I-10 near Casa Grande when the highway patrol pulled over a green Ford Expedition.[1] It was January 5, 2016, and Alex and Jackson were in Nogales to oversee another seizure for a different case they were working on when earlier that afternoon they got a tip from a gun store up in Phoenix about a large purchase of ammunition. Jackson then called a sergeant he knew at the Department of Public Safety and asked him to push a notification to all units in the corridor between Phoenix and Tucson to be on the lookout for the SUV with such-and-such plate numbers. About an hour later, his phone rang—officers stopped the wanted vehicle for a traffic violation: the driver, Jazmin, had a suspended license. She also turned out to be someone the agents already knew about—they had a record of her behind the wheel of another car they connected to the smuggling operation. When the police pulled her over, officers noted that the rear of the SUV was almost scraping the surface of the road, its taillights pointing down. The heavy cargo, which weighed about half a ton—like a grand piano—were twenty-six thousand rounds of ammunition.

The agents left Nogales and headed north to Casa Grande to talk to Jazmin. At first, she told them that she was a member of a shooting club. But when Alex asked her what guns she liked to shoot, she couldn't answer. Most of the ammunition she carried—nineteen thousand rounds—were 7.62 × 39mm; the rest were .223, .38 Super, 9mm, and

.45, all calibers for guns the ATF called "the weapons of choice" for organized crime groups in Mexico. But Jazmin had no clue about which weapons used what ammunition. The agents could see that she knew nothing about guns. After some more questioning, Jazmin finally admitted she got the ammunition for her boyfriend, who lived in Mexico. She said he gave her the money. She also said this was not the only time she had done it. Later, when the agents visited UN Ammo, the store where Jazmin bought the rounds, and asked to see sales receipts, they learned that in the span of three weeks, between December 15, 2015, and January 5, 2016, Jazmin spent $32,000 in cash for 94,500 rounds of ammunition, plus 100 magazines for AK and M4 rifles.

The thing about guns is that they last a long time. An AK-47 will serve for years, likely decades.[2] Unless their rifles are seized by the Mexican military, organized crime groups in Mexico did not need to routinely smuggle replacements. But they did need ammunition, tons of it, and UN Ammo was the place to go. Located at a strip mall on West Glendale Avenue in Phoenix, with a green army jeep parked in front and a picture of Obama with the caption "Greatest gun salesman of the year" on the counter inside, it specialized in bulk sales: piles of large metal bins and wood and cardboard boxes full of cartridges crowded the floor. Gun owners flocked to this place to purchase thousands of rounds at a time for less than they would have to pay at Cabela's or other sporting goods stores. UN Ammo was known for having a large stock of 7.62 cartridges, mostly from Wolf, which imported them from factories in Russia. But they also sold one-hundred-round drums for AR-15 rifles, specialized subsonic .308 Winchester rounds, tracers, and other less usual items. Alex and Jackson began keeping an eye on the store, which seemed to be a major source for the group to get bulk ammunition, and on January 7, only two days after Jazmin's arrest, they received another tip about another woman making a large purchase there. This time they came up with a plan, which, depending on who is telling the story, would be remembered as operation "Box of Rocks" or operation "Rock'N'Roll."

By then the agents were familiar with the cellular structure of the organization: the separation between people who handled the money from those who did the buying from those who transported the goods down to Nogales from those who took them across the border. Not everyone knew each other, which worked in their favor: when someone got arrested, like Darius or Ricky, they could be replaced without the need to rearrange the whole structure. With help from a confidential source in the group, Alex and Jackson were able to insert an undercover agent into this sequence. The agent picked up the ten thousand rounds from the store in Phoenix, where the woman had paid for them, and was to get $400 for delivering it to whoever was supposed to cross it over the border. Once he loaded the ammo into his car, the undercover agent hit I-10, but instead of going straight to Nogales, he got off the highway in Tucson and headed to the ATF office, where Alex and Jackson had been waiting for him.

Their investigation entering its third month, the floor of the ATF evidence vault, where they kept the guns and ammo they were seizing, had begun to sag. They preferred the ATF vault to the one at CBP facilities in Nogales because CBP didn't treat the items they confiscated as evidence. At ATF, each gun was test-fired and the agents entered ballistic imaging results into an integrated database, so that investigators could look for correlations between ballistic evidence recovered from various crime scenes. After that, weapons were tagged and securely stored in the vault, where the agents could easily access them when they needed to bring evidence to the courthouse. By the time this case went to trial, they would have 32 rifles, including a .50 caliber Barrett, and 36,380 rounds of ammunition stored there. Fearing the vault floor would collapse on the offices downstairs, one day the agents brought a U-Haul truck and moved some of the evidence boxes to another location.

That night in early January, even though Jackson and Alex planned to keep surveillance on the undercover agent taking the ammunition to Nogales and were prepared to arrest the person who would come pick it up, they knew things could go wrong. Still reeling from what happened with the guns that Ramiro bought—the guns that his brother Kevin hid and then handed over to the guys from Mexico—they didn't want to risk losing the ammo. The undercover agent got to Tucson a little after ten p.m. and he had to be down in Nogales before sunrise. They had to work fast. First, they unloaded the boxes from the undercover agent's car and emptied them of ammunition, which they put into grey plastic containers and carried to the evidence vault. "Should something catastrophic happen and they take off and get away with those boxes, they wouldn't be getting away with any ammunition," Jackson would later testify about why they decided to swap the rounds with something else—something that "looks and feels and sounds like ammunition."

Had someone accidentally found themselves in the large parking lot between a drive-through Walgreens and a red-brick building with external staircases leading to the second floor that ATF shared with the offices of the Department of Economic Security, they would have witnessed an unusual scene: a handful of men frantically shoveling landscaping rocks and pouring them into empty cardboard boxes. But nobody had any business being there late at night: all the offices and even the Walgreens were closed at that hour. Once the agents filled a few boxes, they weighed them on the scale: not heavy enough. Someone suggested they could use plate weights and they sent him home to bring what he had in his gym. They began calling whoever else they could think of. "We were waking people up in the middle of the night asking if they had any plate weights we could use, preferably 10 pounders," Jackson recalled. When they got the weights, they mixed them with the rocks until they arrived at the right ratio of metal to stone. Each of the ten cardboard boxes now weighed like a thousand rounds of ammunition—thirty-seven pounds, "almost to the ounce"—and, when they shook the boxes, it sounded like there were cartridges inside. For the final touch, they arranged some empty black Wolf WPA ammo boxes on top, so that if the buyer cut the tape to inspect the contents, they would be reassured. They threw a tracking device into one of the boxes and then loaded them all into the undercover agent's car.

With the boxes full of sham ammo in the trunk, the undercover agent proceeded south on empty I-19. He had to be in Nogales by 5:30 a.m. and wait for further instructions. Once there, he was told to go to the parking lot in front of Safeway and the Big Five off West Mariposa Road, where he would be meeting with a person in a white Ford Focus. Alex and Jackson managed to get there ahead of their undercover colleague and set everything up. They were ready. Or so they thought.

At that early hour on a winter morning, the valley was cloaked in darkness and what began as a cold drizzle turned into steady rain drumming on the roof of the car the two were waiting in, engines off, in the parking lot on the opposite side of the street. The surveillance camera on a truck the team had parked up on the hill, in front of the Santa Cruz County complex, was suddenly no more use. Even when the rain relented, they couldn't see a thing through the mist that swallowed the world around them. "The weather was so bad that our great plan about how we're gonna keep an eye on everything was out the window," Jackson told me later.

They had been waiting for less than an hour when a white Ford Focus arrived at the parking lot in front of Safeway. Jackson looked up at the border crossing records and saw that the driver who just entered the United States from Mexico in that car was a seventeen-year-old kid they knew as Junior. Listening in to their conversation, Alex and Jackson heard Junior tell the undercover agent he didn't have the $400 he had been promised for transporting the ammunition to Nogales. Then the two of them, each in their own car, drove half a mile east on Mariposa Road and parked at Motel 6. The undercover agent stayed behind the wheel and watched as Junior, in a red Chicago Bulls cap and a white T-shirt poorly suited for just-above-freezing temperature, stepped out into the chilly rain and hurried inside. A few minutes passed before he emerged through the door carrying two black duffel bags. Somebody inside the motel told Junior that the port was "hot"—there were inspectors on outbound lanes—so he couldn't go through right away. He also still didn't have the payment for the undercover agent because the "money guy" didn't show up. Junior improvised. He collected all the cash he had on him to give to the agent and they agreed to sort out the rest later. Worried about the cardboard boxes getting soaked in the rain and revealing their contents, the agent rushed Junior as they carried them over to the Ford Focus. They placed the boxes next to the duffel bags Junior had brought from the motel and the undercover agent saw what he had feared: the bags were full of guns.

The situation immediately changed. Jackson and Alex started the day being in control. They had taken all the safety precautions. They thought they hadn't left anything to chance. And now there was this teenage boy with two bags of guns in his car and no plan. Junior seemed to be unsure what to do and began driving erratically around Nogales. He was warned not to cross into Mexico, but he didn't know where else to go. When he turned south, the agents contacted inspectors at the port of entry and told them to be ready to stop the vehicle if it entered an outbound lane. But Junior didn't go for the border. He made an unexpected turn and pulled up in front of an apartment complex on Elm Street, then jumped out of the car and ran inside before the police officers arrived on scene. Nobody saw which apartment he had gone into, but this was when the foul weather finally helped them: All the officers had to do was follow the muddy footprints leading from the car to the door. They arrested Junior—as a minor he was prohibited from possessing assault rifles—and seized the bags with weapons from the trunk of his car. When the police called out the address of the residence over the radio, Alex and Jackson recognized it: Jazmin—the woman they questioned just a couple of days earlier, the one who was driving the SUV with the load so heavy that the back of the car was nearly touching the road—used to live in the same building, a few doors down from the apartment where they caught up with Junior.

The ten rifles in the duffel bags were all AK-47s. Alex submitted trace requests, but it turned out that many of the guns had been sold a long time ago. Only two had a short time-to-crime. "Anytime we can get . . . the time to crime of less than a year, we consider that a very good and active lead," Jackson will later explain. Longer than that, and it is more difficult to find the person who bought the gun from the licensed dealer: people move, change addresses, and, as years go by, paper records get damaged or lost. That was the case with some of the AKs they seized from Junior. One of them was sold more than twenty years ago and the dealer told the ATF they no longer had records from that period. But at least there were two good leads: an Egyptian Maadi AK-47 and a RAS47 model made by Century Arms in the United States.

Alex and Jackson went to interview the men whose names were on the 4473 forms as the last recorded owners of those rifles. The men they met had a lot in common: Both had served eight years in the military; both owned multiple firearms and had collections of various AK models; both belonged to Facebook groups where gun enthusiasts bought and exchanged weapons. And both told the agents they sold the AKs to a man whom one knew as "Hugh" and the other as "Hugo." What Hugh was doing "was unusual," one of them later said in court: he was looking to buy multiple rifles, in cash, and would comment on any post by group members willing to sell their AK-47s within a month. The one who sold Hugo the Maadi showed the agents a photo that Hugo sent him of six AK-47 type firearms he had propped up on a couch. Several of them had very distinct characteristics and the agents recognized they were some of the same rifles they seized from Junior in Nogales. This Hugh, or Hugo, became a person of interest.

When he opened the door and saw plainclothesmen with neck badges who introduced themselves as federal agents, Hugo immediately told them he was armed. He was not used to people coming to his house unannounced and had his guard up, a habit from his days in the army. "So are we," Alex said. The agents carried their guns in holsters, so that everyone could see. "Please don't shoot us," Jackson added in a tone that lightened up the mood. He asked Hugo to remove his weapon and Hugo told the agents that his gun was at his waistband. With their approval, he slowly reached for the pistol and placed it on a table in the hallway. Then Hugo invited them inside and offered them to sit down in the kitchen. Jackson could see Hugo's wife and son watching TV in the adjoining living room.

The conversation drifted to the military. Jackson asked Hugo where he deployed to and why he got out—stuff former soldiers talk about when they meet as strangers and learn they have something fundamental in common. They also talked about their dogs: both had pit bulls. Hugo suggested showing the agents his dogs and, when Jackson nodded, he stood up and opened the blinds covering the door to the backyard, where the pits were lounging in mild winter sun. Except for a few nods here and there, Alex stayed out of this chitchat about dogs and deployments, waiting for his partner to finish small talk so they could ask Hugo about the rifles.

That morning on February 4, 2016, neither of them knew much more about the man sitting across the table from them, except that he had military background and that he was into guns and apparently dogs too. The rest of his story they would hear later, some of it only in court.

Hugo was born in Torreón, a city in Coahuila about two hundred miles west of Monterrey, and was six when his family left Mexico for the United States. His parents settled down in Phoenix and, since Hugo didn't speak much English, he was put into an ESL program at his elementary school. By junior high, he had adjusted to life in the new country. He liked American sports and played football and basketball. He also took part in the naval junior ROTC program, which was where he first learned about guns. Cadets drilled and marched with demilitarized M1 Garands, their barrels welded to the receiver so they could not fire. Despite this exposure, military service was not on his mind back then. Hugo wanted to go to college and work for a law enforcement agency, perhaps join the Border Patrol. But then, seventeen years old, he became a father and his priorities changed. He had to find work to support his family. With a new permanent resident card, he got a job at a grocery store and a second at a mechanic's shop. When he could think about school again, a few years later, he enrolled in Phoenix College and began taking courses toward a criminal justice degree.

Then, on what in Arizona was still May 1, 2011, the Navy Seals found and killed Osama bin Laden. The news from Abbottabad left a deep impression on Hugo, and, after talking it over with his girlfriend, he became determined to join the "war on terrorism." He drove to a recruitment center the next day, trying the Marines first, but they told him he would have to remove the large tattoo of his children's names that covered his forearm. The Army, which he visited next, signed some waivers and let him keep the tattoo.

The following year Hugo joined a scout platoon, completed a sixteen-week training in Fort Benning, Georgia, and was sent to Fort Riley, Kansas. After more trainings and certifications, ten days after his third son was born, his unit was deployed to Djibouti, a small country tucked between Somalia, Ethiopia, and Eritrea, and the site of the only permanent US military base in Africa: Camp Lemonnier. The task of US forces in the Horn of Africa, operating under the United States Africa Command, was counterterrorism. "Our sole mission was to help find this guy," Hugo said, about his time there. He didn't specify which rebel leader they were after, only that this warlord recruited child soldiers, or, as Hugo put it, was "creating a kids military."[3]

Before deployment, like many guys in his platoon, Hugo visited the gun stores conveniently located a block or two away from their base in Kansas to buy accessories for his standard issue rifle, an M4, investing in advanced telescopic sights. On weekends, the scouts and the snipers from the base would get together and drive to a mountain range for target practice. Hugo took his M4 to Djibouti, but during his deployment in Africa, he also learned to operate the .50 caliber machine gun— Ma Deuce, as the soldiers called the old-style Browning M2 installed on the Humvee they drove whenever they left the base. The scout group was attached to the sniper unit, and Hugo soon became familiar with their weaponry too, including the Barrett. He liked it so much that when he returned home six months later, he decided to try out for the special forces, hoping to become a sniper.

It seemed like he had found his calling. The military career suited him, and his wife supported his choice. But about a week before Hugo was scheduled to go through the arduous three-week selection process, he went for a run and stepped into a pothole, tearing a ligament in his knee. The doctor told him that the injury was serious and that he would no longer be able to do a lot of the things he once did or wanted to do in the military. His hopes of joining the special forces shattered, Hugo took a medical discharge, and in May 2015 the family packed up and moved back to Phoenix. Although he was receiving disability benefits, it was not enough for them to live on and soon bills started piling up: security deposit and the first month's rent on their home, utility activation fee, medical insurance for his three children who were no longer covered under his military plan. Hugo took up his old job at the garage and used his GI Bill to enroll in technical college. With a degree from the Universal Technical Institute (UTI), in a few years he would qualify for well-paid positions in Arizona's growing automotive industry.

"Are you here to talk about the .50?" Hugo asked the agents sitting across from him at his kitchen table that winter day in 2016.

"No, we are here about something else," Jackson said and immediately regretted it.

"We'll talk about the .50 too if we get to that," Alex quickly corrected his partner.

Neither of them had any clue what .50 Hugo was referring to. They came to ask him about the AK-47 rifles they seized in Nogales, the ones that the two men they talked to following the leads in the trace reports said they sold to Hugo. They asked Hugo about online groups dedicated to trading in firearms that he belonged to and Hugo answered their questions politely, even though they could sense he was nervous. As they kept talking, however, the agents started noticing discrepancies in Hugo's stories. His answers became evasive. They had proof that he had sold more than one AK-47 rifle—they had those guns in their evidence vault—but Hugo insisted it was just one. When the talk turned to the .50 caliber he had inadvertently mentioned and Hugo explained that he was buying this belt-fed machine gun for himself and that he had already made a $10,000 cash deposit on it, the agents couldn't make the math work. It sounded implausible that Hugo, who lived on a military stipend and a few hundred dollars per week from his job at the auto garage, could afford such a purchase. Jackson noted that when Alex began asking more pointed questions, Hugo got uncomfortable: scratched his arm, tapped his foot, blinked more, and kept glancing over to the living room. To him, these were "nonverbal indicators" that Hugo was concerned about his wife overhearing the conversation.

"Look, none of this is tracking," Alex finally said.

Jackson suggested they take the conversation outside. After hesitating for a moment, Hugo agreed, and the three of them stood up and walked out the front door.

"We know you're not telling us the truth," Alex said.

"We have no intent to arrest you since you're being cool, but if you're going to keep lying . . .," Jackson didn't finish the sentence because Hugo interrupted and said he would tell them the truth.

Jackson offered they should talk in the car instead of going back inside, and Hugo didn't object. They walked down the driveway to the street and got inside Jackson's Chevy Equinox. Hugo took the front passenger's seat next to Jackson, Alex sat in the back. Now he laid it all out for them. He told them how many guns he bought and for whom and answered their questions about money and dates. He told them that he was in the process of filling another order for five weapons and he already had four of those: three AK-style rifles and an AK pistol. Hugo explained that he bought the guns with his own money and he was firm about the price he asked for: he charged the buyer $900 per rifle, regardless of how much he spent on them, and, since he never paid more than $750 and sometimes purchased them for as little as $400, he would make at least a $150 profit per firearm, often more. "He knew his guns," Jackson told me later.

While they were talking, Hugo's phone rang and "Guy AK" appeared on the screen. Hugo didn't pick up, telling the agents that coincidentally the man calling was the same person who had placed the order for the five weapons he was working on. "He's calling about the guns," Hugo said. Surprised, even concerned how the buyer knew to call now, the agents instructed Hugo to answer if he called again. He did and Hugo picked up.

"They really want those guns," he said after he hung up. "I'm guessing something broke out in Mexico."

"Is this where you think the guns are going?" Jackson asked then.

"I'm pretty sure that that's where they were fucking taking them," Hugo said.

Since returning to Arizona, Hugo had been hanging out with other military vets he met at the technical institute. They stuck together and on weekends went out for target practice, just like he used to do with his scout unit up in Kansas. Through his new friends, Hugo learned about groups that organized meetups in the desert. A lot of the men who participated in these were military veterans or police; some officers even came while on duty. It wasn't unusual for them to bring their wives and kids. They would arrive at a designated spot, such as the mountain range by Lake Pleasant, set up tents in front of their trucks, and lay their guns on the tables. Everyone could see what each had brought: some had rows of Glocks; others showed off their M4s or AK-47s. These outings could draw a few hundred people, most of whom came to shoot their own guns. But some also used these meetups to trade. Though he was most engaged with a Phoenix-based pro–Second Amendment group, Barter Quality Goods or BQG, Hugo was a member of about a dozen other similar collectives on Facebook, all of them dedicated to selling, swapping, and shooting guns.

But Guy AK was different. Hugo met him through Rudy, the butcher at the store where he went to buy meat for barbecues. Rudy knew Hugo was fixing cars and one day, when he brought his truck to the garage for some touch up, he saw Hugo cleaning a gun. Rudy asked whether Hugo had any guns for sale and Hugo sold him an AK-74, a rifle similar to an AK-47 that uses 5.56 rounds. Rudy told Hugo that his friend, Derek, was also looking to buy guns. After they exchanged a few messages, Hugo decided to meet Derek in the parking lot in front of Cracker Barrel. It was dark when he arrived, so he parked near the entrance to the still open store, late customers streaming in and out. Hugo trusted Rudy, but he was still cautious about meeting this new guy. Derek came in an older, light brown Chevy Tahoe, and, because he smelled of fresh-cut grass and his pants were covered in weeds, Hugo thought he was a landscaper. That first time they met, Hugo also thought that Derek looked like "a really mean cholo." But he turned out to be a nice guy, and they met again and again, always at the same spot, always late in the evening. The people Derek worked for wanted to buy AKs and only AKs. "Cuernos" or "chivitos," as they usually referred to the rifles in their text messages. On his phone, Hugo entered Derek's number and named the contact "Guy AK."

Derek's preferences didn't surprise Hugo. "I don't know if it sounds kind of racial, but, I mean, as a Hispanic, I personally like the AK-47 and a lot of the Hispanic people that I meet like AK-47," he later said. Although Hugo returned from deployment admiring .50 caliber Barretts, he also brought back a regard for AK-47s. African soldiers his unit trained and worked with were armed with AK-47 style rifles, so Americans sent to Camp Lemonnier carrying M4s had to quickly familiarize themselves with the guns the locals were using and learn how they function. Back home in Arizona, Hugo bonded with other vets who liked AKs as much as he did.

Hugo told the agents that Derek wanted more and more AKs. Just the other day he received a text from Derek telling him, "Yo, I need 20 fucking yesterday." The price of AK-47 rifles, especially those made in Eastern Europe, went up when in 2014, in response to the Kremlin's role supporting separatists in Ukraine, the United States banned the imports of semiautomatic rifles as part of sanctions against Russian companies, including Kalashnikov Concern.[4] This was not the first time the government banned foreign-made firearms, but the previous ban of assault rifles with "military configuration," enacted in 1989, was easily skirted by modifying the guns. With these new sanctions against

Russian companies, gun enthusiasts became worried the government would decide on a full ban, so they rushed to buy AKs while they still could. Such was and is the reality of the US gun market: any rumor of impending gun restrictions drives gun sales up. Regardless of whether they believed a ban was coming, people who were buying imported AKs considered the guns to be a good investment, their value guaranteed to rise over time. Those who liked AKs said that European versions were better made, more durable than American ones. The guys Hugo met through Facebook groups were eager to get rid of their US-made AK-47s, which would start malfunctioning after several hundred rounds. Due to all these factors that increased demand, foreign AKs were costing $800 to $1,300, almost twice as much as Century Arms rifles, which went for $500 to $700 a piece. Since Hugo was not buying the guns for himself, he tried to get the cheaper models, whether they were durable or not. Derek wanted AKs, any AKs.

Sitting in the passenger seat of Jackson's truck, Hugo explained all this to the agents. He hoped they would let him go. The final written exam for one of his classes was scheduled for the early afternoon and, if he stayed talking to them any longer, he would miss it and have to retake the class. That would cost him money. "It costs the military money," he said, appealing to common interest. He pleaded with the agents that he wanted to finish school. Jackson was sympathetic. As a vet himself, he supported Hugo's determination to complete his studies. He knew that the technical institute Hugo attended was considered a pipeline to good jobs at high-end car dealerships and in the automotive industry. In fact, Hugo already had a position lined up for him. Alex told Hugo that their conversation was more important and that he should forget school, but since he wasn't in custody, they couldn't make him stay. Before he left, agents took Hugo's phone and asked him to sign a consent form for them to dump it. They agreed to meet up again that evening, after the exam.

By six o'clock, the agents were waiting for Hugo in the parking lot in front of Walgreens at the strip mall on West McDowell Road. When he showed up, they said they had to seize the four AKs he had told them about and so they followed him back to his house. They drove in separate cars and, once they were back at his house, Hugo showed the agents where he kept the guns. Alex gave him an abandonment form to fill out. Before they took the guns, they let him remove the scopes he had put on one of the rifles. Other than that, they were all bare, unlike the other weapons the agents saw in Hugo's closet—the guns he had bought for himself, which had various accessories. To Jackson, who also liked guns and enjoyed target shooting, it was evident that Hugo was a fellow gun enthusiast who invested time and money on them. As they were leaving, Hugo asked the agents whether he would get the four AKs back. "Not very likely," Alex said.

The weapons were not illegal: Like Ramiro, Hugo could buy as many AK-47s or other assault style rifles as he wanted to own. There was also nothing illegal about the secondary market, or person-to-person sales of firearms in Arizona. But Hugo did not have a license to deal in firearms for profit. And his knowledge of the intended purpose—that the guns were going to Mexico—was an issue, even if he only met with Derek and did not know other members of the conspiracy. During their investigation, the agents found that over several months since leaving the military and moving back to Phoenix, Hugo had bought thirty-six guns and, they suspected, sold the majority, if not all of them, to Derek. But they only seized fourteen of them: the four they took from Hugo's house and the ten they recovered from Junior back in January, which matched, gun for gun, the firearms in a photo that the agents found on his phone.[5] Although they could not trace them all, the distinct characteristics of some stood out—one had an ash-colored stock; another had a magazine behind the trigger, called a "bull-pup," which was very uncommon— and they were certain the guns they seized in Nogales and those Hugo photographed on his couch were the same. It appeared Hugo handed them over to Derek at their regular meeting place in Phoenix that same evening, in January, when the agents were busy with their "Box of Rocks" operation. They would never know whether it was Derek or somebody else who took the guns to Motel 6, where Junior, with the undercover agent in tow, picked them up the following morning.

Hugo decided to go to trial. Only three of over twenty people in the gun trafficking case that Alex and Jackson had been working on since the recovery of those AKs in Sonora back in the fall of 2015 chose to do that—Poncho, Kevin, and Hugo. The rest pleaded guilty.[6] That was what most defendants in such cases did. There were no statutory minimums for firearms violations, so most got away with a probation or maybe a short sentence. Going to trial was risky—they could get up to five years in prison for conspiracy (that's what Poncho got) and up to ten years for smuggling. But Hugo didn't know others involved in the trafficking scheme; he didn't know there was a trafficking scheme. He didn't believe he engaged in conspiracy and he never smuggled the guns himself. All he did was buy and sell them to make a little profit to support his family since he took medical leave from the military. He thought he could convince the jury that he was not what the indictment accused him of being—a gun trafficker.

When the day came for the trial, the prosecutor insisted that all four-teen weapons tied to Hugo that the agents had in evidence boxes—thirteen rifles and one semiautomatic pistol—be brought into the court-room. The defense attorney, Rubin Salter Jr., argued that "they're scary looking things to a jury" and would be "unfairly prejudicial," suggest-ing that a picture would be less threatening. But assistant US attorney Angela Woolridge, who had already prosecuted Poncho for his role in this conspiracy, stood firm: Hugo "was directly involved with the han-dling of the firearms. This is the evidence in this case. This is the case itself." Hugo's attorney couldn't convince the judge otherwise. Salter had represented other people charged with gun trafficking, but they were all either supervisors or organizers, much more involved in the schemes. Hugo, on the other hand, only traded guns and was not part of the larger operation. "He was a typical, all-American young man. Good husband, father, worker. Very good mechanic," he said about his client who at the time of the trial had a job as a technician at Scottsdale Ferrari. The jury found Hugo guilty on all three counts: engaging in the business of dealing firearms without a license, conspiracy to smuggle goods from the United States, and smuggling goods from the United States. The judge gave him fifteen months, followed by two years of supervised release. Hugo had to surrender his guns and, with a felony record, he would be prohibited from owning firearms in the future.

After the trials, all firearms and ammunition the agents had seized were destroyed. ATF agents placed thirty-two rifles in specialized locked cases and shipped them to the National Firearms and Ammunition Destruction Branch in Martinsburg, West Virginia, a centralized loca-tion where guns from all over the country are brought for disposal, including retired service weapons from the FBI and DEA.[7] There, the guns were thrown into an industrial shredder, which cut them into pieces. The fate of the cartridges was similar: while some were repur-posed, the rest were sent to a private disposal facility. "Guns and ammo going down the drain," Jackson said, and I thought I heard a tinge of disappointment in his voice.

Metal Afterlives

Ciudad de México

People say that the red ant painted on the white bell tower is slowly advancing toward the sky and, once it reaches the top, the world will end. The church and convent of Santos Apóstoles Felipe y Santiago date back to the sixteenth century when the Spanish conquerors wrested Azcapotzalco from the crumbling Triple Alliance. The Nahuatl word for an "ant" is *azcatl* and Azcapotzalco means "on an anthill." According to legend, ants helped Quetzalcoatl find the realm of the dead and bring the bones of men and grains of corn to re-create life. Dominican friars built their complex over the former Tepaneca ceremonial center, burying the old gods under the weight of the new one.

Today Azcapotzalco is one of sixteen boroughs that make up the country's capital. On a cloudy September morning in 2018, a handful of pedestrians strolled across the walled-in atrium in front of the parish church. A young family pushing a pram slowed down and glanced with curiosity at white tarps bearing government logos and enlarged photographs of firearms behind the backs of soldiers in green digital camouflage. One table was covered with toys: Rubik's cubes, dominoes, coloring books featuring the Avengers, and figurines from *Spiderman* and *Despicable Me*. Those who asked the personnel from the municipal administration wearing bright pink vests learned that the occasion for this gathering was not a job fair or a market, but Mexico City's gun buyback program. The voluntary and anonymous disarmament campaign, "Por tu Familia, Desarme Voluntario," was coordinated between the secretariats of social development and public security, the military, and the archdiocese. Gun exchanges were held on church premises, to reassure people that nobody would be arrested even if they brought in prohibited weapons of suspicious provenance. Children could bring their plastic toy guns and swap them for other games.

Since the inception of the program in 2012, the government had collected and destroyed over thirty thousand firearms, more than two thousand grenades, and nearly two hundred thousand cartridges, at a cost of a 108 million pesos.[1] These numbers would increase in subsequent years and, renamed to "Sí al desarme, sí a la paz" after the 2018 election, the program would continue under the new administration. The yield varied borough to borough, depending less on the number of guns in each part of the city and more on whether residents felt safe where they lived. A few weeks earlier, during the buyback campaign in Benito Juárez, people turned in dozens of firearms each day and brought a total of sixty-six grenades. Nobody expected that much in Azcapotzalco.

Two hours had passed since they set up the module on the campaign's third day in the neighborhood and only one person had showed up thus far—a man in a black T-shirt who looked to be in his forties. He sat down, pulled out a revolver from his leather bag, and placed the gun on the table. He didn't say anything. The *armero*, the officer from the Secretariat of Public Security who acted as the gun expert, picked up the firearm and started examining it. Lieutenant Alfredo García, in military fatigues, stood next to him.

"A .44 Magnum. No markings. No brand name," the policeman said for all of us to hear. It was missing parts and was no longer functional. "It's in bad condition."

The man asked how much he could get for it.

"We don't buy guns," a woman from the city government said. "We provide compensation," she clarified. Then she looked at the sheet on the table in front of her and slid her finger down until she found the right line: "600 pesos" (about $31 US dollars), she said. Had the gun been in good condition, they would have given him 8,400 pesos (approximately $450 US dollars).

"It's from the Revolution," the man objected. The old gun had historic value.

"We don't have proof," the woman replied. "Do you?" When he didn't say anything, she suggested he could try selling it to a collector.

The man lifted the revolver from the pink tablecloth, put it back into his bag, and walked away. Lieutenant García crossed out what he'd written in the form he was filling out. No gun, no paperwork.

Lieutenant García was the battalion's expert in war materials. When he smiled, which he did often, sparkles in his eyes and dimples in his cheeks softened his soldierly appearance. Born and raised in Veracruz, he joined the military at the age of seventeen, against his mother's will, the first in his family to become a soldier. At the Military School for War Materials, he learned about firearms and ballistics as well as explosives and toxic chemicals and graduated as an officer with specialization in weapons.[2] In 2018, he was put in charge of overseeing the voluntary gun buyback program in Mexico City.

"Gun buyback is a grain of sand," Lieutenant García said, as we waited for more people to show up to surrender their weapons. He understood that the program would not solve the issue of violence in the country. The previous year, in 2017, Mexico registered a record high number of homicides: 31,174, up from 24,559 in 2016.[3] And the statistics would get even worse in the years to come. Fractured and reorganized, under command of new leaders vying for power, criminal groups had stepped up extortion rackets and increasingly profited from fuel theft. Before he was assigned to the gun buyback program, García's unit traveled all over the country attached to PEMEX, accompanying fuel tankers to protect them from attacks and guarding oil pipelines to prevent tapping.

Four uniformed soldiers who Lieutenant García brought with him from the army base were hanging out by the truck farther back, FX-05 assault rifles on their shoulders. García's only weapon was a handgun on his right hip. Being in Mexico City was a period of calm for him. One by one, members of his family had been fleeing Veracruz, looking for jobs and safety elsewhere. His sister moved to Chicago. Another relative relocated to Montreal. Even his brother, who owned a business in their hometown, was considering taking up construction work in Canada. García had never been outside of Mexico—as a military officer he had to request permission to leave the country half a year in advance, which made it complicated. But that pleasantly warm morning, as we watched people, trying to guess who may have brought a gun they wanted to exchange for cash, he talked about places he would like to visit. "My son told me that there is less crime in Spain," he said. Security was not only his job. García wanted to live in a safe country. He said he feared for his children. Some time ago he asked a boy they caught with an unregistered firearm how much the gang paid him for what he was doing, and the boy replied that he got nothing, that they threatened him, and he had no choice. García was afraid that the same could happen to his children: that they could be abducted and forced into "a life of crime." He said, proudly, that his oldest son wanted to study medicine at Tec de Monterrey and become a surgeon.

Some people came to the buyback program to turn in guns that belonged to their parents or grandparents. When older family members passed away, their relatives, especially those who lived in the city, had no use for the lethal tools they inherited. They brought century-old rifles and revolvers, from as far back as the revolutionary era, family heirlooms, which they hoped the government would preserve. Once García saw a .44 Magnum revolver with the seal of the Division of the North, a gun that had belonged to Pancho Villa's troops. It could have ended up in a collection, but SEDENA's rules obliged them to destroy all firearms they received. Most often, people brought .22 or .380 caliber semiautomatic pistols; occasionally, revolvers and hunting rifles. But once in a while people would give up powerful assault style weapons. García said that a couple of days ago someone brought an Uzi. He pulled out his phone and showed me a picture of a black submachine gun with a well-worn sand-colored sling still attached. Civilians in Mexico couldn't purchase Uzis, but nobody questioned the person who surrendered the weapon. Here, identity and legality were of no consequence. Although it was the only way to do it, anonymous exchanges had drawbacks. Some said savvy perpetrators could use them to dispose of crime guns. Others speculated that high prices the government was willing to pay would even encourage trafficking of guns and ammo, that people would start buying them cheap in the United States and then selling them to the Mexican state, at a profit.

Every so often, deals broke down. Usually because of disagreements over value: gun owners thought their firearms were worth more than the program offered. During the inauguration of the campaign in Tlalpan in May 2019, as soon as government officials finished their speeches, in which they invited residents to stand up against violence, two women presented several buckets brimming with pen guns. One of them said she found them inside the house they bought in the neighborhood, surmising that the previous owner must have left them behind. She had already taken one bucket to the gun buyback module in Coyoacán and even made the news. "Young woman sells 510 pen guns in CDMX and earns 61,000 pesos," was the headline of the story.[4] In Tlalpan, the officials said that they would not pay the women 120 pesos a piece, as listed on their compensation chart, because the pen guns were "hechizos" (homemade). When they offered to give the women twenty-four pesos for each one, the women objected, accusing the government of making false promises. "It's very unjust," one of them said, addressing the reporters gathered around them. Pen guns could only hold one .22 caliber cartridge, but because they were prone to malfunction, they were even more dangerous, to the shooter as well as to the potential target. "This is not about how much you are paid, but about taking them off the streets," another official said, trying to convince the women to do the right thing. But they didn't relent and we watched as they left, pushing the dollies with plastic buckets full of pen guns in the direction they had come from.

Many residents of Tlalpan, Azcapotzalco, Miguel Hidalgo, Iztapalapa, and other boroughs of Mexico City didn't care much about the program the government brought to their parishes. When I accompanied Alvaro, a stout man with gelled hair and thick eyebrows who volunteered with the gun buyback campaign in Xochimilco, he knew not to knock on closed doors and avoided going down narrow labyrinthine streets that led deep into the neighborhood. We only approached people in places open to the public: a video game salon, a pharmacy, a laundromat, various stores and kiosks and street stalls. Many residents we met had heard about the program either on TV or in church or both. And everybody complained about crime and insecurity and how it was getting worse, telling us they felt unsafe in their neighborhood. Some said they had relatives who owned rifles. More admitted that, if they had a gun, they would not give it up. "Para mí, no vale la pena. I wouldn't exchange it," said a guy at a corner kiosk selling chips and soda. One man said he regretted taking his handgun to the buyback program a few years earlier. Now he wished he still had it. We met a few residents who told us they were more interested in buying a gun than getting rid of one. "Violence generates more violence," Alvaro said, politely disagreeing with one woman who said this, but she didn't change her mind. Nobody came to turn in their guns that day.

In front of the parish church in Azcapotzalco, it was nearing midday when people began trickling in. First, a young man in blue jeans who approached so quickly that the staff were startled when they realized there was someone sitting on the chair. He drew out a firearm. The armero picked it up. The women in pink vests and Lieutenant García got their forms ready. I reached for my notebook.

"It's a Browning. No model. No caliber," the officer said. He pointed the pistol at a trash can behind us and pulled the trigger, to check whether the firing mechanism still worked.

Handing the gun over to García, he said, ".380," but sounded unsure.

"No, it's a .32," García said, as he inspected the gun.

The young man hadn't brought any cartridges, so the officer found a .380 in a box on the table and measured it against the barrel. The cartridge didn't fit. They concurred it was a .32.

The woman with the cost form said, "8,400 pesos. Is that ok?"

"Yes."

She lifted the lid of a box she kept on the table, took out a stack of banknotes, and handed them over. The man flipped through the bills to count them. Satisfied, he stood up and left.

Next was a young woman in long black hair, a white blouse, and pink skirt. She sat down, buried her hand deep into a large purse covered in flowers and pulled out a black pistol with a five-pointed star on its white marbled grip, which she placed on the pink tablecloth.

"Do you have the magazine?" the armero asked.

"Yes!" she said and her hand dove back into the purse to retrieve it.

It was another Browning and again they couldn't tell whether it was .380 or .32. It didn't matter that much. People got 4,800 pesos ($257 US dollars in 2018) for a .380, and 4,200 ($225 USD) for a .32. But there was an error on the form and the .32 caliber pistol was listed twice, which was why the previous man walked away with 8,400 pesos (about $450 US dollars)—the amount the government was only supposed to give in exchange for handguns of restricted calibers, such as a 9mm, .45, and .38 Super. Only an FN Herstal, the "cop killer," which used 5.7 caliber cartridges, was worth more than these. Over two years and two different administrations organizing the campaign in Mexico City, I never saw anyone turn in a five-seven.

"My husband told me it's a .32," the woman said.

"Ok, it's 4,200."

As soon as she stood up, an older man with greying hair who had been waiting a few steps behind her took the seat at the table. He turned in a .357 Magnum revolver and got 6,000 pesos ($320 US dollars).

The last to show up was a boy who could have been in his teens, though nobody asked to see his ID to verify his age. He wore jeans and a grey T-shirt with an image I could not see, white earbuds hanging on a cord around his neck, and a key chain with a colorful crab attached to his belt. From a beige camouflage backpack he pulled out a green plastic box full of ammunition. Four cartridges were Remington 410 Express, used for shotguns, each worth six pesos. The rest were .22s. Once the women finished their calculations, he walked away with 4,230 pesos (about $227 US dollars).

Each transaction took only two or three minutes. Forms were filled out, cash changed hands, photographs of the guns were taken, posted on social media, and then the surrendered firearms were passed on to García's team to be destroyed.

On the opposite side of the atrium, a military technician had set up a table with tools—various screwdrivers, a hammer, and an electric circular saw. He cut Browning pistols twice: first the saw severed the muzzle, then it slashed across the frame, separating the trigger from the hammer. But the revolver, made of quality iron, posed a challenge and they had to bring in a different saw to cut it. "The older the gun, the more difficult it is to destroy," García said, an oblique comment on the poor quality of cheap new guns. Ammunition could not be safely destroyed on-site, so García's team took the cartridges back to the military base.

During ten days in Azcapotzalco, the program yielded 56 handguns, 3 rifles, 1 grenade, and 24,491 rounds of ammo. In 2018, in all the boroughs of Mexico City combined, the government collected 415 handguns, 133 rifles, and 162,221 cartridges.[5] With the exception of the State of Mexico and Coahuila, both of which collected more firearms than Mexico City, these numbers were greater in the capital than in many places with higher gun ownership rates and higher levels of criminal violence. In Guerrero, residents surrendered only nine rifles and twenty-six handguns; in Nuevo León—thirty-six rifles.[6] Some of the weapons people exchanged for money or coupons were AK-47s and AR-15s; one woman in Ciudad Juárez even brought a missile. But gun buyback programs didn't make a dent in criminal violence. Many municipalities in the most violent parts of the country didn't have budgets for them. And residents were not that eager to give their guns up, not even in the capital and much less elsewhere. Most of the weapons SEDENA collected in Tamaulipas, Sinaloa, and Guerrero, among other states, were not surrendered voluntarily and anonymously, but captured during military operations.

GUERRERO, 2018
Handguns voluntarily surrendered: 26
Rifles voluntarily surrendered: 9
Handguns recovered by the military: 184
Rifles recovered by the military: 207

SONORA, 2019
Handguns voluntarily surrendered: 2
Rifles voluntarily surrendered: 0
Handguns recovered by the military: 259
Rifles recovered by the military: 359

TAMAULIPAS, 2019
Handguns voluntarily surrendered: 104
Rifles voluntarily surrendered: 40
Handguns recovered by the military: 92
Rifles recovered by the military: 744

Not all seized guns ended up at the teeth of the metal saw. Some firearms were too precious, literally and figuratively, to be destroyed because of the value they accrued through their association with notorious criminals and their organizations.[7] It was as if the gold-plated and gem-covered guns preserved some of the power held by the crime bosses even after they were killed or imprisoned. Perhaps even more important was their role as the government's booty, as proof of its victory over those who threatened the monopoly of violence it aspired to.

To see them, you needed permission to enter the building that houses the headquarters of the Secretariat of National Defense in Mexico City and take an elevator to one of the top floors, where a windowless room holds a most unusual exhibit: Museo del Enervante, which people have dubbed "the Narco Museum." In the anteroom, visitors are greeted by a plaque filled with names of fallen Mexican servicemen and a mural that depicts the military's fight against drug trafficking: the central figure is a soldier wielding a flaming torch, which rises above red poppies and the green leaves of cannabis plants. There is an eagle in national colors of white, green, and red hovering above the scene, and the architectural icons of Western civilization—the Statue of Liberty, the Eiffel Tower, the Big Ben—visible around the edges.

Inside the museum, samples of dried marijuana and poppy seeds lie next to glass containers for cooking heroin and a metal oven for preparing meth. On the walls are maps, regularly updated, showing routes of cocaine and precursor materials as well as clandestine landing strips in the mountainous area of Sinaloa, Durango, and Chihuahua, which the officer who showed me around called by its popular name: the "Golden Triangle." Objects in the cabinets showcase the ingenuity of smugglers, who have hidden drugs in hollowed-out books, soles of shoes, fresh produce; a photo of a naked woman's backside hangs next to one with bloody packets of drugs recovered from inside her body. There are models of airplanes, trucks, and ships used by drug traffickers as well as those employed by the military that pursues them. There is even a taxidermied German shepherd. The exhibit ends with a room dedicated to "narcocultura," which holds bulletproof shirts and jackets, life-size mounted wild cats, a diamond encrusted cell phone that once belonged to one of the Zetas, and guns.

A lot of guns. Plated in gold and silver. Encrusted with gemstones. Bearing the names of their former owners. Decorated with national and religious symbols, fashion brands and logos, as well as images of tigers, wolves, and dragons. Locked inside display cases, they have green tags that tell an abbreviated version of their stories. On a gold-plated grip, a black Colt .38 Super carries an eagle with a serpent and an inscription "16 de Sep 1810," the day Miguel Hidalgo issued a call to arms that started the Mexican War of Independence. Other markings, including one on the barrel, which is decorated with a golden chain and a Mexican flag, spell out "El Grito de Dolores" and "Viva Mexico." I scribble this in my notebook as I look through the glass at the firearm that used to belong to Osiel Cárdenas Guillén. The card placed next to it says that the pistol was captured in March 2003, when the Mexican military arrested the leader of the Gulf Cartel in Matamoros. All the stories end the same way: the place and date of their capture by the Mexican security forces. Some of them are from the earlier days of organized crime, like the Colt Gold Cup National Match 45 ACP, dipped in yellow and white gold, with 221 diamonds on its grip, which belonged to Stanislao Olmos González, a member of the Arellano Félix organization, "decommissioned" in Tijuana in 1991. Another black .38 Colt with an eagle and initials "ACF," for Amado Carillo Fuentes, on its golden grip, was confiscated from El Chapo when he was first arrested in Guatemala in 1993.

Drug lords admired Colts. There is another Colt .38 Super with an image of Emiliano Zapata, engraved in 24 carat gold, which belonged to

Alfredo Beltrán Leyva, arrested by the Mexican army in Culiacán in 2008. And one more black Colt .38 Super with an image of El Chapo on a wooden grip, which was found in an abandoned vehicle in Sinaloa in the summer of 2017. The card next to a gold-covered pistol with the inscription "El General" and an image of Pancho Villa on the grip says it belonged to a member of the Gulf Cartel nicknamed El Kariz. Rifles hang in display cases on the opposite wall. Most are AKs, including a golden AK-47 with the number "85" which belonged to the leader of CJNG, Érick Valencia Salazar, and which was captured together with its owner during a military operation in Zapopan, Jalisco, in March of 2011.

The practice of marking weapons is old in Mexico. Reliance on foreign tools to forge a sovereign state was mitigated by their symbolic appropriation, inscribing American guns to make them Mexican. But these guns confiscated from crime bosses weren't about national values. They propagated the cult of an individual who wielded power over the life and death of others. Crusted in diamonds and dipped in gold, next to Pancho Villa and Emiliano Zapata, they had brand names, such as "Rolex" and "Versace." The image of Zapata was not even a unique engraving, but a serialized one, a .38 caliber model Colt allegedly made specifically for the Mexican market, one of three special edition models, next to .38 Super pistols branded "El Jefe" and "El Grito."[8] Only later, just before they crossed the border or once they were already in Mexico, did leaders of organized crime groups order them to be personalized with gold and diamonds and mark them with their nicknames.

Most Mexican people don't have such power to transfer value to their guns. Their names don't mean anything to the government and their anonymous weapons, like their lives, are disposable. But, like the trophy guns that are preserved, these anonymous weapons are discarded in ways that serve the official story—that of the Mexican government's righteous fight against the drug trade. The most common of these is the circulation of photographs of carefully arranged guns seized from members of organized crime—a spread of rifles and pistols on a table or on the floor, with security personnel in black masks lined up behind, sometimes holding the men and women they arrested during the raid. These are the easiest to stage. Another, more time-consuming but also lasting method of using captured firearms to prop up the Mexican government's agenda has been molding gunmetal to create art installations.[9]

The Secretariat of National Defense and various military units not only sponsored the creation of artworks, but also selected from among its ranks those artistically inclined to design them. Since 2012, thirty-two colorful sculptures representing each state of the nation, many of them in the shapes of animals—birds, bighorn sheep, a bear, a whale—stand in the gardens of Plaza del Servicio a la Patria, on Paseo de la Reforma in Mexico City, watched over by soldiers in uniform.[10] Celebrating its thirtieth anniversary, the special forces also held a contest and unveiled four sculptures made of firearms along the esplanade at their headquarters in the State of Mexico. One of them, called "Duality," depicts the Mesoamerican deity Mictlantecutli on one side and the Dove of Peace on the other.[11] Similar sculptures made from war materials decorate other military bases around the country, from Tlaxcala to Nayarit to Chihuahua.

The guns collected during the buyback campaigns in Azcapotzalco and other boroughs would have the same fate. In 2019, the government asked artists for ideas to design a sculpture using the metal from the destroyed firearms. The theme was "Culture of Peace and Not Violence in Mexico City." As the culture secretary, José Alfonso Suárez del Real y Aguilera, said: "Each gun given to this sculpture is an expression of peace, of a life saved, of security at home guaranteed. The most important thing is not to defend ourselves with weapons, but to promote peace as a space for community development."[12] In 2021, Mexico City's mayor, Claudia Sheinbaum, unveiled the winning sculpture on the northern edge of Tepito—bronze figures of two children standing in front of a tall corn grinder filled with rifles, their barrels sticking out on top. Created by Miguel Ángel Campos Ortiz from forty-seven hundred voluntarily surrendered guns melted into more than three tons of metal, it was called "Molino por la Paz"—the mill for peace.[13]

Monumental sculptures commissioned by the state are not the only forms recycled gunmetal can take. It has been used to create everyday objects that invite a more intimate reckoning with violence. In Colombia, Antanas Mockus, a mathematician and philosopher who in the 1990s became mayor of Bogotá, sought creative ways to reduce urban crime, among which was a voluntary disarmament campaign with the slogan "Let the firearms rest in peace this Christmas." People received holiday gift cards in exchange for guns and those guns were then melted and molded into spoons, each of them bearing an inscription "ARMA FUI" ("I was a firearm").[14] Over a decade later, after the signing of the peace agreement between the FARC and the Colombian government, sculptor Doris Salcedo used the melted remains of thirty-seven tons of decommissioned weapons to make tiles for a floor in a new museum in Bogotá. To make the tiles, Salcedo invited women who had been sexually assaulted during the armed conflict—by guerillas, paramilitaries, or government soldiers. With mallets in their hands, women pounded the metal from the guns into thirteen hundred tiles, the idea being that, through the process of hammering, they would reassert themselves as survivors. Salcedo called her work an "anti-monument" that inverted "the power relationship that a man carrying a gun has [by] having us Colombians being able to walk on the guns."[15]

When Mexican artist Pedro Reyes received an invitation to do a piece at the botanical garden in Culiacán, Sinaloa, in 2007, he already knew about Mockus and his guns to spoons project. Mockus managed to transform an instrument of violence into a tool "feeding a generation with hope," Reyes told me. His own idea was to use guns to make shovels. He called it "Palas por Pistolas." "I like to think that art can serve a purpose that is not only aesthetic," he said. With support from the city hall and the regional military command, Reyes ran an ad on a local television channel inviting citizens to voluntarily turn in guns in exchange for domestic appliances. Then, those weapons were crushed with a steamroller, wood and plastic components were separated and removed, and the metal parts were sent to the foundry, where they were melted and used to forge 1,527 shovels—one for every gun destroyed.[16] Reyes handed those shovels out to schools and museums, from Tijuana and San Diego to Houston, Boston, and other cities, where volunteers used them to plant trees, to show that "agents of death" could become "agents of life."

The next project Reyes did involving guns was called "Disarm." This time the invitation came from Enrique Betancourt, a Mexican architect and urban designer who oversaw the National Center for Crime Prevention. The government gave Reyes what was left from sixty-seven hundred firearms seized by the military and destroyed in a public ceremony in Ciudad Juárez, and Reyes, in collaboration with an art foundation in Mexico City, made them into an orchestra. Blacksmiths worked with musicians as they molded gunmetal into fifty instruments: guitars, saxophones, flutes, bells.[17] Then Reyes and his team organized a series of concerts, recording sessions, and workshops with community members. He compared the process of transforming weapons into objects of art to "the tradition of alchemy, where, simultaneous with the physical conversion of a substance, a psychological transformation is supposed to occur."[18] Playing music with these instruments is "a sort of exorcism," he said, the way to expel the demons from the material. But Reyes was wary of the ethical risk of such aesthetic transformation. "Making art about guns, you can easily be seduced by the object itself, so the result may wind up praising or glorifying the object rather than critiquing it," he said.[19]

From closer up, I could see that the instruments were made up of guns. Some pistols and rifles assembled into what looked like a harp and a xylophone were nearly intact. Gun shapes stripped to their bare metal carcass, their rough, raw materiality rendered less threatening in the space of an art museum in Salem, Massachusetts, where they stood in a room on a grey carpet, attached to boom boxes, flashing with electric lights—an orchestra of recycled Mexican firearms, playing "a requiem for the lives lost."[20] I listened as the instruments took their turn, playing one by one, like during a sound check before a concert. Then, for a brief moment, they all played together. The screeching, piercing sound of the harp disturbed the quiet atmosphere inside the museum. Like a metal scream.

Some of these recycled guns may have been forged not far from where they were now displayed as art. About one hundred miles southwest from Salem is Springfield, the city that has played a critical role in the history of US gun industry. It was the site of the first federal armory in the United States and the place where mass production of firearms began. Union soldiers carried Springfield rifles and muskets during the American Civil War. Mexican soldiers, too, clutched Springfields when they defended their country from foreign invasions during the nineteenth century and later took them to the battlefields of the Mexican Revolution. Up until its final years, engineers at the armory were designing new weapons, including .50 caliber Browning machine guns. The factory shut down in 1968 and today it is a museum run by the National Park Service. Before seeing its vast collection of old rifles, including muskets assembled into a huge organ, visitors pass through a door with a sign which warns them that bringing their firearms inside is prohibited.

But I didn't come to Springfield for its past. This city, the seat of Hampden County, is among the top ten places in the United States where guns recovered in crime scenes in Mexico come from.[21] On a chilly morning in March, I stopped at the front gate of Smith & Wesson, a mere ten-minute drive from the historic armory. The company that made the black tactical M&P15 rifle Miguel taught me to shoot remains one of the biggest gun manufacturers in the United States. In 2021, citing legislative proposals to ban making assault-style weapons in Massachusetts,

Smith & Wesson announced it would relocate its headquarters to Tennessee.[22] But the company had no plans to leave its massive facility on Roosevelt Avenue just yet. Guns have been made here since the 1850s and, for now, more were being forged every day.

I got out of the car and approached the front gate. When the company began making semiautomatic rifles about seventeen years ago and those rifles began showing up at mass shootings, advocates for gun safety started coming here to protest.[23] The father of Joaquin Oliver—a student at Marjory Stoneman Douglas High School who died from four gunshot wounds inflicted by a Smith & Wesson M&P15 rifle—put up a billboard next to the company's headquarters with his son's image and a message "Gun Laws Save Lives."[24] Because of protestors, visitors are no longer welcome at the facility. I stood there for a few minutes, then left.

In the buildings behind the fence, away from prying eyes, more than a thousand Massachusetts residents continued their work, carefully shaping metal into gun parts and assembling them into rifles and revolvers. Before year's end, Smith & Wesson would make over a quarter million assault-style weapons—about 15 percent of all rifles manufactured in the United States each year.[25] If melted, the metal from them alone would be enough to forge five Statues of Liberty.[26]

Some of these guns will end up south of the border. Not as material for art, but as material for war first.

Epilogue

The last time I took I-35 down to Laredo, in the spring of 2022, I left my rental car in a parking lot on the southern edge of town and walked toward the Juárez-Lincoln international bridge. A thick layer of ashen clouds blocked the sun, causing the temperature to drop by twenty degrees from the day before. With engines rumbling like a swarm of bees, vehicles inched across the river from Mexico, all four northbound lanes crammed bumper to bumper, before they fanned out into over a dozen inspection lanes. Traffic in the other direction was moving faster. Most Semana Santa travelers had already returned home and I saw fewer vehicles wrapped with ropes around half-open trunks stuffed with boxes of video games, inflatable swimming pools, and other bargains found on sale at Walmart or Lowe's.

US federal agents in dark blue uniforms stood in outbound lanes and kept their eyes on the throng of cars advancing south, towards Mexico. They were on alert. A few weeks earlier, Mexican security forces had arrested the latest individual to be titled the leader of CDN and turned him over to US authorities.[1] Armed groups who tried to rescue this man, a nephew of Z-40, set cargo trucks on fire to block roads and spread mayhem in Nuevo Laredo. US agents on duty that night could hear gunfire in Tamaulipas from their posts on the Texas side of the border.

"They went through inventory," Alfredo Flores, the port director, said as we walked over to the inspection area. He knew CDN spent a lot of ammo that night fighting the Mexican military and needed to replenish their arsenal.

Any of those cars sliding into southbound lanes in front of us could be carrying ammunition. The ends of holidays, when ports were packed and agents overwhelmed, were particularly good times for crossing contraband. Even on ordinary days the CBP couldn't search even a fraction of over ten thousand passenger vehicles going over the bridge in both directions.[2] And their efforts weren't evenly distributed. The government continued to prioritize inbound traffic: inspecting vehicles entering the United States, not those leaving. Captured drugs and migrants—not guns—remained the two most important metrics they used to showcase their work protecting the country.

An agent pulled over a Ford F-150 and told the driver to step out of the truck so they could send it through a scanner. They knew that scrupulous smugglers concealed guns in spare tires, modified compartments behind rear seats, in fuel tanks, under bumpers, even in the I-beams of pickup trucks.[3] Last year, they stopped a Dodge Ram and found eight semiautomatic rifles, including a .50 caliber Barrett with scopes, hidden in a futon the driver was taking to Mexico. Having done this for years, the agents knew what to pay attention to. They trusted their senses and those senses told them that something with the F-150 was off. When X-ray images didn't resolve their doubts, they brought in a golden retriever to sniff the truck. Still nothing. Warily, they let the driver go.

Most of the stops ended like that. There were days when agents didn't seize anything. In 2020, they confiscated nearly 100,000 rounds of ammunition and 158 rifles, three times more than in 2019.[4] But that was an unusually good year. Because of the pandemic, the border was closed to nonessential traffic, crossings dramatically fell, and agents, who ordinarily inspected passports and visas of incoming travelers and diligently looked for drugs, were sent over to the southbound lanes. Since they searched more vehicles exiting the United States, they found more guns.

Once they began stopping cars, the agents knew that scouts watching them from the nearby street would alert smugglers that the bridge was "hot." Their only chance was those vehicles already stuck in outbound lanes, like fish caught in a net. The others would wait until the inspectors left and cross their cargo when the port "cooled down."

The lawsuit the Mexican government filed against US gunmakers meandered through the legal system. Smith & Wesson, Barrett, and other companies filed a joint motion to dismiss the case, insisting that gun violence in Mexico was not their responsibility. The companies claimed that they "do not owe any legal duty to protect Mexico from gun violence committed by criminals within its own borders."[5] The long and attenuated chain of actors, from straw buyers to smugglers to criminal groups, made it difficult to establish "proximate cause," they argued. On September 30, 2022, more than a year after the civil lawsuit was filed, Judge F. Dennis Saylor IV dismissed it, writing that "while the Court has considerable sympathy for the people of Mexico, and none whatsoever for those who traffic guns to Mexican criminal organizations, it is duty-bound to follow the law."[6] US law protected gun manufacturers from lawsuits that sought to hold them accountable as long as people used firearms for their "intended purpose." Killing was the gun's intended purpose.

During the time it took me to write this book, US factories made tens of millions of firearms. In 2020 alone, despite economic shutdowns due to the pandemic, US gun manufacturers produced over 6 million handguns and nearly 3 million rifles—more than in years past.[7] In 2021, production ramped up even further, to nearly 8 million handguns and almost 4 million rifles. If researchers are right, about a quarter million of those US-made weapons—and more if we add guns that US companies imported from Europe and Asia—ended up in Mexico.[8] It means that since I started following the guns south in 2018, over a million firearms may have been smuggled across the border. In the same period, more than a hundred thousand Mexican citizens died from gunshot wounds.[9] Over a million tried to flee their country. Hundreds got injured during their attempts to cross into the United States.[10] At least 2,372 died trying.[11]

Wounds that doctors treat at hospital emergency rooms and those forensic pathologists examine during autopsies are only the most tangible forms of gun violence. Social reverberations take longer to see and much longer to heal. People who survive violence live with experiences of trauma. Their families do too. As do relatives of Mexican citizens who have been disappeared—neither alive nor confirmed dead. All over the country there are people who live in fear of potential violence—violence often inflicted by US guns—unable to turn to anyone, least of all the security forces, for protection. With trust between the people and the state strained, guns sever the remaining threads of political and legal accountability. Though distrust of the government is widely shared, the sense of insecurity isn't. Illegal guns have created and exacerbated legal inequality, making access to law and justice patchy, dependent on one's social status and economic resources. While some, like Miguel, could act as if they were impervious to the imperatives of the law, rising above formal rules they knew didn't apply to them, others, like Samara, found themselves below the threshold of the state's care, deemed unworthy of legal protection. Expendable in the government's "drug war," they could be killed and their deaths not even counted, or locked up and never formally tried. Forgotten, as if they never even existed.

Guns have also distorted vocabulary, altering our perception of social reality and pushing truth further out of reach. In Mexico, certain words and names have become taboo in order to safeguard those who risked their lives when uttering them, be they journalists, elected officials, or social workers. Other words took their place, becoming popular shorthand, flattening social discourse into a simple narrative of two sides, the good and the evil, investing the former with legal and moral authority while dehumanizing the latter. The rhetoric of the "drug war" justified violence against civilians who didn't even have to be proven guilty. Alternative narratives, which point to the dirty crimes of the state, always existed, but believing their claims meant abandoning the comfort of the official story about the rule of law for a more messy and scary account of events, and not everyone was ready for that.

In the United States, too, guns have left a mark on language, so deep that it has cut to the core of national identity, magnifying the fault lines that divide American society. Trapped in grammar that may have fit a settler colonial state more than two centuries ago, we are unable to update the terms of social contract to match contemporary reality. We make small alterations to public rhetoric: replacing gun "regulation" with gun "safety" to appease gun rights' advocates, and discarding the discourse of crime in favor of treating gun violence as a public health epidemic. These are crucial, even if tiny steps. Some day we may be able to talk about guns as we do about cars or shovels—as material objects, as practical means to an end, not tokens of national identity. But how long can we afford to wait?

I began following American guns south in order to understand what they were doing to Mexican society. From the stories migrants and refugees told me I already knew I would find communities scarred by gun violence and people who were living in fear, some of whom were choosing to leave their homes in search of safety and better lives. I knew that this journey would eventually take me back to the border, right to where I had started, that the plight of migrants and refugees running away from threats would only lead to further militarization and fortification of the barrier separating "us" from "them." After all, the desire to prevent migrants from crossing is a strong political potion that reliably wins elections in the United States. And yet I was surprised by how few people recognize that it's a circle. Even the language we choose to talk about violence south of the border, using such terms as "narcos" and "cartels," only reinforces the idea that Mexico is a dangerous country and we need to build a barrier lest those people coming from over there—not only Mexico, but also Honduras and Guatemala, Haiti and Venezuela, and many other places—would bring violence here.

Somehow, we fail to connect the dots: that the violence people are fleeing, the violence we are afraid they would spread in the United States is, in large part, of our own making—that the tools come from the factories in Massachusetts, Connecticut, and Tennessee, some smuggled across the borders, others legally exported to foreign military and police forces with records of abuse.[12] Even more: these guns come from the same regions where addiction to opioids has created demand for drugs that continue to enrich smugglers in Mexico; that the money Americans spend on fentanyl, heroin, or meth will be used to buy guns to arm those who supply this contraband. Nor do we realize that the US government's pursuit of the most prominent Mexican traffickers and their extraditions to face trials on this side of the border—the list that includes several leaders of the Gulf Cartel and the Zetas—have deprived communities that have suffered their brutality most directly of recourse to justice, further fraying the social fabric of Mexican society. Osiel Cárdenas Guillén was sentenced in Texas in 2010 to twenty-five years for drug trafficking, money laundering, and threatening to murder US federal agents.[13] Miguel Ángel Treviño Morales, Z-40, who was arrested in Nuevo Laredo in 2013, is locked up in a prison in Mexico, while his lawyers continue blocking his extradition to the United States.[14] His brother Omar Treviño Morales, Z-42, captured in Monterrey in 2015, was sentenced in 2019 to eighteen years in prison for carrying firearms reserved for the exclusive use of the armed forces.[15] So far, neither the Treviño Morales brothers nor numerous other crime bosses already imprisoned for drug-related offenses in the United States have been held accountable for what they have done to Mexican citizens—for threats, assaults, kidnappings, murders.

If you've read this far, you may be asking what can be done about this. How can we begin to unwind this spiral of violence? Although this book is not a policy manual that outlines a plan of action, the inside look it provides into the lives affected by gun trafficking suggests some ideas for where to start. Unfortunately, just like getting into this mess took multiple failed policies that compounded the situation over time, getting out will require various reforms that will take years to show results. The good news is that we can start at home, with small changes that would have far-reaching effects. Any laws that would increase gun safety in the United States would by default reduce the number of guns trafficked to Mexico. These can be very simple, such as mandating gun manufacturers to adopt smart technology, whether based on biometric recognition, like thumb scans on our phones, or radio frequency identification used in car keys. Such personalized firearms wouldn't work in the hands of others, which would not only make guns safer at home, preventing unintentional shootings by children, but also ruin their appeal to thieves and to smugglers.[16]

Another important, though more contentious step would be to follow Mexico's example and limit the types and quantities of firearms that civilians are allowed to buy.[17] There is no reason for common citizens to own .50 caliber rifles. And nobody needs to buy a dozen AR-15s or AK-47s in one year, let alone one month. These weapons are designed for the battlefield and do not have practical uses in everyday life. But they are particularly sought after by organized crime groups in Mexico. Restricting the ownership of military style semiautomatic weapons and sniper rifles would make US citizens feel safer in public places: schools, churches, movie theaters, supermarkets, and other venues where mass shootings have occurred in recent years. And it would curb firearms trafficking, making Mexican citizens feel safer in their country too. An additional step would entail regulating ammunition. Unlike guns, which are durable and can remain operational for decades, cartridges are single-use. Organized crime groups in Mexico depend on replenishments from the United States, where sales of ammunition in amounts exceeding any reasonable legitimate purpose remain unregulated. Capping the quantity of ammunition that gun owners can purchase monthly, as is done in Mexico (and like the United States already does with certain medications, such as pseudoephedrine), would go a long way in helping cut off this lethal supply chain.

As the cases discussed in this book show, smugglers adapt to new law enforcement tactics. When buying guns in licensed firearms dealerships becomes difficult, they turn to gun shows or internet groups to arrange purchases from individuals that entail no paperwork. Making background checks universal and requiring them in private firearms sales would close this loophole. Another loophole that needs attention is the very definition of a firearm. Only a finished frame or receiver—the part of the gun that contains the firing mechanism—has a serial number and is currently regulated by the US government as a firearm. This makes it possible to assemble weapons at home, from parts bought legally, without any oversight. So-called "ghost guns" make up only a tiny fraction of firearms used by organized crime groups in Mexico today because they simply don't need them while they have such easy access to finished products. But once trafficking of regular guns becomes increasingly difficult, this is likely to change. We should be thinking ahead.

Lastly, because smugglers rely on straw buyers who, when caught, often get away on probation, increasing penalties for paperwork violation may discourage people from getting involved in what for years was a low-stakes crime. The new firearms trafficking law passed in June 2022 in response to the mass shooting in Uvalde, Texas, increased sentences for straw purchasing to up to fifteen years in prison.[18] The first person to be indicted under the new law in August 2022 was a US citizen caught driving on I-35 toward the Mexican border in Laredo with seventeen firearms hidden in his car.[19] But such punitive measures that go after people who know little about firearms and may not understand the risks they are taking alone would merely expand the prison industrial complex in the United States. Instead, ATF should focus on gun dealers with a track record of selling guns to straw buyers and make them accountable for negligent business practices.

In Mexico, policy changes that are most urgently needed have almost nothing to do with guns and everything to do with why people seek them. Even comprehensive firearms regulations will be useless unless citizens trust in the government's ability to keep them safe. Gun buyback programs help rid households and communities of unwanted weapons, reducing the chances of them being used in domestic violence situations or to commit suicide, but their impact on gun crimes in most of the country is minimal. Organized crime groups are not interested in surrendering their guns voluntarily, while residents who feel insecure in their neighborhoods don't want to give up their firearms either. Changing this requires addressing both issues: weakening organized crime groups—which involves implementing social and economic programs that provide alternatives to youth who are being recruited to join them, as well as strengthening the criminal justice system—and building trust between citizens and state institutions, which will take time and a lot of goodwill.

One place to start is for the Mexican government to remove the military and the National Guard from domestic affairs and focus on working with local communities in creating public security institutions that are attentive to residents' needs. Training public prosecutors and police detectives, and providing them with adequate resources, will be important. But to make people trust the state and its security forces, government officials, the military, and various police groups must first accept their responsibility for engaging in systemic human rights violations that go back decades. Repairing the social fabric entails a public reckoning with state crimes.

Among other measures the Mexican government should take to stop the circle of violence is ending abuses in the criminal justice system, including doing away with the widespread use of pretrial detention. The authorities should hire more public defenders, and support more educational and vocational programs for the over two hundred thousand people already confined to correctional institutions. Providing them with legal and financial aid to rebuild their lives after incarceration would equip them with tools to refuse recruitment into criminal groups. Civil society organizations, such as Promoción de Paz, are doing a lot, but they can't do it alone. The Mexican government should commit a substantial amount of the compensation it is demanding from US gun makers and dealers in the lawsuits it filed against them to fund such programs.

These changes to laws and policies can only succeed if those implementing them acknowledge that Mexico and the United States are in this together. The demand for drugs in the United States has created the demand for guns in Mexico. The supply of guns in the United States aids the supply of drugs in Mexico. Because of this, solutions to a regional problem, if they are to address the causes of violence and not be distracted by putting a Band-Aid on their most visible effects, must take the binational community as its starting point. Stopping the unregulated sale of 5.7 or 7.62 caliber ammunition in Texas or Arizona would result in fewer wounded police officers in Mexico; at the same time, police detectives in Veracruz and Guerrero who are better trained and paid would be able to investigate extortion, making residents more likely to stay home than flee for refuge across the US border. Investing in addiction treatment programs in Massachusetts and Ohio would help reduce forceful recruitment of Mexican youth to gangs, just as educational and job opportunities for youth in Sonora and Tamaulipas would further slow the flow of drugs to the United States. If this book offers one critical policy lesson, it is that communities on both sides of the border are entangled and so are the solutions.

No matter how many years I've been coming back to southern Arizona, I'm always surprised by the changes in the desert once the monsoons start. With the rains, the dry pale land puts on luxurious green robes: mesquite, acacia, sycamores, and ocotillos compete by showing off their verdant colors. It never looks like the same desert I thought I knew.

"It's beautiful," I said turning to my friend Bob. It was the summer of 2022, seven years after we first met at the volunteer orientation for Tucson Samaritans, the humanitarian group that aids migrants crossing the border through the desert. Sporting dark sunglasses, a broad smile lighting up his suntanned face, Bob didn't seem to have aged at all.

We slowed down and got in line at the Border Patrol checkpoint on I-19—the last stop for cars and trucks heading north; the last chance for the agents to question who belonged in this country; their last effort to find migrants or drugs. Just a month earlier, fifty-three people died in the back of a tractor-trailer, overheated and dehydrated, on a journey past such a checkpoint in Texas. The agent in a dark green uniform waved us through.

We were returning to Tucson after a day at the medical clinic on the Mexican side of the border in Nogales. Bob was driving. I was telling him about what I saw in Laredo and Allende and how ready I was to move on from guns. He was recounting his recent trips to the desert—leaving water and food for the migrants, tending to the crosses for those who didn't make it. Bob had been doing this week after week, month after month, year after year, for more than a decade already, and he was determined to continue, for as long as there were people risking their lives to get to safety.

A few weeks earlier, when the summer rains had just started, Bob and another volunteer reached the very end of the wall in the Pajarito Mountains, about midway between Nogales and Sasabe. They didn't go there that often. There were no roads. No cell phone reception. I remembered putting extra rescue flares in the trunk of a four-wheel drive last time I'd gone to that area. Even Border Patrol agents rarely ventured this far. Bob said they left their SUV with a white Samaritan cross on the dirt path they took from Arivaca and continued on foot, carrying backpacks filled with food and water they planned to leave on the migrant trail, just like they had done on their previous trips.

"Then we saw two guys," Bob said. "They looked very young and were armed with AR-15s." The Samaritans didn't move, waiting to see what the men would do. "They called out to us and asked for help," Bob continued. "They said that they were Mexican and that they were leading a group of eight and that they were out of supplies."

"Did they ask you at gunpoint?" I said, wondering why he mentioned the ARs.

"No," Bob said. "Before they approached, they took off the rifles and propped them against the wall."

That image has stayed with me. Of the guns and the wall. Both forged from steel. Both made in America.

Acknowledgments

A book is a debt and a promise, inevitably only partially fulfilled.

Samara and Miguel, two people I want to thank most of all, cannot be named here. They shared their stories despite the risks of talking to someone they didn't know about things that could put them in prison and introduced me to their friends and their families. Thank you for your trust and for the time we spent together. Without your courage to speak, this book would not exist.

It would also not exist but for the generosity of many others who helped me throughout the years it took me to research and write it. Some of them, too, must remain anonymous to protect their privacy and keep them safe. But there are others I can name. I am grateful to Mauricio Benítez, for taking me to Monterrey for the first time, and to Ana Villarreal, for helping me find someone to talk to about guns while I was there; Consuelo Bañuelos, for inviting me to visit prisons and introducing me to people who were living in and out of them, among them, Ivan and Davíd; Gershon Ben Keren, for listening to my fears and teaching me what to do to be safe; Juan Cedillo, for having patience with my unending questions and for companionship on the road we took across the borderlands; and the special agent I call Jackson, for his patience reliving the past when I asked for ever more minor details about what happened now almost a decade ago.

A number of journalists helped me on this journey: Marcela Turati, who laughed when I brought an empty piñata to her birthday party, and gave me Juan's number; Alfredo Corchado, who was the voice of reason whenever I sought his advice—in Cambridge, Mexico City, and on one snowy day in El Paso; June Erlick, who introduced me to both Marcela and Alfredo and met with me at my favorite bar on Kirkland Street, where she agreed to be my emergency contact. One late spring day in New Bedford, before we went to watch migrant fishermen leaving the shore, Francisco Goldman encouraged me to do more at a time when I desperately wanted this to be over. Sergio Aguayo, Angela Kocherga, Melva Frutos, and Seth Harp were generous with their time, contacts, and information.

Robin Reineke and her colleagues at the Pima County Office of the Medical Examiner showed me exit wounds on human skulls. Ricardo Bojorquez disapproved of my interest in guns, but still drove me around Nogales and Rio Rico to all the places I wanted to see. Bob Kee took me along to the medical aid clinic in Nogales and introduced me to the jack-fruit tacos at Tumerico. Rick Pauza organized my visit to the Laredo Port of Entry, where Albert Flores and his team let me see how they find contraband guns and ammunition. Víctor Castelán helped me imagine what it was like inside the juvenile detention center a decade before I stepped inside. Brian DeLay, over a video call in the middle of winter, talked with me about the history of firearms in Spanish and British colonies. Jason De León helped me think about beginnings and endings and Mexican slang.

Throughout the years, I have turned to other researchers who study gun violence, for guidance and advice, and I am grateful for the conversations I had with David Hemenway, Chelsea Parsons, Eugenio Weigend, John Lindsay-Poland, as well as other members of the Network to Prevent Gun Violence in the Americas. I have benefited from suggestions and support from fellow anthropologists and other scholars, who shared with me everything from details about art exhibits to reading recommendations, especially Rebecca Carter, Elizabeth Ferry, Sandra Rozental, Patricia Alvarez Astacio, Peter Andreas, Davíd Carrasco, Janet McIntosh, David Kertzer, Gabriela Soto-Laveaga, Graham Denyer-Willis, and Lucas Bessire. Elizabeth and Jason, as well as Joe Heyman, Dominic Boyer, and Shaylih Muehlmann, also wrote recommendation letters for the grants and fellowships I applied for to do this research and to write the book—thanks to them I had the institutional support and funding for multiple trips to Mexico and throughout the United States and dedicated time to finish the manuscript.

Since 2018, I worked with a handful of brilliant students who helped collect, systematize, and analyze archival materials and data obtained through public records requests: Kiara Gomez and Stephany Gutierrez scoured newspaper archives for information about the passage of the Mexican federal gun law and how it changed the experiences of gun owners in Mexico; Nina Chandra found out how US media portrayed changing laws in Mexico and looked into past and present gun legislation in the United States; Shania Hurtado explored firearms regulations in British and Spanish American colonies; and Isaac Ochoa reviewed ATF's Fast and Furious operation and the Mérida Initiative.

Institutional and financial support for this research came from the Weatherhead Center for International and Public Affairs and the Dean's Fund for Competitive Scholarship at Harvard University, and the Watson Institute for International and Public Affairs at Brown University. I am grateful to Jessaca Leinaweaver, Edward Steinfeld, and Joel Revill, for enabling me to take a sabbatical leave from Brown one year earlier to finish writing this book. Final revisions were made while I was a 2022–2023 Maury Green Fellow at the Harvard Radcliffe Institute, where my fellow fellows provided company and a caring, engaging intellectual community when I most needed it. I am especially grateful to Omar Dewachi for our conversations about wounds, which he knows better than I do, and to Jenny Boylan, my neighbor at the far end of Byerly Hall, for those Dunkin lattes. During the months we spent together in Cambridge, Tsitsi Dangarembga, Rahul Bhatia, Gaby Calvocoressi, Rebecca Hall, Brodie Fischer, Chris Muller, Caleb Gayle, Maxine Gordon, and Francesca Mari, among others, helped me think through some hard questions and provided encouragement to move forward as the deadline to submit the manuscript approached. Will Cheng's piano improvisations were a special gift. The Radcliffe staff were outstanding and ensured we didn't need to worry about anything but our own work.

At a critical period two winters ago, Kerri Arsenault convinced me that I could write a book I wanted to write. I am grateful to her for introducing me to the community of writers that stretches from Rhode Island to Maine, and for banishing "imaginaries" and other remnants of academic jargon from the manuscript. I shared early drafts of several chapters in Kerri's nonfiction workshop at MWPA's Snowbound Writers Retreat and in Rob Spillman's craft seminar, among other writing classes I took over the past few years, and I received helpful feedback from the instructors as well as fellow participants. The publisher invited three scholars to provide detailed peer review—they read the full manuscript and gave me suggestions for revising both arguments and prose.

Enoch Liao, Genevieve Guenther, and Nina Chandra also commented on the draft. A big thank you to all the early readers.

My editor, Kate Marshall, was excited about this book when it was still a kernel of an idea and (unlike me) never worried that I would not pull it through. When I finished the draft, she printed it out and scribbled on the pages in what turned out to be a magic marker with vanishing ink. Not the one to despair, she read and marked the whole thing again, this time with a regular pen, then mailed me the manuscript and the offending marker as a keepsake. I do not know what kind of writer I would be without Kate as my editor.

My agent, Jessica Papin, understood what I had set out to do from the rough draft I sent her and skillfully steered the book proposal through the publishing world. I was very fortunate to have her on my side every step of the way and I hope she accompanies me on all future journeys.

I am grateful to Chad Attenborough, Jeff Anderson, Alex Dahne, Angela Chen, Lia Tjandra, Katryce Lassle, and the entire team at the University of California Press, for the care they have given to this book, from production to publication and promotion. Lynda Crawford was the most patient and diligent copyeditor. Joan Shapiro made the index. John Wyatt Greenlee drew the map.

Small gestures mean a lot to a writer. Thank you, Paul Sennott, for the legal advice; Heron, for that extra shot of whiskey; Ūla, for that introduction; Kieran, for the "winter is coming" patch; Sylvia, for the matcha; Dahir, for making kombucha to soothe the missed jabs; Vince, for the nickname I haven't yet lived up to; and the elderly bearded man who walks by the river at sunrise, for greeting me when I run past him every morning.

In periods of darkness and doubt, I turned to my friends and family, who listened and cautioned and, no matter what I did, stood by my sometimes questionable choices. Thank you, Aiste, Mary, Deividas, Anna, Arto, Burcu, and Casey for always being there for me when I needed to talk or be silent together. Thank you, mom and dad, for coming to Mexico with me, to see a little of what I had found there, to understand why I keep crossing borders.

About This Project

Methods, Ethics, Sources

Exit Wounds began with an insight that lodged into my mind like a splinter, and moved forward because I let it fester. I knew the border, but I knew nothing about guns, except that getting close to those who smuggled them and used them to perpetrate violence wouldn't be easy. I understood even less what writing about them—those people and the guns—would entail, how their stories would affect me.

This book is the result of over five years of ethnographic and archival research in Mexico and the United States, but it builds on my experience as an emergency responder and an anthropologist in the borderlands that spans more than a decade. My attempts to understand violence started even earlier, trying to make sense of my daily life growing up in Lithuania in the 1980s, when the country was occupied and governed by a repressive state apparatus, in a house blocks away from Soviet military facilities, in a family not afraid to resist. I didn't plan to study violence. My college honor's thesis was on utopian communities. It was only after I arrived in the United States for graduate school that I began to think more critically about the forms of violence in contemporary societies. Looking for answers, I turned to borders, where proximity between social worlds cleaved by boundaries both arbitrary and firm laid bare the presumptions about law and order that we often take for granted. I conducted ethnographic research with journalists on the border between Argentina, Brazil, and Paraguay, examining how media narratives of crime and security are made. And for the past decade I have been working with emergency responders—firefighters, EMTs, paramedics—on the US-Mexico border, studying the materiality of violence and rescue work.

I am an ethnographer, which means that my knowledge of social phenomena comes from immersion in the daily activities of people whose lives and perspectives I seek to understand. Both as a research practice—a method that is embedded and embodied—and as a genre of storytelling, ethnography fore-grounds human experience.[1] But it does more than that. Anthropologist Deborah Thomas, documenting state violence in the Caribbean, described it as a form of witnessing that is "response-able"—it involves assuming responsibility.[2] The focus on people enables ethnographers to tell lesser-known stories and provide new angles from which to see situations that may appear deceptively familiar. At the same time, witnessing is not a passive act. It implicates the one who tells the story.

Ethnography relies on proximity to people, on letting the experiences of others leave an imprint on you, and these human relationships are what makes ethnographic research both thrilling and challenging—physically, emotionally, ethically.[3] Emergency responders I had worked with accepted me as one of their own—they were family to me. I trusted them with my life and they trusted me with theirs. Despite occasional disagreements on matters both political and personal, we shared core values and deep commitment to serving the community. Such camaraderie wasn't possible when I began hanging out with people who engaged in violence. But nor could I close myself off. Writer Alice Munro called it "the pain of human contact." Ethnography is often painful this way, though reasons vary and some relationships hurt more than others. I came to care about the people I met during fieldwork—including some whom I was sometimes afraid of. And caring about them made me anxious about not being able to protect them. As a researcher, I have responsibility to do no harm to those I work with, even though it is not that simple to predict the forms that harm could take in the years ahead. But when people engage in practices that are criminalized, such as smuggling or extortion or murder, the harm to them from participating in research could be immediate—arrest, imprisonment. Being accepted into their lives required me to plan thoroughly in order not to put anyone at risk—neither them, nor me.

Besides the practical steps I took each day, such as not writing down most people's real names, I made two strategic decisions that guided this project. The first was dispersing fieldwork temporally and spatially over several years and a handful of sites. I began with the government and the military in Mexico City, then moved to Monterrey, Nuevo León, to work with people who engaged in gun trafficking and gun violence, not returning to speak to state officials again. I conducted research in the United States with agents pursuing gun traffickers in Arizona instead of Texas, which would have been too close to the region in Mexico—Tamaulipas, Coahuila, Nuevo León—where I met with members of organized crime. I did this so that I would not cross legal and ethical lines and not, even unintentionally, violate anyone's trust. My second decision was to embrace bricolage as a narrative technique and let structure—fractured, intertwining storylines and shifts between ethnographic present and linear sequences of events—be part of the argument. These ethical and stylistic choices enabled proximity while allowing for a degree of distance, which I have found necessary when writing about violence.

Exit Wounds draws on a variety of methods and sources, but it is first and foremost a multi-sited ethnography. I conducted extensive fieldwork in Monterrey and Mexico City, and made multiple research trips to Nogales, Tucson, and

Phoenix in Arizona; Laredo, Austin, and Houston in Texas; the northern Mexican states of Tamaulipas, Nuevo León, and Coahuila; and Washington, DC, as well as once to Glynco, Georgia, where the Federal Law Enforcement Training Center is located. I followed a handful of people in their daily lives, observing and participating, jotting down what I noticed and what I heard, snapshots of activities and conversations that became field notes when I typed them up on my laptop in the evenings or first thing the following morning. But ethnographic fieldwork was not possible when I wanted to learn about events that occurred in the past or when I deliberately chose not to participate in some activities, such as gun smuggling, out of legal and ethical considerations. In those cases, I relied on extensive, often repeated interviews. I interviewed people who were affiliated with organized crime groups and who had committed crimes involving guns as well as gun owners who bought smuggled firearms, but did not engage in other illegal practices. I interviewed government officials, military officers, personnel of the criminal justice and juvenile detention system in Mexico, and current and former federal agents with CBP, HSI, and ATF in the United States. I also spoke with firearms dealers, hunters, collectors, government and defense attorneys, social workers, gun violence researchers, journalists, policy experts, forensic examiners, medical doctors, activists, and artists.

Although I worked on both sides of the border, I spent more time in Mexico than in the United States. After all, I sought to understand the impact of US firearms abroad. In Nuevo León, I hung out with gun owners, accompanying them as they bought ammunition and practiced at the range and shared stories of their hunting trips. During the time we spent together, they taught me practical things, like how to order an illegal gun on WhatsApp and how to manually reload cartridges. Not to be more of an outsider than I already was—a woman and a foreigner in this community of gun aficionados that were all Mexican men—I arrived somewhat prepared. I took a couple of gun safety courses in Boston to learn how to shoot and how to unload firearms. When I moved to Rhode Island, I passed the Blue Card test, which is required to purchase a handgun, and bid on a firearm at an online auction. Though I ended up not buying a gun back then, my rudimentary training made me feel a bit safer around people who liked to shoot.[4]

But getting ready for the part of the project that involved meeting with people who had engaged in gun violence, including committing murder, kidnapping, and extortion, took more than that. By the time I began research in Mexico, I had spent a year training in krav maga, which I continued to do until after my last field trip in 2022. Knowing what to do should someone threaten me with a gun made me believe I had some agency under circumstances I could not otherwise control. At the very least, even mentioning those skills proved useful for stopping several unwanted advances and gave me more confidence during fieldwork than the satellite radio, the emergency app on my phone, and the proof of life I left with my family and friends. These preparations seemed exaggerated at times, but having a plan put me at ease. Above all, what kept me safe were more basic practices I had adopted during previous research trips: relying on advice from local people I trusted, being transparent about who I was and what I was doing, and trying to use common sense. This is not to say everything went well. Plans fell through when I turned down invitations that would have been valuable for the project but I knew that accepting them would mean giving in return something I was not willing to offer. In the end, it was also mere luck that I returned unscathed, at least on the surface.

I met some of the people who had engaged in gun violence inside prisons. Others I got to know after they had been released, as they were trying to rebuild their lives: going to school, looking for jobs, reconciling with their families, all while running into the same neighbors who knew about their past and dealing with the consequences of having a criminal record. We shared each other's company during meals and car rides and social events and, particularly during the pandemic, spent hours chatting on WhatsApp, FaceTime, and over Zoom. I first got to know some of them through Promoción de Paz, a Monterrey-based nongovernmental organization that works with people who have been incarcerated as well as those who live in colonias with a high risk of violence. I also accompanied social workers and volunteers to several carceral institutions in the metropolitan Monterrey area and spent time in their offices, in meetings with politicians and administrators responsible for security, at conferences and public events, and, occasionally, in their homes.

My ethnographic fieldwork in Mexico City focused on gun buyback programs that I observed in four boroughs and under two different local and federal administrations, in 2018 and 2019. I hung out with soldiers and policemen who examined firearms and ammunition people turned in and watched the military technicians destroy them. In September 2018, I also accompanied volunteers with the "*Por tu familia, desarme voluntario*" program as they surveyed borough residents about their perceptions of safety and their opinions about the gun buyback campaign. With permission from SEDENA, I visited Mexico's only gun store at the time located on the army base in the capital and the museum at SEDENA's headquarters that holds gold-plated trophy guns confiscated from organized crime groups. I went to public museums, too, including the Army Museum and the National Museum of Anthropology, and saw numerous exhibits that directly or indirectly engaged with the place of guns in Mexican history and culture, from the murals depicting the revolutionary heroes to contemporary artworks produced in memory of the Ayotzinapa students. These visual narratives demonstrated the tension that exists between the role of gun violence in the official history of the Mexican state and its insidious forms in the lived experiences of the people.

On the US side of the border, I went to multiple gun stores, pawn shops, gun shows, and gun ranges in Tucson and Phoenix in Arizona; and in Austin, Houston, and Laredo in Texas. Other than making me familiar with the vibe and the inventories, these visits were not particularly informative. Sometimes, the stores were too busy, with long lines of customers waiting for their turn to buy a gun, and the staff had no time to chat. When they weren't as crowded, I asked sales clerks about ID and paperwork requirements and whether they carried specific models that were most desired by organized crime groups in Mexico. But once they realized I was not going to purchase a gun, conversations soon wound down. If I brought up the question of gun smuggling, the staff referred me to managers who never responded to my requests to talk. There were some exceptions, though—gun dealers who were very generous. When I told a store clerk in Tucson that I was writing about .50 caliber guns, but had never seen one in real life, he went to the back room and brought out a CDX-50 he had already sold just to let me hold it.

I had been planning to attend court proceedings for several gun trafficking cases in Arizona and Texas, but defendants in most of them pleaded guilty, never going to trial. To understand what they did and how, I scoured through indictments, sentencing memos, and other documents that were available through Public Access to Court Electronic Records (PACER). In the few cases that went to trial in the past, like USA v. *Edgar Vega-Barreras et al.*, USA v. *Andre Rene Garcia and Jorge Acosta-Licerio*, and USA v. *Emilio Villalobos-Alcala and Jose Eluid Lugo-Lopez*, I read thousands of pages of trial transcripts, which contained sworn testimonies by defendants as well as ATF, HSI, and CBP agents who investigated the crimes. The details in those transcripts proved invaluable for describing operations of gun smuggling that I could not observe. While indictments didn't offer such depth as trial transcripts, the sheer number of them and their repetitive nature pointed to the trends in gun trafficking and helped identify patterns. Still, court documents, no matter how thorough, weren't enough. As an ethnographer, I wanted to get closer to the lived experience of those involved, so I reached out to the people whose names appeared in case records, by phone and by email as well as in person. My attempts to speak with the defendants didn't lead anywhere, but I interviewed several prosecuting and defense attorneys and federal agents involved in those cases. I also went to see the locations mentioned in trial transcripts, from mobile homes to gun stores, to get a better sense of those places in order to write about them.

When I teach ethnographic research methods, I tell students about the importance of patience, persistence, and humility when seeking out other people's stories and caution them that in the end, even if they do everything right, they may still hit a wall. I hit many. There were some people I asked for interviews multiple times, sent reminders of my requests, repeatedly called, and once even flew to a city and drove almost five hours to another to knock on the door, and still the answer was no. I accepted refusals. Over the years I lost count of how many people turned me down. Some smugglers wanted to be paid for interviews. Others declined through their attorneys without providing an explanation. Occasionally, people who were willing to talk changed their minds. I understood them: speaking about illegal activities presented risks to them. Gun dealers, smugglers, and buyers were not the only ones refusing to meet with me. Getting the government's side of the story was even harder. Multiple officials declined my interview requests, both on and off the record. In Mexico, for months I sought various channels to speak with forensic examiners performing autopsies at a university hospital morgue in Monterrey. It was only after I learned more about how forensic authorities were disposing of unidentified bodies—by burning, burying, or donating the remains to universities—that I realized why I couldn't get the government's permission to see the morgue.[5] In the United States, despite sending multiple emails to ATF agents and supervisors, and even showing up at their offices, I never got approval for formal interviews with anyone at the Bureau of Alcohol, Tobacco, Firearms and Explosives.

A few ATF agents spoke with me off the record and I conducted one interview with a former agent in Washington, DC, but that was it.

To compensate for this silence, I filed numerous requests for public records with federal, state, and local authorities in both countries. Through Freedom of Information Act (FOIA) in the United States and Plataforma Nacional de Transparencia (PNT) in Mexico, I asked for data on arms confiscated at customs, recovered at crime scenes, and voluntarily surrendered through gun buyback programs. I inquired about prosecutions for gun law violations and asked for information about several noteworthy cases. In Mexico, three agencies granted my requests: SEDENA; the Attorney General's Office (Fiscalía General de la República, FGR); and the General Customs Administration (Administración General de Aduanas). The latter sent me an Excel sheet with detailed descriptions of contraband they seized at land borders and airports between 2006 and 2019. In the United States, Customs and Border Protection provided data on outbound gun and ammunition seizures on the southern border for a period covering twenty years, from 2000 to 2020. The CBP Field Office in Laredo, Texas, allowed me to observe outbound inspections on the Juárez-Lincoln International Bridge, one of the busiest border crossing points between the United States and Mexico. But many more petitions were denied. ATF refused to fulfill my FOIA requests, arguing that the data I sought was "exempt from disclosure."[6] This was not a surprise—ATF routinely denies FOIA requests for firearms trace data, referring to the exclusions for law enforcement and national security records.

Some of the documents I sought were already in the public domain because journalists and investigators had found them earlier and had made them available online. Global Exchange, a nonprofit human rights organization that oversees the project "Stop US Arms to Mexico," shares on their website full datasets obtained through public information requests—among them, the Mexico Police Firearms Database (https://stopusarmstomexico.org). The National Security Archive published key declassified documents, including witness testimonies, from a four-thousand-page dossier compiled by Mexico's National Human Rights Commission (CNDH), following investigations of the Zetas massacre in Allende, Coahuila. CNDH later issued a recommendation relating to what happened in Allende (10 VG/2018) and also published a report on the investigation of the Casino Royale attack in Monterrey, both of which I read carefully. To situate my observations and interviews inside prisons and the juvenile detention center in Monterrey in a broader historical and social context, I drew on investigative reports by Mexican and international human rights organizations, including Amnesty International, the UN Subcommittee on Prevention of Torture and Other Cruel, Inhuman or Degrading Treatment or Punishment, and the Nuevo León State Human Rights Commission (CEDHN), among others.

In the United States, investigations into ATF's Fast and Furious operation provided significant details about the failed gun walking scheme. These included a review prepared by the Office of the Inspector General at the Department of Justice, several reports published by the House Committee on Oversight and Government Reform, and the Senate Committee on the Judiciary. The latter contains transcribed interviews with ATF agents who were involved in the operation. I also made use of reports on firearms trafficking prepared by the Government Accountability Office, as well as data and analyses from the Violence Policy Center, the American Center for Progress, and the *Small Arms Survey*. While ATF has been reluctant to share its gun trace data, it makes other information about gun production and sales available to the public, including annual gun manufacturing reports and lists of federal firearms licensees updated monthly. The agency also publishes statistics on the total number of firearms recovered in Mexico and submitted to ATF for tracing by calendar year. The latest trace statistics available at the time of writing this book were for firearms recovered between January 1, 2014, and December 31, 2019. These reports do not provide details about the calibers of weapons, their manufacturers, locations of dealers, or any information about the places where they were recovered. However, ATF collects this data, and a leaked Excel sheet with trace records on 2,921 firearms sold in the United States and recovered in Mexico between December 2006 and December 2010, which circulated among journalists and gun researchers, has been invaluable for understanding gun trafficking patterns.

Newspapers not only provide a record of the past but also illuminate the historical context of events. The coverage of organized crime in Mexico has changed depending on the threats reporters faced. Tracing these shifts in language was important for examining the impact of firearms on society. Even silences were revealing. In some parts of northern Mexico, getting accurate information was nearly impossible because of the dangers to journalists. News there circulated via blogs and through social media, often anonymously. There are towns and villages where it is still the case to this day. And yet, despite enormous personal risks, some Mexican and American journalists covered the Zetas massacres and this book draws on their firsthand accounts and investigations, including those by Marcela Turati, Juan Cedillo, Alfredo Corchado, Sergio Aguayo, Melva Frutos, Ginger Thompson, Diego Osorno, Daniel de la Fuente, Angela Kocherga, Melissa del Bosque, and others who have been writing about organized crime in northeast Mexico.

Digital archives of Mexican periodicals provided records about the period in the 1990s and 2000s, during which the Zetas were formed. I also consulted newspaper collections of periodicals from the 1970s, when Mexico's Federal Law of Firearms and Explosives came into effect. Not all of the papers from those years were digitized and during my last trip to Monterrey before the pandemic, I spent hours at the newspaper library at the Autonomous University of Nuevo León in San Nicolás, flipping through binders of old *El Norte* issues, their pages fraying at the edges and falling apart. Historical records of those days helped situate what gun owners who remembered the passage of the law told me about that time, just as reading the forums on México Armado, a popular online site for Mexican gun owners, let me understand their reactions to current events and changing regulations.

Social scientists, many of them women, have done important research examining violence, insecurity, and organized crime in Mexico. I learned a lot from the work of Ana Villarreal, Severine Durin, Guadalupe Correa-Cabrera, and Shaylih Muehlmann, among others studying these topics. Jennifer Carlson's research on gun culture in the United States has been particularly illuminating for trying to understand what firearms mean to American society and why. I read general interest books about guns, including weapons encyclopedias and historical accounts of the Winchester, Colt, and AK-47, as well as more specialized military ballistics studies and forensic pathology textbooks on gunshot wounds. I read memoirs and biographies by and about gun dealers, gangsters, and law enforcement agents. There was so much I had to learn about guns—their history, their design, their politics.

I read fiction, too. Fernanda Melchor and Toni Morrison, Yuri Herrera and Cormac McCarthy. I was looking for a language to write about violence, for words to give knowledge the right story form, because research was not the only difficult part about working with guns—writing wasn't easy either. When I began this book, I wrestled with the question: How do I talk about crime and violence without resorting to the language and categories that foreclose inquiry? How do I avoid cliches and the traps of policy-speak? Even more importantly: How do I not make it worse? Oswaldo Zavala, who worked as a journalist in Ciudad Juárez before he became a literature scholar, suggests that words, not armies, begin wars: that the Mexican government's strategic use of language, which it copied from the United States and which journalists began repeating without questioning, has established the primacy of the "narco" narrative, which legitimized the militarization of the country.[7] But do we know how to tell this story in a different way? How do I write about the Zetas—the organization of "the last letter"[8]—without using such words as "cartel," "narcos," and "sicario"? How do I find ways to represent people without assigning them to preestablished roles? I was inspired by Mexican writer Yuri Herrera who makes lists of words he doesn't use because of their loaded meanings.[9] Ethnography, like literature, entails political responsibility and thus requires finding a language that allows us to see social problems with an open mind.

Before I started, I took a yellow Post-it note, wrote down "cartel," and taped it onto my desk as a reminder that I should find another word to refer to organized crime groups in Mexico whenever possible. Policy analysts in the United States and those who draft United Nations documents prefer abbreviations, such as TCO (transnational criminal organization) or DTO (drug trafficking organization). But these are too rigid and don't reflect the dynamic forms these groups take—not always transnational and not limited to moving drugs. The most all-encompassing term—"organized crime group"—is accurate, yet clumsy. It is not the way people talk. I heard locals call those they feared as "*los malandros*" or "*los mañosos.*" I also heard them referred to as "the mafia" or "*la maña.*" Those who worked for the CDG and the Zetas, before the two split, called their organization "La Compañía," the company. Oftentimes, in private conversations as well as in court testimonies, people who worked with the Zetas, simply opted for the pronoun "they." Others called them "*aquellas gentes*"—those people. Everyone knew who "they" or "those people" were. I use all of these in the narrative, depending on the situation, who is talking, and what words they choose. The word "cartel" appears only when it is part of the official name the organization has adopted, like "the Gulf Cartel" or the "Northeast Cartel." When it comes to individual members of these groups, I prefer the concept of "violence worker," which is descriptive and expresses the nature of their labor without an evaluative undertone that comes from using legal categories or getting lost in the game of assigning names. It also doesn't differentiate between, on the one hand, the military and the police, whose violence is designated as a legitimate use of force, and, on the other, the outlaws, whose violence is categorized as a crime. It allows us to see the fluidity and continuity between the two domains—state and crime, legal and illegal—a continuity that is conceptual as well as empirical.

Too often, the talk of crime and violence is dominated by a fascination with numbers. Counting deaths, counting working hours lost, counting guns and spent bullet casings found at homicide scenes, confiscated at customs, collected during buyback programs. We use them because, as legal anthropologist Sally Engle Merry argued in *The Seductions of Quantification*, "numbers convey an aura of objective truth and scientific authority."[10] Quantitative information appears to be transparent, but its political impartiality is deceptive. There is a great deal of interpretive work that goes into making indicators that measure rule of law, for example. They are social constructs. But even when the matter is simpler, when it is about counting objects, such as guns smuggled across the border, numbers hide as much as they show.[11] It is important to ask what gets counted and when and how and why. It is also critical to understand that when it comes to criminal practices and informal economies counting means merely estimating. We can only count the number of guns that are confiscated at customs. We can't count how many guns get across the border undetected. In response to my public records requests, both US and Mexican governments sent me Excel sheets and I made lists, arranging numbers in sequences. They say something, but they don't tell the whole story.

Such research as this is inevitably marked by uncertainty—the past lives in our memory, and memory is a particularly sensitive matter for survivors of violence. Time and trauma shape how people remember.[12] How do I write in a way that acknowledges this impossibility to know without giving up trying to understand what happened? Anthropologist Yael Navaro observed that research in the aftermath of mass violence requires a "negative methodology" which, rather than assuming the presence of evidence, begins with the premise of its absence: denial, erasure, inaccessibility, loss.[13] Such methodological pessimism regarding what is and isn't possible helps avoid writing over experiences that cannot be recovered. We are left to work with shards of the past that can't be assembled into a coherent narrative of violence.

I couldn't fact-check all the details. In Mexico, homicides go unreported and unrecorded. People spend years in jail without hearing their sentences. It is impossible to verify some parts of their stories.[14] It is too dangerous to try to pursue others. But there is more to this than the impossibility of verification. It is about research ethics. Reflecting on how refugees are asked for dates and places to establish the truthfulness and authenticity of their asylum claims, anthropologist Michael Jackson noted that for people in crisis life is not narratable in the way that we are accustomed to.[15] Hannah Arendt described such events as "an unbearable sequence of sheer happening." Survivors of the Holocaust experienced time not as chronology, but as duration. Inmates in Stalin's Gulag not only had no memory for dates or the passage of time but struggled to distinguish between their experiences and the stories they heard from others.[16] When interviewing people who had engaged in organized crime and gun violence, my repetitive questions about when this or that happened, about dates and places with which I tried to double-check the stories I was hearing, resulted in approximations and repetitions that were not always neatly compatible with each other nor easy to pin down on the calendar and on the map. What people told me did happen. Maybe not in that order. Maybe at a different time, in another place. But such confusion doesn't deny the reality of their experiences. In the end, to rephrase anthropologist Clifford Geertz, we care about the stories we tell ourselves about ourselves.[17]

With several exceptions, the names of the people in this book are pseudonyms, to ensure their privacy and their safety. The conversations are usually verbatim quotes from my own recordings and field notes or plucked from court transcripts, investigative documents, or media reports. Some quotes from interviews originally conducted in Spanish and translated into English were minimally edited for clarity. Occasionally, I reconstructed the dialogue from people's recollections, the way they remembered those conversations when they shared them with me. I did not attribute to them any comments they did not make, and I did not change any details about places or dates, which I tried to cross-check from multiple sources to the extent that I could. But I did leave out some information that could help identify and put in danger people who trusted me with their stories.

For writing, too, can wound.

Notes

THE WORKSHOP

1. Charles Bowden, *Jericho* (Austin: University of Texas Press, 2020), 97.

SHAPE OF WOUNDS

1. The names of public officials and of individuals listed in public records are real. The only exception are people in USA v. Edgar Vega-Barreras et al., and USA v. Andre Rene Garcia and Jorge Acosta-Licerio. As several individuals involved in these cases were concerned about the safety of their families and requested that I use pseudonyms, I changed all the names. For privacy reasons, I also use pseudonyms for other people throughout the book, except for those who specifically asked me to use their real names.

2. For testimonios by migrants staying at the center run by the Kino Border Initiative, see Tobin Hansen and María Engracia Robles Robles, eds., *Voices of the Border: Testimonios of Migration, Deportation, and Asylum* (Washington, DC: Georgetown University Press, 2021).

3. Between 2001 and 2022, 45,266 Mexican nationals applied for asylum in the United States. Asylum was granted to 5,700 people and 1,586 others received "other relief." Asylum was denied to 37,980 Mexican nationals who had requested it. "Asylum Decisions," TRAC Immigration, accessed August 13, 2022, https://trac.syr.edu/phptools/immigration/asylum/.

4. In fiscal year 2021, which began in October 2020 and ended in September 2021, US Customs and Border Protection (CBP) apprehended 655,594 Mexican nationals. "Southwest Land Border Encounters," CBP, accessed August 17, 2022, https://www.cbp.gov/newsroom/stats/southwest-land-border-encounters.

5. In fiscal year 2022, which began in October 2021 and ended in September 2022, CBP apprehended 808,339 Mexican nationals. This number includes

692,363 individuals expelled under Title 42 and 115,976 Title 8 apprehensions. "Southwest Land Border Encounters," accessed Oct 24, 2022.

6. Jeanine Vellema and Hendrik Johannes Scholtz, "Forensic Aspects of Ballistic Injury," in *Ballistic Trauma: A Practical Guide*, 2nd edition, ed. Peter F. Mahoney (London: Springer, 2005), 91–121.

7. Since 2020, the average number of mass shootings per year has exceeded six hundred. Gun Violence Archive, accessed March 23, 2023, https://www.gunviolencearchive.org/past-tolls.

8. Robert Gebeloff et al., "Childhood's Greatest Danger: The Data on Kids and Gun Violence," *New York Times*, December 18, 2022, https://www.nytimes.com/interactive/2022/12/14/magazine/gun-violence-children-data-statistics.html.

9. "Gun Violence Disproportionately and Overwhelmingly Hurts Communities of Color," Center for American Progress, June 30, 2022, https://www.americanprogress.org/article/gun-violence-disproportionately-and-over whelmingly-hurts-communities-of-color/.

10. "UChicago Harris/AP-NORC Poll: About 1 in 5 Americans Say Gun Violence Has Touched Their Lives and Even More Fear Being a Victim," University of Chicago Harris School of Public Policy, August 22, 2022, https://harris.uchicago.edu/news-events/news/uchicago-harrisap-norc-poll-about-1-5-americans-say-gun-violence-has-touched-their.

11. "One-Third of US Adults Say Fear of Mass Shootings Prevents Them from Going to Certain Places or Events," American Psychological Association, August 15, 2019, https://www.apa.org/news/press/releases/2019/08/fear-mass-shooting.

12. About three-fifths (59 percent) of crime guns recovered in other countries and submitted for tracing came from Mexico. During a five-year period from 2017 to 2021, ATF traced 97,791 guns recovered in Mexico; 74.1 percent of these firearms were traced to a purchaser in the United States; only 1.7 percent had been legally exported. Canada submitted 24,586 tracing requests to ATF for guns recovered at crime scenes in that country, which accounted for 14.8 percent of international trace requests; 11.9 percent of these guns recovered in Canada were traced to a purchaser in the United States; 33.5 percent involved firearms that had been legally exported. Data from National Firearms Commerce and Trafficking Assessment (NFCTA): Crime Guns, Volume Two, Part IV ("Crime Guns Recovered Outside the United States and Traced by Law Enforcement"), January 11, 2023, https://www.atf.gov/firearms/docs/report/nfcta-volume-ii-part-iv-crime-guns-recovered-outside-us-and-traced-le/download.

13. Data from Secretariado Ejecutivo del Sistema Nacional de Seguridad Pública, Centro Nacional de Información, CNSP/38/15, "Víctimas de delitos de fuero común, 2019"; includes 34,582 homicides and 1,006 murders classified as feminicides. Public health researchers who tried to estimate the impact of American guns on Mexican society noted that trafficked firearms account for about half of all homicides in the country: in 2020 alone, at least 17,000 people were killed by guns trafficked from the United States. The numbers are based on the following calculation: 70 percent of homicides committed by firearms; 70 percent of guns from the United States. The numbers were cited in a presentation by Alejandra Cortés Rodríguez (Anáhuac University), "Awareness, Action,

and Advocacy against Gun Violence and Crime in Mexico," at the Stockholm Criminology Symposium, streamed live on June 15, 2021.

14. "Crime in the United States by Volume and Rate per 100,000 Inhabitants, 2000–2019," FBI, accessed March 23, 2023, https://ucr.fbi.gov/crime-in-the-u.s/2019/crime-in-the-u.s.-2019/tables/table-1. Firearm suicides, which outnumber firearm homicides in the United States, are not included. In 2019, 23,941 Americans died by firearm suicide; see "Statistics," Prevent Firearm Suicide, Educational Fund to Stop Gun Violence, https://preventfirearmsuicide.efsgv.org/about-firearm-suicide/statistics/.

15. "Victims of Intentional Homicide," UN Office on Drugs and Crime, accessed October 14, 2022, https://dataunodc.un.org/dp-intentional-homicide-victims. This does not include the number of people who survived gun injuries. Researchers estimate that around 150,000 people may have suffered gunshot wounds during robberies, assaults, kidnappings, and other crimes between 2013 and 2019. See Eugenio Weigend Vargas and Carlos Perez Ricart, "Nonfatal Gunshot Injuries during Criminal Acts in Mexico, 2013–2019," *Injury Prevention* 28 (December 9, 2021): 238–42.

16. According to Sistema Nacional de Seguridad Pública (SNSP, National System for Public Security), between January and June 2016, 59 percent of homicides, or 5,586 out of 9,413, were committed using firearms. In 2015, firearms were used in 57 percent of homicides; in 2014—in 56 percent. Source: Paulina Arriaga and Maura Roldán Álvarez, "Armas De Fuego En México: Panorama En 2016" (Ciudad de México, Colectivo de Análisis de la Seguridad con Democracia, 2016).

17. Estados Unidos Mexicanos v. Smith & Wesson et al., No. 1:21-cv-11269 (Boston, August 4, 2021).

18. In January 2022, Arizona had 1,274 federally licensed gun dealers and pawnbrokers; Texas 6,028; New Mexico 545; California 1,904. Source: "Report of Active Firearms Licenses—License Type by State Statistics," ATF, printed January 10, 2022, https://www.atf.gov/firearms/docs/undefined/ffltypebystate01-10-2022pdf/download.

19. Secretariat of Defense opened the second store on the military base in Apodaca, near Monterrey, Nuevo León, in 2019.

20. "Firearms Recovered in Mexico and Submitted to ATF for Tracing," US Department of Justice, Bureau of Alcohol, Tobacco, Firearms and Explosives, updated March 10, 2020, https://www.atf.gov/file/144886/download.

21. Personal conversations with Mexican government officials in 2019; the estimate is also cited in GAO-21-322 report published on February 22, 2021, https://www.gao.gov/products/gao-21-322. Other sources suggest that the estimated number of guns crossing the border is higher. In the lawsuit Estados Unidos Mexicanos v. Smith & Wesson et al., the Mexican government suggests that as many as 873,000 guns could be smuggled from the United States to Mexico annually. Their calculation is based on a study, according to which 2.2 percent of US domestic arms sales are attributable to the US-Mexico traffic; see Topher L. McDougal et al., "The Way of the Gun: Estimating Firearms Trafficking across the US-Mexico Border," *Journal of Economic Geography* 15, no. 2 (2015): 297–327.

22. US Customs and Border Protection, response to FOIA request no. CBP-2021–030251, February 10, 2021.

23. Administración General de Aduanas, response to public information request no. 0610100039520, Ciudad de México, February 18, 2020.

24. According to a recent report, which analyzes trends of guns recovered in crime scenes abroad and traced by ATF in 2017–2021, most crime guns found in Mexico were sold in Texas (43 percent, or 14,216 firearms), followed by Arizona (17.3 percent, or 5,737), California (13.1 percent, or 4,335), New Mexico (3.2 percent, 1,051), and Florida (2 percent, 662). From Table IRT-23: International Crime Gun Traces to a Purchaser by Top 5 Source States and Recovery Country or Grouping, 2017—2021, National Firearms Commerce and Trafficking Assessment (NFCTA): Crime Guns, Volume Two, Part IV ("Crime Guns Recovered Outside the United States and Traced by Law Enforcement"), January 11, 2023, https://www.atf.gov/firearms/docs/report/nfcta-volume-ii-part-iv-crime-guns-recovered-outside-us-and-traced-le/download.

25. Brian DeLay, "How Not to Arm a State: American Guns and the Crisis of Governance in Mexico, Nineteenth and Twenty-First Centuries," *Southern California Quarterly* 95, no. 1 (Spring 2013), 5–23.

26. Pablo Ferri, "La Comisión para la Verdad concluye que Ayotzinapa 'fue un crimen de Estado,'" *El País*, August 18, 2022, https://elpais.com/mexico/2022-08-18/la-comision-para-la-verdad-concluye-que-ayotzinapa-fue-un-crimen-de-estado.html.

27. The weapons used on the night Ayotzinapa students were abducted included German Heckler and Koch G-36 rifles that had been sold, in violation of international law, to Guerrero police; see Alexander Gorski, "From Germany to Ayotzinapa," NACLA, June 26, 2018, https://nacla.org/news/2018/06/26/germany-ayotzinapa. US company Colt also shipped to Mexico AR-6530 rifles—a variant of AR-15—which were used by Guerrero police who attacked the Ayotzinapa students; see John Lindsay-Poland, "How US Guns Sold to Mexico End Up with Security Forces Accused of Crime and Human Rights Abuses," *The Intercept*, April 26, 2018, https://theintercept.com/2018/04/26/mexico-arms-trade-us-gun-sales/. Furthermore, police in Guerrero reported that they "lost" one fifth of their weapons, which were likely sold to criminal groups; see Stop US Arms to Mexico and the Mexican Commission for the Defense of Human Rights (CMDPDH), "Gross Human Rights Abuses: The Legal and Illegal Gun Trade to Mexico," August 2018, https://www.stopusarmstomexico.org/wp-content/uploads/2018/08/THE-LEGAL-AND-ILLEGAL-GUN-TRADE-TO-MEXICO_August2018.pdf.

28. Elizabeth Malkin, "Mexican Authorities Disarm Acapulco Police Amid Corruption Inquiry," *New York Times*, September 26, 2018, https://www.nytimes.com/2018/09/26/world/americas/mexico-acapulco-police.html.

29. These figures vary year to year. In 2019, about 79 percent of Mexican people said they felt insecure. By 2022, the number dropped to 66 percent. The percentage also varied widely by state and city. See "Percepción sobre seguridad pública," INEGI, accessed August 21, 2022, https://www.inegi.org.mx/temas/percepcion/.

30. "Mexico: Dark Landmark of 100,000 Disappearances Reflects Pattern of Impunity, UN Experts Warn," UN Office of the High Commissioner for Human Rights, May 17, 2022, https://www.ohchr.org/en/statements/2022/05/mexico-dark-landmark-100000-disappearances-reflects-pattern-impunity-un-experts.

31. Estados Unidos Mexicanos v. Smith & Wesson et al., No. 1:21-cv-11269 (August 4, 2021).

32. The only reason Remington, the company that made the AR-15-style Bushmaster rifle used in the Sandy Hook school shooting, was compelled to settle with families of the victims was because the gunmaker's aggressive marketing tactics violated Connecticut consumer protection law. See Rick Rojas, Karen Zraick, and Troy Closson, "Sandy Hook Families Settle with Gunmaker for $73 Million over Massacre," *New York Times*, February 15, 2022, https://www.nytimes.com/2022/02/15/nyregion/sandy-hook-families-settlement.html.

33. As historian Pamela Haag has shown, after the Civil War, when domestic demand for firearms dried out, US gun capitalists turned to international markets, vying for orders from rulers and revolutionaries alike, from Russia to France, and from Egypt to Chile. Pamela Haag, *The Gunning of America: Business and the Making of American Gun Culture* (New York: Basic Books, 2016), 112–17. Today, firearms export to foreign countries is a multimillion-dollar business in the United States and it continues to grow. In 2019, the oversight of this trade shifted from the US Department of State to the Department of Commerce, which made exporting firearms even easier. According to the Stockholm International Peace Research Institute (SIPRI), the United States is the world's largest arms exporter: during 2017–2021, US arms exports accounted for 39 percent of the global total (14 percent more than between 2012–2014). Saudi Arabia accounted for 23 percent of total US arms exports in 2017–2021. See "Trends in International Arms Transfers," SIPRI Fact Sheet, March 2022, https://www.sipri.org/sites/default/files/2022-03/fs_2203_at_2021.pdf.

34. It is estimated that US exports of firearms, ammunition, and explosives to Mexico average more than $40 million annually and that these exports increased significantly since the launch of the Mérida Initiative. Based on data in the 2018 report by Mexican Commission for the Defense and Promotion of Human Rights and Stop US Arms to Mexico, SEDENA has received thousands of rifles from Arizona-based Nammo Talley, while the Navy has been buying semiautomatic pistols and submachine guns from New Hampshire–based Sig Sauer. But even more guns are sold to state police forces, which, between 2007 and 2017, have imported more than two hundred thousand firearms, most of them from European companies Beretta and Glock, but also from Colt, Bushmaster, and Mossberg, located in the United States. There is evidence that firearms legally imported from the United States have been used in some of the worst human rights violations in Mexico in recent years. See Stop US Arms to Mexico, "Gross Human Rights Abuses." The report is based on data on firearms sales provided by SEDENA in response to public records' requests and data from the US Census Bureau. For the use of guns imported from the United States by Mexican security forces implicated in human rights abuses, also see Ryan Devereaux, "The U.S. Is Organizing a $5 Million Gun Sale to Mexican

Forces Accused of Murder and Kidnapping," *The Intercept*, October 6, 2021, https://theintercept.com/2021/10/06/mexico-weapons-sale-biden-murder -kidnapping/.

35. Stop US Arms to Mexico, "Gross Human Rights Abuses."

36. US exports of guns to Mexico were on par with its exports of fish and a hundred times less than that of cement. According to the United Nations COM-TRADE database on international trade, in 2021 US exports of stone, plaster, cement, asbestos, mica, or similar materials to Mexico was US$397.63 million; tobacco and tobacco substitutes—US$82.5 million; fish, crustaceans, and mollusks—US$40.36 million; arms and ammunition—$38.54 million. Data from "United States Exports to Mexico," Trading Economics, accessed February 3, 2023, https://tradingeconomics.com/united-states/exports/mexico.

37. Estados Unidos Mexicanos v. Smith & Wesson et al., No. 1:21-cv-11269 (Boston, November 22, 2021).

38. According to the popular definition by sociologist Max Weber, the state is a political organization or institutional form of rule that "(successfully) claims the monopoly of the legitimate use of physical force within a given territory" (1994 [1919]: 310). Cited from Max Weber, "Politics as Vocation," in *The Vocation Lectures* (Indianapolis: Hackett Pub, 2004 [1919]), 32–94.

39. French philosopher and anthropologist Bruno Latour suggested we "study the gun and the citizen as propositions." Refuting materialist accounts ("guns kill people") and sociological narratives ("people kill people"), Latour argued that neither subject nor object are fixed. When a person picks up a gun, the two of them articulate a new proposition. Although Latour didn't expand his brief discussion of guns beyond that, it is clear that this coupling of the subject and object doesn't happen in a social vacuum. See Bruno Latour, *Pandora's Hope: Essays on the Reality of Science Studies* (Cambridge, MA: Harvard University Press, 1999), 180.

40. Roxanne Dunbar-Ortiz, *Loaded: A Disarming History of the Second Amendment* (San Francisco: City Lights Books, 2018), 35, 61. See also *The Records of the Colony of New Plymouth in New England*, The Plymouth Colony Archive Project, modified April 26, 2003, http://www.histarch.illinois.edu /plymouth/laws1.html. For example, the section dedicated to arms states "That each [person] for himselfe [etc.] accord to Jan. 2d l632 haue peece powder [and] shott vizt a [sufficient] musket or other serviceable peece for war wth bandeleroes sword [and] other [appurtenances] for himselfe [and] each man servt he keepeth able to beare Armes. And that for himselfe [and] each such [person] under him he be at all times furnished wth two [pownds] of powder and ten [pownds] of [bullets] [and] for each default to forfeit ten shillings."

41. The Second Amendment of the United States Constitution reads, "A well regulated Militia, being necessary to the security of a free State, the right of the people to keep and bear Arms, shall not be infringed." Cited from https://www .law.cornell.edu/wex/second_amendment.

42. Scott Neuman, "The 'Gun Dude' and a Supreme Court Case that Changed Who Can Own Firearms in the U.S.," NPR, August 14, 2022, https://www .npr.org/2022/08/14/1113705501/second-amendment-supreme-court-dick -heller-gun-rights.

43. Dunbar-Ortiz, *Loaded*, 49.

44. Dunbar-Ortiz suggests that another rationale for the Second Amendment was controlling Black communities through armed slave patrols. *Loaded*, 71.

45. Virginia and John Purvis, *A Complete Collection of All the Lavvs of Virginia Now in Force: Carefully Copied from the Assembly Records: To Which Is Annexed an Alphabetical Table* (London: Printed by T. J. for J. P. and are to be sold by Tho. Mercer at the sign of the Half Moon the corner shop of the Royal-Exchange in Cornhil, 1684), https://searchworks.stanford.edu/view /12714050.

46. For discussion on Colt and Winchester marketing, see Haag, *Gunning of America*; William N. Hosley, *Colt: The Making of an American Legend* (Amherst: University of Massachusetts Press, 1996). Also see Phil Klay, "A History of Violence," in *Uncertain Ground: Citizenship in an Age of Endless, Invisible War* (New York: Penguin Press, 2022), 139–62. Klay writes: "This market has been created out of a mixture of myths about American history, antigovernment rhetoric, paranoia, fear of crime, fascination with military hardware, and appeals to the insecurities of American men. These myths are the software American consumers are buying along with their hardware," 161.

47. Jennifer Carlson, *Policing the Second Amendment: Guns, Law Enforcement, and the Politics of Race* (Princeton, NJ: Princeton University Press, 2020), 13. Carlson argues that this private violence is said to be directed against potential threats arising from above (a tyrannical government), but in reality it targets the perceived threats from below, posed by marginalized groups.

48. For a discussion of US expansion, race wars, and martial nationalism in nineteenth-century United States, see Greg Grandin, *The End of the Myth: From the Frontier to the Border Wall in the Mind of America* (New York: Metropolitan Books, 2019), chap. 5.

49. As María Josefina Saldaña-Portillo argues in her book *Indian Given*, while in the United States "indigenous peoples as first inhabitants are scripted to disappear, either fortuitously or tragically," in Mexico "the state monumentalizes its indigenous past and present in the service of nationalism," 9. She contrasts the Mexican and US visions of citizenship, calling the former "incorporative" and the latter "exclusionary," 138. Saldaña-Portillo, *Indian Given: Racial Geographies across Mexico and the United States* (Durham, NC: Duke University Press, 2016).

50. On the Yaqui rebellion see, for example, Kelly Lytle Hernández, *Bad Mexicans: Race Empire and Revolution in the Borderlands* (New York: W. W. Norton, 2022), 46–48.

51. When Mexico passed bounty laws for Apache and Comanche scalps in the nineteenth century, US mercenaries, though they were not the only bounty hunters, came to dominate the business (Saldaña-Portillo, *Indian Given*, 130). For a more in-depth study of interethnic violence and warfare in the US-Mexico borderlands, see Brian DeLay, *War of a Thousand Deserts: Indian Raids and the U.S.-Mexican War* (New Haven, CT: Yale University Press, 2008).

52. The Federal Firearms and Explosives Law also established rigorous procedures for the licensing and registration of firearms. Although it was stricter than the Gun Control Act of 1968 in the United States, the two laws had some

similarities. The US Gun Control Act was also passed in response to political assassinations and violence. The Gun Control Act implemented age restrictions for purchasing firearms, prohibited felons and people with mental illnesses from purchasing guns, required all manufactured or imported guns to have a serial number, and imposed federal licensing of gun dealers and manufacturers.

53. The NPR/Ipsos poll of 1,116 US adults was conducted online in July 2022, finding 28 percent of participants strongly agreed and 25 percent somewhat agreed that the United States is "experiencing an invasion" at the southern border. "A majority of Americans see an 'invasion' at the southern border, NPR poll finds," NPR, August 18, 2022, https://www.npr.org/2022/08/18/1117953720/a-majority-of-americans-see-an-invasion-at-the-southern-border-npr-poll-finds.

54. Following the example set by the United States, the Mexican government's militarized approach to the illicit production and circulation of narcotics is usually referred to by the shorthand *"guerra contra el narco"* (war on drug traffickers) or *"narco guerra"* (drug war). These terms are inaccurate: it is not a conventional war and it is not about drugs, or not only about them. These shorthands describe a violent process that concerns much more than antidrug policies. Throughout this book, I try to avoid these terms whenever possible, opting for more precise, factual descriptions of the relationship between Mexican security forces and organized crime groups. However, because of the widespread use of these terms in public discourse, there are a few places where I decided to include them in order to critique the phenomenon they refer to. I added quotation marks to indicate that these are phrases borrowed from public discourse and should not be taken for granted.

55. I wrote about this violence exchange in Ieva Jusionyte, "Violence Exchange," *Anthropology Now* 13, no. 1 (2021): 49–54. For an ethnographic account of how northbound smuggling of drugs is intertwined with southbound smuggling of money, see Shaylih Muehlmann, *When I Wear My Alligator Boots: Narco-Culture in the US-Mexico Borderlands* (Berkeley: University of California Press, 2013).

56. Cristina Rivera Garza, *Grieving: Dispatches from a Wounded Country* (New York: Feminist Press, 2020), 168–69.

57. Russell Contreras, "FBI Stats Show Border Cities Are among the Safest," *Axios*, December 1, 2020, https://www.axios.com/2020/12/01/border-cities-safest-fbi-data.

58. Michael T. Light, Jingying He, and Jason P. Robey, "Comparing Crime Rates between Undocumented Immigrants, Legal Immigrants, and Native-Born US Citizens in Texas," *Proceedings of the National Academy of Sciences of the United States of America* 117, no. 51 (December 20, 2020), 32340–47.

ARMING THE STATE

1. For more on the history of iron mining in New Spain, specifically the contributions by Andrés Manuel del Río in developing the mines in Real del Monte and the establishment of a preindustrial iron smelter in the Coalcomán highlands, see José Alfredo Uribe Salas, "Labor de Andrés Manuel Del Río en México: Pro-

fesor en el Real Seminario de Minería e Innovador tecnológico en Minas y ferrerías," *Asclepio* 58, no. 2 (2006): 231–60, https://doi.org/10.3989/asclepio.2006. v58.i2.15. I thank Elizabeth E. Ferry for help finding this source and others on iron mining in New Spain.

2. Uribe Salas, "Labor de Andrés Manuel Del Río en México," 252.

3. Thomas Frank Schilz and Donald E. Worcester, "The Spread of Firearms among the Indian Tribes on the Northern Frontier of New Spain," *American Indian Quarterly* 11, no. 1 (1987): 1–10, https://doi.org/10.2307/1183724.

4. The original document, dated November 22, 1771, and stored at Biblioteca Nacional de España, was reproduced in Bernardo Ibarrola et al., *Centenario de la industria militar mexicana: 1916–2016* (Ciudad de México: Secretaría de la Defensa Nacional, 2016), 74.

5. Ibarrola et al., *Centenario de la industria militar mexicana*, 73.

6. The royal government also held monopoly (*estanco*) over the commerce of tobacco, salt, mercury, and some other products. Revenue from the sales of these products was deposited into a separate treasury and remitted directly to Spain.

7. Two more gunpowder factories—in Veracruz and Zacatecas—were established in the 1820s.

8. Ibarrola et al., *Centenario de la industria militar mexicana*, 70.

9. Haag, *The Gunning of America*, 122.

10. Haag, *The Gunning of America*, 123–24.

11. John Mason Hart, *Empire and Revolution: The Americans in Mexico Since the Civil War* (Berkeley: University of California Press, 2005), chap. 1 "Arms and Capital," 9–45. Also see Grandin, *The End of the Myth*, 154.

12. Kelly Lytle Hernández, *Bad Mexicans: Race, Empire, and Revolution in the Borderlands* (New York: W. W. Norton, 2022), chap. 10, "Cananea."

13. Lytle Hernández, *Bad Mexicans*, 38.

14. More than a million Mexicans fled the country during the Revolution, settling down in the United States and giving rise to the first generation of Mexican Americans. Lytle Hernández argues that "the 1910 Mexican Revolution is a seminal event in U.S. history: it changed who we are as people" (*Bad Mexicans*, 8). The scholarship on the Mexican Revolution is too vast to summarize here. For those interested, the following studies provide more in-depth historical analysis: Adolfo Gilly, *The Mexican Revolution* (New York: New Press, 2005); Gilbert M. Joseph and Jürgen Buchenau, *Mexico's Once and Future Revolution: Social Upheaval and the Challenge of Rule Since the Late Nineteenth Century* (Durham, NC: Duke University Press, 2013); Alan Knight, *The Mexican Revolution*, vol. 1 and vol. 2 (New York: Cambridge University Press, 1986).

15. Lytle Hernández, *Bad Mexicans*, 148–50, 186–87.

16. Lytle Hernández, *Bad Mexicans*, 265–66.

17. "Troops to Stop All Arms into Mexico," *New York Times*, March 15, 1912, 2.

18. For a detailed discussion of how Pancho Villa acquired guns and ammunition from the United States, see Christopher R. Stewart, "Pancho Villa's Munitions," MA thesis, University of Montana, 1979.

19. The arms embargo was lifted on February 3, 1914, and reinstated on April 24, 1914.

20. For more on El Plan de San Diego, see Hernández, *Bad Mexicans*, 298–300.

21. Called "la Matanza," this retaliation is, according to Lytle Hernández, one of the least-known episodes of racial terror in the US history. Although the number of victims is not known, some scholars estimate that as many as five thousand people were killed in the reprisal. See Lytle Hernández, *Bad Mexicans*, 299–300.

22. Luis Cabrera, *La Herencia De Carranza* (Mexico: [Imprenta nacional, s. a.], 1920), 38, https://babel.hathitrust.org/cgi/pt?id=mdp.39015051117557 &view=1up&seq=37.

23. Lytle Hernández, *Bad Mexicans*, 282.

24. According to Lytle Hernández, Porfirio Díaz asked the US government to arrest Francisco Madero and Ricardo Flores Magón, but US authorities declined. They also did not stop gunrunning across the border. See *Bad Mexicans*, 277–78.

25. George T. Díaz, *Border Contraband: A History of Smuggling Across the Rio Grande* (Austin: University of Texas Press, 2015), 75.

26. Juries comprised of borderland residents continued to accept arms smuggling and find defendants accused of violating the law not guilty at least until the 1940s. See Díaz, *Border Contraband*, 77, 126–28.

27. The concept of "moral economy" refers to a system of exchange that is not reduced to materialist considerations and includes social norms and obligations. It was first developed by social historian E. P. Thompson. See E. P. Thompson, "The Moral Economy of the English Crowd in the Eighteenth Century," *Past & Present* 50, no. 1 (February 1971), 76–136.

28. Stopping the flow of guns across the US border, which continued during the Cristero Rebellion and into later decades of the twentieth century, was the priority of the Mexican government. So much so that the government even chose to tolerate petty smuggling of consumer goods that was common in the borderlands as long as local residents cooperated in the state's efforts to arrest arms traffickers. See Díaz, *Border Contraband*, 120–25.

29. Ibarrola et al., *Centenario de la industria militar mexicana*, 228.

30. Cabrera, *La Herencia De Carranza*, 36–37.

31. This is similar to current requirements for arms exporters to obtain end-user certificates from the buyers.

32. On October 16, 1916, Carranza founded Departamento de Establecimientos Fabriles e Industriales Militares. See Ibarrola et al., *Centenario de la industria militar mexicana*, 167.

33. Cabrera, *La Herencia De Carranza*, 38. Also see Francisco L. Urquizo, *Carranza: El hombre. El político. El caudillo. El patriota* (México, D.F.: Instituto Nacional de Estudios Históricos de las Revoluciones de México, 2015), 47, https://archivos.juridicas.unam.mx/www/bjv/libros/9/4354/14.pdf.

34. In 1919, Mexico imported 5,000 Winchester .30–30 rifles and 499 Remington .45 caliber rifles, among others. See Ibarrola et al., *Centenario de la industria militar mexicana*, 167.

35. "Industria Militar: Produciendo nuestras armas y municiones. 100 años," brochure published by SEDENA, 2016.

36. In addition to Mauser and Mendoza models, the factory began making 60mm and 81mm mortars and munition rounds, manufactured with equipment imported from the United States.

37. Initially the Mexican government chose the FAL (Fusil Automatique Léger) made by FN Herstal in Belgium. Chambered for a 7.62 × 51mm NATO cartridge, it was one of the most widely used rifles in the world. But the company sold only complete weapons and forbade manufacturing of its parts in local factories. See Ibarrola et al., *Centenario de la industria militar mexicana*, 196.

38. Ignacio Alzaga, "Sedena busca autosuficiencia en la producción de armas," *Milenio*, January 30, 2016, https://www.milenio.com/policia/sedena-busca-autosuficiencia-en-la-produccion-de-armas.

39. Constitución Política de los Estados Unidos Mexicanos, as amended, Diario Oficial de la Federación [D.O.], February 5, 1917, errata, D.O., February 6, 1917. Translated by Norma C. Gutiérrez, Senior Foreign Law Specialist at the Law Library of Congress, February 2013. Retrieved from https://www.loc.gov/law/help/firearms-control/mexico.php#f1 (on November 27, 2018). An alternative translation, from Constitución Política de los Estados Unidos Mexicanos, Trigésima Quinta Edición, 1967, Editorial Porrua, S.A., México, D.F., originally published by the Pan American Union, General Secretariat, Organization of American States, Washington, DC, 1968, is as follows: "The inhabitants of the United Mexican States are entitled to have arms of any kind in their possession for their protection and legitimate defense, except such as are expressly forbidden by law, or which the nation may reserve for the exclusive use of the army, navy, or national guard; but they may not carry arms within inhabited places without complying with police regulations." Retrieved from https://www.oas.org/juridico/mla/en/mex/en_mex-int-text-const.pdf (accessed November 27, 2018).

40. Articles 160–163, Código Penal Federal, adopted August 14, 1931. Full text (in Spanish) is available here: http://www.diputados.gob.mx/LeyesBiblio/pdf_mov/Codigo_Penal_Federal.pdf. The original text reads "antecedentes de honorabilidad y prudencia."

41. Pablo Piccato, *City of Suspects: Crime in Mexico City, 1900–1931* (Durham, NC: Duke University Press, 2001), 99–100.

42. Piccato, *City of Suspects*, 100.

43. Alexander Aviña, *Specters of Revolution: Peasant Guerrillas in the Cold War Mexican Countryside* (Oxford, UK: Oxford University Press, 2014).

44. Aviña, *Specters of Revolution*, 5.

45. For an important account of the massacre, based on eyewitness testimonies, see Elena Poniatowska, *La Noche De Tlatelolco: Testimonios De Historia Oral* (México: Era, 2014).

46. See, for example, the front page of *Excelsior* on August 1, 1968, which includes an article about the arrests of communist youth leaders who allegedly signed a manifesto committing to open rebellion against the government. http://www.ahunam.unam.mx:8081/uploads/r/archivo-historico-de-la-unam/a/7/6/a76481ac99e965de1611d7e508568c7f810146391876876f810c939f8bc1bd04/HM68_01.JPG

47. "Mexico Blames Rebels for Raids," *New York Times*, September 20, 1971, 8.

48. FARC-EP (Fuerzas Armadas Revolucionarias de Colombia—Ejército del Pueblo), ELN (Ejército de Liberación Nacional), and EPL (Ejército Popular de Liberación) were three major leftist guerilla movements in Colombia, all established in the 1960s.

49. For more detailed examination of student organizing in Mexico during the 1960s and 1970s, see Jaime M. Pensado and Enrique Ochoa, *México Beyond 1968: Revolutionaries Radicals and Repression during the Global Sixties and Subversive Seventies* (Tucson: University of Arizona Press, 2018).

50. Héctor Daniel Torres Martínez, "Monterrey Rebelde 1970–1973. Un estudio sobre la Guerrilla Urbana, la sedición armada y sus representaciones colectivas" (master's thesis, El Colegio de San Luis, 2014), 61.

51. Caen dos del M.A.R., *El Norte*, January 12, 1972.

52. In the early 1970s, these groups included las Fuerzas de Liberación Nacional, los Procesos, los Macías, la Liga Comunista 23 de Septiembre, and la Liga de Comunistas Armados.

53. Torres Martínez, "Monterrey Rebelde," 152.

54. Camouflage paraphernalia, especially when seen next to guns and propaganda, was incriminating evidence for the government intent on squashing social disturbances. This anxiety was centuries old and not exclusive to Mexico. Historian E. P. Thompson wrote about the circumstances that led to the passage of the Black Act in 1723 in Britain: "A stick and a dirty face would do for arms and disguise" (195). The Black Act applied to "person or persons . . . armed with swords, fire-arms, or other offensive weapons, and having his or their faces blacked, or being otherwise disguised, shall appear in any forest, chase, park, paddock, or grounds inclosed with any wall, pale, or other fence, wherein any deer have been or shall be usually kept" (213); being armed and disguised made an offense into a felony (162). In what Thompson called a "legislative overkill," the state made covering one's face with a mask or smearing it with gunpowder while poaching or stealing deer from a forest into crimes worthy of capital punishment. The armory of sanctions the act established went far beyond restricting hunting—it provided a model for outlawing the practices of Scottish and Irish rebels, English smugglers, and any other organized expressions of social grievance that the British government saw as resistance to and displacement of its authority. See E. P. Thompson, *Whigs and Hunters: The Origin of the Black Act* (London: Breviary Stuff Publications, 2013). Many countries have since borrowed items from this legal repertoire, including prohibitions of wearing masks to conceal identity. See, for example, the Code of Virginia § 18.2-422: "It shall be unlawful for any person over 16 years of age to, with the intent to conceal his identity, wear any mask, hood or other device whereby a substantial portion of the face is hidden or covered so as to conceal the identity of the wearer, to be or appear in any public place, or upon any private property in this Commonwealth without first having obtained from the owner or tenant thereof consent to do so in writing." The law makes some exceptions, including for holiday costumes and public health emergencies. https://law.lis.virginia.gov /vacode/title18.2/chapter9/section18.2-422/ (accessed October 14, 2022).

55. "La Portación y Posesión de Armas de Fuego se Reglamentará Debidamente," *El Informador*, October 24, 1971, 1A.

56. Editorial: Legislación Sobre Armas, *El Informador*, October 28, 1971, 4A.

57. Ley Federal de Armas de Fuego y Explosivos. Published in Diario Oficial de la Federación on January 11, 1972. Regulations of the Federal Law on Firearms and Explosives (Reglamento de la Ley Federal de Armas de Fuego y Explosivos) was passed a year later, in 1972. http://ordenjuridico.gob.mx /Federal/Combo/R-99.pdf (accessed November 27, 2018).

58. Approximately $5 to $5,000 US dollars in 2019.

59. "Mexico, Land of the 'Pistolero,' Plans a Strict Gun-Control Law," *New York Times*, November 7, 1971, 27.

60. "Mexico, Land of the 'Pistolero,' Plans a Strict Gun-Control Law," 27.

61. Francis B. Kent, "Strict Mexico Law to Control Guns Expected," *Los Angeles Times*, November 19, 1971, A19.

62. After the Federal Firearms Law came into effect, Productos Mendoza suspended manufacturing guns. In the 1980s, the company reoriented its operations to producing office supplies. Mendoza Productos resumed gun manufacturing in 1997, with authorization from SEDENA. The company has been making submachine guns for public security agencies as well as handguns and .22 caliber rifles for the civilian market. See "Productos Mendoza," accessed April 18, 2023, http://www.productosmendoza.com/Historia .html.

63. "Quedó Aprobada la Ley Sobre Armas de Fuego," *El Informador*, December 30, 1971, 2A.

64. "Quedó Aprobada la Ley Sobre Armas de Fuego," 2A.

65. "Quedó Aprobada la Ley Sobre Armas de Fuego," 1A.

66. "Este Asunto Compete Sólo a la Policía," *El Informador*, January 14, 1972, 1A.

67. Kent, "Strict Mexico Law to Control Guns Expected," A19.

68. "Around the World: Mexican Firearms," *Washington Post*, June 30, 1972, A26.

69. In 2019, the federal registry contained 3,544,625 firearms. SEDENA, response to public records request, no. 0000700068219, Lomas de Sotelo, Ciudad de México, March 22, 2019. These numbers contradict the report from *Small Arms Survey*, which estimates that in 2007 Mexicans owned 15.5 million firearms and 4.5 million were properly registered with the army. See Nick Wagner, "At Mexico's Lone Gun Store, even the Boss Discourages Sales," Associated Press, August 17, 2016, https://www.apnews.com/c29ecc229f0846bobfa 4f4ecf8eca7d5.

70. Aaron Karp, "Estimating Global Civilian-Held Firearms Numbers," *Small Arms Survey*, June 2018, https://www.smallarmssurvey.org/sites/default /files/resources/SAS-BP-Civilian-Firearms-Numbers.pdf.

71. Since there is no gun registry in the United States, and recently more people have been refusing to answer survey questions about firearm possession, the US numbers are rough estimates. See Karp, "Estimating Global Civilian-Held Firearms Numbers."

WITH A SIDE OF BEANS

1. See, for example, Jo Tuckman, "Mexico Casino Arson Attack Shows Violence Is Spreading," *The Guardian*, August 26, 2011, https://www.theguardian.com/world/2011/aug/26/52-die-arson-mexico-casino.

2. It is estimated that as of 2020, almost nine out of every ten homicides in Mexico goes unpunished. See "OAS Rights Group: 'Critical' Levels of Impunity in Mexico," Associated Press, April 25, 2021, https://apnews.com/article/health-mexico-coronavirus-a178e2582c6coa21881ab66535ae97c0.

3. See, for example, Séverine Durin, *¡Sálvese Quien Pueda! Violencia Generalizada y Desplazamiento Forzado en el Noreste de México* (Ciudad de México: CIESAS Centro de Investigaciones y Estudios Superiores en Antropología Social, 2019), 400.

4. Ana Villarreal, "Domesticating Danger: Coping Codes and Symbolic Security amid Violent Organized Crime in Mexico," *Sociological Theory* 39, no 4 (December 2021): 225–44.

5. "Critical Defense," Hornady Manufacturing Inc., accessed September 3, 2020, https://www.hornady.com/ammunition/critical-defense#!/.

6. The Arellano Félix family founded what was once one of the most powerful organized crime groups in Mexico, known both as Cártel Arellano Félix (el C.A.F.) and the Tijuana Cartel. In US academic literature it is also called the Arellano Félix Organization (AFO). For more about the AFO, see David A. Shirk, "A Tale of Two Mexican Border Cities: The Rise and Decline of Drug Violence in Juárez and Tijuana," *Journal of Borderlands Studies* 29, no. 4 (2014), 481–502.

7. Like elsewhere in Mexico, an increase in violent crime in Tijuana during this period is usually explained as resulting from infighting between organized crime groups. However, the rise in violence starting in 2007 coincided with the arrival of federal security forces to the area. The military was deployed in January 2007, as part of Operation Baja California, and their presence contributed to the escalation of violence and the general sense of insecurity in the border region. Because local police officers were suspected of collaborating with organized crime groups, some units were disarmed. In his analysis of violence in Tijuana and Ciudad Juárez, political scientist David Shirk suggested that it increased both because of dynamics within and among drug trafficking organizations and due to pressures from US and Mexican law enforcement. See Shirk, "A Tale of Two Mexican Border Cities."

8. Eugenio Weigend Vargas and Carlos Pérez Ricart, "Gun Acquisition in Mexico 2012–18: Findings from Mexico's National Crime Victimization Survey," *British Journal of Criminology* 61, no. 4 (July 2021), 1066–85. Authors claim that mistrust in neighbors as well as in the municipal and state police forces are associated with higher levels of gun acquisition, but mistrust in the federal police and the military are not.

9. David Pérez Esparza and David Hemenway, "What Is the Level of Household Gun Ownership in Urban Mexico? An Estimate from the First Mexican Survey on Gun Ownership 2017," *Injury Prevention* 25 (2019), 93–97. The research firm contacted 9,611 respondents in nine cities with more than 500,000 inhabitants (CDMX, Guadalajara, Monterrey, Puebla, Tijuana, Mérida,

Veracruz, Oaxaca, and Ciudad Victoria), but only 1,361 completed the survey, for a response rate of 14.2 percent. For comparison, a national web-based survey conducted in 2015 found that 22 percent of respondents in the United States reported owning at least one firearm. See Deborah Azrael et al., "The Stock and Flow of U.S. Firearms: Results from the 2015 National Firearms Survey," *RSF: The Russell Sage Foundation Journal of the Social Sciences* 3, no. 5 (2017), 38–57. About half of all respondents said that if the government loosened regulations, allowing residents to carry guns in their vehicles or take them to their workplaces, crime would increase. Urban dwellers appeared to be in favor of keeping strict gun laws in Mexico over the weaker regulations in the United States.

10. Information obtained through interviews with buyers of smuggled guns in Monterrey and Tijuana in 2018–2019.

11. For more on the history of how La Isla became a vacation destination for tourists from Monterrey, see Efrén Sandoval, *Infraestructuras transfronterizas: etnografía de itinerarios en el espacio social Monterrey-San Antonio* (Ciudad de México: CIESAS, Centro de Investigaciones y Estudios Superiores en Antropología Social; Tijuana: El Colegio de la Frontera Norte, 2012), 237–39.

12. Administración General de Aduanas, response to public information request, no. 0610100039520, Ciudad de México, February 18, 2020. The breakdown of 2019 seizures by border crossing is as follows: Agua Prieta, Sonora—1 firearm, 93 cartridges; Colombia, Nuevo León—10 firearms, 8 magazines, 617 cartridges; Juárez, Chihuahua—4 firearms, 53 magazines, 12,158 cartridges; Mexicali, Baja California—19 firearms, 57 magazines, 4,815 cartridges; Naco, Sonora—1 magazine; Nogales, Sonora—5 firearms, 1 magazine, 12,880 cartridges; Nuevo Laredo, Tamaulipas—46 firearms, 64 magazines, 4,225 cartridges; Ojinaga, Chihuahua—462 cartridges; Piedras Negras, Coahuila—40 cartridges; Reynosa, Tamaulipas—14 firearms, 66 magazines, 2,195 cartridges; Tijuana, Baja California—23 firearms, 17 magazines, 3,632 cartridges.

13. According to data provided in response to FOIA request no. CBP-2021-0302510, outbound firearm and ammunition seizures in 2019 in El Paso Sector consisted of 3 rifles, 37 pistols, 1 revolver, 37,874 cartridges; in Laredo Sector—56 rifles, 8 shotguns, 68 pistols, 1 revolver, 2 receivers, 75,900 cartridges; in San Diego Sector—2 shotguns, 1 pistol, 38 cartridges; in Tucson Sector—7 rifles, 1 shotgun, 4 pistols, 5 receivers, 40,280 cartridges. All in all, CBP confiscated 66 rifles, 11 shotguns, and 149 handguns that year.

COLLATERAL DAMAGE

1. Narcocorridos are songs that fall within the genre of corrido-style ballads historically associated with Mexico's northern borderlands. They became popular in the 1970s. The main protagonists of these songs—prototypical modern outlaws—are drug traffickers riding in pickup trucks armed with assault rifles. See Sophie Esch, *Modernity at Gunpoint: Firearms Politics and Culture in Mexico and Central America* (Pittsburgh, PA: University of Pittsburgh Press, 2018), 196–203.

2. C. J. Chivers, *The Gun* (New York: Simon & Schuster, 2010), 343.

3. Chivers, *The Gun*, 383.

4. Chivers, *The Gun*, 9.

5. This reputation of AK-47 as the common man's gun is still part of its branding today. For example, Century Arms advertises one of its AK-47 models, the BFT47, as "a reliable, durable, and accurate AK at a price point the blue collar American can afford" (https://www.centuryarms.com/bft47-series). In March 2023, the rifle cost around $800.

6. Chivers, *The Gun*, 360.

7. We may never know the number of guns that left Eastern Europe in the 1980s and 1990s. When Ukrainian Ministry of Defense tried to assess its inheritance of Soviet arms and ammunition that was stockpiled and abandoned in hundreds of deposits, they counted about 7 million military small arms, in addition to about 3 million tons of ammunition. See Chivers, *The Gun*, 368.

8. Even when American soldiers fighting in Vietnam complained about the routine jamming of their M16s—the military version of AR-15—the US government was reluctant to admit the problem. For a detailed account on what went wrong with the M16 and the cover-up of problems with the gun, see the chapter "The Accidental Rifle" in Chivers, *The Gun*, 263–336.

9. Many Viet Cong and North Vietnamese Army combatants carried the Type 56 assault rifle, a clone of the AK-47 made in China based on specifications provided by the Soviets. See Chivers, *The Gun*, 265.

10. Chivers, *The Gun*, 287.

11. "The Militarization of the U.S. Civilian Firearms Market," Violence Policy Center, June 2011, https://www.vpc.org/studies/militarization.pdf.

12. The ban was enacted under the authority of the Gun Control Act of 1968, which allowed the US government to prohibit imports of guns lacking a "sporting purpose." See United States Department of the Treasury, Bureau of Alcohol, Tobacco and Firearms, "ATF Determines Semiautomatic Assault Rifles Cannot Be Imported into the United States," July 7, 1989, https://www.atf.gov/files/publications/newsletters/ffl/ffl-newsletter-1989-07.pdf. As for fully automatic weapons, including automatic AK-47s, they are legal in the United States as long as they were registered before May 1986, with the passage of the Firearm Owners Protection Act. Also see Clay Boggs and Kristen Rand, "GUN-RUNNING NATION: How Foreign-Made Assault Weapons Are Trafficked from the United States to Mexico and What to Do About It," Washington Office on Latin America and Violence Policy Center, July 2015, 8–9, https://vpc.org/studies/Gun_Running_Nation.pdf.

13. Not all AK-47 style rifles are imported. Some are made in the United States. Florida-based company Century Arms, which has been importing military surplus since the 1960s, now manufactures AK-47 style rifles in the United States. In 2015, Kalashnikov USA opened a factory in Pennsylvania, moving it to Florida in 2016.

14. President Lyndon B. Johnson explained the purpose of the law by saying that "the Government can help protect its citizens against the random and the reckless violence of crime at gun point" and that "the key to effective crime control remains, in my judgment, effective gun control." Lyndon B. Johnson,

Remarks Upon Signing the Gun Control Act of 1968, October 22, 1968, https://www.presidency.ucsb.edu/documents/remarks-upon-signing-the-gun-control-act-1968.

15. See Jeanne Marie Laskas, "Inside the Federal Bureau of Way Too Many Guns," *GQ*, August 30, 2016, https://www.gq.com/story/inside-federal-bureau-of-way-too-many-guns. According to the article, the center handles about 370,000 trace requests per year, running up to 1,500 requests on any given day. In 65 percent of the cases, workers at the tracing center identify the original purchaser.

16. US Department of Justice (DOJ), Office of the Inspector General. "A Review of ATF's Operation Fast and Furious and Related Matters (Redacted)." September 2012 (reissued November 2012), https://oig.justice.gov/reports/2012/s1209.pdf, 109.

17. Ioan Grillo, *Blood Gun Money: How America Arms Gangs and Cartels* (New York: Bloomsbury Publishing, 2021), 233.

18. United Nations Convention against Transnational Organized Crime. Article 2(i), accessed June 15, 2021, https://www.unodc.org/documents/middleeastandnorthafrica/organised-crime/UNITED_NATIONS_CONVENTION_AGAINST_TRANSNATIONAL_ORGANIZED_CRIME_AND_THE_PROTOCOLS_THERETO.pdf.

19. Module 8: Law Enforcement Tools and Cooperation. UNODC online resource, accessed June 15, 2021, https://www.unodc.org/e4j/en/organized-crime/module-8/key-issues/special-investigative-techniques/controlled-deliveries.html.

20. US DOJ, "A Review of ATF's Operation Fast and Furious," 67. Of the 474 firearms purchased during Operation Wide Receiver, 42 firearms were recovered in Mexico between January 2007 and August 2011, 22 were recovered in the United States. At the time this OIG review was published in 2012, the rest of the guns remained at large.

21. Mike Detty, *Operation Wide Receiver: An Informant's Struggle to Expose the Corruption and Deceit That Led to Operation Fast and Furious* (New York: Skyhorse Publishing, 2015).

22. Two notable operations run by ATF agents in Arizona were the Fidel Hernandez case in 2007 and the Alejandro Medrano case in 2008.

23. See Grillo, *Blood Gun Money*, chap. 2, "The Draco," for a comprehensive account of Jaime Zapata's assassination and the investigation into the origins of the guns used in the attack.

24. US DOJ, "A Review of ATF's Operation Fast and Furious," 238.

25. "Seven Straw Purchasers in Arizona Firearms Trafficking Case Sentenced to Federal Prison," Department of Justice, US Attorney Laura E. Duffy, Southern District of California, December 12, 2012, https://www.justice.gov/archive/usao/cas/2012/cas12-1212-ReleaseSDCA_Seven_Sentencing.pdf (accessed June 20, 2021). Also, Grillo. *Blood Gun Money*, 253.

26. John Dodson, *The Unarmed Truth: My Fight to Blow the Whistle and Expose Fast and Furious* (New York: Threshold Editions, 2014), chap. 2, "The Phoenix Way," 48–51.

27. US DOJ, "A Review of ATF's Operation Fast and Furious," 237.

28. Transcribed interview of ATF Special Agent John Dodson, April 26, 2011, quoted in "Department of Justice's Operation Fast and Furious: Accounts of ATF Agents," Joint Staff Report prepared for Representative Darrell E. Issa and Senator Charles E. Grassley, June 14, 2011.

29. Transcribed interview of ATF Special Agent Lawrence Alt, April 27, 2011, quoted in "Department of Justice's Operation Fast and Furious: Accounts of ATF Agents."

30. Alfredo Corchado, *Midnight in Mexico: A Reporter's Journey through a Country's Descent into the Darkness* (New York: Penguin Books, 2014), 228.

31. Corchado writes about his experiences of living in Mexico and the United States in his second book, Alfredo Corchado, *Homelands: Four Friends Two Countries and the Fate of the Great Mexican-American Migration* (New York: Bloomsbury, 2018).

32. The Juárez cartel is a criminal organization based in Ciudad Juárez, Chihuahua. At different times, the organization has been both an ally of and a brutal rival of the Sinaloa cartel. La Línea, formed by Juárez police officers, started as an enforcer group for the organization and over the years became one of its strongest factions. In 2011, La Línea formed an alliance with the Zetas. In 2021, they allied with the Jalisco New Generation Cartel (Cártel Jalisco Nueva Generación, CJNG).

33. "Death Toll at 16 in Juarez Party Shooting," CNN, February 1, 2010, https://web.archive.org/web/20120511194935/http://articles.cnn.com/2010-02 -01/world/mexico.juarez.shooting_1_juarez-reyes-death-toll?_s=PM%3 AWORLD.

34. Letter signed by Rigoberto Vega Garcia, on behalf of SEDENA, addressed to Felipe de Jesús Espitia Hernández, March 9, 2010, https://s3.documentcloud .org/documents/443681/mexican-army-salvarcar-documet.pdf; also see Abel Barajas, "Va PGR Por Ligados a 'Rápido y Furioso,'" *El Norte*, October 4, 2012.

35. Corchado, *Midnight in Mexico*, 232.

36. Marcela Turati, "Entre el miedo y desconfianza," *Proceso*, February 21, 2010, https://marcelaturati.wordpress.com/2011/07/18/entre-el-miedo-y-la -desconfianza-2/.

37. "Anuncia Calderón nuevo plan contra el narco en Juárez," *Proceso*, February 2, 2010, https://www.proceso.com.mx/nacional/2010/2/2/anuncia -calderon-nuevo-plancontra-el-narco-en-juarez-10082.html. Mexico's top officials have been accused of meddling in this rivalry between organized crime groups. In 2023, Genaro García Luna, who was Mexico's secretary of public security under President Calderón, stood trial in the United States, accused of collaborating with organized crime groups. The federal jury in Brooklyn convicted him on five counts, including "engaging in a continuing criminal enterprise." See "Ex-Mexican Secretary of Public Security Genaro Garcia Luna Convicted of Engaging in a Continuing Criminal Enterprise and Taking Millions in Cash Bribes from the Sinaloa Cartel," US Attorney's Office, Eastern District of New York, press release, February 21, 2023, https://www.justice.gov/usao -edny/pr/ex-mexican-secretary-public-security-genaro-garcia-luna-convicted -engaging-continuing. This case revealed how one of Mexico's highest ranking government officials, charged with implementing Calderón's "drug war," took

bribes from some organized crime groups in return for favors. Likely, he was not the only one. For more on García Luna's trial, see José Olivares, "Mexico's Former Top Cop Is on Trial in New York. Will the U.S. Be Implicated?" *The Intercept*, January 18, 2023, https://theintercept.com/2023/01/18/genaro -garcia-luna-trial/; and Alan Feuer, "Mexican Ex-Lawman Took Money from Cartels He Pursued, Prosecutors Say," *New York Times*, January 23, 2023, https://www.nytimes.com/2023/01/23/world/americas/genaro-garcia-luna -corruption-trial-mexico.html.

38. For discussion of the link between militarization under Calderón and an increase in violence, see Dawn Paley, *Drug War Capitalism* (Oakland, CA: AK Press, 2014), 111, 124–125; and Oswaldo Zavala, *Drug Cartels Do Not Exist: Narcotrafficking in US and Mexican Culture* (Nashville, TN: Vanderbilt University Press), 8, 62. Both Paley and Zavala reference several studies that show the correlation between military presence and homicides. According to the study conducted by the Drug Policy Program at the Center for Research and Teaching in Economics (CIDE), 84 percent of the 3,327 clashes in which Mexican military and the federal police were involved between 2007 and 2011 were *caused* by the Mexican armed forces; only 7 percent were direct attacks against them (Zavala, *Drug Cartels Do Not Exist*, 62).

39. For details about Mérida Initiative, see "Mexico: Evolution of the Mérida Initiative, FY2008–FY2021," Congressional Research Service Report, September 20, 2021, https://crsreports.congress.gov/product/pdf/IF/IF10578/21. When it was signed in 2008, critics dubbed the agreement "Plan Mexico" after Plan Colombia, a similar agreement the United States had with the Colombian government, which involved the United States providing foreign and military aid to the Colombian government to fight drug production and trafficking. See Paley, *Drug War Capitalism*, 30–33.

40. According to Paley, US funding appropriations for the Mérida Initiative in 2008–2014 amounted to $2.35 billion. Some years, Mexico's expenditures on the Mérida Initiative were thirteen times that of the United States. See Paley, *Drug War Capitalism*, 86–87. Most of the funds went to private US security firms. See Mica Rosenberg, "U.S. Security Firms Vie for Mexican Drug War Work," Reuters, July 16, 2009, https://www.reuters.com/article/idUSN16445904.

41. "Mexico: Evolution of the Mérida Initiative."

42. Corchado, *Midnight in Mexico*, 234.

43. Documents published by Judicial Watch, accessed March 29, 2023, https://www.judicialwatch.org/wp-content/uploads/2016/05/ATF-Fast-and -Furious-records-1.pdf.

44. Richard A. Serrano, "Fast and Furious Guns Turned Up at Cartel Enforcer's Home," *Los Angeles Times*, October 9, 2011.

45. Assistant Attorney General Peter J. Kadzik's letter to Charles E. Grassley and Jason Chaffetz, March 15, 2016. https://www.judiciary.senate.gov/imo /media/doc/2016-3-15%20DOJ%20to%20CEG%20%28El%20Chapo%20 F+F%20recovery%29.pdf.

46. The autopsy report says the gunshot wound was "an oblique, 1 1/4-inch oval perforation with an approximately one-fourth inch tear at the 1 o'clock position. After penetrating the skin and soft tissues of the left lower back, the

bullet passed forward, rightward and upward to penetrate the spinal column and cord at the level of L2. The bullet continued on to perforate the aorta, mesentery, small intestines, distal stomach, and left lobe of the liver before causing subcutaneous hemorrhage of the anterior midline abdominal wall, 22 inches from the top of the head." Brady McCombs, "Border Boletín: Bullet That Killed Agent Terry Went in Back, Traveled Upward," *Arizona Daily Star*, March 4, 2011, updated April 2, 2015, https://tucson.com/news/local/border/border -bolet-n-bullet-that-killed-agent-terry-went-in-back-traveled-upward/article _83809dd6-45f6-11e0-9802-001cc4c002e0.html.

47. "Seven Straw Purchasers in Arizona Firearms Trafficking Case Sentenced to Federal Prison," Department of Justice, US Attorney Laura E. Duffy, Southern District of California, December 12, 2012, https://www.justice.gov/archive /usao/cas/2012/cas12-1212-ReleaseSDCA_Seven_Sentencing.pdf.

48. See Grillo, *Blood Gun Money*, 231–33, for a description and discussion of these conspiracy theories.

49. Grillo, *Blood Gun Money*, 256.

50. See Shane Bauer, "Undercover with a Border Militia," *Mother Jones*, November/December 2016, https://www.motherjones.com/politics/2016/10 /undercover-border-militia-immigration-bauer/.

51. Alt transcript, April 27, 2011, cited in "Department of Justice's Operation Fast and Furious: Accounts of ATF Agents."

52. Transcribed interview with Carlos Canino, ATF Attaché to Mexico, cited in "Department of Justice's Operation Fast and Furious: Fueling Cartel Violence," Joint Staff Report prepared for Representative Darrell E. Issa and Senator Charles E. Grassley, July 26, 2011.

53. Transcribed interview with ATF Special Agent Olindo James Casa, April 28, 2011, cited in "Department of Justice's Operation Fast and Furious: Accounts of ATF Agents."

54. Voth's email, cited on p. 36 in "The Department of Justice's Operation Fast and Furious: Accounts of ATF Agents."

55. USA v. Avila et al., no. CR 11-126-PHX-JAT (Phoenix, Arizona, January 19, 2011).

56. Cindy Carcamo, "'Straw' Buyer of Arms Linked to Border Agent's Death Is Sentenced," *Los Angeles Times*, December 12, 2012, https://www.latimes .com/world/la-xpm-2012-dec-12-la-na-fast-furious-20121213-story.html.

57. US DOJ, "Review of ATF's Operation Fast and Furious and Related Matters," 471.

58. "Diputado Recrimina a EU Por 'Rápido y Furioso,'" *El Universal*, March 9, 2011.

59. Ken Ellingwood, Richard A. Serrano, and Tracy Wilkinson, "Mexico Still Waiting for Answers on Fast and Furious Gun Program," *Los Angeles Times*, September 19, 2011, https://www.latimes.com/archives/la-xpm-2011 -sep-19-la-fg-mexico-fast-furious-20110920-story.html.

60. "Operation Fast and Furious: Management Failures at the Department of Justice." Hearing before the Committee on Oversight and Government Reform, House of Representatives, 112th Congress, 2nd session, February 2, 2012. Serial No. 112–103, https://www.govinfo.gov/content/pkg/CHRG-112hhrg72915

/html/CHRG-112hhrg72915.htm. See also "Eduardo Medina Mora, otro de los nombres en los documentos sobre 'Rápido y Furioso,'" *Infobae*, June 16, 2020, https://www.infobae.com/america/mexico/2020/06/17/eduardo-medina-mora -otro-de-los-nombres-en-los-documentos-sobre-rapido-y-furioso/.

61. Luciano Campos Garza, "Ejército destruye 500 armas de 'Rápido y Furioso' en Nuevo León," *Proceso*, January 17, 2017, https://www.proceso.com .mx/nacional/2017/1/17/ejercito-destruye-500-armas-de-rapido-furioso-en -nuevo-leon-177258.html. These guns were a portion of 5,097 firearms the military captured during operations in Tamaulipas, San Luis Potosí, and Nuevo León. See also "Destruyen Más De 5 Mil Armas Decomisadas," *El Universal*, January 18, 2017, https://www.eluniversal.com.mx/articulo/estados/2017/01/17 /destruyen-en-nl-500-armas-del-operativo-rapido-y-furioso.

62. Luciano Campos Garza, "Abogada mexicana alista demanda civil contra ATF por 'Rápido y Furioso,'" *Proceso*, June 5, 2012, https://www.proceso .com.mx/nacional/2012/6/5/abogada-mexicana-alista-demanda-civil-contra -atf-por-rapido-furioso-103722.html. The news piece about the civil lawsuit included contact information for those who wanted to reach out to the lawyer, Diana Eugenia González Saldaña. The email address given to the public was named "victims of the ATF" (victimasdelatf@hotmail.com).

63. Sharyl Attkisson, "Family of Second Murdered Federal Agent Files Lawsuit against the US Government over 'Fast and Furious,'" CBS News, February 13, 2013, https://www.cbsnews.com/news/family-of-second-murdered-federal -agent-files-lawsuit-against-us-government-over-fast-and-furious/. On the dismissal of the Terry family's lawsuit, see Paul Ingram, "9th Circuit Dismisses Terry Family's Lawsuit over BP Agent's Death," *Tucson Sentinel*, June 27, 2016, https://www.tucsonsentinel.com/local/report/062716_terry_lawsuit/9th -circuit-dismisses-terry-familys-lawsuit-over-bp-agents-death/.

64. Claudia Salazar, "Condenan operaciones de EU en México," *El Norte*, December 6, 2011.

65. Catherine E. Shoichet, "Mexico's President to U.S.: 'No more weapons,'" CNN, February 17, 2012, https://www.cnn.com/2012/02/17/world/americas /mexico-us-weapons/index.html.

GHOST HIGHWAY

1. Leopoldo Ramos, "Policía frena a comando armado que intentaba entrar a Coahuila," *La Jornada*, August 26, 2021, https://www.jornada.com.mx/notas /2021/08/26/estados/comando-armado-se-enfrenta-a-policias-en-intento-por -ingresar-a-coahuila/.

2. "Enfrentamiento entre civiles con policías y militares deja 9 muertos," *Animal Politico*, September 16, 2021, https://www.animalpolitico.com/2021/09 /enfrentamiento-militares-policias-civiles-muertos-coahuila/.

3. "Control . . . Over the Entire State of Coahuila," An Analysis of Testimonies in Trials against Zeta Members in San Antonio, Austin, and Del Rio, Texas. Human Rights Clinic, University of Texas School of Law, November 2017, https://law.utexas.edu/wp-content/uploads/sites/11/2017/11/2017-HRC -coahuilareport-EN.pdf, 21.

278 | Notes to Pages 71–78

4. "Control . . . Over the Entire State of Coahuila," 24.

5. Between 2005 and 2012, Zetas exercised control over various government institutions in Coahuila: the state and municipal police, some federal police and the military, the state attorney general's office, the prisons, and even elected state officials. See "Control . . . Over the Entire State of Coahuila."

6. México: Asesinatos, desapariciones y torturas en Coahuila de Zaragoza constituyen crímenes de lesa humanidad. Open letter to the prosecutor's office by Federación Internacional de Derechos Humanos and a coalition of organizations, June 2017, https://www.cmdpdh.org/publicaciones-pdf/cmdpdh-comunicacion -coahuila.pdf.

7. For more on Santa Muerte, see Alberto Hernández Hernández, *La Santa Muerte: Espacios Cultos y Devociones* (Tijuana, B.C: El Colegio de la Frontera Norte/El Colegio de San Luis, 2016).

8. "Destruyen capillas de la Santa Muerte en Nuevo Laredo," *Excelsior California*, March 26, 2009, https://www.excelsiorcalifornia.com/2009/03/26 /religion-y-folclore-destruyen-capillas-de-la-santa-muerte-en-nuevo-laredo/.

9. With the onset of the Covid-19 pandemic, on March 21, 2020, the US government closed the US-Mexico border to "non-essential travel." The border was reopened on November 8, 2021.

10. Testimony of Mario A. Cuellar, USA v. José Treviño-Morales, no. 12-cr-210 (Austin, Texas, April 16, 2013), 111.

11. Juan Alberto Cedillo, "En la mira del FBI: la carretera Monterrey-Nuevo Laredo, un 'hoyo negro," *Proceso*, July 7, 2021, https://www.proceso.com.mx /reportajes/2021/7/7/en-la-mira-del-fbi-la-carretera-monterrey-nuevo-laredo -un-hoyo-negro-267378.html.

12. The full name of the program is "Federal Mechanism for the Protection of Human Rights Defenders and Journalists." It is run by the Special Prosecutor's Office for Attention to Crimes Committed Against Freedom of Expression (Fiscalía Especial para la Atención de Delitos cometidos contra de la Libertad de Expresión, FEADLE). When a journalist seeks protection, a committee is formed to conduct a risk assessment and determine what kind of protection is most appropriate, from police escorts and video surveillance to panic buttons. In cases where journalists are in immediate danger, they can be relocated to another city or state. Between 2012 and 2022, FEADLE enrolled 563 journalists and 449 human rights defenders into the protection mechanism. For more, see Paroma Soni, "2022 Is Already the Deadliest Year for Journalists in Mexico," *Columbia Journalism Review*, April 29, 2022, https://www.cjr.org/special_report/journalism-mexico -margarito-martinez-lourdes-maldonado.php.

13. According to Article 19, which monitors attacks on freedom of expression, including violence against journalists, in Mexico, the impunity rate for crimes against freedom of expression was at 99.75 percent, and more than half of the attacks against the press in 2017 were thought to have involved public officials. See "In Focus: Mexico and Central America," Article 19, accessed March 30, 2023, https://www.article19.org/regional-office/mexico-and-central-america/.

14. In Mexico, *huachicol* can refer to adulterated alcohol or gasoline. Recently, fuel theft has become so extensive that now the term *huachicoleo* generally refers to the practice of stealing and illicitly selling gasoline, which is

done both by large criminal organizations and smaller, local groups. The people engaged in huachicoleo are called *huachicoleros*. In 2018, Petróleos Mexicanos (PEMEX) reported a loss of 66 billion pesos ($3.4 billion USD) due to theft of 21,242,000 barrels of fuel. For more on fuel theft, see Samuel Leon, "Confronting Mexico's New Black Market in Fuel Theft and Trafficking," *Oxford University Politics Blog*, January 21, 2019, https://blog.politics.ox.ac.uk/confronting -mexicos-new-black-market-in-fuel-theft-and-trafficking/.

15. Jannet López Ponce, "Túneles, nueva modalidad para huachicoleo en Hidalgo, Puebla, Guanajuato y NL," *Milenio*, June 30, 2020, https://www .milenio.com/policia/tuneles-modalidad-huachicol-hidalgo-puebla-guanajuato.

16. Charles Tilly, "War Making and State Making as Organized Crime," in *Bringing the State Back In*, edited by Peter B. Evans, Dietrich Rueschemeyer, and Theda Skocpol (New York: Cambridge University Press, 1985), 169–91, 169. Tilly grounded his analysis of organized means of violence in sixteenth- and seventeenth-century Europe, but his insights had far broader implications and offer us a novel way to look at contemporary statecraft. Not only is the Mexican state operating a protection racket—which, if we agree with Tilly, all states do: they create and even simulate threats against which the government then vows to protect its citizens—but it has lost "the advantage of legitimacy."

THE LAST LETTER

1. Sam Dillon, "Canaries Sing in Mexico, but Uncle Juan Will Not," *New York Times*, February 9, 1996. A4.

2. See Paul Gootenberg, *Andean Cocaine: The Making of a Global Drug* (Chapel Hill: University of North Carolina Press, 2008).

3. For the discussion of how the organization became known as Guadalajara Cartel and why this moniker is inaccurate, see Carlos Pérez Ricart and Jack Pannell, "The Guadalajara Cartel Never Existed," *Noria Research*, November 2021, https://noria-research.com/the-guadalajara-cartel-never -existed/.

4. Federal Judicial Police (Policía Judicial Federal, PJF) was founded in 1908 and for nearly a century served as Mexico's top law enforcement organization responsible for investigating crimes. It operated under the auspices of the Attorney General's Office. Due to widespread corruption, PJF was dissolved in 2002 and replaced by the Federal Investigative Agency (Agencia Federal de Investigaciones, AFI).

5. Juan Alberto Cedillo, *Las Guerras Ocultas Del Narco* (Ciudad de México: Grijalbo, 2018), 23.

6. From photocopies of redacted military files shared with me by Juan A. Cedillo.

7. "Ofrecen 'Zetas' Empleo," *El Norte*, April 14, 2008, ProQuest; "La banda de sicarios Los Zetas 'te quiere a ti, militar o ex militar,'" *El País*, April 14, 2008, https://elpais.com/internacional/2008/04/15/actualidad/1208210403 _850215.html.

8. "Ofrece 'Prestaciones' El Cártel Del Golfo," *Reforma*, April 17, 2008, ProQuest.

9. José Meléndez, "'Zetas' Reclutan Por Radio a Kaibiles; no Indagará Guatemala," *El Universal*, April 24, 2008, ProQuest.

10. "Refuerza a Zetas Deserción Militar, Advierten En EU," *Reforma*, September 26, 2006.

11. Juan Veledíaz, "Hasta 2003, Mil 382 Elementos De Élite Dejaron El Ejército," *El Universal*, November 5, 2007, ProQuest.

12. Abel Barajas, "Va El Ejército Tras Traidores," *Reforma*, October 1, 2006.

13. Manuel Pineda, "La hidra del narco ajusta cuentas," *Revista Contralínea*, May 2003.

14. Decena was killed by the members of a special organized-crime unit. The story about his death, based on interviews with witnesses, appeared in the Tamaulipas-based journal *Vertical* on December 2, 2002.

15. Juan J. Ramirez, "Balean a Testigo De Enfrentamiento," *El Norte*, December 14, 2002, ProQuest.

16. See Abel Barajas, "Consignan a Narcotraficante; Dan Libertad a Cuatro Mujeres," *El Norte*, October 7, 2001, ProQuest; Eduardo Hernández, "Consignan a integrante de los zetas," *El Economista*, March 8, 2005, ProQuest.

17. "Breves De Estado," *El Economista*, March 29, 2005, ProQuest.

18. Silvia Otero, "Reos De Cárteles Del Golfo y De Sinaloa, Los Que Más Escapan," *El Universal*, May 18, 2005, ProQuest.

19. Francisco Gómez, "Vive Nuevo Laredo Una 'Guerra De Sicarios,'" *El Universal*, June 26, 2005, ProQuest.

20. Francisco Gómez," Cárteles En Guerra Al Norte Del País," *El Universal*, June 26, 2005, ProQuest.

21. Rubén Torres, "Heriberto Lazcano, El Z-3, Un Sicario Formado En Las Fuerzas Especiales," *El Economista*, January 10, 2006, ProQuest.

22. Ricardo Raphael, *Hijo de la guerra* (Ciudad de México: Editorial Planeta Mexicana, 2019), 105–8.

23. Testimony of Jorge De León-Navarro, USA v. Marciano Millan Vasquez, no. SA:13-CR-655-XR (San Antonio, TX, July 13, 2016), 196–97. Also in "Control . . . Over the Entire State of Coahuila," An Analysis of Testimonies in Trials against Zeta members in San Antonio, Austin, and Del Rio, Texas, University of Texas School of Law, November 2017. https://law.utexas.edu/wp-content/uploads/sites/11/2017/11/2017-HRC-coahuilareport-EN.pdf, 34–35.

24. "Control . . . Over the Entire State of Coahuila," 34.

25. For the history of the School of the Americas, see Lesley Gill, *The School of the Americas: Military Training and Political Violence in the Americas* (Durham, NC: Duke University Press, 2004).

26. According to the cable, the United States trained 440 Mexican military personnel in 1996, 236 in 1997, 693 in 1998, and 1,271 in 1999. From 1996 to 1998, the United States provided unit-specific training to 422 GAFEs. Records from years prior to 1996, maintained by the US Embassy in Mexico as well as by the US Army at Fort Bragg, are in the form of hard copies and they are incomplete. To date, only one individual was found to have received US training and worked for the Zetas: Rogelio López Villafana, a former Mexican infantry

lieutenant who retired from the special forces, was forcibly recruited by the Zetas, and was arrested after he was implicated in a plan to assassinate the former deputy attorney general for legal and international affairs, José Luis Santiago Vasconcelos in January 2008. See Setting the Record Straight on Zetas and U.S. Military Training. August 21, 2009, 09MEXICO2473_a, https://wikileaks.org/plusd /cables/09MEXICO2473_a.html. See also Jason Buch, "Cable: Founding Zetas Did Not Train in U.S.," February 1, 2011, https://www.mysanantonio.com/news /mexico/article/Cable-Founding-Zetas-did-not-train-in-U-S-990849.php.

27. For more on using animals in military training, see Gary Martinic, "Military 'Live Tissue Trauma Training' Using Animals in the US—Its Purpose, Importance and Commentary on Military Medical Research and the Debate on Use of Animals in Military Training," *Journal of Military and Veterans' Health* 20, no. 4 (November 2012), https://jmvh.org/article/military-live-tissue-trauma-training -using-animals-in-the-us-its-purpose-importance-and-commentary-on-military -medcal-research-and-the-debate-on-use-of-animals-in-military-training/.

28. Raphael, *Hijo de la guerra*, 275.

29. "Ubican rancho de ejecuciones," *El Universal*, June 29, 2005, ProQuest.

30. Laurie Freeman, "State of Siege: Drug-Related Violence and Corruption in Mexico," WOLA Special Report, June 2006, https://www.wola.org/sites /default/files/downloadable/Mexico/past/state_of_siege_06.06.pdf.

31. Sergio Flores, "Dejan Cabeza De Ejecutado En Alcaldía," *El Norte*, June 30, 2006.

32. Rolando Herrera, "Advierten Endurecimiento De Violencia Entre Narcos," *Reforma*, July 10, 2006.

33. Rodrigo Ramírez, "Escala Crudeza: Tiran Cuerpo En Tres Bolsas," *El Norte*, July 31, 2006, ProQuest.

34. Ioan Grillo, "How Mexico's Drug Cartels Are Profiting from the Pandemic," *New York Times*, July 7, 2020, https://www.nytimes.com/2020/07/07 /opinion/sunday/mexico-drug-cartels-coronavirus.html.

35. "Nuevo León: Sería una venganza de un narco el crimen de Marcelo Garza," *Proceso*, September 6, 2006, https://www.proceso.com.mx/221047 /nuevo-leon-seria-una-venganza-de-un-narco-el-crimen-de-marcelo-garza; and Raúl Martínez, "Marcelo Garza, una carrera policiaca truncada por dos balas," *Milenio*, September 1, 2019, https://www.milenio.com/opinion/raul-martinez /historias-negras/marcelo-garza-carrera-policiaca-truncada-balas.

36. An article in *El Norte* suggested that the firearm was likely purchased north of the border, in the United States. In Texas, a gun of that caliber cost more than fifteen hundred dollars. Mario A. Álvarez and Rodrigo Ramírez, "Es Fácil Comprar El Arma En EU," *El Norte*, September 8, 2006.

37. Juan Cedillo and Jaime Márquez, "Ejecutan a Comandante De San Nicolás De Los Garza," *El Universal*, November 14, 2006, ProQuest.

38. Víctor Hugo Michel and David Vicenteño, "Mandan Más Tropas a NL y Tamaulipas," *El Norte*, February 19, 2007, ProQuest.

39. "Arrecian En El Norte Las 'Narcoprotestas,'" *Mural*, February 18, 2009, 8. ProQuest.

40. "Señoras y Niños Al Frente," *El Norte*, February 18, 2009, ProQuest.

41. "Atacan Consulado," *El Norte*, October 13, 2008.

42. Gabriel Talavera and José García, "Investigan FBI y PGR El Ataque Al Consulado," *El Norte*, October 14, 2008, ProQuest.

43. "Ataque Contra Televisa Destapa La Vulnerabilidad De La Prensa En Mexico," EFE News Service, January 7, 2009, ProQuest.

44. "Capturan En Mexico a Presunto Asesino De Militares y Ataques a Consulado EEUU," EFE News Service, March 21, 2009, ProQuest.

45. Investigators found over two hundred spent bullet casings at the site, mostly of calibers used in AR-15 and AK-47 style rifles. "Acribillan a General," *El Norte*, November 5, 2009, ProQuest.

46. Guadalupe Correa-Cabrera, *Los Zetas Inc.: Criminal Corporations, Energy, and Civil War in Mexico* (Austin: University of Texas Press, 2017), 137.

47. Journalist Gary Moore defines it as "a geographical area of influence" and writes that "a plaza is where you squeeze out profits." See Gary Moore, "Heating Up the Plaza: How Mexico's Gangs Use Scorched Earth Tactics," *InSight Crime*, December 6, 2011, https://www.insightcrime.org/news/analysis/heating-up-the-plaza-how-mexicos-gangs-use-scorched-earth-tactics/.

48. Correa-Cabrera, *Los Zetas Inc.*, 158.

49. Emmanuel Salazar, "Afirman Que Granada Lanzada Al Consulado Pertenecía Al Ejército," *El Norte*, November 2, 2008, ProQuest; "Vinculan En EU Ataques Con Granadas En Monterrey y Texas," Notimex, February 13, 2009, ProQuest.

50. The article, published in numerous newspapers simultaneously, suggests that these guns belonged to men planning to assassinate Deputy Attorney General Vasconcelos. "Usan 'Zetas' Armas Del Ejército De EU," *El Norte*, February 4, 2008, ProQuest. Also see María de la Luz González, "Operación 'Hormiga,' En El Tráfico De Armas," *El Universal*, December 22, 2008, ProQuest.

THE CAMP

1. Silvia Otero, "'Los Estacas,' Escoltas De Los 'Capos' Del Golfo," *El Universal*, December 17, 2007; Francisco Gómez, "'Los Zetas' Por Dentro," *El Universal*, December 31, 2008.

2. Humberto Padgett, "Yo Maté Con El Z-40: La Historia de 'Karen,'" *Sin Embargo*, July 17, 2013.

3. One of the biggest of these training camps was in the mountainous area close to Ejido Aura. See Cedillo, *Las Guerras Ocultas Del Narco* (Ciudad de México: Grijalbo, 2018), 120.

4. Ioan Grillo, *El Narco: Inside Mexico's Criminal Insurgency* (New York: Bloomsbury Press, 2012), 213; Correa-Cabrera, *Los Zetas Inc.: Criminal Corporations, Energy, and Civil War in Mexico* (Austin, TX: University of Texas Press, 2017) 72.

5. Silvia Otero, "Los Zetas Tenían Un Almacén De Arsenal," *El Universal*, February 9, 2008.

6. See the interview with Édgar Huerta Montiel, known as "El Wache," the former leader of the Zetas in San Fernando: "Declara 'El Wache' sobre caso San

Fernando," *La Jornada Online*, June 2011, June 22, 2011, https://www
.youtube.com/watch?v=UycQoP9jCts&feature=youtu.be (accessed November
29, 2019).

7. "Alertan en EU por 'los zetas,'" *El Norte*, December 10, 2005.

8. Alfredo Corchado, "Drug Cartels Operate Training Camps near Texas
Border Just Inside Mexico," *McClatchy—Tribune News Service*, March 29,
2008.

9. Testimony of Jorge De León-Navarro, USA v. Marciano Millan Vasquez,
No. SA:13-CR-655-XR (San Antonio, TX, July 13, 2016). See also "Control
... Over the Entire State of Coahuila," An Analysis of Testimonies in Trials
against Zeta Members in San Antonio, Austin, and Del Rio, Texas, University
of Texas School of Law, November 2017. https://law.utexas.edu/wp-content
/uploads/sites/11/2017/11/2017-HRC-coahuilareport-EN.pdf, 43–44.

10. Testimonies of Saúl Fernández and other witnesses, USA v. José Treviño-
Morales et al., No. 12-CR-210 (Austin, TX, April 2013).

11. For more on the risks migrants were taking to cross the militarized US-
Mexico border, see Jason De León, *The Land of Open Graves: Living and
Dying on the Migrant Trail* (Berkeley: University of California Press, 2015);
and Maria Jimenez, "Humanitarian Crisis: Migrant Deaths at the U.S.-Mexico
Border," American Civil Liberties Union, October 1, 2009, https://www.aclu
.org/legal-document/humanitarian-crisis-migrant-deaths-us-mexico-border.

12. US Border Patrol Fiscal Year Southwest Border Sector Deaths (FY 1998–
FY 2020), https://www.cbp.gov/sites/default/files/assets/documents/2021-Aug
/U.S.%20Border%20Patrol%20Fiscal%20Year%20Southwest%20Border
%20Sector%20Deaths%20%28FY%201998%20-%20FY%202020%29%20
%28508%29.pdf.

13. Manny Fernandez, "A Path to America, Marked by More and More
Bodies," *New York Times*, May 4, 2017, https://www.nytimes.com/interactive
/2017/05/04/us/texas-border-migrants-dead-bodies.html.

14. Padgett, "Yo Maté Con El Z-40."

15. Shaylih Muehlmann, *When I Wear My Alligator Boots: Narco-Culture
in the US-Mexico Borderlands* (Berkeley: University of California Press, 2013),
chap. 1.

16. For a deeper, historical look at women's roles in organizations dedicated
to smuggling drugs from Mexico to the United States, see Elaine Carey, *Women
Drug Traffickers: Mules, Bosses and Organized Crime* (Albuquerque: University of New Mexico Press, 2014); and Deborah Bonello, *Narcas: The Secret
Rise of Women in Latin America's Cartels* (Boston: Beacon Press, 2023).

17. For more on women combatants in insurgent movements, see Luisa
Maria Dietrich Ortega, "Looking Beyond Violent Militarized Masculinities,"
International Feminist Journal of Politics 14, no. 4 (2012): 489–507; Maya E.
Berry, *War, Women, and Power: From Violence to Mobilization in Rwanda
and Bosnia-Herzegovina* (New York: Cambridge University Press, 2018); Joce-
lyn Viterna, *Women in War: The Micro-Processes of Mobilization in El Salvador* (New York: Oxford University Press, 2013); Máximo Badaró, "'One of the
Guys': Military Women, Paradoxical Individuality, and the Transformations of
the Argentine Army," *American Anthropologist* 117, no. 1 (2015): 86–99.

18. Javier Méndez Araya, "'Las panteras,' jóvenes y temibles mujeres al servicio de los narcos mexicanos," *El Mercurio*, April 5, 2009.

19. "'La Comandante Bombón,' cómo fue capturada la asesina que hizo temblar a Cancún," *Infobae*, August 15, 2019, https://www.infobae.com/america /mexico/2019/08/15/la-comandante-bombon-como-fue-capturada-la-asesina -que-hizo-temblar-a-cancun/.

20. Not only does the presumption of women's inherent pacifism reify the binary between feminine vulnerability and masculine aggression, but it glances over the much more nuanced realities of the few women who become perpetrators of violence. See Jennifer Carlson, "Troubling the Subject of Violence: The Pacifist Presumption, Martial Maternalism, and Armed Women in Contemporary Gun Culture," *Political Power and Social Theory* 30 (2016): 81–107.

21. "¿Qué es el feminicidio y cómo identificarlo?," Comisión Nacional para Prevenir y Erradicar la Violencia Contra las Mujeres, October 19, 2016, https://www .gob.mx/conavim/articulos/que-es-el-feminicidio-y-como-identificarlo?idiom=es.

22. "'A Rapist in Your Path': Chilean Protest Song Becomes Feminist Anthem," *Guardian News*, December 6, 2019, https://www.youtube.com/watch?v= s5AAscy7qbI.

23. Anabel Hernandez, "Los Treviño, una familia de Zetas," *El Proceso*, October 28, 2012, https://www.proceso.com.mx/347497/los-trevino-una -familia-de-zetas.

24. These descriptions of Z-40 are from the testimony of Rodrigo Humberto Uribe Tapia, USA v. Marciano Millan Vasquez, No. SA:13-CR-655-XR (San Antonio, TX, July 6, 2016), 74; and "Un Líder De Zetas Que Está En La Mira," *El Norte*, December 6, 2010.

25. Scott C. Johnson, "Miguel Angel Trevino Morales's Legacy on Mexico's Drug War," *Daily Beast*, July 17, 2013, https://www.thedailybeast.com/miguel -angel-trevino-moraless-legacy-on-mexicos-drug-war.

26. Cedillo, *Las Guerras Ocultas Del Narco*, 67–68.

THE PLAYER

1. Events reconstructed using testimonies in the trial USA v. Vega-Barreras et al., no. 4:16-cr-00478-JGZ-LAB (Tucson, AZ, 2017). Although court documents are public records, names of individuals in this case have been changed to respect their privacy.

2. Curt Prendergast, "Ceremony Marks Completion of Renovation at Mariposa Port of Entry," *Nogales International*, October 17, 2014, https://www .nogalesinternational.com/news/ceremony-marks-completion-of-renovation-at -mariposa-port-of-entry/article_od123510-560f-11e4-9b8d-e3831ebbd6a2 .html.

3. MS-13, also known as Mara Salvatrucha, is a gang that was founded by Salvadoran immigrants in Los Angeles, California, in the 1980s. When the US government began deporting gang members to El Salvador, the criminal organization started recruiting new members in Central America and has since become one of the major transnational gangs in the region.

4. These task forces, abbreviated to BESTs, were created to coordinate the work of DHS with other federal, state, tribal, and local law enforcement agencies. Authorized under the Jaime Zapata act, named in memory of the HSI special agent who was killed in 2011 by the Zetas with an AK-47 style rifle sold to a man in Dallas, Texas, and trafficked into Mexico, the units investigate transnational criminal organizations that smuggle drugs, people, guns, and money across land and maritime borders.

5. This mismatch resulted in somewhat divergent views of gun smuggling tactics and trends. For example, according to HSI, the main type of firearms smuggled across the border to Mexico in 2017 were rifles, while ATF analysis showed that about two-thirds (64 percent) of US firearms recovered in Mexico were handguns. The agencies also disagreed about how the guns were diverted from the legal market in the United States: ATF claimed it was primarily through secondary purchases (private sales), but HSI suggested the most common way was to use straw buyers. See US Government Accountability Office, "Firearms Trafficking: U.S. Efforts to Disrupt Gun Smuggling into Mexico Would Benefit from Additional Data and Analysis," GAO-21–322, February 2021, 12–23, https://www.gao.gov/assets/gao-21-322.pdf.

6. Oscar bought the cheapest AK-47 variants available, including models manufactured by Romarm and Zastava, each costing approximately $500 to $700. According to agents' estimates, he must have paid around $4,000–$5,000 for eight firearms he purchased in a month. The average monthly wage in Pima County, Arizona, in 2015 was $3,312. See "County Employment and Wages in Arizona—Second Quarter 2015," US Bureau of Labor Statistics, February 16, 2016, https://www.bls.gov/regions/west/news-release/2016/countyemploymentandwages_arizona_20160216.htm.

7. "Listing of Federal Firearms Licensees (FFLs)—2015," Bureau of Alcohol, Tobacco, Firearms and Explosives, accessed June 6, 2022, https://www.atf.gov/firearms/listing-federal-firearms-licensees-ffls-2015.

8. Jonathan Clark, "Lawyer Says Driver Shot at Mariposa Port Was Struck in Head," *Nogales International*, September 16, 2016, https://www.nogalesinternational.com/news/lawyer-says-driver-shot-at-mariposa-port-was-struck-in/article_0364b6be-7b8d-11e6-bf07-6b1906480a75.html.

9. USA v. Melchor Enrique Urquides-Tapia, no. CR-16-0478-TUC-JGZ (Tucson, AZ, August 18, 2017).

10. USA v. Melchor Enrique Urquides-Tapia, no. CR-16-0478-TUC-JGZ (Tucson, AZ, September 19, 2017).

11. USA v. Melchor Enrique Urquides-Tapia, no. CR-16-0478-TUC-JGZ (Tucson, AZ, September 19, 2017).

12. Keith Wood, "Best States for Gun Owners (2019)," *Guns & Ammo*, October 23, 2019, https://www.gunsandammo.com/editorial/best-states-for-gun-owners/369075. For more, see Jennifer Carlson, *Policing the Second Amendment: Guns, Law Enforcement, and the Politics of Race* (Princeton, NJ: Princeton University Press, 2020), 17–18.

13. According to US Census Bureau trade records, between 2015 and 2017, the United States sold to the Mexican military $123 million worth of firearms and ammunition. Bushmaster, Browning, Remington, Barrett, Smith & Wesson,

and others have exported thousands of firearms to Mexico. See John Lindsay-Poland, "How U.S. Guns Sold to Mexico End Up with Security Forces Accused of Crime and Human Rights Abuses," *The Intercept*, April 26, 2018, https://theintercept.com/2018/04/26/mexico-arms-trade-us-gun-sales/.

POISONED CITY

1. Based on reporting in *El Norte*, including "El fuego nos rebasó," *El Norte*, August 26, 2011; "Prenden la tragedia en sólo 2.5 minutos," *El Norte*, August 27, 2011, 8; Luis Castro, "'Con poco hicimos lo que pudimos,'" *El Norte*, August 28, 2011, 5.

2. "Se quema un casino: El testimonio de un bombero," *Multimedios Digital*, August 25, 2014, https://www.multimedios.com/telediario/local/quema-casino-testimonio-bombero.html.

3. Juan Alberto Cedillo, *Las Guerras Ocultas Del Narco* (Ciudad de México: Grijalbo, 2018), 173.

4. Luciano Campos Garza, "Casino Royale: Historias de una tragedia," October 4, 2012, *El Proceso*, https://www.proceso.com.mx/321637/casino-royale-historias-de-una-tragedia.

5. Daniel de la Fuente, "Antes del fuego," *El Norte*, September 3, 2011.

6. De la Fuente, "Envueltos en fuego y humo," *El Norte*, August 24, 2012.

7. Daniel de la Fuente, "El día del fuego," *El Norte*, August 24, 2012.

8. De la Fuente, "El día del fuego."

9. Dulce Ramos, "Las vidas apagadas en el Casino Royale," *Animal Político*, August 29, 2011, https://www.animalpolitico.com/2011/08/las-vidas-apagadas-en-el-casino-royale/.

10. Comisión Nacional de los Derechos Humanos (CNDH) México, Recomendación No. 66/2012, sobre el caso de V1 a V63, víctimas del delito con motivo de los hechos ocurridos en el 'Casino Royale,' en Monterrey, Nuevo León (México, D.F., November 29, 2012), https://www.stps.gob.mx/gobmx/transparencia/documentos/Recomendacion66.pdf.

11. There is inconsistency among sources as to whether the fee was weekly or monthly. Ioan Grillo, "Paying for Your Life in Mexico," *Global Post*, September 6, 2011, https://theworld.org/stories/2011-09-06/paying-your-life-mexico, and Juan Martinez Ahrens, "Capturado el último prófugo de la matanza del Casino Royale," *El País*, April 8, 2016, say it was 130,000 pesos per *month*; while Michael Deibert, *In the Shadow of Saint Death: The Gulf Cartel and the Price of America's Drug War in Mexico* (Guilford, CT: LP Lyons Press, an imprint of Rowman & Littlefield, 2015), says it was the same amount of pesos per week.

12. "Calderón tilda de 'acto de terror y barbarie' el ataque al casino de Monterrey," EFE, August 26, 2011, https://www.elmundo.es/america/2011/08/26/mexico/1314367905.html.

13. "Colitas" is Spanish slang for marijuana buds.

14. Their full names are as follows: Roberto Carlos López Castro ("El Toruño); Baltazar Saucedo Estrada ("El Mataperros"); and Carlos Oliva Castillo ("La Rana"). For more on their arrests, see Javier Estrada, "Uno de los

principales sospechosos del ataque al Casino Royale es detenido," CNN México, September 30, 2011, https://web.archive.org/web/20120216164233/http://mexico.cnn.com/nacional/2011/09/30/uno-de-los-principales-sospechosos-del-ataque-al-casino-royale-es-detenido; "Detenido el líder de los Zetas que ordenó el ataque al casino de Monterrey," EFE, January 6, 2012, https://elpais.com/internacional/2012/01/06/actualidad/1325844863_882401.html; Luis Prados, "Detenido el líder de los Zetas responsable del ataque al Casino de Monterrey," *El País*, October 13, 2011, https://elpais.com/internacional/2011/10/13/actualidad/1318521074_086482.html. For more on Zetas' leadership structure, see Steven Dudley, "The Zetas and Monterrey Math," *InSight Crime*, December 16, 2012, https://insightcrime.org/investigations/zetas-monterrey-math/.

15. "Death of 'El Quemado' Confirmed." Justice in Mexico, April 9, 2012, https://justiceinmexico.org/death-of-el-quemado-confirmed/.

16. "Un policía de Nuevo León, detenido por participar en el ataque a casino," CNN México, September 2, 2011, https://web.archive.org/web/20120216163509/http://mexico.cnn.com/nacional/2011/09/02/un-policia-de-nuevo-leon-detenido-por-participar-en-el-ataque-a-casino. Also see Jan Martínez Ahrens, "Capturado el último prófugo de la matanza del Casino Royale," *El País*, April 8, 2016, https://elpais.com/internacional/2016/04/08/actualidad/1460086679_222259.html.

17. Email to author from Samara Pérez Muñiz, mother of Xavier Muraira, who died in the casino attack, December 11, 2019.

18. David Carrizales, "Acusan familiares corrupción e impunidad en caso del Casino Royale a 9 años del incendio," *El Universal*, August 24, 2020, https://www.eluniversal.com.mx/estados/acusan-familiares-corrupcion-e-impunidad-en-caso-del-casino-royale-9-anos-del-incendio.

19. David Carrizales, "Destruyen memorial de víctimas de incendio del Casino Royale por demolición del inmueble," *El Universal*, April 28, 2021, https://www.eluniversal.com.mx/estados/nuevo-leon-destruyen-memorial-de-victimas-de-incendio-del-casino-royale.

20. Ma. Elena Sánchez y Emmanuel Aveldaño, "Hallan muerto a procesado por Caso Royale," *El Norte*, July 14, 2022, https://www.elnorte.com/hallan-muerto-a-procesado-por-caso-royale/ar2436085.

21. José García, "Investigarán colocación de narcomantas," *El Norte*, February 23, 2010; see also Nik Steinberg, "The Monster and Monterrey: The Politics and Cartels of Mexico's Drug War," *The Nation*, May 25, 2011, https://www.thenation.com/article/archive/monster-and-monterrey-politics-and-cartels-mexicos-drug-war/.

22. According to Jesús Enrique Rejón Aguilar, the Zetas were loyal to Cárdenas Guillén until his sentencing in Houston, Texas, in February 2010, when they learned that he took a plea deal. See Alfredo Corchado and Kevin Krause, "Deadly Deal," *Dallas Morning News*, April 14, 2016, http://interactives.dallasnews.com/2016/cartels/.

23. Consulate Monterrey, "Border Violence Spreads to Nuevo Leon," Wikileaks Cable: 10MONTERREY43, dated February 26, 2010.

24. José García, "Investigarán colocación de narcomantas," *El Norte*, February 23, 2010.

25. In Spanish: "el veneno se combate con el mismo veneno." See Cedillo, *Las Guerras Ocultas Del Narco*, 77.

26. During the raid, the military also seized five rifles, four pistols, four grenades, magazines, ammunition, and bulletproof vests, and charged the detained men with violating federal firearms laws. See "Tenían Narcos Listas De Servidores De NL," *El Norte*, February 3, 2009, ProQuest.

27. Elyssa Pachico, "How Much Is Guatemala Arming the Zetas?" *InSight Crime*, April 12, 2011, https://insightcrime.org/news/analysis/how-much-is -guatemala-arming-the-zetas/. Zetas also got guns from El Salvador and Honduras, among other countries, a portion of which were initially sold to their militaries by the United States. According to one investigation, three hundred FAL assault rifles and three hundred thousand bullets that disappeared from the Honduran police's special forces were sold to the Zetas; see "How the Honduran Military and Police Profit from the Illegal Arms Trade," Transparency International, November 9, 2017, https://www.transparency.org/en/news/how -the-honduran-military-and-police-profit-from-the-illegal-arms-trade.

28. In addition to the author's interviews, the details on gun smuggling are drawn from testimonies by Adolfo Efren Tavira-Alverado and Saul Fernandez in USA v. Marciano Millan Vasquez, no. SA:13-CR-655-XR (San Antonio, TX, July 7 and July 14, 2016); testimonies of Julio Cesar Salazar, Sarai Longoria-Rivas, and Leroy Milligan in USA v. Emilio Villalobos-Alcala and Jose Eluid Lugo-Lopez, no. DR-13-CR-217-AM (Del Rio, TX, June 16, 17, 18, 2014); and testimony of José Luis Vasquez Jr. in USA v. José Treviño-Morales, no. 12-CR-210 (Austin, TX, April 17, 2013).

29. In the video of the interview released by the Secretariat of Public Security, one of the founding members of the Zetas explained that they got their guns from buyers in the United States who were not affiliated with their organization. Policía Federal interview with Jesús Enrique Rejón Aguilar, El Mamito, shared by Secretaría de Seguridad Pública, July 8, 2011, https://www .youtube.com/watch?v=9ZLoKvx2J6k&list=FLQCeCLsgouoTnmvszvg-oOg.

30. Details from USA v. Emilio Villalobos-Alcala and Jose Eluid Lugo-Lopez, no. DR-13-CR-217-AM (Del Rio, TX, 2014).

31. If law enforcement appeared to show interest in the vehicle carrying the guns, the scout would speed up or do another violation to be pulled over, allowing the loaded vehicle to escape. See Julio Aguirre testimony in USA v. Emilio Villalobos-Alcala and Jose Eluid Lugo-Lopez, no. DR-13-CR-217-AM (Del Rio, TX, June 17, 2014), 14–15.

32. Border Patrol agents stopped Sarai's truck on Highway 57, about fifteen miles east of Eagle Pass, on August 7, 2012. After the mobile X-ray scanner didn't show anything unusual, the agents took the vehicle with the auxiliary fuel tank to the Eagle Pass port of entry and used a more powerful scanner (known as VACIS), which revealed "an anomaly" in the gas tank and helped them find the weapons. In addition to forty-three assault-style rifles, the tank contained three handguns, twenty-one rifle magazines, three pistol magazines, and seventy-nine loose rounds of ammo. See USA v. Emilio Villalobos-Alcala and Jose Eluid Lugo-Lopez, no. DR-13-CR-217-AM (Del Rio, TX, June 16, 2014).

33. For a while, gun shipments arrived in Monterrey a few times a week, bringing hundreds of firearms to be distributed to the foot soldiers in the neighborhoods. Later, when the authorities stepped up border inspections on the bridges in Eagle Pass and Laredo, deliveries of firearms and ammunition became more sporadic, as few as once a month. See Policía Federal interview with Jesús Enrique Rejón Aguilar, El Mamito, shared by Secretaría de Seguridad Pública, July 8, 2011.

34. "Asesina comando a un empresario tras fallar secuestro," *Dossier Politico*, May 24, 2008, https://www.dossierpolitico.com/vernoticiasanteriores.php ?artid=37089&relacion=dossierpolitico.

35. Luis Brito, "Usan Fama De Sicarios En Extorsión," *El Norte*, January 9, 2009, ProQuest.

36. Diego Gambetta, *The Sicilian Mafia: The Business of Private Protection* (Cambridge, MA: Harvard University Press, 1993).

37. Robin Emmott, "If Monterrey Falls, Mexico Falls," Reuters, June 1, 2011, https://www.reuters.com/article/uk-mexico-drugs-monterrey/if-monterrey -falls-mexico-falls-idUSLNE75004G20110601.

38. "Mexico Apologizes for 2010 Murder of Tec Monterrey Students," *Telesur English*, March 20, 2019, https://www.telesurenglish.net/news/Mexico -Apologizes-for-2010-Murder-of-Tec-Monterrey-Students-20190320-0028 .html.

39. "Five People Killed in Stampede at Mexican Concert," Reuters, May 2, 2010, https://www.reuters.com/article/uk-mexico-stampede/five-people-killed -in-stampede-at-mexican-concert-idUKTRE6411Z220100502.

40. Cedillo, *Las Guerras Ocultas Del Narco*, 79.

41. Cedillo, *Las Guerras Ocultas Del Narco*, 84.

42. "Car Bombs Explode Near Mexico TV Station, Transit Office," CNN, August 27, 2010, https://www.cnn.com/2010/WORLD/americas/08/27/mexico .car.bomb/index.html.

43. Her name was Marisol Macías Castañeda, but in news reports she was often referred to as Maria Elizabeth Macías Castro. "Mexican Newspaper Editor Maria Macias Found Decapitated," BBC, September 25, 2011, https:// www.bbc.com/news/world-latin-america-15055458.

44. See Séverine Durin, "La prensa noreste bajo fuego," in *¡Sálvese Quien Pueda! Violencia Generalizada Y Desplazamiento Forzado En El Noreste De México* (Ciudad de México: CIESAS Centro de Investigaciones y Estudios Superiores en Antropología Social, 2019), chap. 5, 211–54.

45. Mike O'Connor, "El Mañana Cedes Battle to Report on Mexican Violence," Committee to Protect Journalists, May 23, 2012, https://cpj.org/2012/05 /el-manana-cedes-battle-to-report-on-mexican-violen/.

46. "Medios mexicanos pactan un decálogo para la cobertura de la violencia," *El País*, March 24, 2011, https://elpais.com/internacional/2011/03/24 /actualidad/1300921220_850215.html.

47. Ignacio de los Reyes, "México: entre la responsabilidad y la censura de los medios," BBC Mundo, March 25, 2011. The full quote from *Milenio* cited in the news piece is as follows: "A partir de hoy, nos referiremos eufemísticamente a dichos fenómenos como . . . *Narco: Agricultor alternativo y under-*

ground y *Enfrentamiento entre el Ejército y sicarios: Cita a ciegas entre dos que se aman con loca pasión."*

48. Daniel Hernandez, "In Monterrey, Mexico, a Culture of Fear Is Evident," *Los Angeles Times*, April 12, 2012, https://www.latimes.com/archives/la-xpm-2012-apr-03-la-fg-mexico-monterrey-fear-20120403-story.html.

49. Durin, *¡Sálvese Quien Pueda!*, 174.

50. Ana Villarreal, "Fear and Spectacular Drug Violence in Monterrey," in *Violence at the Urban Margins: Global and Comparative Ethnography*, edited by Javier Auyero, Philippe Bourgois, and Nancy Scheper-Hughes (New York: Oxford University Press, 2015), 135–61, 138.

FALLEN SOVEREIGNS

1. People who were incarcerated also had a right to continue intimate relationships with their partners and spent nights in conjugal cells together, an arrangement which had less to do with respect for human rights and more with maintaining both the formal and the informal economy of the prison. See, for example, Anthony Fontes and Kevin O'Neill, "La Visita: Prisons and Survival in Guatemala," *Journal of Latin American Studies* 51, no. 1 (2019): 85–107.

2. "'Limpian' penales Topo Chico, Apodaca, Cadereyta . . . de reos peligrosos," *Excelsior*, March 27, 2019, https://www.excelsior.com.mx/nacional/limpian-penales-topo-chico-apodaca-cadereyta-de-reos-peligrosos/1304095; "Reportan disparos al interior del penal de Topo Chico en Monterrey," *Infobae*, March 27, 2019, https://www.infobae.com/america/mexico/2019/03/27/reportan-disparos-al-interior-del-penal-de-topo-chico/.

3. La Silla Rota (@lasillarota), video posted on Twitter, August 8, 2019.

4. It was in Topo Chico that American writer Thomas Harris met the doctor-murderer who inspired him to write *The Silence of the Lambs*. See Elia Baltazar, "El médico asesino de Monterrey que inspiró al creador de Hannibal Lecter," *Infobae*, October 7, 2018, https://www.infobae.com/america/mexico/2018/10/07/el-medico-asesino-de-monterrey-que-inspiro-al-creador-de-hannibal-lecter/.

5. Melva Frutos, "Un 'reino' criminal en territorio del gobierno: así son las cárceles del norte de México," *Vice News*, June 21, 2017, https://www.vice.com/es_latam/article/bjvxja/un-reino-criminal-en-territorio-del-gobierno-asi-son-las-carceles-del-norte-de-mexico.

6. In the aftermath of the February 2016 massacre, the authorities implemented changes. But the effects of inspections and transfers were short-lived and old structures were soon reconstituted, which brought more violence. That same year, in June, three inmates were assassinated and at least fourteen others were wounded in another riña. The following year, after thirty-eight leaders of organized crime groups were transferred to other states, rumors about new prison leadership prompted a motín. More than three thousand inmates participated. Smoke from burned mattresses rose above the prison walls; at least one inmate was stabbed. See Melva Frutos and David Carrizales, "Otro motín en Topo Chico . . . ahora por el traslado de reos," *El Universal*, June 6, 2017, https://www.eluniversal.com.mx/articulo/estados/2017/06/20/otro-motin-en

-topo-chico-ahora-por-el-traslado-de-reos. The last riot before my visit happened in the spring of 2019.

7. Comisión Nacional de los Derechos Humanos (CNDH) Mexico, "Diagnóstico Nacional de Supervisión Penitenciaria 2018." México, https://www.cndh.org.mx/sites/all/doc/sistemas/DNSP/DNSP_2018.pdf.

8. This phenomenon is not limited to Mexico. Scholars and journalists have documented how prisons function as a central node in organized crime activities in Central America, Brazil, and elsewhere. For a detailed account of criminal governance in São Paulo prisons, see Graham Denyer Willis, *The Killing Consensus: Police, Organized Crime and the Regulation of Life and Death in Urban Brazil* (Berkeley: University of California Press, 2015).

9. Frutos, "Un 'reino' criminal en territorio del gobierno."

10. This account is based on Comisión Nacional de los Derechos Humanos (CNDH), Recomendación No. 40/2013: Sobre el caso de los internos del Centro de Reinserción Social de Apodaca, Nuevo León (México, D.F., October 22, 2013).

11. CNDH, Recomendación No. 40/2013.

12. According to the CNDH report, the agents providing perimeter security during the operation carried rifles that included the Panther caliber .308, the Bushmaster .223, the Galil IWI ACE caliber .223, and 9mm Glock pistols. See CNDH, Recomendación No. 40/2013.

BLURRED LINES

1. Luciano Campos Garza, "Dejan restos humanos en hieleras cerca de penales y un edificio ministerial de NL," *El Proceso*, February 4, 2019, https://www.proceso.com.mx/570339/dejan-restos-humanos-en-hieleras-cerca-de-penales-y-un-edificio-ministerial-de-nl.

2. "Déjense de mamadas" can be translated as "stop fucking around." Denisse López, "Nueva ola violenta golpea al estado más rico de México; analistas culpan a cárteles del narco," *Infobae*, February 7, 2019, https://www.infobae.com/america/mexico/2019/02/07/nueva-ola-violenta-golpea-al-estado-mas-rico-de-mexico-analistas-culpan-a-carteles-del-narco/.

3. Sandra González, "Abandono de restos humanos es para llamar la atención: Fasci," *Milenio*, February 4, 2019, https://www.milenio.com/policia/abandono-restos-humanos-llamar-atencion-fasci.

4. Melva Frutos, "Dejan hieleras con restos humanos cerca de penales en NL," *Aristegui Noticias*, February 4, 2019, https://aristeguinoticias.com/0402/mexico/dejan-hieleras-con-restos-humanos-cerca-de-penales-en-nl/.

5. "Por segunda vez en dos meses aparecieron restos humanos afuera de cárceles de Nuevo León," *Infobae*, February 4, 2019, https://www.infobae.com/america/mexico/2019/02/04/por-segunda-vez-en-dos-meses-aparecieron-restos-humanos-afuera-de-carceles-de-nuevo-leon/.

6. SEDENA, response to public information request, no. 0000700068219, March 22, 2019.

7. On the abandonment of ranches and rural properties due to violence in the northeast, see Séverine Durin, *¡Sálvese Quien Pueda! Violencia Generalizada Y*

Desplazamiento Forzado En El Noreste De México (Ciudad de México: CIESAS Centro de Investigaciones y Estudios Superiores en Antropología Social, 2019), 380–81. Citing data from *El Norte*, Durin notes that in 2010, the value of *fincas campestres* (country farms) fell between 25 percent and 50 percent during a period of less than a year.

8. Durin, *¡Sálvese Quien Pueda!*, 151. On police working for the Zetas, see also Guadalupe Correa-Cabrera, *Los Zetas Inc.: Criminal Corporations, Energy, and Civil War in Mexico* (Austin: University of Texas Press, 2017), 94.

9. Consulate Monterrey, "San Pedro Mayor-Elect Plans Hardhitting Campaign to Improve Security," Wikileaks Cable: 09MONTERREY344_a, September 17, 2009, https://wikileaks.org/plusd/cables/09MONTERREY344_a.html.

10. Patrick Signoret, "A Force for Change: Nuevo León Bolsters Police Capacity in Tough Times, 2011–2015," Innovations for Successful Societies, July 2018, https://successfulsocieties.princeton.edu/sites/g/files/toruqf5601/files /PS_Mexico_NL%20Police_Formatted_ToU_962018_1.pdf.

11. "Balean y calcinan al director del C5," *El Norte*, February 14, 2011.

12. "Ahora utilizan lanzagranadas en ataque al C5," *El Norte*, November 28, 2010.

13. Ana Villarreal, "Domesticating Danger: Coping Codes and Symbolic Security amid Violent Organized Crime in Mexico," *Sociological Theory* 39, no. 4 (December 2021): 225–44; Durin, *¡Sálvese Quien Pueda!*, 161.

14. Durin, *¡Sálvese Quien Pueda!*, 397.

15. Durin, *¡Sálvese Quien Pueda!*, 164.

16. On Fuerza Civil, see Signoret, "A Force for Change, 2011–15"; Lucy Conger, "The Private Sector and Public Security: The Cases of Ciudad Juárez and Monterrey," in *Building Resilient Communities in Mexico: Civic Responses to Crime and Violence* (Washington, DC: Wilson Center Mexico Institute, 2014), 173–209; Horacio Salazar, *Fuerza Civil: La Fuerza de Todos*. Secretaría de Gobernación, "Plan de Implementación del Nuevo Modelo de Policía Estatal Acreditable," 2013.

17. For more on the Mérida Initiative and its role in the militarization of police in Mexico, see Dawn Paley, *Drug War Capitalism* (Oakland, CA: AK Press, 2014), chaps. 4–5. In Nuevo León, the Mérida Initiative also funded police training; see, for example: "Capacitan a Policías De NL Con Apoyo De La Iniciativa Mérida," Notimex, July 3, 2017, ProQuest; "Reciben Curso De Inteligencia En NL Por Iniciativa Mérida," Notimex, January 28, 2013, ProQuest; "Suman 3 Mil Elementos Reclutados Para Fuerza Civil De NL," Notimex, February 17, 2013, ProQuest. For more on Mérida Initiative funds used to support police training, see Clare Ribando Seelke and Kristin Finklea, "U.S.-Mexican Security Cooperation: The Mérida Initiative and Beyond," CRS report R41349, June 29, 2017, https://fas.org/sgp/crs/row/R41349.pdf. Although the 2011 budget in Salazar's "Plan de Implementación del Nuevo Modelo de Policía Estatal Acreditable" mentions equipment costs, including long and short guns, no other information could be found on the firearms used by Fuerza Civil, nor whether Mérida Initiative was used to finance the purchase of these weapons.

18. Nevertheless, concerns with Fuerza Civil, as a militarized, reactionary force implicated in human rights violations, remained. See Hector Eduardo Mendoza Marquez, "Gobernanza para la gobernabilidad. La construcción de 'Fuerza Civil', la nueva policía de Nuevo León." *Revista Mexicana de Análisis Político y Administración Pública* IV, no. 1 (January–June 2015); Sandra Ley and Magdalena Guzmán, "Doing Business amid Criminal Violence: Companies and Civil Action in Mexico," in *Civil Action and the Dynamics of Violence,* edited by Deborah Avant, Marie Berry, Erica Chenoweth, Rachel Epstein, Cullen Hendrix, Oliver Kaplan, and Timothy Sisk (New York: Oxford University Press, 2019), 147–74.

19. Leonardo González, "Sorprende Fasci Con Panorámico," *El Norte,* May 9, 2018, 2.

20. In Spanish: "Fiscal de hierro, pero con dedos de pianista." Luis A. Rivera, "Promueve Subprocurador Su Inspiración," *El Norte,* January 14, 2007, ProQuest.

21. Consulate Monterrey. "New Nuevo Leon Security Director's Ambitious Plans to Overhaul Corrupt Police Forces," Wikileaks Cable: 07MONTERREY828, September 7, 2007, https://wikileaks.jcvignoli.com/cable_07MONTERREY828.

22. Gabriel Talavera, "No Me Puedo Confiar. Fasci," *El Norte,* November 11, 2011, ProQuest. See also Gabriel Talavera, "Va Al Penal Por Asesinar a Un Policía," *El Norte,* December 12, 2011, ProQuest.

23. Daniel Reyes, "'Ni con Supermán se arregla violencia.'" *El Norte,* May 23, 2019, https://www.elnorte.com/ni-con-superman-se-arregla-violencia/ar1682909.

24. Luis Astorga, *El Siglo De Las Drogas: El Narcotráfico Del Porfiriato Al Nuevo Milenio* (México, D.F.: Plaza y Janés, 2005), 180.

25. As of October 2017, the General Directorate of Private Security (Dirección General de Seguridad Privada, DGSP) listed 4,587 private security companies registered at the state level across the country. Mexico City had 814 private security companies; Monterrey (Nuevo León)—294; and Guadalajara (Jalisco)—250. See "Regulating Mexico's Private Security Sector," report by Robert Strauss Center for International Security and Law, University of Texas at Austin, and Mexico's National Security Commission, April 2018, https://www.strausscenter.org/wp-content/uploads/MSI-CNS_Report_06.pdf. Authors of the report note that there are significant limitations to their analysis based on data from registered companies because of a sizable informal market for private security, which makes up over 40 percent of all providers (13).

26. "Regulating Mexico's Private Security Sector." The report cites INEGI data, according to which there were 218,649 police officers across Mexico in 2016 ("Censo Nacional de Gobierno, Seguridad Pública y Sistema Penitenciario Estatales 2017"), and 331,000 police officers in 2017 ("Encuesta Nacional de Ocupación y Empleo"). The report estimates there were 460,000 to 600,000 private security personnel operating around the country.

27. Mexico's 2006 Federal Private Security Law (Ley Federal de Seguridad Privada) forbids private security companies from hiring individuals who were previously dismissed from the country's public security forces for reasons related to a lack of personal honesty or for divulging government information, but it is not clear to what extent this prohibition has been enforced. For data on

salaries in public and private security, see "Regulating Mexico's Private Security Sector," app. 6, p. 32. According to the report, the average salary of private security guards in charge of protecting people is higher than that of employees in public security agencies.

28. This is based on analysis of 1,465 registered attacks. Three quarters of the attacks against armored vehicles were carried out by handguns. Esteban Hernández López, "Las armas más utilizadas por la delincuencia en México," Asociación Mexicana de Blindadores de Automotores (AMBA), March 2, 2023.

29. Daniel de la Fuente, "Recordando a Don Alejo," *El Norte*, June 21, 2020, https://www.elnorte.com/recordando-a-don-alejo/ar1970859.

30. "El valiente ve la muerte solo una vez," Ambulante, accessed April 2, 2023, https://www.ambulante.org/en/documentales/el-valiente-ve-la-muerte-solo-una-vez/.

31. Porfirio Ibarra, "Policía de Nuevo León registra robo de 50 armas dentro de instalaciones," *Expansión*, July 28, 2015, https://expansion.mx/nacional/2015/07/28/policia-de-nuevo-leon-registra-robo-de-50-armas-dentro-de-instalaciones.

32. Mario Álvarez, "De policía élite a secuestrador," *El Norte*, September 1, 2021, https://www.elnorte.com/de-policia-elite-a-secuestrador/ar2249951.

33. Gabino Arriaga y Gabriel Talavera, "Caen otros tres polis plagiarios," *El Norte*, September 2, 2021.

BROTHERS

1. Events reconstructed based on court documents, including trial transcripts, of USA v. Andre Rene Garcia and Jorge Acosta-Licerio, no. CR-16-00478-TUC-JGZ (Tucson, AZ, 2017), and interviews with individuals involved in the case. The names have been changed for privacy reasons.

2. For more on Nogales and its binational community, see Ieva Jusionyte, *Threshold: Emergency Responders on the US-Mexico Border* (Oakland: University of California Press, 2018).

REVENGE

1. St. John Barned-Smith, "A Shootout in Mexico Left 23 Dead and Led ATF Agents to Houston," *Houston Chronicle*, August 13, 2020, https://www.houstonchronicle.com/news/houston-texas/houston/article/mexico-shootout-23-dead-houston-tx-crime-guns-15481531.php.

2. "Ataque en Villa Unión lo hicieron 130 sicarios en 25 camionetas; hay 10 detenidos," *El Universal*, December 3, 2019, https://www.eluniversal.com.mx/estados/villa-union-ataque-lo-hicieron-130-sicarios-en-25-camionetas-hay-10-detenidos.

3. Preliminary examination and hearing in USA v. Victor Ricardo Camacho, no. 4:20-CR-00026 (Houston, TX, December 23, 2019), 19.

4. At the time this book went into production (April 2023), public information request no. 050105700004322, submitted to Coahuila's attorney general's

office on November 7, 2022, asking for details about the types of guns recovered at the scenes of shootouts in Villa Unión, was still pending response.

5. USA v. Victor Ricardo Camacho, no. 4:20-CR-00026 (Houston, TX, December 23, 2019, and July 15, 2020).

6. Both Chapa and Camacho were indicted in Texas. On March 23, 2021, Chapa pleaded guilty to one count of "aiding and abetting false statements on ATF Form 4473" and was sentenced to thirty-two months in prison. Camacho pleaded guilty on March 1, 2022, to two counts of "aiding and abetting false statements on ATF Form 4473" and one count of "possession of firearm with obliterated serial number"; he was sentenced to fifty-seven months in prison. The surviving ten men who participated in the attack were tried in Piedras Negras, Coahuila, in November 2022. Each received a sentence of eighty-five years in prison, for kidnapping; they are also facing charges for terrorism (René Arellano, "Dan 85 años de prisión a implicados en caso Villa Unión," *El Siglo de Torreón*, November 9, 2022, https://www.elsiglodetorreon.com.mx/noticia /2022/dan-85-anos-de-prision-a-implicados-en-caso-villa-union.html).

7. Juan Alberto Cedillo, *Las Guerras Ocultas Del Narco* (Ciudad de México: Grijalbo, 2018), 77–98.

8. Most were migrants from Central and South America on their way to the United States. Migrants were easy prey for the Zetas who kidnapped them for mixed reasons, including robbing them of their money and possessions, demanding ransom from their families, and forcibly recruiting them to work for the group as foot soldiers or drug mules. One of the members of the Zetas, Edgar Huerta Montiel, known as El Wache, said in a video testimony that his group was kidnapping migrants because of their fear that they were coming from other states to join their rivals, the CDG.

9. The August 2010 massacre is sometimes called the first massacre of San Fernando. In March 2011, there was another massacre, in which the Zetas killed at least 193 people at La Joya ranch, also located in the municipality of San Fernando, which is known as the second massacre of San Fernando. Many victims of this second massacre were Mexican citizens traveling by passenger buses when they were hijacked on Mexican federal highway 101.

10. Marcela Turati, "Pese al acoso judicial, nosotras solo buscamos desenterrar la verdad en México," *Washington Post*, November 25, 2021, https://www .washingtonpost.com/es/post-opinion/2021/11/25/investigacion-espionaje-pgr -san-fernando-marcela-turati/.

11. Perla Reséndez, "A diez años de masacre de 72 migrantes en Tamaulipas, no hay una sola sentencia," *El Financiero*, August 24, 2020, https://www .elfinanciero.com.mx/estados/a-diez-anos-de-masacre-de-72-migrantes-en -tamaulipas-no-hay-una-sola-sentencia/.

12. Juan Alberto Cedillo, "El apocalipsis en Coahuila," *Proceso*, December 24, 2012, https://www.proceso.com.mx/reportajes/2012/12/24/el-apocalipsis -en-coahuila-112377.html.

13. The checkpoint was staffed by personnel from the National Migration Institute (Instituto Nacional de Migración, INM), as well as federal and state police that received support from the Mexican army. See Comisión Nacional de

los Derechos Humanos (CNDH), Recomendación No. 10VG/2018. Sobre la investigación de violaciones graves a los derechos humanos, por los hechos acontecidos del 18 al 20 de marzo de 2011, en el municipio de Allende, Coahuila, así como por las detenciones arbitrarias y desapariciones forzadas cometidas con posterioridad a dicho evento, CNDH (Mexico City, March 16, 2018), https://www.cndh.org.mx/sites/default/files/doc/Recomendaciones/Violaciones Graves/RecVG_010.pdf.

14. Juan Alberto Cedillo, "Masacre de Allende: el silencio del general," *Proceso*, June 19, 2021, https://www.proceso.com.mx/reportajes/2021/6/19/masacre-de-allende-el-silencio-del-general-266215.html.

15. Cedillo, *Las Guerras Ocultas Del Narco*, 143–62.

16. Testimony of Adolfo Efren Tavira-Alverado. U.S.A. v. Marciano Millan Vasquez, no. 5:13-cr-00655-XR (San Antonio, TX, July 14, 2016).

17. Testimonies of Cuellar and Vásquez are covered in Melissa del Bosque's book about the Zetas' involvement in the horse-racing industry and their money laundering scheme. Melissa del Bosque, *Bloodlines: The True Story of a Drug Cartel, the FBI, and the Battle for a Horse-Racing Dynasty* (New York: HarperCollins, 2017). The Zetas were also suspecting that Vásquez and his associates in Piedras Negras had stolen money from the organization.

18. Ginger Thompson, "How the U.S. Triggered a Massacre in Mexico," *ProPublica*, June 12, 2017, https://www.propublica.org/article/allende-zetas-cartel-massacre-and-the-us-dea.

19. Declaration of Allende firefighter Jesús Gerardo De León Ramos, December 17, 2014. Translation from Michael Evans, "The Allende Massacre in Mexico: A Decade of Impunity," National Security Archive, March 18, 2021. Full document, released by Mexico's National Human Rights Commission (CNDH), is available at https://nsarchive.gwu.edu/sites/default/files/documents/20515960/28-20141217-jesusgerardodeleonramos-v1.pdf.

20. Declaration of Allende firefighter Luis Gerardo Herrera Estrada, November 23, 2014, https://nsarchive.gwu.edu/document/20718-25-20141123-luisgerardoherrera-v1.

21. Thompson, "How the U.S. Triggered a Massacre in Mexico."

22. Cedillo, *Las Guerras Ocultas Del Narco*, 153.

23. Sergio Aguayo, Delia Sánchez del Ángel, Manuel Pérez Aguirre, and Jacobo Dayán Askenazi, *Mexico: State of Neglect. Los Zetas, the State, Society, and the Victims of San Fernando, Tamaulipas (2010) and Allende, Coahuila (2011)* (Ciudad de México: El Colegio de México, 2016), 20.

24. Declaration of former Allende police shift commander, September 18, 2016. Cited in Michael Evans, "The Allende Massacre in Mexico: A Decade of Impunity," National Security Archive, March 18, 2021, https://nsarchive.gwu.edu/document/20733-35-20160918-policeshiftcommander-7.

25. Cedillo, *Las Guerras Ocultas Del Narco*, 161–62; CNDH, Recomendación No. 10 VG/2018.

26. Declaration of Allende firefighter Luis Gerardo Herrera Estrada, November 23, 2014. The police used those radios to report suspicious vehicles that arrived in Allende and inform the plaza bosses when federal authorities came in.

27. The money police officers received monthly depended on their rank: the director got 20,000 pesos, the chief 10,000, shift commanders 12,000; even police who refused to collaborate got 1,500 pesos; at the time, the average salary for municipal police in the region was approximately 6,000 pesos per month. See Aguayo et al., *Mexico: State of Neglect*, 20.

28. Aguayo et al., *Mexico: State of Neglect*, 14.

29. See Diego Enrique Osorno, "El manantial masacrado," *Vice*, July 17, 2016 (originally published in 2014), https://www.vice.com/es_latam/article /qbqdpq/el-manantial-masacrado.

30. Some agents speculated that this method of extermination, colloquially referred to as "cooking," became more popular after the discovery of the mass grave in San Fernando, Tamaulipas, where the Zetas killed seventy-two migrants. Burning the remains was a cover-up of a crime. It made it more difficult to find mass graves and draw attention to the operations of organized crime.

31. Aguayo et al., *Mexico: State of Neglect*, 24.

32. Aguayo et al., *Mexico: State of Neglect*, 16.

33. In a letter dated January 4, 2023, Comisión Ejecutiva Estatal de Atención a Víctimas del Estado de Coahuila confirmed it recognized fifty-seven "direct victims" of the Allende massacres. This number did not include people killed in Piedras Negras. The copy of the letter was shared with me by Juan Cedillo.

34. Jury verdict in USA v. Marciano Millan Vasquez, no. SA-13-CR-655-5-XR (San Antonio, TX, July 19, 2016).

35. CNDH, Recomendación No. 10VG/2018.

36. Secretaría de Gobernación, June 27, 2019, Boletín No. 155/2019, https:// www.gob.mx/segob/prensa/enfrentamos-como-pais-y-como-estado-mexicano -uno-de-los-sucesos-mas-dolorosos-en-la-historia-el-de-allende-olga-sanchez -cordero-206812.

37. Juan Alberto Cedillo, "Los Garza, el rancho maldito," *Revista Proceso*, January 23, 2022, 22.

38. Cited in Evans, "The Allende Massacre in Mexico."

50 BMG

1. For a biography of Ronnie Barrett and the story of how he invented the .50-caliber Barrett rifle, see Linda Hoff, "Ronnie Barrett: High-Caliber Innovator," *NRA Family*, September 27, 2019, https://www.nrafamily.org/articles /2019/9/27/ronnie-barrett-high-caliber-innovator/.

2. Jack Lewis, *Guide Book of Assault Weapons*, 6th ed. (Iola, WI: Gun Digest Books, Krause Publications Inc., 2004), 106–7.

3. Seth Harp, "Arming the Cartels: The Inside Story of a Texas Gun-Smuggling Ring," *Rolling Stone*, August 7, 2019, https://www.rollingstone.com/culture /culture-features/arming-mexican-cartels-inside-story-of-a-texas-gun-smuggling -ring-866836/.

4. Lewis, *Guide Book of Assault Weapons*, 110.

5. Barrett 2020 Catalog, https://barrett.net/wp-content/uploads/2020/07 /barrett-catalog.pdf.

6. Gary Reisenwitz, "ArmaLite Brings on the 'Big Boy' AR-50," *Small Arms Review* 3, no.6 (March 2000), http://www.smallarmsreview.com/display.article.cfm?idarticles=3052.

7. Glenn M. Gilbert, "The Barrett Model 82A1 Rifle," *American Rifleman*, April 29, 2016, https://www.americanrifleman.org/articles/2016/4/29/the-barrett-model-82a1-rifle/.

8. "Voting from the Rooftops: How the Gun Industry Armed Osama bin Laden, Other Foreign and Domestic Terrorists, and Common Criminals with 50 Caliber Sniper Rifles." Violence Policy Center, October 2001, https://vpc.org/publications/voting-from-the-rooftops/voting-from-the-rooftops-section-one-the-capability-of-the-50-caliber-sniper-rifle/.

9. In 2018, Barrett manufactured 6,187 rifles in their facility in Murfreesboro, Tennessee; in 2019, 5,710; in 2020, 6,815; and in 2021, the last year for which numbers are available as of March 2023, 5,812. Source: ATF Annual Firearms Manufacturing and Export reports, https://www.atf.gov/resource-center/2021-annual-firearms-manufacturers-and-export-report-afmer.

10. "Machine Guns and 50 Caliber," Giffords Law Center to Prevent Gun Violence, accessed April 3, 2023, https://lawcenter.giffords.org/gun-laws/policy-areas/hardware-ammunition/machine-guns-50-caliber/.

11. From a listing of Barrett M107A1 .50 BMG semiautomatic rifle on the auction website GunBroker.com, accessed July 11, 2020, https://www.gunbroker.com/item/869136670.

12. Andy Sher, "Tennessee Names the Barrett .50 Caliber as the State's Official Rifle," *Chattanooga Times Free Press*, February 24, 2016, https://www.timesfreepress.com/news/politics/state/story/2016/feb/24/tennessee-names-barrett-50-cal-states-official-rifle/351788/.

13. Quote from a letter from Gatling to Miss Lizzie Jarvis on June 15, 1877, as cited in C. J. Chivers, *The Gun* (New York: Simon & Schuster, 2010), 25–26. Like Ronnie Barrett, Gatling had no experience with designing weapons before he began tinkering with this invention. In 1862, he received the patent for the "battery gun," a weapon that was manually operated, but could provide continuous rapid fire. Whether the Gatling gun and its descendants spared more lives than they took is impossible to know, but the idea that it was created as a tool to save lives by taking them more efficiently endures in history books.

14. "50 Caliber Rifle Crime," briefing paper, GAO/OSI-99-15R, United States General Accounting Office, Office of Special Investigations, August 4, 1999, https://www.gao.gov/products/OSI-99-15R, 2.

15. "50 Caliber Rifle Crime," 4. The common version of the story says that Barrett rifles started appearing in the hands of organized crime groups in Mexico through the ATF's Fast and Furious operation in 2009–2010, but, according to this briefing paper, .50 caliber rifles were already reaching Mexico in the 1990s.

16. Verónica Díaz, "Ejército y Marina incautaron 6 Barrett al mes durante 2019," *Milenio*, February 24, 2020, https://www.milenio.com/policia/incautaron-ejercito-marina-6-fusiles-barrett-mes-2019.

17. Alex Yablon, "American-Made .50-Caliber Rifles Help Fuel Mexican Cartel Violence," *The Trace*, October 29, 2019, https://www.thetrace.org/rounds/american-made-50-caliber-rifles-help-fuel-mexican-cartel-violence/.

18. A leaked database of firearms trace requests includes detailed records on 2,921 firearms sold in the United States and recovered in Mexico between December 2006 and December 2010, representing a portion (5–6 percent) of the approximately 50,000 firearms recovered and traced by the United States during that period. The database was leaked to a journalist in 2011 and was posted on several websites over the years. As of September 25, 2022, it was posted on the website of Stop US Arms to Mexico, https://stopusarmstomexico .org/atf-leaked-data-of-guns-recovered-in-mexico-2007-2010/.

19. The full list of crimes is available in the previously cited database of ATF trace requests in 2006–2010. Since 2006, more than 415 members of the Mexican Federal Police or National Guard were killed and over 840 wounded by guns, most of them smuggled from the United States. From March 2009 to March 2021, guns sold in the United States were also used to kill twenty-five and wound eighty-four members of the Mexican military. Estados Unidos Mexicanos v. Diamondback Shooting Sports Incorporated et al., no. 4:22-cv-00472 (Tucson, AZ, October 10, 2022), 110.

20. Fiscalía General de la República, Response to Public Information Request No. 330024622002873, October 10, 2022.

21. Jacobo García, "Sobrevivió a 414 disparos: Omar García Harfuch, el policía más amenazado del mundo," El País, June 20, 2021, https://elpais.com /mexico/2021-06-20/sobrevivio-a-414-disparos-omar-harfuch-el-policia-mas -amenazado-del-mundo.html.

22. "Más de 400 disparos, granadas, y 5 Barret: el arsenal asegurado tras ataque a García Harfuch," Animal Politico, June 27, 2020, https://www .animalpolitico.com/2020/06/granadas-barret-armas-aseguradas-atentado-garcia -harfuch/.

23. "Éste es el blindaje que resistió el impacto de una Barrett en ataque contra García Harfuch," Milenio, June 27, 2020, https://www.milenio.com/policia /blindaje-camioneta-garcia-harfuch-atentado-cdmx.

24. García, "Sobrevivió a 414 disparos."

25. Three more police officers and two civilians, including Gabriela's sister Tania, were injured in the attack. Abraham Reza, "Mujer que murió en ataque contra García Harfuch dejó 2 hijas huérfanas," Milenio, June 26, 2020, https:// www.milenio.com/politica/caso-omar-garcia-harfuch-gabriela-murio-ataque-2 -huerfanas; Jacobo García, "Gabriela, la víctima que estaba en el lugar equivocado," El País, June 26, 2020, https://elpais.com/internacional/2020-06-26 /gabriela-la-victima-que-estaba-en-el-lugar-equivocado.html.

26. "Atentado contra Omar García Harfuch: lo que se sabe del ataque contra el jefe de la policía de CDMX, según la Fiscalía," BBC News Mundo, June 28, 2020, https://www.bbc.com/mundo/noticias-america-latina-53208584.

27. Falko Ernst (@falko_ernst), Twitter post, June 26, 2020. See also Benito Jiménez, "Salvan a mando fallas de sicarios," El Norte, June 28, 2020, https:// www.elnorte.com/salvan-a-mando-fallas-de-sicarios/ar1975958.

28. This was the explanation given by the director of Global Risk Prevention, Gonzalo Senosian; see Benito Jiménez, "Salvan a mando fallas de sicarios," El Norte, June 28, 2020, https://www.elnorte.com/salvan-a-mando-fallas -de-sicarios/ar1975958; Jannet López Ponce, "'Se rompió la línea roja'; atentado

marca un antes y un después en CdMx: expertos," *Milenio*, June 26, 2020, https://www.milenio.com/policia/atentado-omar-garcia-harfuch-marca-cdmx.

29. Ángel Hernández, "Desde Estados Unidos y en partes, así se abastece de armamento el CJNG," *Milenio*, June 26, 2020, https://www.milenio.com/policia/desde-estados-unidos-y-en-partes-asi-se-abastece-de-armamento-el-cjng.

30. In February 2018, the US Department of Justice indicted Ovidio Guzmán on drug trafficking charges. Mexican security forces arrested him in Culiacán on January 5, 2023, and extradited him to the United States on September 15, 2023.

31. Jo Tuckman, "'Call It Off, Please': Video Shows How Operation against El Chapo's Son Fell Apart," *The Guardian*, October 30, 2019, https://www.theguardian.com/world/2019/oct/30/mexico-el-chapo-son-ovidio-guzman-lopez-operation.

32. In a surreal turn of events that further shamed the government, lawyers for the Guzmán family held a televised news conference Friday afternoon in which they thanked President López Obrador for freeing the leader of the organization.

33. Jo Tuckman, "'We Do Not Want War': Mexico President Defends Release of El Chapo's Son," *The Guardian*, October 18, 2019, https://www.theguardian.com/world/2019/oct/18/el-chapo-son-ovidio-guzman-lopez-release-amlo.

34. See, for example, León Krauze, "La liberación del hijo del Chapo es una gran derrota para México," *Washington Post*, October 19, 2019, https://www.washingtonpost.com/es/post-opinion/2019/10/19/la-liberacion-del-hijo-de-el-chapo-es-una-gran-derrota-para-mexico/; Azam Ahmed, "The Stunning Escape of El Chapo's Son: It's Like 'a Bad Netflix Show,'" *New York Times*, October 18, 2019, updated October 21, 2019, https://www.nytimes.com/2019/10/18/world/americas/mexico-cartel-chapo-son-guzman.html.

35. After nine US citizens were killed in an attack on the LeBaron family in Sonora in 2019, President Trump talked about labeling Mexican organized crime groups as terrorist organizations and in 2020 considered launching missiles into Mexico to destroy drug labs. See "Mexico Rejects US Intervention after Trump Outlines Drug Cartel Plan," BBC, November 27, 2019, https://www.bbc.com/news/world-latin-america-50577522; Maggie Haberman, "Trump Proposed Launching Missiles into Mexico to 'Destroy the Drug Labs,' Esper Says," *New York Times*, May 5, 2022, https://www.nytimes.com/2022/05/05/us/politics/mark-esper-book-trump.html.

36. Among the guns used during a series of shootouts that day, technical intelligence experts identified at least one Barrett M82-series anti-material rifle, several M2-type heavy machine guns, one M72-series shoulder-fired rocket launcher, one FN Herstal Minimi / M249 SAW light machine gun, Romanian-made AKs, and Beretta and Glock handguns. See "Weapons Used by Sinaloa Cartel Sicarios in Culiacán, Mexico," ARES Team, October 18, 2019, https://armamentresearch.com/weapons-used-by-cartel-sicarios-in-culiacan-mexico/; and Phineas Rueckert, "An Ocean of Guns: Mexico's Journalists in the Crossfire of the International Arms Trade," Forbidden Stories, December 9, 2020, https://forbiddenstories.org/an-ocean-of-guns-mexicos-journalists-in-the-crossfire-of-the-international-arms-trade/.

ATTITUDE

1. In 2019, annual membership at Club Deportivo de Cazadores cost 3,000 pesos ($150 USD) and there was a 2500 peso ($125 USD) inscription fee.

2. Todd C. Frankel et al., "The Gun That Divides a Nation," *Washington Post*, March 27, 2023, https://www.washingtonpost.com/nation/interactive/2023/ar-15-america-gun-culture-politics/.

3. Estados Unidos Mexicanos v. Smith & Wesson et al., 84.

4. Nick Wagner, "At Mexico's Lone Gun Store, Even the Boss Discourages Sales," Associated Press, August 17, 2016, https://www.apnews.com/c29ecc229f0846b0bfa4f4ecf8eca7d5.

5. Wagner, "At Mexico's Lone Gun Store."

6. SEDENA, response to public information request no. 0000700068219, Ciudad de México, March 22, 2019. These numbers don't match with those reported in Wagner, "At Mexico's Lone Gun Store." According to the AP piece, 52,147 firearms were sold from 2009 to 2014. The discrepancy could be because firearms sold to police and private security forces were not included in the count.

7. SEDENA, response to public information request no. 0000700068219.

8. The store sold 549 guns in 2000; by 2015, sales had increased eighteen times. See Wagner, "At Mexico's Lone Gun Store"; Ioan Grillo writes that the shop sells about nine thousand guns a year to the public and seven thousand to private security companies: *Blood Gun Money: How America Arms Gangs and Cartels* (New York: Bloomsbury Publishing, 2021), 159. Also see Estados Unidos Mexicanos v. Diamondback Shooting Sports Incorporated et al., 59.

9. Sales data show that Mexican police like European firearms. More than a third of all weapons they bought between 2006 and 2018—over a hundred thousand guns—were from the Italian manufacturer Beretta and they purchased almost seventy thousand pistols from the Austrian company Glock. See Database of firearms sold to police in Mexico, 2006–2018, compiled by Stop US Arms to Mexico from documents released by SEDENA, public information request no. 0000700176018, https://www.stopusarmstomexico.org/police-firearms-database. German HK and Sig Sauer, which had a factory in the United States, also sold well, as did military-grade fully and semiautomatic Galil and Tavor assault rifles made by Israel Weapons Industries (I.W.I.). Mexican police bought 16,442 of these guns, equipping forces all over the country, from Mexico City to Sonora to Veracruz. See "Deadly Trade: How European and Israeli Arms Exports Are Accelerating Violence in Mexico," Stop US Arms to Mexico, 13. Some of Galil assault rifles ended up in the hands of municipal police agents in Nuevo León, though the majority of 5.56 caliber rifles used by state and local forces in and around Monterrey were manufactured by Beretta, Colt, Bushmaster, and Heckler and Koch.

10. Sophie Esch, *Modernity at Gunpoint: Firearms Politics and Culture in Mexico and Central America* (Pittsburgh, PA: University of Pittsburgh Press, 2018), 50.

11. Daniel Flores, "Va al Penal por arma de su abuelo," *El Norte*, March 11, 2006.

12. Rodrigo Ramírez, "Aseguran que 30–30 es arma deportiva," *El Norte*, April 1, 2006, 16.

13. Gabriel Talavera, "Demanda detener a verdaderos pistoleros," *El Norte*, March 31, 2006, 10.

14. El Abogado del Pueblo, "Fricasé: Duro a los inocentes," *El Norte*, March 28, 2006, 9.

15. César Cubero, "Séptima Zona Militar abrirá comercializadora de armas en NL," *Milenio*, July 29, 2019, https://www.milenio.com/politica/gobierno /septima-zona-militar-abrira-comercializadora-armas-leon.

16. Comments posted on a forum hosted by México Armado (www .mexicoarmado.com) between July 27 and August 12, 2019.

CAGED

1. "Mexico: Events of 2018," Human Rights Watch, accessed November 25, 2021, https://www.hrw.org/world-report/2019/country-chapters/mexico #49dda6.

2. "Torture Around the World: What You Need to Know," Amnesty International, accessed July 29, 2022, https://www.amnesty.org/en/latest/news /2015/06/torture-around-the-world/. The other four countries that Amnesty International's Stop Torture campaign focused on during its first year were Morocco, Nigeria, the Philippines, and Uzbekistan.

3. "Failed Justice. Prevalence of Torture in Mexico's Criminal Justice System," document prepared by a team led by Roberto Hernández, Juan Salgado, and Laura Aquino, under the executive direction of Elizabeth Andersen and Alejandro Ponce, https://worldjusticeproject.mx/wp-content/uploads/2019/11 /GIZ-Report_Failed-Justice.pdf.

4. The data by Amnesty International is for the period between 2003 and 2013. See "Torture Around the World."

5. "Principales Resultados. Encuesta Nacional de Población Privada de la Libertad (ENPOL) 2016," INEGI, July 2017, accessed July 28, 2020, https:// www.inegi.org.mx/contenidos/programas/enpol/2016/doc/2016_enpol _presentacion_ejecutiva.pdf.

6. "Failed Justice."

7. "Report on the Visit of the Subcommittee on Prevention of Torture and Other Cruel, Inhuman or Degrading Treatment or Punishment to Mexico," U.N. Subcommittee on Prevention of Torture, May 31, 2010, https://docstore.ohchr .org/SelfServices/FilesHandler.ashx?enc=6QkG1d%2fPPRiCAqhKb7yhsrYQAh dCTgawvygbo%2biRuazURllYd43CARogddBzX8xqNYtJ1hwbKJm97xB87U O%2fUDEd9ne1kEUmtJVQSwoZL5UOMHBjdO6ZgM1hBao458RZ, 34.

8. "Control . . . Over the Entire State of Coahuila," an Analysis of Testimonies in Trials against Zeta Members in San Antonio, Austin, and Del Rio, Texas. University of Texas School of Law, November 2017, https://law.utexas.edu/wp -content/uploads/sites/11/2017/11/2017-HRC-coahuilareport-EN.pdf, 24.

9. Until 2016, the penalties for youths who committed serious crimes, like homicide, were more strict in Nuevo León compared to many other Mexican states, with sentences of eight to ten years permitted. Since the new national law was passed in 2016, the length of sentencing was reduced. Now the maximum

sentencing permitted for children who are twelve or thirteen years of age is one year; fourteen- and fifteen-year-olds could get up to three years (used to be eight in NL); and sixteen- and seventeen-year-olds up to five years (used to be ten in NL). The juvenile detention center in Monterrey also houses youths in their twenties because every youth had to complete their sentence in the same institution where they had started. This meant that a seventeen-year-old sentenced for homicide before 2016 would not leave the juvenile detention center until they turned twenty-seven. Transferring inmates to adult prisons when they turned eighteen happened only in exceptional circumstances. See Ley del Sistema Especial de Justicia para Adolescentes del Estado de Nuevo León (adopted in 2006, revised in 2012), http://www.hcnl.gob.mx/trabajo_legislativo/leyes/pdf /LEY%20DEL%20SISTEMA%20ESPECIAL%20DE%20JUSTICIA%20 PARA%20ADOLESCENTES%20DEL%20ESTADO%20DE%20 NUEVO%20LEON.pdf; Ley Nacional del Sistema Integral de Justicia Penal para Adolescentes (adopted in 2016, revised in 2020 and 2022), https://www .diputados.gob.mx/LeyesBiblio/pdf/LNSIJPA.pdf.

10. Centro de Internamiento y de Adaptación de Adolescentes Infractores (CIAAI).

11. Mexico signed and ratified the Convention on the Rights of the Child in 1990, but the constitutional modifications guaranteeing due process rights to juveniles between twelve and eighteen years old were not made until 2005. The constitutional reform established a comprehensive system of juvenile justice, which considers institutionalization an extreme measure applicable only to felonies and only to juveniles older than fourteen. In 2006, all Mexican states began following the new legal framework, formally aligning the Mexican juvenile justice law with the Convention on the Rights of the Child. For more, see Frías Armenta, Martha, and Livier Gómez Martínez, "Juvenile Justice in Mexico," *Laws* 3 no. 3 (2014): 580–97, https://doi.org/10.3390/laws3030580.

12. "Report on the Visit of the Subcommittee on Prevention of Torture."

13. Héctor Castro and Camilo Lizcano, "Desatan trifulca en el Tutelar," *El Norte*, February 23, 2009.

14. Rodrigo Ramírez, "Moviliza a Policía rebelión en Tutelar," *El Norte*, April 7, 2009.

15. In Spanish, the banners read "No queremos a los Z" and "No queremos a los Zetaz." See "Arman menores motín en Tutelar," *El Norte*, September 1, 2011.

16. The youths complained that they were not offered activities that the law promised them, that they spent weeks or even months without seeing a psychologist. See Comisión Estatal de Derechos Humanos Nuevo León, July 10, 2014, https://www.cedhnl.org.mx/bs/secciones/recomendaciones/2014 /RECOM%20033-2014.pdf.

HOMEFRONT

1. Events are reconstructed based on court documents, including trial transcripts, of USA v. Andre Rene Garcia and Jorge Acosta-Licerio, no. CR-16-

00478-TUC-JGZ-LAB (Tucson, AZ, December 18, 2017), and interviews with individuals involved in the case. The names have been changed for privacy reasons.

2. In 2010, the US military in Afghanistan captured an AK-47 from the Taliban, which was still functional after fifty years in service. See C. J. Chivers, "What's Inside a Taliban Gun Locker?" *New York Times*, September 15, 2010, https://archive.nytimes.com/atwar.blogs.nytimes.com/2010/09/15/whats -inside-a-taliban-gun-locker/.

3. The time line of Hugo's deployment coincides with the years when the US military was providing support to African Union–led forces trying to capture the rebel leader of the Lord's Resistance Army, Joseph Kony, indicted for war crimes and crimes against humanity by the International Criminal Court in 2005, and still at large a decade later. Kony continued violently recruiting child soldiers into his group, sowing fear in the borderlands between Uganda, South Sudan, Central African Republic, and the Democratic Republic of Congo. In his testimony in court, Hugo spoke about his mission in Africa in general terms, without naming the person his team was after, nor locations outside Djibouti that they traveled to, so it is possible that his unit was assigned to help find a different individual. For more on the US role in looking for Kony, see Marthe van der Wolf, "Task Force Wants More Resources in Hunt for Elusive African Warlord," VOA, November 15, 2014, https://www.voanews.com/a/resources -time-need-to-neutralize-kony/2517248.html.

4. Aaron Smith, "AK-47s Become Hot Commodity after U.S. Sanctions," CNN Money, July 18, 2014, https://money.cnn.com/2014/07/18/news/companies /ak-47-kalashnikov/.

5. The belt-fed .50 caliber machine gun that Hugo told them about was not connected to this investigation. It was for another group, which, unlike the Nogales crew, sought expensive Barrett .50 caliber rifles. Hugo admitted they promised him a $1000 for being a straw buyer. He paid the FFL dealer a 10,000 deposit in $5 and $10 bills that some man brought over to his house. The gun was for that man's friend. The agents did not know anything about this other group operating through Douglas yet, so they asked Hugo to wear a wire to the meeting with the buyers. He cooperated and agents arrested the people involved in ordering the rifle.

6. The sentences they received varied, ranging from probation to several years imprisonment. Oscar was sentenced to fifteen months; Jazmin to four years' probation; Kevin was acquitted.

7. For the description of the process, see "Audit of the Bureau of Alcohol, Tobacco, Firearms and Explosives Controls over Weapons, Munitions, and Explo-sives," US Department of Justice, Office of the Inspector General, March 2018, https://oig.justice.gov/reports/2018/a1821.pdf. In 2019, a guard at the facility in Martinsburg admitted to stealing thousands of guns and gun parts slated for destruction and selling them; some of those weapons were later recovered in Mex-ico. See John Diedrich, "ATF Agents Searching for Thousands of Guns Stolen from Their Facility Before They Could Be Destroyed," *Milwaukee Journal Senti-nel*, June 13, 2019, https://www.jsonline.com/story/news/investigations/2019/06 /13/atf-looking-guns-and-glock-parts-stolen-and-sold-guard/1425467001/.

METAL AFTERLIVES

1. Between 2012 and mid 2017, the program registered 30,497 long and short guns; 2,432 grenades; and 199,611 bullets. "Datos de Desarme Voluntario por Etapas," Gobierno del Distrito Federal, Ciudad de México, accessed November 20, 2018, http://data.sds.cdmx.gob.mx/desarme/.

2. The school, Escuela Militar de Materiales de Guerra, located in the state of Mexico, is part of the Secretariat of National Defense. It prepares officers who specialize in arms, munitions, and explosives.

3. Data from INEGI, the Mexican National Institute of Statistics and Geography, cited in "2017, el año más violento de la historia del país; se registraron 31 mil 174 homicidios: Inegi," *Aristegui Noticias*, July 30, 2018, https://aristeguinoticias.com/3007/mexico/2017-el-ano-mas-violento-de-la-historia-del-pais-se-registraron-31-mil-174-homicidios-inegi/.

4. At May 2019 exchange rates, 61,000 pesos was just over $3,120. "Joven vende 510 plumas pistola a CDMX y gana 61 mil pesos," *El Sol de México/Excélsior*, May 3, 2019, https://www.angulo7.com.mx/2019/05/03/joven-vende-510-plumas-pistola-a-cdmx-y-gana-61-mil-pesos/.

5. SEDENA, Response to public information request no. 0000700034520, February 28, 2020.

6. SEDENA, Response to public information request no. 0000700034520.

7. The value of the gun changes as it crosses borders between states and passes from the legal economy into an informal market, but also when it is used by particular people in specific contexts. For an in-depth study on the "active and processual nature of value," see Elizabeth E. Ferry, *Minerals, Collecting, and Value across the U.S.-Mexico Border* (Bloomington: Indiana University Press, 2013).

8. Estados Unidos Mexicanos v. Smith & Wesson Brands, Inc. et al., no. 1:21-cv-11269-FDS (Boston, Massachusetts, August 4, 2021).

9. See Sophie Esch, *Modernity at Gunpoint: Firearms Politics and Culture in Mexico and Central America* (Pittsburgh, PA: University of Pittsburgh Press, 2018), chap. 6, "Golden AK-47s and Weapon Displays." Esch argues that such installations show how easily "art can be appropriated by a government intent on depoliticizing and moralizing the narrative" (193).

10. Mauricio Nava, "De las esculturas hechas con armas en Campo Marte," *Chilango*, September 17, 2019, https://www.chilango.com/cultura/esculturas-hechas-con-armas-en-campo-marte/.

11. See the images accompanying these articles: "Con armas de fuego decomisadas, crearon esculturas para fomentar la paz en México," *Infobae*, January 26, 2021, https://www.infobae.com/america/mexico/2021/01/27/con-armas-de-fuego-decomisadas-crearon-esculturas-para-fomentar-la-paz-en-mexico/; Verónica Díaz, "Ejército honra con 4 esculturas 30 años de las Fuerzas Especiales," *Milenio*, December 21, 2020, https://www.milenio.com/policia/ejercito-honra-esculturas-30-anos-fuerzas-especiales; and Daniela Wachauf, "Sedena realiza esculturas con armas decomisadas al crimen," *24 Horas*, February 15, 2021, https://www.24-horas.mx/2021/02/15/sedena-realiza-esculturas-con-armas-decomisadas-al-crimen-video/.

12. "Cultura de paz dará forma escultórica a más de una tonelada de armas," Secretaría de Cultura, Gobierno de la Ciudad de México, October 24, 2019, https://www.cultura.cdmx.gob.mx/comunicacion/nota/1342-19.

13. For an image of the sculpture, see "Sheinbaum devela escultura 'Sí al desarme, sí a la paz,'" *Capital 21*, March 30, 2021, https://www.capital21.cdmx .gob.mx/noticias/?p=16779.

14. Antanas Mockus, *Cultura ciudadana, programa contra la violencia en Santa Fe de Bogotá, Colombia, 1995–1997* (Washington, DC: Inter-American Development Bank, 2002), 13. During Mockus's term as mayor, the homicide rate in Bogotá fell from eighty per one hundred thousand inhabitants in 1993 to twenty-two per one hundred thousand inhabitants in 2003. Traffic fatalities also dropped by more than half in the same time period, from an average of thirteen hundred per year to about six hundred. See Mara Cristina Caballero, "Academic Turns City into a Social Experiment," *Harvard Gazette*, March 11, 2004, https://news.harvard.edu/gazette/story/2004/03/academic-turns-city-into-a -social-experiment/.

15. John Otis, "In Colombia, Artist Renders Tons of Rebel Guns into Floor Tiles," NPR, November 6, 2018, https://www.npr.org/2018/11/06/663473304 /in-colombia-artist-renders-tons-of-rebel-guns-into-floor-tiles.

16. José Luis Falconi et al., *Pedro Reyes: Ad Usum* (Cambridge, MA: Department of History of Art and Architecture, Harvard University, 2017), 78.

17. These projects are described on Pedro Reyes's website: http://pedroreyes .net/palasporpistolas.php?szLang=en&Area=work and http://pedroreyes.net /disarm.php?szLang=en&Area=work.

18. Pedro Reyes, "Disarm: Transforming Guns into Art, from Mexico to the U.S.," *Creative Time Reports*, May 20, 2013, https://creativetimereports .org/2013/05/20/disarm-transforming-guns-into-art-from-mexico-to-the-united -states/.

19. Quoted from the description of the project on the author's website, accessed August 4, 2020, http://pedroreyes.net/disarm.php?szLang=en&Area= work.

20. "Pedro Reyes: Disarm. 27 March–4 May 2013," Lisson Gallery press release, https://www.lissongallery.com/exhibitions/pedro-reyes-disarm.

21. Data shared by Edgar Guerrero, director general of the National Analysis at el Centro Nacional de Planeación, Análisis e Información para el Combate a la Delincuencia (CENAPI) at Mexico's Attorney General's Office, at the conference "El negocio de letalidad: El Tráfico de Armas a México," El Colegio de México, November 3, 2022. The list also includes Hartford, Connecticut, the home of Colt. The rest of the top ten counties are in border states: five in Texas, two in Arizona, one in California.

22. Like other military-style semiautomatic rifles, Smith & Wesson M&P15s, made in Springfield, are not available for purchase in Massachusetts, which has a state law prohibiting sale and possession of assault weapons (G.L. c. 140, §§ 128 and 131M). A bill to ban manufacturing such rifles in Massachusetts was introduced in April 2021, but, as of early 2023, it has not been passed.

23. Historically, Smith & Wesson manufactured handguns. The company only began making semiautomatic M&P15 rifles, modeled on assault-style AR-

15s, in 2006. Smith & Wesson's M&P15 rifle was used in the mass shooting in Aurora, Colorado, in 2012 and in the massacre at the Marjory Stoneman Douglas High School in Parkland, Florida, in 2018. Since then, student activists and gun safety groups have organized numerous protests in front of Smith & Wesson headquarters in Springfield.

24. See the image of the billboard and read more in Douglas Hook, "'I Feel Joy Because I Can Bring Everybody to Know about Joaquin'; Father of Slain Parkland Teen Designs Billboard That Overlooks the Smith & Wesson Factory in Springfield," *MassLive*, August 4, 2021, https://www.masslive.com/springfield/2021/08/i-feel-joy-because-i-can-bring-everybody-to-know-about-joaquin-father-of-slain-parkland-teen-designs-billboard-that-overlooks-the-smith-wesson-factory-in-springfield.html.

25. The company made 4,650 M&P15 semiautomatic rifles when it first started manufacturing them in 2006. By 2009, the plant in Springfield was making over 100,000 such weapons, some years three times as many (in 2013, it made 348,731; in 2016—396,710). In 2021, the last year for which data is available as of March 2023, the company made 427,368 rifles, the vast majority at their new plant in Columbia, Missouri; see "2021 Annual Firearms Manufacturers and Export Report," Bureau of Alcohol, Tobacco, Firearms and Explosives, accessed April 3, 2023, https://www.atf.gov/resource-center/2021-annual-firearms-manufacturers-and-export-report-afmer. Because of annual differences, for production estimates I am using the average of three years, 2014–2016 (159,807 in 2014; 209,180 in 2015, and 396,710 in 2016), which is 255,232 rifles. This data is from ATF's annual firearms manufacturing and export reports (AFMER) and "Understanding the Smith & Wesson M&P15 Semiautomatic Assault Rifle," Violence Policy Center, February 16, 2018, https://vpc.org/wp-content/uploads/2018/02/FloridashootingSmithWesson.pdf. These Smith & Wesson rifles account for over 2.5 percent of some 10 million firearms made in the United States per year. For this estimate, too, I am using the average of three years (2014–2016). In 2014, manufacturers in the United States made 3,379,549 rifles (9,050,626 firearms total); in 2015, 3,691,799 (9,358,661 total); in 2016, 4,239,335 (11,497,441 total). Data from "Firearms Commerce in the United States, Annual Statistical Update 2021," Bureau of Alcohol, Tobacco, Firearms and Explosives, accessed April 3, 2023, https://www.atf.gov/firearms/docs/report/2021-firearms-commerce-report/download. The average number of rifles made in the United States per year is therefore 3,770,228 (average number of all firearms 9,968,909). This does not include firearms that are imported to the United States.

26. The weight of the M&P15, which slightly varies by model, is just over six pounds. The copper and steel in the Statue of Liberty weighs 310,000 lbs. or 156 US tons; "Facts and Figures," Statue of Liberty Club, accessed April 3, 2023, https://www.statueoflibertyclub.com/facts-figures/.

EPILOGUE

1. The captured man, Juan Gerardo Treviño Chávez, nicknamed "El Huevo," was the nephew of Z-40, and was charged with trafficking and terrorism.

2. This estimate was according to the Bureau of Transportation Statistics (BTS) Border Crossing Data, which provide statistics for inbound crossings at the port level collected by CBP. See "Border Crossing/Entry Data," Bureau of Transportation Statistics, accessed April 3, 2023, https://www.bts.gov/browse -statistical-products-and-data/border-crossing-data/border-crossingentry-data. CBP does not collect comparable data on outbound crossings. According to the City of Laredo, in recent years the passenger vehicle crossings have been very similar in both directions, with a difference of less than 1 percent; see "Laredo International Bridge System Master Plan, 2021," City of Laredo, accessed April 3, 2023, https://www.cityoflaredo.com/LaredoPlanning/wp-content/uploads /2021/07/2021-Laredo-Bridge-Master-Plan-Draft-Compressed.pdf, 37.

3. "Dribs and Drabs. The Mechanics of Small Arms Trafficking from the United States. Issue Brief," *Small Arms Survey* no. 17, March 2016, https:// www.smallarmssurvey.org/sites/default/files/resources/SAS-IB17-Mechanics-of -trafficking.pdf.

4. They also seized 42 shotguns and 261 handguns, both four times their seizures in 2019. For comparison, in 2019, agents in Laredo confiscated 56 rifles, 8 shotguns, and 69 handguns, as well as 75,900 cartridges. Data from US Customs and Border Protection, response to FOIA request no. CBP-2021-030251.

5. Estados Unidos Mexicanos v. Smith & Wesson et al. (November 22, 2021).

6. Estados Unidos Mexicanos v. Smith & Wesson et al. (September 30, 2022).

7. Based on the Annual Firearms Manufacturing and Export report, in 2020, US gunmakers manufactured 5,509,183 pistols, 993,078 revolvers, 2,760,392 rifles, and 476,682 shotguns. See "2020 Annual Firearms Manufacturers and Export Report," https://www.atf.gov/resource-center/2020-annual-firearms -manufacturers-and-export-report-afmer. In 2021, US manufacturers made 6,751,919 pistols, 1,159,918 revolvers (7,911,837 handguns total), 3,934,374 rifles, and 675,426 shotguns; "2021 Annual Firearms Manufacturers and Export Report," https://www.atf.gov/explosives/docs/report/afmer2021finalwebreportpdf /download. At the time this book went into production (April 2023), data for 2022 was not yet available.

8. The complaint cites estimates that nearly 2.2 percent of all guns manufactured in the United States are trafficked to Mexico. Estados Unidos Mexicanos v. Smith & Wesson et al. (August 4, 2021). The quarter million cited here doesn't include guns that were imported to the United States and then smuggled to Mexico, of which there is a substantial quantity. The Mexican government's lawsuit estimates 873,000 guns smuggled annually.

9. According to INEGI, 20,005 people were killed by firearm in 2018 (in addition to 130 dead by involuntary manslaughter and 195 cases of feminicidio); 24,420 in 2019 (71; 218). Similar trends continued in 2020 (24,617), 2021 (24,484), and 2022; about 70 percent of homicides each year are committed by firearm. Total homicides by firearm over a five-year period (2018–2022) will likely exceed 120,000. For comparison, during the five-year period from 2016 to 2020, Mexico registered 117,433 homicides by firearm; see Lidia

Arista, "México cierra 2020 con 34,515 homicidios, el 70% con armas de fuego," *Expansión*, https://politica.expansion.mx/mexico/2021/01/20/mexico -cierra-con-34-515-homicidios-en-2020-el-70-con-armas-de-fuego.

10. Mexico's Secretariat of Foreign Affairs (Secretaría de Relaciones Exteriores, SRE) publishes data on the number of repatriated/returned Mexican nationals. One category of the returnees is for people who are sick or "have been injured during attempt to cross the border." In 2018, this group consisted of 281 men and 62 women; in 2019, 336 men and 122 women; in 2020, 331 men and 101 women; in 2021, 551 men and 156 women. See "Migratorio—Casos de protección y/o asistencia consular atendidos por la RDCM en el mundo," Gobierno de México, accessed September 25, 2022, https://datos.gob .mx/busca/dataset/migratorio—casos-de-proteccion-y-o-asistencia-consular -atendidos-por-la-rdcm-en-el-mundo. The Mexican Consulate in Tucson registered 187 Mexican migrants wounded during attempts to cross the border in Arizona between January 2020 and December 2021.

11. The number includes Mexican nationals who died crossing the border in the five-year period of 2018–2022. According to the Mexican government data, 7,773 Mexican nationals died crossing the border since 2001. "Personas mexicanas fallecidas en su intento de cruce indocumentado a Estados Unidos," Secretaría de Relaciones Exteriores, accessed March 20, 2023, https://datos .gob.mx/busca/dataset/personas-mexicanas-fallecidas-en-su-intento-de-cruce -indocumentado-a-estados-unidos.

12. Documents leaked to the press by hackers in October 2022 exposed how some Mexican military officials sold guns, ammunition, and grenades to organized crime groups.

13. "Osiel Cardenas-Guillen, Former Head of the Gulf Cartel, Sentenced to 25 Years' Imprisonment," US Attorney's Office, Southern District of Texas, February 24, 2010, https://archives.fbi.gov/archives/houston/press-releases /2010/ho022410b.htm.

14. Z-40 and Z-42 are high on the priority list of people that the US government wanted Mexico to extradite. See Elías Camhaji and Zedryk Raziel, "Caro Quintero, Los Zetas: US Prioritizing Extradition of Notorious Drug Lords, Mexican Leaked Security Emails Show," *El País*, October 21, 2022, https://english .elpais.com/international/2022-10-21/caro-quintero-los-zetas-us-prioritizing -extradition-of-notorious-drug-lords-mexican-leaked-security-emails-show .html.

15. David Saúl Vela, "Sentencian a 18 años de prisión a Óscar Omar Treviño Morales, 'El Z-42,'" *El Financiero*, July 21, 2019, https://www.elfinanciero .com.mx/nacional/sentencian-a-18-anos-de-prision-a-oscar-omar-trevino -morales-el-z-42/.

16. Marissa Edmund, "Smart Guns: Technology That Can Save Lives," Center for American Progress, March 29, 2022, https://www.americanprogress .org/article/smart-guns-technology-that-can-save-lives/.

17. There is precedent: the US government has issued regulations prohibiting certain types of firearms before, including outlawing possession and transfer of machine guns. However, the law had loopholes. The Firearms Owners' Protection Act, which outlawed machine guns, has an exception for "those lawfully

possessed before the effective date of the prohibition, May 19, 1986." The most challenging part of any type of prohibition will be to decide what to do with powerful weapons already circulating in the country.

18. 18 USC 933, SEC. 12004. Stop Illegal Trafficking in Firearms Act, https://www.congress.gov/117/plaws/publ159/PLAW-117publ159.pdf. The law was passed as part of a larger legislative package called "Bipartisan Safer Communities Act."

19. "Mexican Resident Indicted for Trafficking Firearms under New Law," US Department of Justice press release, August 9, 2022, https://www.justice.gov/usao-sdtx/pr/mexican-resident-indicted-trafficking-firearms-under-new-law. Isaac Hernandez purchased a total of 231 handguns between January 21, 2020, and July 11, 2022, following directions from a contact in Mexico. He pleaded guilty to one count of trafficking firearms and, on February 10, 2023, the judge in Texas sentenced him to eighty months in prison. See César Rodriguez, "Man Sentenced in Firearm Trafficking Scheme," *Laredo Morning Times*, February 14, 2023, https://www.lmtonline.com/local/article/man-sentenced-firearm-trafficking-scheme-17784132.php.

ABOUT THIS PROJECT

1. This description is based on Loïc Wacquant's suggestion to define ethnography as "embedded and embodied social inquiry based on physical co-presence with(in) the phenomenon in real time and space." See Loïc Wacquant, "For a Sociology of Flesh and Blood," *Qualitative Sociology* 38, no. 1 (2015), 4.

2. Deborah A. Thomas, *Political Life in the Wake of the Plantation: Sovereignty, Witnessing, Repair* (Durham, NC: Duke University Press, 2019), 2–3.

3. For a compelling argument on using proximity as a method in social science, see the appendix of Reuben Jonathan Miller's *Halfway Home: Race, Punishment, and the Afterlife of Mass Incarceration* (New York: Little, Brown, 2021), 283–97.

4. According to research, living in a house with a gun would significantly increase the chances of dying from a gunshot wound. See Charles C. Branas et al., "Investigating the Link between Gun Possession and Gun Assault," *American Journal of Public Health* 99, no. 11 (2009): 2034–40.

5. Luis Herrera, "Universidades reciben cadáveres sin identificar del IJCF," *Reporte Indigo*, October 3, 2019, https://www.reporteindigo.com/reporte/universidades-reciben-cadaveres-sin-identificar-del-ijcf-peritajes-disposicion-final/.

6. The response explained that the agency's refusal to provide information was supported by the Second Circuit decision in Everytown for Gun Safety Support Fund v. ATF. The Ninth Circuit reached a different conclusion on trace data in Center for Investigative Reporting v. US Department of Justice, but that didn't change ATF's disposition.

7. Oswaldo Zavala, *La Guerra En Las Palabras: Una Historia Intelectual Del "Narco" En México (1975–2020)* (Ciudad de México: Debate, 2022), 39–40.

8. Juan Alberto Cedillo, *Las Guerras Ocultas Del Narco* (Ciudad de México: Grijalbo, 2018), 78.

9. "Literature as a Political Responsibility: An Interview with Yuri Herrera," *Latin American Literature* 1, no. 2 (April 2017), http://www.latinamerican literaturetoday.org/en/2017/april/literature-political-responsibility-interview -yuri-herrera-radmila-stefkova-and-rodrigo.

10. Sally E. Merry, *The Seductions of Quantification: Measuring Human Rights, Gender Violence, and Sex Trafficking* (Chicago: University of Chicago Press, 2016), 1.

11. For a more extensive discussion of the politics of numbers, especially when trying to quantify illicit flows, see Peter Andreas and Kelly M. Greenhill, *Sex, Drugs, and Body Counts: The Politics of Numbers in Global Crime and Conflict* (Ithaca, NY: Cornell University Press, 2010).

12. Lee Ann Fujii suggests that silences, rumors, and inventions can be as valuable for researchers as verifiable testimonies—not for their accurate descriptions of what happened, but because of the meaning with which narrators endow what they narrate. These stories, even when vague or embellished, are not lies; instead, they may be saying more about the present social and political situation in which the narrator lives than about their past. Lee Ann Fujii, "Shades of Truth and Lies: Interpreting Testimonies of War and Violence," *Journal of Peace Research* 47, no. 2 (2010): 231–41.

13. Yael Navaro, "The Aftermath of Mass Violence: A Negative Methodology," *Annual Review of Anthropology* 49, no. 1 (2020): 161–73.

14. Dealing with a similar conundrum, Mexican journalist Ricardo Raphael, who interviewed one of the early members of the Zetas, decided to call his book a "novela": some of the stories that Galdino Mellado told him could not be verified, so he chose a genre that is based on reality—his journalistic investigation—but strays into fiction. What Mellado told him could be true, but there was no way to know. In the only scholarly book on the Zetas, political scientist Guadalupe Correa-Cabrera admits that "solid" information was not always available, therefore she was left to work with hypotheses. Her statements in *Los Zetas Inc.* are often qualified as "according to this view," "some thought," "allegedly." Similarly, writing about gangs in Guatemala, geographer Anthony Fontes embraced a narrative filled with lacunae and ellipses, refusing to tell truth from fantasy. Because he couldn't. See Anthony W. Fontes, *Mortal Doubt Transnational Gangs and Social Order in Guatemala* (Oakland: University of California Press, 2018).

15. Michael Jackson, *The Politics of Storytelling: Variations on a Theme by Hannah Arendt* (Copenhagen: Museum Tusculanum Press, 2019), 102–3.

16. See the work of Lawrence Langer and Nadezhda Mandelstam, discussed in Jackson, *Politics of Storytelling*, 102–4.

17. Clifford Geertz, *The Interpretation of Cultures* (New York: Basic Books, 2008), 448.

Selected Bibliography

This book draws extensively on court records, information obtained through FOIA requests, and reporting in newspapers, including El Norte, Proceso, Milenio, Infobae, El País, *the* Dallas Morning News, *the* Washington Post, *and the* New York Times, *among others. Due to the sizable number of these references, full citations for all primary sources appear only in the endnotes, to facilitate the use of the following bibliography.*

Administración General de Aduanas. Response to public information request no. 0610100039520. Ciudad de México, February 18, 2020.

Aguayo, Sergio, Delia Sánchez del Ángel, Manuel Pérez Aguirre, and Jacobo Dayán Askenazi. *Mexico: State of Neglect. Los Zetas, the State, Society and the Victims of San Fernando, Tamaulipas (2010) and Allende, Coahuila (2011).* Ciudad de México: El Colegio de México, 2016.

Andreas, Peter, and Kelly M. Greenhill. *Sex, Drugs, and Body Counts: The Politics of Numbers in Global Crime and Conflict.* Ithaca, NY: Cornell University Press, 2010.

Astorga, Luis. *El Siglo De Las Drogas: El Narcotráfico Del Porfiriato Al Nuevo Milenio.* México, D.F.: Plaza y Janés, 2005.

Aviña, Alexander. *Specters of Revolution: Peasant Guerrillas in the Cold War Mexican Countryside.* New York: Oxford University Press, 2014.

Boggs, Clay, and Kristen Rand. "Gun-Running Nation: How Foreign-Made Assault Weapons Are Trafficked from the United States to Mexico and What to Do about It." Washington Office on Latin America and Violence Policy Center, July 2015, 8–9. https://vpc.org/studies/Gun_Running_Nation.pdf.

Bowden, Charles. *Jericho.* Austin: University of Texas Press, 2020.

Carey, Elaine. *Women Drug Traffickers: Mules, Bosses, and Organized Crime.* Albuquerque: University of New Mexico Press, 2014.

Carlson, Jennifer. *Policing the Second Amendment: Guns, Law Enforcement and the Politics of Race.* Princeton, NJ: Princeton University Press, 2020.

———. "Troubling the Subject of Violence: The Pacifist Presumption, Martial Maternalism, and Armed Women in Contemporary Gun Culture," *Political Power and Social Theory* 30 (2016), 81–107.

Cedillo, Juan Alberto. *Las Guerras Ocultas Del Narco.* Ciudad de México: Grijalbo, 2018.

Chivers, C.J. *The Gun.* New York: Simon & Schuster, 2010.

Comisión Nacional de los Derechos Humanos (CNDH) México. "Diagnóstico Nacional de Supervisión Penitenciaria 2018." https://www.cndh.org.mx /sites/all/doc/sistemas/DNSP/DNSP_2018.pdf.

———. Recomendación No. 40/2013. Sobre el caso de los internos del Centro de Reinserción Social de Apodaca, Nuevo León. México, D.F., October 22, 2013.

———. Recomendación No. 66/2012. Sobre el caso de V1 a V63, víctimas del delito con motivo de los hechos ocurridos en el 'Casino Royale,' en Monterrey, Nuevo León. México, D.F., November 29, 2012. https://www.stps.gob .mx/gobmx/transparencia/documentos/Recomendacion66.pdf.

———. Recomendación No. 10VG/2018. Sobre la investigación de violaciones graves a los derechos humanos, por los hechos acontecidos del 18 al 20 de marzo de 2011, en el municipio de Allende, Coahuila, así como por las detenciones arbitrarias y desapariciones forzadas cometidas con posterioridad a dicho evento. Mexico City, March 16, 2018. https://www.cndh.org.mx/sites /default/files/doc/Recomendaciones/ViolacionesGraves/RecVG_010.pdf.

"Control . . . Over the Entire State of Coahuila." An Analysis of Testimonies in Trials against Zeta Members in San Antonio, Austin, and Del Rio, Texas. University of Texas School of Law. November 2017. https://law.utexas.edu /wp-content/uploads/sites/11/2017/11/2017-HRC-coahuilareport-EN.pdf.

Corchado, Alfredo. *Midnight in Mexico: A Reporter's Journey through a Country's Descent into the Darkness.* New York: Penguin Books, 2014.

Correa-Cabrera, Guadalupe. *Los Zetas Inc.: Criminal Corporations, Energy, and Civil War in Mexico.* Austin: University of Texas Press, 2017.

Deibert, Michael. *In the Shadow of Saint Death: The Gulf Cartel and the Price of America's Drug War in Mexico.* Guilford, CT: LP Lyons Press, an imprint of Rowman & Littlefield, 2015.

DeLay, Brian. "How Not to Arm a State: American Guns and the Crisis of Governance in Mexico, Nineteenth and Twenty-First Centuries." *Southern California Quarterly* 95, no. 1 (Spring 2013), 5–23.

Del Bosque, Melissa. *Bloodlines: The True Story of a Drug Cartel, the FBI, and the Battle for a Horse-Racing Dynasty.* New York: HarperCollins, 2017.

Denyer Willis, Graham. *The Killing Consensus: Police, Organized Crime, and the Regulation of Life and Death in Urban Brazil.* Berkeley: University of California Press, 2015.

Detty, Mike. *Operation Wide Receiver: An Informant's Struggle to Expose the Corruption and Deceit That Led to Operation Fast and Furious.* New York: Skyhorse Publishing, 2015.

Díaz, George T. *Border Contraband: A History of Smuggling Across the Rio Grande*. Austin: University of Texas Press, 2015.

Dodson, John. *The Unarmed Truth: My Fight to Blow the Whistle and Expose Fast and Furious*. New York: Threshold Editions, 2014.

Dunbar-Ortiz, Roxanne. *Loaded: A Disarming History of the Second Amendment*. San Francisco: City Lights Books, 2018.

Durin, Séverine. *¡Sálvese Quien Pueda! Violencia Generalizada Y Desplazamiento Forzado En El Noreste De México*. Ciudad de México: CIESAS Centro de Investigaciones y Estudios Superiores en Antropología Social, 2019.

Esch, Sophie. *Modernity at Gunpoint: Firearms Politics and Culture in Mexico and Central America*. Pittsburgh, PA: University of Pittsburgh Press, 2018.

Estados Unidos Mexicanos v. Diamondback Shooting Sports Incorporated et al., no. 4:22-cv-00472 (Tucson, AZ, October 10, 2022).

Estados Unidos Mexicanos v. Smith & Wesson et al., no. 1:21-cv-11269 (Boston, MA, August 4, 2021).

Evans, Michael. "The Allende Massacre in Mexico: A Decade of Impunity." *National Security Archive*, March 18, 2021. https://nsarchive.gwu.edu/briefing -book/mexico/2021-03-18/allende-massacre-decade-impunity.

"Failed Justice. Prevalence of Torture in Mexico's Criminal Justice System." Document prepared by a team led by Roberto Hernández, Juan Salgado, and Laura Aquino, under the executive direction of Elizabeth Andersen and Alejandro Ponce. https://worldjusticeproject.mx/wp-content/uploads/2019/11 /GIZ-Report_Failed-Justice.pdf.

Ferry, Elizabeth E. *Minerals, Collecting, and Value across the U.S.-Mexico Border*. Bloomington: Indiana University Press, 2013.

"50 Caliber Rifle Crime." Briefing paper. US General Accounting Office, GAO/ OSI-99-15R, August 4, 1999. https://www.gao.gov/products/OSI-99-15R.

Fiscalía General de la República. Response to Public Information Request No. 330024622002873, October 10, 2022.

Fontes, Anthony W. *Mortal Doubt: Transnational Gangs and Social Order in Guatemala*. Oakland: University of California Press, 2018.

Fontes, Anthony, and Kevin O'Neill. "La Visita: Prisons and Survival in Guatemala." *Journal of Latin American Studies* 51, no. 1 (2019), 85–107.

Fujii, Lee Ann. "Shades of Truth and Lies: Interpreting Testimonies of War and Violence." *Journal of Peace Research* 47, no. 2 (2010): 231–41.

Gambetta, Diego. *The Sicilian Mafia: The Business of Private Protection*. Cambridge, MA: Harvard University Press, 1993.

Gill, Lesley. *The School of the Americas: Military Training and Political Violence in the Americas*. Durham, NC: Duke University Press, 2004.

Grandin, Greg. *The End of Myth: From the Frontier to the Wall in the Mind of America*. New York: Metropolitan Books, 2019.

Grillo, Ioan. *Blood Gun Money: How America Arms Gangs and Cartels*. New York: Bloomsbury, 2021.

———. *El Narco: Inside Mexico's Criminal Insurgency*. New York: Bloomsbury Press, 2012.

Haag, Pamela. *The Gunning of America: Business and the Making of American Gun Culture*. New York: Basic Books, 2016.

Hansen, Tobin, and María Engracia Robles Robles, eds. *Voices of the Border: Testimonios of Migration, Deportation, and Asylum.* Washington, DC: Georgetown University Press, 2021.

Harp, Seth. "Arming the Cartels: The Inside Story of a Texas Gun-Smuggling Ring." *Rolling Stone,* August 7, 2019. https://www.rollingstone.com /culture/culture-features/arming-mexican-cartels-inside-story-of-a-texas -gun-smuggling-ring-866836/.

Hart, John Mason. *Empire and Revolution: The Americans in Mexico Since the Civil War.* Berkeley: University of California Press, 2005.

Ibarrola, Bernardo, Alejandro Cisneros Méndez, María Eugenia Ibarra Cano, and Jorge Armando de Luna Zamora. *Centenario de la industria militar mexicana: 1916–2016.* Ciudad de México: Secretaría de la Defensa Nacional, 2016.

Jackson, Michael. *The Politics of Storytelling: Variations on a Theme by Hannah Arendt.* Copenhagen: Museum Tusculanum Press, 2019.

Karp, Aaron. "Estimating Global Civilian-Held Firearms Numbers." *Small Arms Survey,* June 2018. https://www.smallarmssurvey.org/sites/default /files/resources/SAS-BP-Civilian-Firearms-Numbers.pdf.

Klay, Phil. "A History of Violence." In *Uncertain Ground: Citizenship in an Age of Endless, Invisible War,* 1–21. New York: Penguin Press, 2022.

Lindsay-Poland, John. "How U.S. Guns Sold to Mexico End Up with Security Forces Accused of Crime and Human Rights Abuses." *The Intercept,* April 26, 2018. https://theintercept.com/2018/04/26/mexico-arms-trade-us-gun-sales/.

Lytle Hernández, Kelly. *Bad Mexicans: Race, Empire, and Revolution in the Borderlands.* New York: W. W. Norton & Company, 2022.

McDougal, Topher L., David A. Shirk, Robert Muggah, and John H. Patterson. "The Way of the Gun: Estimating Firearms Trafficking across the US–Mexico Border." *Journal of Economic Geography* 15, no. 2 (2015): 297–327.

Merry, Sally E. *The Seductions of Quantification: Measuring Human Rights, Gender Violence, and Sex Trafficking.* Chicago: University of Chicago Press, 2016.

"Mexico: Evolution of the Mérida Initiative, FY2008–FY2021." Congressional Research Service, September 20, 2021. https://crsreports.congress.gov/product /pdf/IF/IF10578/21.

Miller, Reuben Jonathan. *Halfway Home: Race, Punishment, and the Afterlife of Mass Incarceration.* New York: Little, Brown, 2021.

Muehlmann, Shaylih. *When I Wear My Alligator Boots: Narco-Culture in the US-Mexico Borderlands.* Berkeley: University of California Press, 2013.

National Firearms Commerce and Trafficking Assessment (NFCTA): Crime Guns, Volume Two, Part IV ("Crime Guns Recovered Outside the United States and Traced by Law Enforcement"). January 11, 2023. https://www .atf.gov/firearms/docs/report/nfcta-volume-ii-part-iv-crime-guns-recovered -outside-us-and-traced-le/download.

Navaro, Yael. "The Aftermath of Mass Violence: A Negative Methodology." *Annual Review of Anthropology* 49, no. 1 (2020): 161–73.

Paley, Dawn. *Drug War Capitalism.* Oakland, CA: AK Press, 2014.

Pensado, Jaime M., and Enrique Ochoa. *México Beyond 1968: Revolutionaries, Radicals, and Repression during the Global Sixties and Subversive Seventies.* Tucson: University of Arizona Press, 2018.

Pérez Esparza, David, and David Hemenway. "What Is the Level of Household Gun Ownership in Urban Mexico? An Estimate from the First Mexican Survey on Gun Ownership 2017." *Injury Prevention* 25 (2019): 93–97.

Piccato, Pablo. *City of Suspects: Crime in Mexico City, 1900–1931.* Durham, NC: Duke University Press, 2001.

Poniatowska, Elena. *La Noche De Tlatelolco: Testimonios De Historia Oral.* México: Era, 2014.

"Principales Resultados. Encuesta Nacional de Población Privada de la Libertad (ENPOL) 2016." July 2017, accessed July 28, 2020. https://www.inegi.org.mx /contenidos/programas/enpol/2016/doc/2016_enpol_presentacion_ejecutiva .pdf.

Raphael, Ricardo. *Hijo de la Guerra.* Ciudad de México: Editorial Planeta Mexicana, 2019.

"Report on the Visit of the Subcommittee on Prevention of Torture and Other Cruel, Inhuman or Degrading Treatment or Punishment to Mexico." UN Subcommittee on Prevention of Torture, May 31, 2010. https://docstore .ohchr.org/SelfServices/FilesHandler.ashx?enc=6QkG1d%2fPPRiCAqhKb7 yhsrYQAhdCTgawvygbo%2biRuazURllYd43CARogddBzX8xqNYtJ1hwb KJm97xB87UO%2fUDEd9ne1kEUmtJVQSwoZL5UOMHBjdO6ZgM1hB a0458RZ.

Rivera Garza, Cristina. *Grieving: Dispatches from a Wounded Country.* New York: Feminist Press, 2020.

Saldaña-Portillo, María Josefina. *Indian Given: Racial Geographies across Mexico and the United States.* Durham, NC: Duke University Press, 2016.

Secretaría de Defensa Nacional (SEDENA). Response to public information request no. 0000700034520, February 28, 2020.

———. Response to public information request, no. 0000700068219, March 22, 2019.

Stop US Arms to Mexico and the Mexican Commission for the Defense of Human Rights (CMDPDH). "Gross Human Rights Abuses: The Legal and Illegal Gun Trade to Mexico." August 2018. https://www.stopusarmstomexico .org/wp-content/uploads/2018/08/THE-LEGAL-AND-ILLEGAL-GUN -TRADE-TO-MEXICO_August2018.pdf.

Thomas, Deborah A. *Political Life in the Wake of the Plantation: Sovereignty, Witnessing, Repair.* Durham, NC: Duke University Press, 2019.

Thompson, E. P. *Whigs and Hunters: The Origin of the Black Act.* London: Breviary Stuff Publications, 2013.

Thompson, Ginger. "How the U.S. Triggered a Massacre in Mexico." *ProPublica*, June 12, 2017. https://www.propublica.org/article/allende-zetas-cartel -massacre-and-the-us-dea.

Tilly, Charles. "War Making and State Making as Organized Crime." In *Bringing the State Back In*, edited by Peter B. Evans, Dietrich Rueschemeyer, and Theda Skocpol, 169–91. New York: Cambridge University Press, 1985.

Torres Martínez, Héctor Daniel. "Monterrey Rebelde 1970–1973. Un estudio sobre la Guerrilla Urbana, la sedición armada y sus representaciones colectivas." Master's thesis, El Colegio de San Luis, 2014.

US Customs and Border Protection. Response to FOIA request no. CBP-2021-030251. February 10, 2021.

US Department of Justice. Bureau of Alcohol, Tobacco, Firearms and Explosives. "Firearms Recovered in Mexico and Submitted to ATF for Tracing." Updated March 10, 2020. https://www.atf.gov/file/144886/download.

———. Bureau of Alcohol, Tobacco, Firearms and Explosives. "Report of Active Firearms Licenses—License Type by State Statistics." January 10, 2022. https://www.atf.gov/firearms/docs/undefined/ffltypebystate01-10-2022pdf /download.

———. Office of the Inspector General. "A Review of ATF's Operation Fast and Furious and Related Matters (Redacted)." September 2012 (reissued November 2012). https://oig.justice.gov/reports/2012/s1209.pdf.

US Government Accountability Office. "Firearms Trafficking: U.S. Efforts to Disrupt Gun Smuggling into Mexico Would Benefit from Additional Data and Analysis." GAO-21-322, February 2021. https://www.gao.gov/assets /gao-21-322.pdf.

Villarreal, Ana. "Domesticating Danger: Coping Codes and Symbolic Security amid Violent Organized Crime in Mexico." *Sociological Theory* 39, no. 4 (December 2021): 225–44.

———. "Fear and Spectacular Drug Violence in Monterrey." In *Violence at the Urban Margins: Global and Comparative Ethnography*, edited by Javier Auyero, Philippe Bourgois, and Nancy Scheper-Hughes, 135–61. New York: Oxford University Press, 2015.

Weigend Vargas, Eugenio, and Carlos Pérez Ricart. "Gun Acquisition in Mexico 2012–18: Findings from Mexico's National Crime Victimization Survey." *British Journal of Criminology* 61, no. 4 (July 2021): 1066–85.

Yablon, Alex. "American-Made .50-Caliber Rifles Help Fuel Mexican Cartel Violence." *The Trace*, October 29, 2019. https://www.thetrace.org/rounds /american-made-50-caliber-rifles-help-fuel-mexican-cartel-violence/.

Zavala, Oswaldo. *Drug Cartels Do Not Exist: Narcotrafficking in US and Mexican Culture*. Nashville, TN: Vanderbilt University Press.

———. *La Guerra En Las Palabras: Una Historia Intelectual Del "Narco" En México (1975–2020)*. Ciudad de México: Debate, 2022.

Index

tracing, 59–60, 105–7, 160, 177–79, 210, 258n12, 260n23; HSI vs. ATF on gun types and diversion, 285n5; lack of acknowledgment of, 186; logistics of, 51–55; into prisons, 130–31; private sales for, 153–60, 285n5; registered guns, documentation required, 50–51; scout tactics of, 123; seizure by Mexico, 277n61; seizure by US, 54–55, 110; statistics (2018–2023), 235; trials and incarceration for, 109, 110, 113–16; unregistered guns as self-defense, 45–50; US exports to Mexico, 8–13, 262n36; vocabulary of, 49–50. *See also* AK-47 rifle and variants; ammunition; AR-15 rifle and variants

gun violence: Apodaca prison massacre (2016), 133–34, 290–91n6; author's recommendations to reduce gun violence in Mexico, 237–41; coolers incident/threat, 139–40; Corpus Christi Massacre (El Halconazo), 41; domestic violence, 239; exit wounds, defined, 5–7; grenade attack, US consulate (Monterrey), 91–92; gun injuries, statistics, 259n15; homicide statistics, Mexico, 67; kidnapping, 26–27, 45–50, 72–74, 151, 152, 165–73, 235; Marjory Stoneman Douglas High School, 232, 305–6n23; mass shootings (US), 5–7, 183, 258n7; at National Autonomous University of Mexico (UNAM), 40–41; Sabino Gordo bar shootout, 164; Sandy Hook Elementary School shootings, 261n32; San Fernando massacre, 165–66; statistics (2018–2023), overview, 235; suicide, 239, 259n14; trauma care for injuries, 5–7; and US vs. Mexico weapons sales, 7–8, 44; and victim blaming, 47–48, 64; Villas de Salvárcar massacre, 63; Villa Unión shootout, 161–62. *See also* Garza ranch massacre (Allende); kidnapping; organized crime; *individual names of gangs*

gunwalking, 15, 60–69, 112
Gustavo, 110, 111
Guy AK (Derek), 215
Guzmán, Ovidio, 181
Guzmán Loera, Joaquín (El Chapo), 65, 84, 87, 181, 227, 228

Haag, Pamela, 31, 261n33
El Halconazo (Corpus Christi Massacre), 41

halcones (lookouts), 75
Los Halcones (paramilitary group), 41
Harfuch, Omar García, 179–80
Harris, Thomas, 290n4
Hart, John, 31
"Heating Up the Plaza: How Mexico's Gangs Use Scorched Earth Tactics" (Moore), 282n47
Heckler & Koch (H&K), 36–37
Hernandez, Isaac, 310n19
Hernández, Kelly Lytle, 32, 265n14, 266n21
Herrera, Yuri, 254
Hidalgo, Miguel, 29, 227
Hijo de la guerra (Raphael), 88, 89
hobbyists, gun ownership by, 182–84. *See also* hunters, gun ownership by
Homeland Security Investigations (HSI, US): ATF collaboration initiative with, 106–7; vs. ATF on gun types and diversion, 285n5; Border Enforcement Security Task Force (BESTs), 106, 285n4; private gun sales investigated by, 153–60; Zapata's murder by Zetas, 61, 68, 285n4
homicide: in Colombia (1993–2003), 306n14; feminicide, 99, 258–59n13, 308–9n8; Mexico (2016–2017), 221; Mexico (2016–2020), 308–9n8. *See also* gun violence
Honduras, Zetas' weapons from, 122, 288n27
Hornady "critical defense" cartridges, 48
Houston Chronicle, on Villa Unión shootout, 161–62
huachicoleo (fuel theft), 78, 221
Huerta, Victoriano, 33
El Huevo (Juan Gerardo Treviño Chávez), 307n1
Hugo, 17, 160, 205, 210–18
Huitzilopochtli (deity), 35
hunters, gun ownership by, 42, 50–51, 182, 186, 188–90

Illinois, .50 caliber rifles sold in, 178
Immigration and Customs Enforcement (ICE, US), 61, 105, 106
incarceration, 128–38, 194–204; author's recommendations to reduce US incarceration, 239, 240; author's research methods about, 250; Brazil/Central America, organized crime in prisons of, 291n8; conjugal visits, 290n1; gang violence in Mexican

regulation in Mexico vs., 8–11; Los
Angeles Police Department, 177, 180;
police violence toward Black Americans,
7. *See also* Bureau of Alcohol, Tobacco,
Firearms and Explosives; Customs and
Border Protection (CBP, US); Homeland
Security Investigations
Lazcano Lazcano, Heriberto, 85, 87–88,
100, 165
lethality tests, 58
La Línea (gang), 63
Llama semiautomatic pistol, 141
*Loaded: A Disarming History of the Second
Amendment* (Dunbar-Ortiz), 12
Lohmann Iturburu, Jens Pedro, 190, 192
Lone Wolf Trading Company, 62, 65
López Castro, Roberto Carlos (El Toruño),
286–87n14
López Obrador, Andrés Manuel, 78, 181,
190
López Villafana, Rogelio, 280–81n26
Lord's Resistance Army, 304n3
Los Angeles Police Department, 177, 180
Los Angeles Times: on ATF's gunwalking
operations, 68; on crime reporting in
Monterrey, 127; on Federal Law on
Firearms and Explosives (1971), 43
Los Zetas Inc. (Correa-Cabrera), 92
Luna, Vaneli, 171

Maadi (gun manufacturer), 210
Macías, Marisol (Castañeda/Castro), 126,
289n43
Madero, Francisco, 32–33
Madison, James, 11
mafias. *See* organized crime; *individual
names of gangs*
Mafia (Sicilian), 124
Magón, Ricardo Flores, 32
El Mañana (Nuevo Laredo), crime writing
stopped by, 126
Mara Salvatrucha (MS-13), 106, 140–41,
284n3
Marco, 186–88
Marine Corps, US, 175
Marjory Stoneman Douglas High School,
232, 305–6n23
marking of weapons, 228
Márquez, Martín, 167–68
Maryland, .50 caliber rifles regulations, 176
Massachusetts: assault weapons ban,
306n22; and Mexico's lawsuit against
US gunmakers (*Estados Unidos
Mexicanos v. Smith & Wesson et al.*),

8–11, 234–35, 259n21; Springfield, gun
manufacturing in, 231–32
"la Matanza," 266n21
El Mataperros, 119, 286–87n14
Mateo, 184
Mauser rifles and carbines, 36
Maximilian (emperor of Mexico), 31
McNamara, Robert S., 57
el mecanismo de protección (Mexican
protection program), 77–78, 163,
278n12
Medina, Rodrigo, 146
Medina Mora, Eduardo, 68
Mellado Cruz, Galdino, 88, 311n14
Mendoza, Rafael, 36
Mendoza machine guns, 36
Mérida Initiative, 64, 68, 146, 181, 261n34
Merry, Sally Engle, 255
mestizaje (mixed race) ideology, 12–13
Mexica (Aztec) Empire, Spanish conquest
of, 28–29
Mexican Commission for the Defense and
Promotion of Human Rights, 261n34
Mexican Railway Association, 20–21
Mexico, wars: Aztec (Mexica) Empire,
Spanish conquest of, 28–29; Battle of
Puebla, 46; Civil War, 231; Mexican
Revolution, 32–38, 43, 191; Seven
Years War, 29; and Texas insurgency
(1915), 34; War of Independence, 29;
and World War I, 33, 36
México Armado (online discussion group),
192
Mexico City: *armería* (Mexico City army
store), 185–86; "Culture of Peace and
Not Violence in Mexico City" (art
sculpture), 229; gun buyback program
in, 219–26
Mexico government: Air Force, 38; Alliance
for Security, 146; Army, 38; assassinations of government officials by Zetas,
90–92; Attorney General's Office,
119–20, 252; author's policy recommendations for, 239–41; Chamber of
Deputies, 68; civilian permit and
licensing process, 42, 50–51, 54, 142,
183–89; civil lawsuit against US
gunmakers (*Estados Unidos Mexicanos
v. Smith & Wesson et al.*), 8–11,
234–35, 259n21; Coahuila state police,
70–72, 80; Constitution, 13, 37–39;
Convention on the Rights of the Child,
303n11; DCAM (Directorate of
Commercialization of Arms and

registration with, 183, 185, 186, 189, 190, 192; Museo del Enervante ("the Narco Museum"), 226–27; Nuevo León firearm shipment theft, 151; US guns purchased by, 261n34; weapons passed to Zetas from, 94; and Zetas inception, 86

The Seductions of Quantification (Merry), 255

serial numbers on guns, 239

7.62 × 39 mm ammunition, 206

7.62 × 51mm ammunition, 2

Seven Years War, 29

Sheinbaum, Claudia, 229

Shirk, David, 270n7

shovels, from guns, 230

"Sí al desarme, sí a la paz" program, 220. *See also* gun buyback program

Sigifredo Nájera Talamantes (El Canicón), 91–92

Sig Sauer, 261n34

The Silence of the Lambs (Harris), 290n4

Sinaloa Cartel: gunwalking and collateral damage, 56, 64–65; smuggling by, 110, 113; and Zetas' rise to power, 84, 90, 95

Small Arms Review, on ArmaLite's AR-50, 175

Small Arms Survey (Mexican gun ownership), 269n69

smart technology, 238

Smith & Wesson (manufacturer), 10, 183, 231–32, 234–35, 259n21, 305–6n23

Soler, Isidro, 29–30

Soviet Union. *See* Russia

Spain, Aztec (Mexica) Empire conquest by, 28–29

Special Operations Command, US, 180

Special Prosecutor's Office for Attention to Crimes Committed Against Freedom of Expression (FEADLE, Mexico), 278n12

Specters of Revolution (Aviña), 39

spoons, from guns, 229–30

Sportsman's Warehouse, 176

Springfield rifles and muskets (Civil War), 231

State Department, US, 261n33

Stockholm International Peace Research Institute (SIPRI), 261n33

Stop Illegal Trafficking in Firearms Act (2017, US), 310n18

"Stop US Arms to Mexico" (Global Exchange), 252, 261n34

straw purchasing cases: author's recommendations to reduce gun violence in

Mexico, 239; and "dead-dropping," 111–12; gunwalking and collateral damage of, 61–69

Suárez del Real y Aguilera, José Alfonso, 229

suicide: prevention, 239; statistics, 259n14

tableada (torture tactic), 136, 168

Taft, William, 33

Talamantes, Sigifredo Nájera (El Canicón), 91–92

Taliban, 10, 304n2

Tamaulipas: La Ribereña region, 72–74; Zetas' inception in, 83

Tandera, Danny, 162

Tec de Monterrey students, murder by soldiers, 125

Televisa Monterrey, television host's murder, 126

Televisa news, 91; attack on studio of, 126; on crime reporting agreement, 126

Téllez Moreno, Eduardo, 185–86

Tennessee, and Barrett rifles, 174–78

Terry, Brian, 65, 68

Texas: .50 caliber rifles sold in, 178; gun purchases reported to ATF by, 107; gun sales in, overview, 8; guns traced back to, 260n23; Mexican insurgency (1915), 34; Zetas' weapons from, 122

Texas State University, 96

".30-30 case," 190–92

Thomas, Deborah, 248

Thompson, E. P., 268n54

Thompson, Ginger, 167, 168

.308 Winchester, 2, 134, 191

Tijuana, violent crime in, 48–49

Tijuana Cartel, 270n6

Tilly, Charles, 78

time-to-crime, in gun tracing, 105, 210

Tito, 190

Tomás, 183, 184

Topo Chico prison, 131–33, 138, 139, 191, 202

Torres Marufo, Jose Antonio, 64

El Toruño, 119, 286–87n14

The Trace (web site), on Barrett rifles, 177–78

trauma care for injuries, 5–7, 125

Treasury Department, US, 59

Treviño Chávez, Juan Gerardo (El Huevo), 307n1

Treviño Morales, José, 75

Treviño Morales, Miguel Ángel, 100–101, 167, 237

CALIFORNIA SERIES IN PUBLIC ANTHROPOLOGY

The California Series in Public Anthropology emphasizes the anthropologist's role as an engaged intellectual. It continues anthropology's commitment to being an ethnographic witness, to describing, in human terms, how life is lived beyond the borders of many readers' experiences. But it also adds a commitment, through ethnography, to reframing the terms of public debate—transforming received, accepted understandings of social issues with new insights, new framings.

Series Editor: Ieva Jusionyte (Brown University)

Founding Editor: Robert Borofsky (Hawaii Pacific University)

Advisory Board: Catherine Besteman (Colby College), Philippe Bourgois (UCLA), Jason De León (UCLA), Laurence Ralph (Princeton University), and Nancy Scheper-Hughes (UC Berkeley)

Founded in 1893,
UNIVERSITY OF CALIFORNIA PRESS
publishes bold, progressive books and journals
on topics in the arts, humanities, social sciences,
and natural sciences—with a focus on social
justice issues—that inspire thought and action
among readers worldwide.

The UC PRESS FOUNDATION
raises funds to uphold the press's vital role
as an independent, nonprofit publisher, and
receives philanthropic support from a wide
range of individuals and institutions—and from
committed readers like you. To learn more, visit
ucpress.edu/supportus.